Studying Global Pentecostalism

The editors want to thank the following institutions for their financial assistance toward the conferences on which this publication is based: British Academy, University of Heidelberg, Royal Netherlands Academy of Arts and Sciences, Vrije Universiteit Amsterdam, Church in Action (Protestant Church in the Netherlands).

Studying Global Pentecostalism

Theories and Methods

———

Edited by

Allan Anderson, Michael Bergunder,
André Droogers, and
Cornelis van der Laan

UNIVERSITY OF CALIFORNIA PRESS
Berkeley   Los Angeles   London

University of California Press, one of the most distinguished university presses in the United States, enriches lives around the world by advancing scholarship in the humanities, social sciences, and natural sciences. Its activities are supported by the UC Press Foundation and by philanthropic contributions from individuals and institutions. For more information, visit www.ucpress.edu.

University of California Press
Berkeley and Los Angeles, California

University of California Press, Ltd.
London, England

© 2010 by The Regents of the University of California

Library of Congress Cataloging-in-Publication Data

Studying global Pentecostalism : theories and methods / edited by
Allan Anderson . . . [et al.].
    p.   cm.—(The anthropology of christianity ; 10)
Includes bibliographical references and index.
ISBN 978-0-520-26661-2 (cloth : alk. paper)
ISBN 978-0-520-26662-9 (pbk. : alk. paper)
1. Pentecostalism—Congresses.   I. Anderson, Allan.
BR1644.S79   2010
270.8′2—dc22   2010003229

19   18   17   16   15   14   13   12   11   10
10   9   8   7   6   5   4   3   2   1

CONTENTS

ABBREVIATIONS

AJPS	*Asian Journal of Pentecostal Studies*
CoUP	Columbia University Press
CPCR	*Cyberjournal for Pentecostal-Charismatic Research*
CUP	Cambridge University Press
DPCM	*Dictionary of Pentecostal and Charismatic Movements*, ed. Stanley M. Burgess and Gary McGee, asst. ed. Paul Alexander. Grand Rapids: Zondervan, 1988
EPCRA	European Pentecostal Charismatic Research Association
EPTA	European Theological Asscociation
Exchange	*Exchange: Journal of Missiological and Ecumenical Research*
GPH	Gospel Publishing House
Glopent	European Research Network on Global Pentecostalism
HUP	Harvard University Press
IBMR	*International Bulletin of Missionary Research*
IJPR	*International Journal for the Psychology of Religion*
IMR	*International Review of Mission*
IUP	Indiana University Press
IVP	Inter Varsity Press
JBV	*Journal of Belief and Values*
JEPTA	*Journal of the European Theological Assocation*
JES	*Journal of Ecumenical Studies*
JPC	*Journal of Psychology and Christianity*
JP&T	*Journal of Psychology and Theology*
JPT	*Journal of Pentecostal Theology*

JRA	*Journal of Religion in Africa*
JSSR	*The Journal for the Scientific Study of Religion*
MHRC	*Mental Health, Religion and Culture*
Missiology	*Missiology: An International Review*
NIDPCM	*New International Dictionary of Pentecostal and Charismatic Movements*, ed. Stanley M. Burgess, asst. ed. Eduard M. van der Maas. Grand Rapids: Zondervan, 2002
OGS	Office of the General Secretary (Springfield, Missouri)
OUP	Oxford University Press
PentecoStudies	*PentecoStudies: Online Journal for the Interdisciplinary Study of Pentecostalism and Charismatic Movements*
Pneuma	*Pneuma: Journal of the Society for Pentecostal Studies*
SAP	Sheffield Academic Press
SPS	Society for Pentecostal Studies
UCP	University of California Press
Unisa	University of South Africa Press
WCC	World Council of Churches

Introduction

Allan Anderson, Michael Bergunder, André Droogers,
and Cornelis van der Laan

A RAPIDLY EXPANDING MODALITY OF CHRISTIANITY

With one estimate of 500 million adherents worldwide, converted in the course of one century, Pentecostalism has become one of the main branches of Christianity.[1] A popular theory locates the origin of Pentecostalism in a 1906 revival meeting at the Azusa Street Mission in Los Angeles. In this community the gifts of the Holy Spirit—for example, speaking in tongues, healing, and prophecy—were discovered and celebrated. There are reports, however, of the more or less simultaneous occurrence of similar movements in other parts of the world. Within a few years of the 1906 upsurge Pentecostalism had in fact established itself worldwide. Today the majority of Pentecostal believers are found in non-Western countries, especially in the Global South. In the short history of its existence, Pentecostalism has reshaped the face of Christianity and has also developed a rich and varied repertoire of doctrines, rituals, strategies, and organizations, which makes it difficult to generalize about the phenomenon.

Without losing its identity and despite its stereotypical reputation as a movement of conservative orthodox Christians, Pentecostalism has shown a remarkable ability to adapt to diverse cultural contexts. Through its adaptability, its impact has been global, both in its geographic distribution and in its presence as a religious movement capable of producing local versions of its universal message. As a successful global movement, it has served to give its many converts the possibility of integrating into the widening modernized world. In Pentecostalism they have found the means to facilitate their adaptation to the increasing scale of modern life. Especially to inhabitants of developing countries, now known as "the majority world," this was an important factor in the attraction of Pentecostal churches. Though viewed by outsiders as focused on saving souls, Pentecostalism owes its success to addressing the corporeal and material aspects of peoples' lives, including problems caused by modernization processes. An intriguing question concerns the interplay between Pentecostal practice, local traditions, and a global modernizing context. More particularly, questions of continuity and discontinuity are calling for detailed interdisciplinary research and a profound analysis of the processes that take place.

In the course of the past century Pentecostalism has put itself on the world map. Initially it was mostly missionaries from northern churches who founded churches in the south and east. Later in the century, independent local leaders founded important churches in the south and east. In sending missionaries to the Northern Hemisphere, especially secularized Western Europe, southern Pentecostalism has now taken the lead, inverting the classic mission movement in Christianity.

The number and spread of the Pentecostal faithful is impressive in view of the relatively recent start of the movement. Pentecostalism can be viewed today as the most rapidly expanding religious movement in the world. Within the past thirty years there has been an estimated 700 percent increase in the number of Pentecostal believers, who represent about a quarter of the world's Christian population and two-thirds of all Protestants. The rapid expansion of Pentecostalism has pushed so-called mainstream Protestantism into a minority position. It is not uncommon to see Pentecostalism presented as a modality on its own, at the same level as Catholicism and Protestantism. The growth of Pentecostalism has raised a challenge to ecumenical cooperation.

Pentecostal churches show a wide variety of forms, from back-room churches with a dozen members directed by one pastor, to mega-churches with millions of members, run as a religious enterprise by CEO-style leaders. This organizational diversity is part of Pentecostals' capacity to adapt to local demands. It also reflects their able use of market strategies and entrepreneurial tools. The larger churches mark their public presence by the large auditoriums that have been built. A characteristic of the approach followed by some mega-churches is the use of secular buildings, such as abandoned cinemas, for their daily services. Migrants from the south in Europe often occupy church buildings deserted by older European denominations. A local church community may rent a garage in a neighborhood, furnish it with plastic garden chairs, and install a sound system, to hold its meetings as close as possible to where potential converts live. An essential part of the global perspective adopted in Pentecostal mega-churches is the use of mass media and modern communication, efficiently applied to facilitate contacts between leaders and followers, wherever they live. A few of the large churches have been able to buy television time, or even a network.

In addition to establishing its own churches, Pentecostalism has deeply influenced sectors of the mainline churches. From the sixties onward the so-called Charismatic renewal movements emerged within established churches, first in Protestantism and subsequently in the Catholic Church. These Charismatic movements and believers gave a new boost to Pentecostal expansion in the United States but soon elsewhere. They are commonly viewed as an integral part of Pentecostalism, despite being part of mainline churches. In the Latin American context the Catholic Charismatic renewal has been a strategic tool of the clergy to combat the exodus of members to Pentecostal churches.

Pentecostal churches have not only produced local adaptations of their identity to accommodate cultural conditions but also attracted a variety of social categories. Churches often specialize in particular audiences defined by (for example) class, ethnicity, age, and profession. Though often making its base in urban areas, Pentecostalism has spread to rural areas also. A characteristic of Pentecostal churches is that the leadership is usually male, whereas most of the followers are female. In some churches women occupy formal leadership positions.

SCHOLARLY INTEREST

Considering its relatively short history, Pentecostalism has become a remarkable religious phenomenon. In view of the description just given, five typifying characteristics of this modern Christian movement can be identified. First, there is the new form it has given to the Christian message, emphasizing the role of the Holy Spirit and creating an environment in which the gifts of the Spirit can be practiced. Second, there is its surprising numerical growth, an achievement by itself, that contradicts all predictions on the supposedly secularizing effect of modernization processes. Third, it is flexible: throughout its expansion this form of Christianity has shown itself to be gifted with the capacity to adapt to the world's cultural heterogeneity while remaining loyal to its identity. It thereby represents a laboratory in which globalization processes can be observed in concrete practice. It also illustrates what a religious approach to the body and to the material side of life can do. Accordingly, it has produced a rich variety of manifestations, not only in its organization, but also in its strategies and uses of communication technology. Fourth, it has been capable of attracting a wide variety of audiences, each of which has selected from the rich Pentecostal repertoire and made its own adaptations. The presence of a majority of female adherents is an important characteristic of Pentecostal audiences. Fifth and finally, that most Pentecostals live in the Southern Hemisphere, in the heart of Christianity's new center of gravity, has contributed to its fame as a special case in the religious field.

A field with these characteristics cannot but raise scholarly interest. Each of the five characteristics identified above or some combination of them represents an attractive research theme. Yet it was only in the 1950s that serious academic work on Pentecostalism began. Especially over the past two decades the study of global Pentecostalism has gained strength, parallel to the movement's major expansion. The common expressions of an established academic field, such as study associations, networks, research centers, conferences, journals, and books, are now found with regard to the study of Pentecostalism. Research on Pentecostalism has achieved an accepted position in academia.

Yet, just as Pentecostal history is short, Pentecostal studies is young and explorative. This is also because of the dynamics of Pentecostalism as a study object. Scholars sometimes appear to have difficulty keeping up with the activist rhythm of Pentecostalism. Before the ink on research reports is dry, new developments have already presented themselves. Thus as a new study area Pentecostalism is still very much under construction. From its inception it has met with at least three difficulties that still have not been fully resolved.

The first problem is the delineation of the field and the search for a good definition. It is not easy to reduce the huge diversity of Pentecostal phenomena to a generalized formula acceptable to all. Statistical questions and disputes are of course closely linked to the debate on the definition. Although the worldwide Pentecostal expansion can hardly be questioned, there are diverging opinions on the actual size of the global Pentecostal community. Authors differ with regard to the inclusion or exclusion of groups such as African independent churches or even Charismatic renewal movements.

The second difficulty is the interdisciplinary nature of this scholarly field. More modestly put, the multidisciplinary nature of the research already represents a challenge. The advantage of a particular discipline's study of Pentecostalism is usually not contested, but common ground has hardly been defined. From the start researchers from various disciplines developed an interest in Pentecostalism, each attracted by a particular aspect. Gradually the motive for doing research changed from a biased interest in a deviating and competing form of Protestantism to the challenging and more objectively approached riddle of the spectacular growth of Pentecostalism. Theologians studied Pentecostalism for its emphasis on the Holy Spirit and for its competitive position. Moreover, the everyday practice of putting experience over doctrine drew attention, in part because it did not exclude rather orthodox stances. Church historians among the theologians started to study the short history of Pentecostalism and its expansion, and they were soon joined by researchers from Pentecostal churches, often describing the history of their own churches. Psychologists of religion were primarily interested in the manifestations of the Holy Spirit and in believers' experiences with the charismata. Sociologists of religion, especially those studying Christianity, shared with theologians an interest in Pentecostal groups as examples of what was labeled a "sect." For quite some time sociologists of religion produced work on church-sect typologies, nourished in part by the Pentecostal example. The mainline churches' distrust of Pentecostalism's success appears to have influenced the choice of Pentecostalism as a topic and sometimes also the outcome of research, putting Pentecostal churches in a second-rank position as a modus of being Christian. The stereotypical and erroneous image of Pentecostals as focused on souls and the hereafter may be interpreted as a result of this mainline view, ignoring the this-worldly and corporeal aspects of Pentecostal practice. Anthropologists came relatively late to this field, studying Pentecostal groups initially as examples of religious movements in Third World contexts and emphasizing the functions they shared with other such movements, including evangelical revival groups. Once they had made the turn from "pure" cultures to changing cultures, and from "primitive" societies to culture as a global phenomenon, their interest in global Pentecostalism grew significantly.

With each of these disciplines producing a particular type of approach and thematic interest, academic work in the field is still much more multidisciplinary than interdisciplinary. It is not uncommon for scholars to be unaware of what colleagues in other disciplines are doing or publishing. A sign of change is the increased interest theologians have shown in the work of their colleagues from the social sciences and the humanities. There is accordingly a tendency to rehabilitate Pentecostalism from its second-rank status, sometimes leading to the other extreme, romantic idealization of its expansion and flexibility. Cooperation between scholars from different disciplines, such as occurs in the network that took the initiative for this book,[2] is a result of these trends, although still in its initial, exploratory stages.

The third problem, partly connected with the previous set of challenges, is the way in which a good practice for academic work on Pentecostalism can be developed. Developing interdisciplinary methods and a common vocabulary is a major task, but there is more. The participation of scholars from various disciplines introduces a variety of views on the mission of science. One of the questions in this regard is the competition or cooperation between scholars working with quantitative methods on the one hand and those who prefer qualitative methods on the other. The increasing activity of researchers who themselves are Pentecostal believers—a welcome and interesting development—adds a dimension to the debate on issues of objectivity and subjectivity. The former theological bias in work with a mainline background may now be substituted with another theological bias, this time from a Pentecostal perspective. One issue that may emerge is the question of whether the study of Pentecostalism should contribute to effective recruitment and successful marketing through the choice of themes and the application of results. In historical studies, the discussion of objectivity and subjectivity may concern how the role of the leadership is depicted: in a critical way or as a form of modern hagiography, to mention only the extreme positions. Another issue is the preference for either an insider's or an outsider's point of view. This may take the form of a debate between those scholars, mainly from the social sciences and the humanities, who tend to reduce any religious activity, including Pentecostalism, to nonreligious aspects and functions, and those, in particular theologians and scholars from Pentecostal backgrounds, who maintain the truth of their religion, as manifested through the Holy Spirit. For Pentecostal scholars the view from the social sciences and the humanities may cause a crisis in personal faith. If the success of Pentecostalism is attributed to the combined effect of internal characteristics and external conditions, not to the working of the Holy Spirit, some personal soul-searching may result. On the other hand, the scholar who is an agnostic outsider may view typical Pentecostal practice as just another functional religious phenomenon in this confusing modern world, thereby missing idiosyncratic elements that may be relevant for a complete analysis.

THIS BOOK

The question to be answered now is what contribution this book hopes to make to the study of Pentecostalism. The three problem areas mentioned in the preceding section have been instrumental in the design and organization of the book. As editors we thus sought to address the issue of defining the field of global Pentecostalism, to summarize and stimulate multidisciplinary efforts, and to explore examples of good research practice. In view of the demands of these challenges we did not consider ourselves able to produce this book without the help of others. Authors were selected for their eminence in disciplinary, theoretical, thematic, methodological, or regional sectors of research. We invited both Pentecostal and non-Pentecostal scholars. We invited authors who were able to address the overarching themes mentioned above in our description of Pentecostalism and in our appraisal of the problems our study field is confronted with. Taken together, their contributions summarize the achievements and challenges of the current study of Pentecostalism.

That this is the first publication to undertake a general inventory of the study of Pentecostalism since serious academic work on it began illustrates how young the field is; in fact, it is still coming of age. Our volume completes the change from research motivated by a polemical theological interest in a phenomenon that meant competition to mainline churches to a focus on Pentecostalism's success in moving easily throughout a globalizing world, adapting to any cultural context without losing its basic identity markers. Because Pentecostalism has grown into a global religion, we as editors sought to offer a global perspective, making up for what is still lacking. Our intention was to cover as many angles as possible from which global Pentecostalism can be studied. We made an effort to map the field, trace its boundaries, and describe the various landscapes it encompasses.

With regard to readership, this collective work is meant to serve as a useful tool in the development of this area of study, both for those already part of this research effort and for those, such as graduate students, who as newcomers want to catch up with what has been done so far. In addition, it offers the opportunity for researchers to become acquainted with work in other disciplines and thus overcome a strict monodisciplinary perspective. Moreover, we hope to stimulate reflection on the form authentic interdisciplinary work may take. In this respect we hope that readers will find this book helpful for making responsible choices of themes, cases, and methods. But it is not only important to learn what has been achieved so far. The various contributions assembled here should inspire those who are looking for a conceptual framework for future research initiatives, especially when moving to an interdisciplinary approach, taking into account the global and yet localized nature of current Pentecostalism. It should also help to overcome possible biases, whether of reductionist, mainline, or Pentecostal origin, in the study of Pentecostalism.

We have a special interest in theoretical developments, as these may nourish our quest for interdisciplinary work on global Pentecostalism. Bringing together perspectives that are dear to disciplinary work, we intend to take a step toward a combined approach to our field. Admittedly, the disciplinary lines visible in the composition of the second and third parts of this book reflect the still-common subdivision of the field. The second part includes contributions from the social sciences and humanities, while the third part explores work done in theological subdisciplines. Yet part 1 discusses some of the interdisciplinary themes of the field, seeking to contribute to the search for common ground. The importance of moving from a multidisciplinary to a true interdisciplinary approach and developing good research practice is explicitly reflected in part 1.

Allan Anderson opens part 1, "Interdisciplinary Perspectives," with a chapter about defining Pentecostalism. He outlines ways in which the movement can be identified by using the family resemblance analogy. He discusses parameters by which we make categories and then offers a flexible and overlapping taxonomy. In chapter 2 André Droogers draws a map of the various options available when scholars in the field of Pentecostalism have to position themselves with regard to essentialist and normative elements. His overview results in a short checklist that is meant to make scholars more conscious of their often-implicit preferences.

Michael Bergunder, in chapter 3, shows that debates in cultural and postcolonial studies are also of interest for the research of Pentecostal and Charismatic movements. He illustrates this with three exemplary cases: the question of defining Pentecostalism, Pentecostal historiography, and the relationship between the researcher and the researched. In chapter 4 Elizabeth Brusco seeks to answer why women convert to Pentecostalism in greater numbers than men, when Pentecostal doctrine and practice seem so oppressive to women. Although women make up the majority of Pentecostals, they rarely hold leadership positions in their churches, but more surprisingly neither are they discussed in academic treatments of Pentecostalism as a worldwide religious movement. In chapter 5 Henri Gooren shows how to analyze conversion stories as told by Pentecostals. Using a conversion career approach, he addresses the core rituals involved in the Pentecostal conversion process: accepting Christ as your Savior, baptism by full immersion, sanctification (or holiness), and praising (speaking, singing, or praying) in tongues. Birgit Meyer, in chapter 6, guides us toward new theoretical directions in the study of Pentecostalism as a global religion par excellence. Key terms from the Pentecostal vocabulary relevant to globalization are taken as points of departure. Pentecostal imaginaries of the world imply material practices, involving bodies, things, and technologies. Meyer advocates moving beyond the dualism of matter and spirit that has informed much of our thinking about modern religion and that is challenged by global Pentecostalism today.

Part 2, "Social Sciences and Humanities," opens with a contribution from the psychology of religion by Stefan Huber and Odilo W. Huber. The chapter is structured by the distinction between two research perspectives. The first conceptualizes Pentecostal religiosity as a phenomenon caused by general psychological factors and has psychological consequences. The second, in contrast, focuses on inner structures and dynamics of the religiosity of Pentecostals. The authors review recent psychological studies on Pentecostal piety concerning findings indicating inner structures and dynamics of Pentecostals' personal religious systems. In chapter 8 Joel Robbins disentangles the elaborate interdisciplinary discourse of Pentecostal studies to determine the distinctly anthropological threads. He focuses on three areas: issues of Pentecostalism and the cultural process, Pentecostalism as a lived religion, and the relationship of Pentecostalism to modernity. In chapter 9 Stephen Hunt first explores old dominant themes in the sociological study of Pentecostalism, for example, deprivation, sectarianism, and the responses to routinization by organized Pentecostal bodies. More recently sociologists of religion have engaged in new and innovating frameworks for understanding the changing forms of Pentecostalism. Cornelis van der Laan, in chapter 9, compares methodological developments in historical research with some of the interpretive approaches to Pentecostal history. He discusses the difficulties of facing issues of origin, definition, and statistics and the challenges of doing archival research.

In part 3, "Theology," Veli-Matti Kärkkäinen looks at the state of Pentecostal theological scholarship in the area of pneumatology. Whereas Pentecostals themselves have not produced much constructive systematic theology, their interest in the Spirit and pneumatology has inspired a number of contemporary theologians to begin to develop distinctively Pentecostal contributions arising from different global and local settings. Pentecostals have always been heavily involved in missions but traditionally have not given much thought to a theology of religions or interreligious dialogue and encounter. In chapter 12 Amos Yong and Tony Richie argue that Pentecostal scholars can no longer avoid these topics. After a survey of these issues they offer a suggestive sketch of fruitful developments and directions. Mark Cartledge is the first to map the nature of practical theology in the context of Pentecostal-Charismatic Christianity. He does so by looking at the dominant methodological approaches that characterize contemporary practical theology and by distinguishing between writers from inside the movement and those outside it. Chapter 14, by Cecil M. Robeck, rounds off part 3 and the book with a discussion of ecumenism. Robeck explains why this is another difficult subject for most Pentecostals. He suggests an ecumenical methodology and provides a bibliography and series of recommendations on how to proceed.

IN SUM

This book is intentionally designed to assist anyone involved in the academic research of global Pentecostalism to think about and, we hope, avoid pitfalls that commonly occur in the research process. That this book approaches the field from different disciplinary angles is, we believe, its strength—for it underscores the need for and shows the way to an interdisciplinary perspective that especially includes an encounter between the social sciences, theology, and the humanities. The editors commend this volume to our readers with the conviction that together the contributions will change the way we do Pentecostal studies.

NOTES

1. See chapter 1 of this book.

2. This book is an initiative of the European Research Network on Global Pentecostalism (GloPent). GloPent was founded in 2004 by three academic institutions committed to the study of Pentecostalism: the Centre for Pentecostal and Charismatic Studies at the University of Birmingham, represented by Allan Anderson; the Hollenweger Center at the Vrije Universiteit Amsterdam, represented by André Droogers and Cornelis van der Laan; and the Department of History of Religions and Mission Studies at the faculty of Theology, University of Heidelberg, represented by Michael Bergunder.

The main objective of GloPent is to connect researchers on global Pentecostalism and Charismatic Christianity in order to encourage and promote international and interdisciplinary approaches to the study of Pentecostal/Charismatic movements. GloPent, especially through its Web site (www.glopent .net), links research activities, promotes study exchange, facilitates the discussion of methods and theoretical frameworks as well as common research projects, and stimulates academic publications on Charismatic movements and Pentecostalism, especially through its journal, *PentecoStudies*. In January 2006 Glopent started a cycle of annual workshops with the intent to produce this book on the study of Pentecostal and Charismatic Christianity. To this end three workshops were held in Birmingham, Amsterdam, and Heidelberg during 2006–8.

PART ONE

Interdisciplinary Perspectives

1

Varieties, Taxonomies, and Definitions

Allan Anderson

This chapter is about defining Pentecostalism/s, in view of the fact that definitions are often static and prone to generate confusion. It seeks to give some clarity to the discussion of ways in which Pentecostalism can be described and analyzed, and it tries to offer direction through the maze of different shifting forms of Pentecostalism/s. In addition, it outlines some of the ways in which this movement can be identified by using the family resemblance analogy. It looks at the parameters by which we make categories, offers a flexible and overlapping taxonomy, and examines how various scholars have approached the subject.

DEFINING GLOBAL PENTECOSTALISM

The globalization of various kinds of Pentecostalism is a fact of our time, and its proliferation into such a complex variety is bewildering. With its offer of the power of the Spirit to all, regardless of education, language, race, class or gender, Pentecostalism in its early years became a movement that subverted the conventions of the time. Its methods were not so dependent on Western specialists and the transmission of Western forms of Christian liturgy and leadership. Part of our new task in the twenty-first century is to reflect on the role of Pentecostalism in the majority world in the transformation of Christianity, or what Andrew Walls has called "the change in Christianity's centre of gravity."[1] Pentecostalism in all its diversity, both inside and outside the older churches, was probably the fastest expanding religious movement worldwide in the twentieth century, and by the beginning of this century it had expanded into almost every nation on earth. According to one debatable estimate, it had well over half a billion adherents by the end of the

13

century, a quarter of the world's Christian population.[2] However, much depends on what is included in these figures, which are considerably inflated by including such large movements as African and Chinese independent churches and Catholic Charismatics.

Although the term *Pentecostalism* is now widely used by scholars of religion, most of them assuming they know what it means, it embraces churches as widely diverse as the celibacy-practicing Ceylon Pentecostal Mission; the sabbatarian True Jesus Church in China, with a "Oneness" theology; the enormous, uniform-wearing, ritualistic Zion Christian Church in southern Africa; and Brazil's equally enormous and ritualistic, prosperity-oriented Universal Church of the Kingdom of God. These are lumped together with the Assemblies of God, various Churches of God, the Catholic Charismatic movement, "neo-Charismatic" independent churches that espouse prosperity and "Word of Faith" theologies, the "Third Wave" evangelical movement, with its use of spiritual gifts framed within a theology that does not posit a subsequent experience of Spirit baptism, and many other forms of Charismatic Christianity as diverse as Christianity itself. All these are labeled "Pentecostalism." Clearly, such a widely inclusive definition is problematic and leads to wild speculations about the extent of the movement. Some American Pentecostal scholars tend to use Barrett's statistics as proof of the numerical strength of their specific form of Pentecostalism.[3] Looking at Barrett's latest offering more closely, in which he states that in 2008 there were some 601 million Pentecostals, "Charismatics," and "Neocharismatics" in the world (a figure projected to rise to 798 million by 2025),[4] three distinct forms are included—and the term *neo-Charismatics* embraces the largest numerically of the three. Although not expressly stated, presumably "Pentecostal" here means "classical Pentecostal"; "Charismatic," those who practice spiritual gifts in the older Catholic and Protestant denominations (with Catholic Charismatics forming the great majority); and "Neocharismatics," all others, especially the vast number of independent churches—perhaps two-thirds of the total. The mind boggles at the possible permutations.

The study of Pentecostalism is a developing field, and this book attempts to embrace its different methodological and theoretical aspects from a global perspective. In all academic writing, authors have their own agendas and influences that determine the nature of their work.[5] An insider (emic) paradigm makes academic reflection quite different from those outsider (etic) paradigms that might not admit to the influence of divine agency (such as a theological analysis might do). This means that emic observers sometimes refer to testimonies and accounts of healing and miracles at face value, as they were narrated, and sometimes the boundaries between truth, confession, and science are blurred. A researcher must in any case take others' experiences as they are and offer an interpretation. The paradigms we use to do research fundamentally change what and how we write and how we make our definitions. Most so-called Pentecostal theology has been written by insiders and emerges from a paradigm serving a particular interest group, often with denominational and national pressures and intent to preserve a "pure" Pentecostal theology. Although etic observers sometimes make use of these studies, their scholarly orientation is completely different. The emic/etic distinction is basic to understanding this discussion on definitions. For all these and many other reasons, knowing more precisely what we mean by the term *Pentecostalism* is very important, even if such precision is elusive. Indeed, is a label like "Pentecostalism," which emerged at the beginning of the twentieth century, an altogether appropriate term to use today? It is probably more correct to speak of Pentecostalism*s* in the contemporary global context, though the singular form will continue to be used here to describe these movements as a whole. Droogers has observed that the task of defining any religious phenomenon is "necessary, explorative and useful" but paradoxically also "superfluous, impossible and ethnocentric."[6] The terms *Pentecostal* and *Pentecostalism* refer to a wide variety of movements scattered throughout the world that can be described as having "family resemblance."[7] Wittgenstein argued that family resemblance does not mean that there is something that all have in common but that all have certain similarities and relations with each other. Describing or defining something must allow for "blurred edges," so an imprecise definition can still be meaningful.[8] Defining Pentecostalism may be considered in this way. The term itself is one with shortcomings but despite its inadequacy refers to churches with a family resemblance that emphasize the working of the Holy Spirit.

Definitions depend on which range of criteria one takes. Criteria are always subjective and arbitrary, and differences may not be perceived as significant by the movements on which these criteria are imposed. On the other hand, there is also the possibility of overlooking differences that may be quite important to church members. Emic and etic views always create such differences of viewpoint. The phenomenon of Pentecostalism is, however, much more complex than any neat categorizing will allow. Different scholars in different disciplines have different criteria. If we are to do justice to this global movement, we must include its more recent expressions in the independent, Charismatic, and neo-Charismatic movements. But even more fundamentally, do we actually need definitions, and if so, do they serve any useful function? Whatever we consider for inclusion needs to be completely flexible, so that we make room for the fringes where constantly changing new developments deviate from the "normal." Despite the seeming diversity within global Pentecostalism, the movement does have family resemblances, certain universal features and beliefs throughout its many manifestations, most of which emerged in the early twentieth century. Although this is not at all a homogeneous movement, and acknowledging their very significant differences, the thousands of different denominations and movements could all be described as Pentecostal in character, theology, and ethos. One of the tasks would be to describe and analyze these so-called Pentecostal characteristics and to trace the complex historical developments that led to the emergence of the various global movements that make up contemporary Pentecostalism/s.

Below I discuss four disciplinary criteria for defining Pentecostalism. It will be seen that these are by no means exclusive approaches but are mutually dependent. The first, typological approach attempts to produce a taxonomy of the different types of the Pentecostal family. This takes up the most attention, because all the approaches that follow depend on it in different ways.

TYPOLOGICAL APPROACH

No taxonomy of such a wide variety of churches, networks, and movements is a straightforward undertaking. Attempts to classify religious movements and churches into types have sometimes been oversimplistic and have lacked the depth of understanding usually facilitated by empirical research and participant observation. Any attempt at classification therefore can be only preliminary and tentative and should clarify, not confuse, issues. As Martin West pointed out in his 1975 study of independent churches in Soweto, South Africa, any attempt at a taxonomy may become information that is pigeonholed and whose terms of reference are inadequately explained.[9] There is also the possibility that the categorization into different types will emphasize the differences to such an extent that it will go beyond that recognized by church members themselves.

An inclusive definition will allow for diversity in understanding these movements. Using the family resemblance analogy, by combining the "ideal" with the deviations, is the best way to proceed. Walter J. Hollenweger divided Pentecostalism into three types: classical Pentecostals, the Charismatic renewal movement, and Pentecostal or "Pentecostal-like" independent churches.[10] Although there is the danger of reductionism in this threefold classification of global Pentecostalism, it is a useful starting point, to which I will add a fourth type. No working definition answers all the objections or altogether avoids generalizations, but at least parameters acceptable to most scholars can be set. Using a narrower theological definition such as "initial evidence," "speaking in tongues," or even "baptism in the Spirit" (as Pentecostal theologians tend to do) is fraught with difficulties when there are exceptions all over the world. This is even the case with those who can indirectly trace their origins to North America, such as most forms of European classical Pentecostalism. Similarly, a historical definition that depends on established links alone is difficult to maintain in the plethora of mutations of Pentecostalism worldwide. Although we must resist any simple definition in such a diverse movement, a multidisciplinary definition of Pentecostalism might follow that suggested by Robert M. Anderson. His definition does not rely exclusively on theological dogma, cultural characteristics, or historical precedents. Situating

Pentecostalism within the broad framework of those movements and churches "concerned primarily with the *experience* of the working of the Holy Spirit and the *practice* of spiritual gifts" (this could then be unpacked further) may be a satisfactory way to deal with the problem and lend a family likeness in keeping with the analogy.[11]

Within this broad family resemblance described in terms of an emphasis on the Spirit and spiritual gifts, a taxonomy of global Pentecostalism can be further divided into at least four overlapping types, each with its own family characteristics influenced by historical, theological, and cultural factors. These include the following, each with its own subtypes.

1. Classical Pentecostals are those whose diachronous and synchronous links can be shown, originating in the early-twentieth-century revival and missionary movements. The first decade of the twentieth century was the time when these movements began to emerge, and although it took a few years before they were known by the term *Pentecostal,* their gradual ostracizing by their holiness and evangelical relatives resulted in new denominations being formed just before and after the Great War. In North America the first major schism in Pentecostalism occurred in 1911, when the Chicago preacher William Durham went to Azusa Street and set up a rival mission after the doors of the revival center were locked against him. At issue was his insistence that the Holiness doctrine of sanctification as a second work of grace was not scriptural; instead he advocated a doctrine of "Finished Work" in which sanctification was a gradual process beginning at conversion. Ultimately this was to result in a schism in American Pentecostalism that exists to this day. Most African American Pentecostals followed Seymour as "Holiness" Pentecostals, whereas the largest group of white Pentecostals, the Assemblies of God, formed in 1914, followed Durham's Finished Work doctrine. For various reasons and in part as a result of missionary activity within this group and those who joined them in the global South, this has become the largest group of classical Pentecostals worldwide. In 1916 another acrimonious division occurred in the Assemblies of God between Trinitarian and "Oneness" or "Jesus Name" Pentecostals (who denied the Trinity while reaffirming the deity of Christ).[12]

Thus classical Pentecostalism can now be divided into four subtypes as follows: (a) *Holiness Pentecostals,* with roots in the nineteenth-century holiness movement and a belief in a second work of grace called sanctification, followed by the third experience of Spirit baptism, which includes the largest African American denomination in the United States, the Church of God in Christ, the Church of God (Cleveland, Tennessee), and the International Pentecostal Holiness Church (among others); (b) *Baptistic or Finished Work Pentecostals,* who differ in their approach to sanctification, seeing it as an outgrowth from conversion, and including the Foursquare Church, the Pentecostal Church of God, and the Assemblies of God; and, stemming from the latter, (c) *Oneness Pentecostals,* who reject the doctrine of the Trinity and posit a unitarianism that includes the deity of Christ, including the True Jesus Church in China, the United Pentecostal Church, and the Pentecostal Assemblies of the World; and (d) *Apostolic Pentecostals,* both Oneness and Trinitarian, who emphasize the authority of present-day "apostles" and "prophets," including some of the older Apostolic Church groups and African independent churches, the Church of Pentecost founded in Ghana, and some newer independent churches. These categories apply mostly to Western-originating Pentecostals, although (d) includes the significant number of West African Apostolic Pentecostal churches influenced by the British Apostolic Church, some of which were founded by Africans. All these four groups have a theology of a subsequent experience of Spirit baptism, usually accompanied by speaking in tongues.

2. *Older Independent and Spirit Churches,* especially in China, India, and sub-Saharan Africa, that sometimes have diachronous (but usually not synchronous) links with classical Pentecostalism. These churches do not always have a clearly defined theology, nor do they necessarily see themselves as "Pentecostal," but their practices of healing, prayer, and spiritual gifts are decidedly so.[13] Here the True Jesus Church in China could also be appropriately placed, and so could other churches of Pentecostal origin such as the Jesus Family, called Old Three-Self Churches in China. In this country and in India, several independent churches emerged in the 1920s and 1930s influenced by Pentecostal missionaries.[14] The independent churches are referred to in the literature by many different terms, and here I rely on the continent I know best, Africa. In southern Africa there are Zionist and Apostolic groups that were first formed in the 1910s and 1920s with influences from John Alexander Dowie's Zion City near Chicago and Apostolic Faith missionaries in South Africa, resulting in "Zion-type" and "Spirit-type" churches. In central Africa the independent churches include the Kimbanguists, originating in a healing revival movement that was severely repressed by Belgian authorities. In West Africa "spiritual," "prophet healing," and "aladura" (prayer) churches emerged in healing revival movements at the same time, and in East Africa "Pentecostal" and "spiritual" churches came out of various African revivals in this region.[15] Most of these independent churches prefer to be known as "churches of the Spirit." There is abundant historical evidence that many of these churches were influenced by indigenous Pentecostal revival movements in the early stages of their formation, and some were in direct contact with classical Pentecostals. Some observers feel that these churches should be separated from Pentecostal ones because of the relative enormity of this African phenomenon. Others in "classical Pentecostalism" in the West try to distance themselves from churches they pejoratively view as "syncretistic."[16] When looked at from a global perspective, however, this tends to blur the Pentecostal identity of these churches and to obscure common characteristics and historical links. The various terms

used to describe these churches also suggest that at least they are *inclined* to be Pentecostal. Scholars increasingly recognize their Pentecostal character, as do the churches themselves.[17]

3. Older Church Charismatics, including *Catholic Charismatics, Anglican Charismatics,* and *Protestant Charismatics.* These movements remain in established older churches, are widespread and worldwide, and often approach the subject of Spirit baptism and spiritual gifts from a sacramental perspective. Although the Charismatic movement is usually thought to have begun in the United States in 1960 in an Episcopalian church in California and in 1967 in Catholic circles in the American Midwest, there are several examples of earlier Charismatic movements in older churches in Germany, the United Kingdom, France, and Scandinavia. The movements originating in the 1960s, however, have been more widespread and more heavily influenced by classical Pentecostalism in their initial stages.[18] Today, in countries like France, Nigeria, Brazil, India, and the Philippines, they have established their own denominational organizations that constitute a significant percentage of the Christian population. Catholic Charismatics in particular make up a large percentage of the total numbers given in statistics and may be at least a tenth of all practicing Catholics.

4. Neo-Pentecostal and neo-Charismatic Churches, often regarded as Charismatic independent churches, including megachurches, and influenced by both classical Pentecostalism and the Charismatic movement. Most of these churches emerged from the 1970s onward and are of various kinds: (a) *Word of Faith churches* and similar churches in which the emphasis is on physical health and material prosperity by faith, according to some originating in the Rhema movement of Kenneth Hagin in Tulsa, Oklahoma, whose ideas were in turn influenced by the independent Baptist pastor E. W. Kenyon and the healing evangelist Oral Roberts; (b) *Third Wave churches,* which usually conflate Spirit baptism with conversion and see spiritual gifts as available to every believer, including such church movements as Vineyard and Calvary Chapel and mostly originating in the 1980s; (c) *new Apostolic churches,* which have reintroduced an apostolic leadership to their governance not unlike that of the earlier Apostolic Pentecostals, promoting the idea of "apostolic teams" that establish new churches globally; and (d) probably the largest and most widespread group consisting of many other *different independent churches* that vary considerably in their theology between Third Wave, Word of Faith, apostolic, and classical Pentecostal and are therefore difficult to categorize. Communities of believers led by Charismatic preachers often form international networks and loose associations, which have occasionally been organized into new denominations. These are often the fastest growing sections of Christianity and appeal especially to the younger, better-educated urban population.

Some have suggested that this is a form of "Americanization,"[19] but there is also the danger of generalizing and failing to appreciate reconstructions and innovations made by Pentecostals in adapting to a very different social context. Pentecostalism has quickly become a non-Western, majority world church movement. Some of the churches in the "new church" category are among the largest Pentecostal churches in the world, including the Brazilian Universal Church of the Kingdom of God and the Nigerian Redeemed Christian Church of God, whose widespread use of the media and public relations is becoming a defining characteristic. It should also be noted that *neo-Pentecostal* is a fluid term that has been used in various ways over the past fifty years, at one stage referring to older church Charismatics ([2], above), later to independent Charismatic churches, Third Wave churches, and more recently to a wide range of newer independent Pentecostal churches that embrace contemporary cultures, use contemporary methods of communication, media, and marketing, form international networks or "ministries," and often have a prosperity emphasis.[20]

SOCIAL SCIENTIFIC APPROACH

The social scientific approach is one in which Pentecostalism is defined according to certain perceived common characteristics or phenomena. Social scientists sometimes assume that readers know what Pentecostalism is and do not define it in their studies. But when they do, they might look for social and cultural characteristics that, for example, place the movements they study into a church/sect typology, depending on their theoretical framework. They usually place a wide variety of different movements under the generic label "Pentecostalism" based not only on phenomenological evidence but also on theological and historical factors. The first sociological studies were somewhat polemical, and the various presuppositions of the writers were often transparent. Many of them assumed that Pentecostals were religious fanatics who were psychologically unstable, neurotic, and deprived, various forms of what is called the "relative deprivation theory." Lalive d'Épinay's study of Chilean Pentecostalism in the 1960s characterized Pentecostalism as "a popular form of Protestantism in which emotion prevails rather than reason" and suggested that it "belongs to Troeltsch's 'sect' type."[21] He described "Pentecostal propaganda" that convinces potential converts of a new mystical experience, "the baptism of fire made tangible by the gift of tongues."[22] He also wrote that his "sociological definition owes much to theology" because Pentecostalism is grounded in "belief in the gifts of the Spirit."[23] Applications of the relative deprivation theory are found in the British sociologist Malcolm Calley's study of African Caribbean Pentecostals in Britain and in the study of the social historian Robert Mapes Anderson, whose groundbreaking work saw Pentecostalism as a refuge for the socially marginalized and underprivileged poor, the "vision of the disinherited," where "ecstatic religious experience" was "a surrogate for success in the social struggle."[24] Social scientists usually make their generalizations from the particular case they know best.

Later studies have been more sympathetic. The sociologist David Martin makes a distinction between the Charismatic movement and Pentecostalism. The latter is "an indigenous enthusiastic Protestantism" and an extension of Methodism that cannot be regarded as an "imported package" from American Methodism because of its "multi-cultural transfers."[25] The anthropologist Simon Coleman uses a whole chapter to describe "Charismatic Christians" as subtypes of "conservative Protestants," where "conservative" refers to traditional Christian beliefs in miracles, the second coming of Christ, and biblical literalism in contrast to liberalism. In this sense he also speaks of them as "fundamentalists" and refers to their roots in Pentecostalism, with its Methodist heritage and glossolalia and other spiritual gifts, with origins in Azusa Street and new expressions in the Charismatic and neo-Pentecostal movements.[26] Social scientists also provide helpful indicators for defining what is meant by "global" Pentecostalism. Coleman suggests that "elements of belief and practice" of particular Charismatic churches are "paralleled but also transformed . . . throughout the world." His study of a Charismatic church in Sweden demonstrated "the globalization of Charismatic Christianity" by reference to three dimensions: (1) the use of mass communications media to disseminate its ideas; (2) a social organization that promotes internationalism through global travel and networking, conferences, and megachurches that function like international corporations; and (3) a "global orientation" or global Charismatic "metaculture" that transcends locality and denominational loyalty and displays striking similarities in different parts of the world.[27] Coleman's appraisal of Charismatic Christianity shows that the "meta-culture" embraces many of the theological emphases of Pentecostalism. Global Pentecostalism in its many different forms is a complex and variegated example of Coleman's thesis. It has developed its own characteristics and identities over a century, including transnational connections and international networks.

André Droogers has outlined three broad but common features of transnational Pentecostalism that are helpful for understanding the ideology that makes Pentecostals feel part of a global community. These features include what might also be termed theological categories: (1) the central emphasis on the experience of the Spirit, accompanied by ecstatic manifestations such as speaking in tongues; (2) the "born again" or conversion experience that accompanies acceptance into a Pentecostal community; and (3) the dualistic worldview that distinguishes between the "world" and the "church," the "devil" and the "divine," "sickness" and "health."[28] These are features of all the different kinds of Pentecostalism, and have been so throughout its history. Droogers and others discuss the ideas of the social scientific approach in detail in this volume; but it must also be said that these definitions depend on and are informed by both theological and historical considerations.

HISTORICAL APPROACH

The third approach is a *historical* one, in which Pentecostalism consists of all those movements that can be shown to have diachronic and synchronic links. These historical roots in the radical fringes of "free church" Evangelicalism tend to create a certain fundamentalist rigidity, while paradoxically, Pentecostalism's emphasis on "freedom in the Spirit" renders it inherently flexible in different cultural and social contexts and has made its central tenets transplanted in different parts of the world more easily assimilated. With the passing of a century, the historical roots are not as easily recognizable. Pentecostalism began as a restoration or revitalization movement at the beginning of the twentieth century among radical Evangelicals and their missionaries, expecting a worldwide, Holy Spirit revival before the imminent coming of Christ. The fundamental conviction of these early Pentecostals was that before the cataclysmic eschatological events, the "old-time power" of the Acts of the Apostles would be restored to the church and "signs and wonders" would enable the Christian gospel to be preached rapidly all over the world. The message traveled quickly as its messengers spread out into a world dominated by Western colonial powers. As the the twentieth century lurched through two devastating world wars that created disillusionment with Western "civilization" and the colonial empires crumbled, Pentecostalism changed with it. It saw itself no longer as a form of Christianity imported from the West but by the end of the century had developed thousands of local mutations varying from large urban megachurches with high-tech equipment and sophisticated organizations to remote village house churches meeting in secret with a handful of believers.

Pentecostal historical approaches have also changed. Pentecostals themselves have moved from a providential view of their history ("suddenly from heaven") through one of origins in the white holiness movement in the United States, with its "fourfold gospel," to a more generally accepted view of multiple origins, with the African American church in Los Angeles, the Azusa Street revival, as one of its several centers. Scholars are now more appreciative of the forces and influences of Pentecostalisms outside the Western world. Toward the end of the twentieth century, a number of scholars from Africa, Asia, and Latin America began to challenge previously held assumptions of power and privilege and long-cherished theories.[29] This will continue unabated in the twenty-first century, as more discoveries are made from an entirely different perspective. Historians in the Western world speak of classical Pentecostalism, referring to those denominations with roots in the early revivals in North America. Others follow the church growth guru Peter Wagner's lead and write of successive waves or historical phases of

Pentecostalism. In this schema, the first wave is classical Pentecostalism formed at the beginning of the twentieth century; the second wave is the Charismatic movement in the older churches that began in North America in the 1960s; and the third wave consists of the neoevangelical, independent Charismatic churches that arose in the 1970s and 1980s. Wagner now speaks of a "Fourth Wave" and a "New Apostolic Reformation."[30] Each of these categories has its own personal heroes and catalysers in the emergence of the category. But these terms are over-used, clichéd, and totally inappropriate in a global context. Even in the Western context there are large groups of churches that would fall somewhere between the different "waves." Historians like to be precise and to present factual evidence of continuity between different movements and to define Pentecostalism by reference to its origins. Chesnut does this in his study on Brazilian Pentecostalism,[31] Bergunder with regard to South Indian Pentecostalism;[32] and Robeck traces the influence of the Azusa Street revival in Los Angeles in what for him amounts to the "birth of the global Pentecostal movement."[33] The synchronic and diachronic links between the various movements can be demonstrated historically,[34] and the links and influences between classical Pentecostalism and independent churches throughout the world on the one hand and those in the middle of the century between classical Pentecostals and the Charismatic movement on the other are illustrated in these and other texts.

Michael Bergunder has helped researchers think seriously about what Pentecostalism *is* and *who* represents it in academic discourse. His central thesis is one of setting historical criteria for identifying Pentecostalism: diachronous and synchronous links must be proven. However, Bergunder adds that definitions also cannot be proven. "Pentecostalism" is simply a name that various interested parties give to a particular discourse on religion and culture and not a preconceived or reified concept. So, starting with synchronous networks, he writes that boundaries are necessarily contested. I have found substantial support for Bergunder's thesis that Pentecostalism had its origins in a global network of evangelical missions.[35] The belief in "missionary tongues" coupled with a premillennial expectation of a worldwide revival to precede the imminent second coming of Christ was undoubtedly the reason for the frantic missionary migrations that took place a century ago, migrations that involved Pentecostal missionaries from the West as well as others. Azusa Street played a prominent role, perhaps even (as Robeck maintains) *the* most prominent role in this regard. Missionaries from Azusa Street were instrumental in introducing the Pentecostal gospel to many parts of the world, and their diachronous links with many parts of global Pentecostalism can be satisfactorily established.

However, it must also be noted that because these missionaries did not speak the languages of the nations as they expected, they were ineffectual in reaching local people with their message. There *were* key people who reached the locals (including experienced foreign missionaries on the "field" who became Pentecostal), but mostly it was the work of the so-called native Evangelists and Bible women that began the spread of Pentecostalism—people like the unnamed young women from the Mukti Mission, Ramankutty Paul, Alwin De Alwis and K. E. Abraham in India and Ceylon; Mok Lai Chi and Zhang Lingshen in China; Wade Harris and Sokari Braide in West Africa; Alfayo Mango and Zakayo Kivuli in Kenya; Engenas Lekganyane and Christina Nku in South Africa—to mention a few. Some of these pioneers were ardently nationalistic and anticolonial, and their work resulted in churches fiercely independent of Western missions. Many of them were formerly "native workers" connected to existing missions. Unfortunately, although diachronous links may be identified in most cases, in others this is much more difficult to establish. Do we leave them out of our "Pentecostal" definition because we have not established these diachronous and synchronous links? Although Bergunder answers this question in the affirmative, he qualifies this with the statement, "It is of utmost importance that the bias of Western archival sources and indigenous hagiographical traditions is not reproduced by the historian but is critically broken up and put under hermeneutical suspicion."[36] This qualification I heartily endorse.

The links are often not there because the native workers did not write letters or pamphlets as their Western missionary contemporaries did, or because their followers chose not to acknowledge such links for ideological or anti-imperialistic motives, or because they want to represent their particular movement as uniquely divine. These motives are certainly found in the cases of the vast number of independent churches in Africa and China, which possess the "Pentecostal" characteristics Hollenweger and others describe. In some—like the Zion Christian Church and many other independent churches in southern Africa, the Christ Apostolic Church and connected churches in Nigeria, and the True Jesus Church and the Jesus Family (and their secessions) in China—such diachronous and synchronous links are clear. But this approach evokes questions like where to draw the lines without essentializing and what to do when we cannot find links for the various reasons outlined above. Moreover, if movements and churches can move in and out of synchronous networks, then how are they not "Pentecostal" if their reasons for leaving the network have nothing to do with the theological and phenomenological criteria that would otherwise make them fully pentecostal? In Bergunder's example of the Ceylon Pentecostal Mission as a contested case, he makes the important point that a researcher should not decide but argue and retrace conflicting claims of representation.[37]

I support Bergunder's suggestion that Pentecostalism was not fully birthed until it had established its networks, so that one must consider its historical origins from that perspective. I also agree substantially with his suggestion that its boundaries are found in mapping its splits, frictions, and exclusive and competing strategies, remembering that these boundaries can never be fixed. It seems that using a strict historical approach to defining Pentecostalism has difficulties, not least of which situates it strictly within Western Evangelicalism. As I have argued elsewhere,[38] the role of other revival movements like that of the Welsh revival (1904–5) and Pandita Ramabai's Mukti Mission revival in India (1905–7), which predated Azusa Street, and even earlier revivals in North America, must be given sufficient recognition in tracing diachronic links in early Pentecostalism. This is especially true of the Mukti revival, because the Pentecostal phenomena of healings, tongues, and prophecy also occurred there, and it was a must-see place of pilgrimage for international travelers. The Mukti revival, which was not primarily the work of American missionaries, was the single most important reason for the rapid early spread of Pentecostal ideas in India and as far away as Chile. It is for these reasons that I advocate a polycentric approach to the question of Pentecostal origins.[39] The formulating of a postcolonial reading of Pentecostal history needs new attention and painstaking research. Establishing diachronous and synchronous networks will be helpful in understanding pentecostal identity, just as theological, cultural, and phenomenonological considerations should not be neglected in this exercise.

THEOLOGICAL APPROACH

The fourth approach is *theological,* where Pentecostalism is defined as those who share a particular theology and emphasis on the Holy Spirit. Theological definitions sometimes tend towards essentialism, and even though in most forms of Pentecostalism experience and practice are usually more important than dogmatic formulations, these too can be essentialized. Once again, the use of definitions is problematized.[40] The word *Pentecostal* is derived from the Day of Pentecost experience. The fourth verse of Acts 2 is probably the most important distinguishing "proof text" in classical Pentecostalism, when the disciples in Jerusalem were "filled with the Holy Spirit and began to speak in other tongues as the Spirit enabled them."[41] This experience of being "filled" or "baptized" with the Holy Spirit is that which distinguishes many Pentecostals, in their own opinion, from most others. But there is a difference between Pentecostalism in its first, "Charismatic" generation and that in the second, more formalized one. It is usually in the third generation that a revitalization movement arises promoting "revival," which often has a different emphasis from that of the first generation. In later forms of Pentecostalism this so-called distinguishing doctrine is given less prominence—in fact, the insistence on tongues is often absent and certainly of relatively minor significance. In any case, many contemporary pentecostal churches seldom use speaking in tongues in public worship. Dayton wrote about the "theological *patterns*" of Pentecostalism,[42] and people generally have at least a vague idea of what those patterns are. But his exposition of a "common four-fold pattern" to distinguish what Pentecostalism is can only neatly be applied to classical Pentecostalism in North America.[43] Jacobsen has pointed out that from its earliest times Pentecostalism has defied precise definition. Like Wittgenstein's family resemblance, it is "clear to everyone with regard to its general meaning but impossible to define in detail in a way that will satisfy everyone." The nearest Jacobsen gets to a definition is, "In a general sense, being pentecostal means that one is committed to a Spirit-centred, miracle-affirming, praise-oriented version of the Christian faith," but he concludes that "there is no meta-model of Pentecostalism—no essence of pentecostalism or normative archetype."[44] Using preconceived discourses to define Pentecostalism may evoke Asad's critique of such definitions as ethnocentric and neglecting the power dimension in religion.[45]

On the other hand, Hollenweger insisted that there *are* certain theological criteria for defining what Pentecostalism is. If such criteria can be established, then questions of historical origins and phenomenological categories should harmonize with those criteria. Hollenweger considers the growth of Pentecostalism to have taken place not because of adherence to a particular doctrine but because of its roots in the spirituality of nineteenth-century African American slave religion. In his well-known analysis, he outlines the main features of this spirituality to include an oral liturgy and a narrative theology and witness, maximum participation of the whole community in worship and service, visions and dreams in public worship, and an understanding of the relationship between the body and the mind manifested by healing through prayer.[46] These would be Hollenweger's characteristics of a family resemblance. The thousands of Spirit churches throughout Africa and the various house churches in China are Pentecostal movements in this sense, where the features outlined by Hollenweger have persisted, although their form of Christianity is often quite different from Western forms of Pentecostalism. Hollenweger argues that the essence of Pentecostalism is found in its oral nature and that one should look for a founding figure who best represents that characteristic. He concludes that the founder is William Seymour (with his background in African American spirituality) and his Azusa Street revival. His characteristics of this spirituality mentioned above constitute his theological criteria.[47] Hollenweger's essentializing and hagiography aside, however, we could also borrow from Robertson and argue that the identity of Pentecostalism could be found in its "glocalization"—that combination of a global metaculture with a certain local particularity.[48] The Pentecostal family resemblance transcends locality and denominational loyalty and displays striking similarities in different parts of the world.[49] The vast majority of Pentecostals are situated in places where local cultural characteristics are resilient in the face of globalization and where local perceptions are often very different from those found in Western contexts.

Pentecostals, like many other confessing Christians, claim that their experiences are the result of encounters with God. There will always be religious or "mystical" reasons given for people joining or continuing to adhere to religious movements. An etic approach might exclude the possibility of a "non-physical realm of reality,"[50] or what Pentecostals believe is the presence of the Holy Spirit in their experience. Acknowledging this will ensure that a theological approach to global Pentecostalism will have integrity and transparency. So, however we use the term *Pentecostal,* it has to be inclusive enough. The affinities of the global metaculture justify a much more inclusive use of the term than that usually understood in the West. This inclusive theological approach will avert both hasty generalizations and overlooking obvious differences. In referring to many different kinds of churches as "Pentecostal," we neither overlook their distinct character in liturgy, healing practices, and, especially, different approaches to religion and culture nor ignore their unique contribution to Christianity in a broader global context.

CONCLUSION

In the multidisciplinary study of global Pentecostalism, a broad taxonomy must use the family resemblance analogy to include its historical links and its theological and sociological foci. Pentecostalism continues to renew and reinvigorate itself in countless new forms of expression. Seen from this perspective, it is not a movement that has a distinct beginning in America or anywhere else, or a movement based on a particular theology; it is instead a series of movements that emerged after several years and several different formative ideas and events. In seeking a working definition of *Pentecostalism* we need to acknowledge that such a definition might prove elusive and always depends on the paradigms and criteria of the individual attempting to make it.

NOTES

1. Andrew F. Walls, *The Missionary Movement in Christian History: Studies in the Transmission of Faith* (Maryknoll: Orbis, 1996), 145.

2. David B. Barrett, Todd M. Johnson, and Peter F. Crossing, "Missiometrics 2008: Reality Checks for Christian World Communions," *IBMR* 32:1 (2008): 30.

3. Vinson Synan, *The Holiness-Pentecostal Tradition: Charismatic Movements in the Twentieth Century* (Grand Rapids: Eerdmans, 1997), ix, 281; Vinson Synan, *The Century of the Holy Spirit: 100 Years of Pentecostal and Charismatic Renewal* (Nashville: Thomas Nelson, 2001), 373.

4. Barrett, Johnson, and Crossing, "Missiometrics 2008," 30.

5. Walter J. Hollenweger, *The Pentecostals* (London: SCM, 1971); Walter J. Hollenweger, *Pentecostalism: Origins and Developments Worldwide* (Peabody: Hendrickson, 1997).

6. André Droogers, "Defining Religion: A Social Science Approach," in *The Oxford Handbook of the Sociology of Religion,* ed. Peter B. Clarke (Oxford: OUP, 2008), 263.

7. In this book the proper nouns *Pentecostalism* and *Charismatic* and the adjectives *Pentecostal* and *Charismatic* are capitalized.

8. Ludwig Wittgenstein, *Philosophical Investigations* (Oxford: Blackwell, 2001), 66, 71.

9. Martin West, *Bishops and Prophets in a Black City* (Cape Town: David Philip, 1975), 17–18.

10. Hollenweger, *Pentecostalism*, 1.

11. Robert Mapes Anderson, *Vision of the Disinherited: The Making of American Pentecostalism* (Peabody: Hendrickson, 1979), 4; Allan Anderson, *An Introduction to Pentecostalism: Global Charismatic Christianity* (Cambridge: CUP, 2004), 14.

12. Anderson, *Introduction*, 45–57.

13. Harold W. Turner, *Religious Innovation in Africa: Collected Essays on New Religious Movements* (Boston: G. K. Hall, 1979), 97.

14. Anderson, *Introduction*, 124–28, 132–36.

15. Anderson, *Introduction*, 103–22.

16. Gary B. McGee, "Pentecostal Missiology: Moving beyond Triumphalism to Face the Issues," *Pneuma* 16:2 (1994): 276.

17. Harvey Cox, *Fire from Heaven: The Rise of Pentecostal Spirituality and the Reshaping of Religion in the Twenty-first Century* (London: Cassell, 1996), 246.

18. Anderson, *Introduction*, 144–55.

19. Steve Brouwer, Paul Gifford, and Susan D. Rose, *Exporting the American Gospel: Global Christian Fundamentalism* (New York: Routledge, 1996).

20. Anderson, *Introduction*, 155–65.

21. Christian Lalive d'Épinay, *Haven of the Masses: A Study of the Pentecostal Movement in Chile* (London: Lutterworth, 1969), xvii.

22. Lalive, *Haven of the Masses*, 7–8.

23. Lalive, *Haven of the Masses*, 14.

24. Malcolm J. Calley, *God's People: West Indian Pentecostal Sects in England* (London: OUP, 1965); Anderson, *Vision of the Disinherited*, 152.

25. David Martin, *Tongues of Fire: The Explosion of Protestantism in Latin America* (Oxford: Blackwell, 1990), 2–3; David Martin, *Pentecostalism: The World Their Parish* (Oxford: Blackwell, 2002), 1, 6–7.

26. Simon Coleman, *The Globalisation of Charismatic Christianity: Spreading the Gospel of Prosperity* (Cambridge: CUP, 2000), 20–27.

27. Coleman, *Globalisation of Charismatic Christianity*, 19, 66–69.

28. André Droogers, "Globalisation and Pentecostal Success," in *Between Babel and Pentecost: Transnational Pentecostalism in Africa and Latin America*, ed. André Corten and Ruth Marshall-Fratani (Bloomington: IUP, 2001), 44–46.

29. Various doctoral theses at the University of Birmingham in the past two decades are examples, such as J. Sepúlveda, "Gospel and Culture in Latin American Protestantism: Toward a New Theological Appreciation of Syncretism" (1996); R. S. Beckford, "Towards a Black Pentecostal Theology of Liberation" (1999); O. Onyinah, "Akan Witchcraft and the Concept of Exorcism in the Church of Pentecost" (2002); T. J. Padwick, "Spirit, Desire and the World: Roho Churches of Western Kenya in the Era of Globalization" (2003); M. A. Olaniyi, "The Meaning of Religious Conversion in the Christ Apostolic Church of Nigeria: Towards the Incarnation of Christianity in Yorubaland" (2007).

30. C. Peter Wagner, *Churchquake: How the New Apostolic Reformation Is Shaking up the Church as We Know It* (Ventura: Regal Books, 1999).

31. R. Andrew Chesnut, *Born Again in Brazil: The Pentecostal Boom and the Pathogens of Poverty* (New Brunswick: Rutgers University Press, 1997), 25–48.

32. Michael Bergunder, *The South Indian Pentecostal Movement in the Twentieth Century* (Grand Rapids: Eerdmans, 2008).

33. Cecil M. Robeck Jr., *The Azusa Street Mission and Revival: The Birth of the Global Pentecostal Movement* (Nashville: Nelson, 2006).

34. This has been attempted most recently in Allan Anderson, *Spreading Fires: The Missionary Nature of Early Pentecostalism* (London: SCM, 2007).

35. Michael Bergunder, "Constructing Indian Pentecostalism: On Issues of Methodology and Representation," in *Asian and Pentecostal: The Charismatic Face of Christianity in Asia,* ed. Allan Anderson and Edmond Tang (Oxford: Regnum, 2005), 177 213.

36. Bergunder, "Constructing Indian Pentecostalism," 190.

37. Bergunder, "Constructing Indian Pentecostalism," 195.

38. Allan Anderson, "Pandita Ramabai, the Mukti Revival and the Origins of Pentecostalism," *Transformation* 23:1 (January 2006): 37–48. See also chapter 2 of Anderson, *Spreading Fires.*

39. Allan Anderson, "Revising Pentecostal History in Global Perspective," in Anderson and Tang, *Asian and Pentecostal,* 152–57.

40. Western Pentecostals often define themselves theologically in terms of the *doctrine* of the "initial evidence" for Spirit baptism of speaking in tongues, yet Pentecostalism is more correctly seen in a much broader context regarded as a movement or movements concerned primarily with the *experience* of the working of the Holy Spirit and the *practice* of spiritual gifts. Anderson, *Vision of the Disinherited,* 4.

41. Acts 2:4, *Holy Bible,* New International Version.

42. Donald W. Dayton, *Theological Roots of Pentecostalism* (Metuchen: Scarecrow, 1987), 174.

43. Dayton, *Theological Roots,* 21; emphasis added.

44. Douglas Jacobsen, *Thinking in the Spirit: Theologies of the Early Pentecostal Movement* (Bloomington: IUP, 2003), 11–12.

45. Talal Asad, *Genealogies of Religion: Discipline and Reasons of Power in Christianity and Islam* (Baltimore: Johns Hopkins University Press, 1993), 29–30.

46. Walter J. Hollenweger, "After Twenty Years' Research on Pentecostalism," *IMR* 75:297 (1986): 5–6.

47. Hollenweger, *Pentecostalism,* 18–19; Walter J. Hollenweger, "The Black Roots of Pentecostalism," in *Pentecostals after a Century: Global Perspectives on a Movement in Transition,* ed. Allan Anderson and W. J. Hollenweger (Sheffield: SAP, 1999), 42–43.

48. Roland Robertson, "Glocalization: Time-Space and Homogeneity-Heterogeneity," in *Global Modernities,* ed. M. Featherstone et al. (London: Sage, 1995), 25–44.

49. Coleman, *Globalisation of Charismatic Christianity,* 66–69.

50. Donald E. Miller and Tetsunao Yamamori, *Global Pentecostalism: The New Face of Christian Social Engagement* (Berkeley: UCP, 2007), 4, 13.

2

___

Essentialist and Normative Approaches

André Droogers

In this chapter the role of essentialist and normative elements in the study of Pentecostalism is discussed. These elements are part of any academic effort. In studying Pentecostalism, essentialist and normative tendencies may also stem from the identity of Pentecostalism itself and from its perception by others. Any scholar studying this form of Christianity must therefore reflect on them, especially when interdisciplinary work is proposed. The overview given in this chapter serves to raise scholarly awareness of the pitfalls connected with essentialist and normative approaches. Yet both essentialist and normative tendencies can be shown to have a challenging, useful side as well. The argument results in a short checklist that is meant to make scholars aware of the options available.

SUSAN'S CASE

Meet Susan.[1] She is a white Ph.D. student from a social science department at a North American university, planning to do fieldwork on gender relations in a local Pentecostal community with an Afro-Brazilian membership in a slum area of a major Brazilian city. Raised in a middle-class Episcopalian family, participating in a high-church-style parish, she has been brought up with a rather stereotypical image of Pentecostal believers, especially because her parents do not sympathize with Charismatic renewal groups in their church. Susan, however, is fascinated, both as an Episcopalian and as a social scientist, by the totally different faith praxis in Pentecostal and Charismatic groups and by the role of these groups and their members in society.

In addition, Susan has a special interest in gender issues, inspired by her feminist convictions. What she wants to find out during her fieldwork is why poor black women give the Holy Spirit such an important place in their lives. She cannot escape the impression that the male church leadership relegates women to a second-rank position. She suspects that this tendency will be even more pronounced in the case of black women from a slum area. Yet from her readings she also knows that Pentecostalism may soften patriarchal tendencies and is able to empower women.[2] People's image of the Holy Spirit may even gain feminine characteristics.[3] She is excited by the chance to study this paradox.[4]

Susan tries to prepare herself. For her research proposal she has studied the relevant literature on gender, development, Pentecostalism, and urbanization. She wants her research to contribute to the improvement of the quality of life of the slum women she will be studying. During a short explorative trip to Brazil, in preparation for her fieldwork, Susan has selected her research site. Colleagues from the gender studies department of a Brazilian university have helped her to find the right place.

Susan's case can illustrate some of the essentialist and normative issues that may emerge in research on a Pentecostal subject. The conjunction of several elements in her background and interests makes her amenable to essentialist and normative standpoints. Though not always made explicit, essentialist and normative tendencies may appear in any research effort in the study of Pentecostalism. Perhaps more than other fields, religious studies in general are by their specific nature open to such leanings.[5] The study of Pentecostalism is no exception. Because of its idiosyncratic characteristics it even seems a preeminent case. Insiders may take an apologetic position, experiencing their religion as ultimate, whereas outsiders may have their own biases, encountering difficulties understanding and appreciating what happens in Pentecostal practice. Insiders usually have a more positive image of Pentecostalism than do outsiders, who tend to be more critical. In both cases, stereotypes and subjective evaluations may arise. Being an outsider, Susan has her own set of biases and must find a way to handle them.

What characterizes essentialist and normative approaches? Susan's training helps us to understand these tendencies. First, with regard to essentialism, she has learned that essentialist clichés reduce complex phenomena in a commonsense manner to a small number of stereotypical characteristics, thought to be the essence of a phenomenon.[6] Susan has been trained to avoid essentialism, as it obfuscates the research perspective. It does not accommodate nuances and exceptions. The risk of the essentialist perspective is that cultural, religious, and social elements and characteristics are viewed as static, bounded, and autonomous, thus ignoring the dynamics brought about by both internal tensions and external influences.

Susan has also learned that an essentialist view very often has a power dimension. As a social scientist she has a trained eye for the role of power in contexts where essentialist notions appear to be prominent—understanding power as the human capacity to influence other people's behavior.[7] Because of its simplified version of reality, essentialism easily serves the purposes and interests of the powers that be, just as it can be a weapon in the hands of those who oppose those same powers. In either case, essentialism can take the form of both affirmative and critical stereotypes. Gender theory has, for example, shown her that the dominant male view of women is often essentialist, constraining women according to what are supposed to be nature-given characteristics. Women's self-image can also be essentialist, whether submissive or emancipating.

Regarding essentialist approaches, Susan is also aware that her parents have a rather essentialist view of the Charismatic members of their church, just as these Charismatic believers have their own essentialist views of themselves and their fellow Episcopalians. Both factions have their own convictions as to the ideal church. Susan's interest in Pentecostalism was nourished by her awareness of the power struggle in her church, both factions seeking to influence the other and to gain dominance.

However, while being conscious of the risks of essentialism, Susan knows that it can be useful as well. Stereotypes are common in social relations because they facilitate communication and make behavior predictable. That they present a reduced version of reality can be an asset instead of an inconvenience. Besides, essentialism appears to be the inevitable consequence of the basic idea in the social sciences that in the final analysis people's behavior is predetermined by their position in society and therefore shows some regularity that can be viewed as its essence.[8] Moreover, in her methodology class Susan has been told that one of the founding fathers of the social sciences, Max Weber, used a form of stereotype as a sociological tool to discover the essence of a phenomenon.[9] He called this heuristic instrument the "ideal type" and used it to reduce inchoate complexity to analyzable proportions. He emphasized that the ideal type is in fact a construct and does not occur in pure form in reality. Susan thus knows that the ideal type of the Pentecostal believer does not exist, just as there is no essential Episcopalian or a stereotypical social scientist. Ideal types may nevertheless facilitate analysis.

Next to the essentialist approaches, Susan has to reckon with normative tendencies. Her teachers have made her aware of the need to come to grips with her subjectivity.[10] She has become acquainted with two positions in this regard. Some of her lecturers have taught a positivist view of scientific work.[11] From them Susan has learned to always keep some distance from a phenomenon and look at it in a detached way, as an objective outsider. A scholar should not interfere in the situation she studies. Being an enthusiastic swimmer, she has labeled this the "high and dry springboard position." A few other lecturers have proposed a constructivist perspective instead.[12] They have shown her that when human beings study human beings it is virtually impossible to reach absolute objectivity and distance.

What could be true for the physics lab need not apply to the humanities' and social sciences' study field. What is more, turning a seeming shortcoming into an advantage, they have suggested that close contact and looking at reality from the informants' perspective may even be rewarding.[13] Knowledge finding needs the interaction between the researcher and the researched. Participant observation is a tried and tested method. Besides, since the field-worker cannot leave her personality at home, she may as well make efficient use of it. Susan has labeled this the "soaked to the skin swimming pool position." She knows that the metaphors she invented suffer from didactic exaggeration and are in fact the extreme ends of a spectrum. Yet they help her to accept on the one hand that subjectivity cannot be avoided and on the other that subjective and personal choices have implications for her research results. Thus she tries to keep the best of two worlds, positivist and constructivist.

As a consequence, Susan considers maintaining objectivity in her project a relevant goal. She has been taught how to work with more objective quantitative methods such as surveys, just as she has become acquainted with more qualitative methods, such as participant observation and the life history method, in which subjectivity is given a controlled role.[14] She is aware of the delicate boundary between objectivity and subjectivity, especially given her consciousness of the role her personal characteristics may play in research. In deciding to use mainly qualitative methods in her fieldwork, Susan has chosen to live as close as possible to the women and men studied and to participate in their lives as much as she can. Taking into consideration that objectivity cannot be fully realized, her solution is to make her presuppositions as explicit as possible. Though immersing herself along the lines of qualitative methodology, she considers using quantitative methods toward the end of her research, organizing a small survey, to test some of her provisional conclusions. She is ready to admit that her background and normative preferences have influenced some of the decisions that she has made regarding her topic and field site. Thus her feminist views have influenced her choice of the gender theme, just as her opinions on poverty have led her to opt for this particular Brazilian slum site.

There are other aspects of her personal history that may intervene. Coming from an Episcopalian family that is skeptical of Charismatic renewal, she intends nevertheless to be as open as possible to the Pentecostal faith and practice. Yet, having been warned by several people, she is on her guard against efforts to convert her, even though she intends to be "soaked to the skin." Being white and relatively well off, as is apparent from her clothes and the mere fact that she has been able to buy a ticket to Brazil, she is aware that she will attract attention when working among poor black people. Besides, as a North American, she knows she has to overcome a cultural barrier, especially if she wants to use the method of participant observation. She acknowledges that she not only has to be fluent in

Portuguese; she will have to discover the codes of Brazilian society and culture, the social and body languages, at the lower-class level as well.

Like Susan, any scholar studying Pentecostalism will have to find a way to manage choices with essentialist and normative dimensions in a responsible manner. In fact, for at least four reasons any researcher doing studies in Pentecostalism is confronted with dilemmas. First, normal academic work demands that scholars define their position with regard to essentialist and normative tendencies. Susan's positivist and constructivist teachers reflect the two most current positions. Second, Pentecostalism itself is characterized by a number of essentialist and normative tendencies. A researcher should be aware of these. Third, non-Pentecostal sectors of society and Christianity, in expressing their views, easily support stereotypical representations of Pentecostalism, containing essentialist and normative elements. These as well may influence researchers. And fourth, interdisciplinary work puts essentialist and normative issues on the agenda.

This last aspect needs more clarification, since one of the goals of this book is to explore the possibilities of *inter*disciplinary work, moving beyond the still rather separate efforts of a *multi*disciplinary approach.[15] In developing interdisciplinary work, it is necessary to agree on common ground with regard to questions of ontology, epistemology, and methodology: what is the nature of what is studied, how are the inquirer and the knowable related, and how should the inquirer go about finding reliable knowledge?[16] In the contacts between disciplines, whether theology, the social sciences, or the humanities, awareness of essentialist and normative elements is part of good scholarly practice. These elements may occur in the ontology, epistemology, and methodology of a discipline. Accordingly each discipline involved in the study of Pentecostalism carries its own biases in making sense of this phenomenon. Each has for example its own genealogy of normative essentialist concepts, such as the term *Pentecostalism* itself, but also a concept like sect. In the contact between scholars from different disciplines a comparative appreciation of each other's essentialist and normative leanings is necessary if an effort at interdisciplinary work is to be undertaken. If scholars seek to give meaning to people giving meaning to their life, for example, through Pentecostalism, essentialist and normative trends do occur. Nontheologians may tend to think that they are free from these trends, especially if they emphasize that the theological idea of the existence of God is an unscientific axiom. Yet the social sciences and the humanities have their own presuppositions, many of which have to do with essentialist and normative approaches. The methodology of these disciplines abounds with examples of hermeneutic concerns.[17] Moreover, many theologians with a hermeneutic awareness will view their task as an ongoing quest for meaning. They will emphasize the tentative nature of their search for reliable knowledge, even the knowledge of God or the Holy Spirit.[18]

In this chapter Susan and all her fellow researchers will find some help to make a more conscious choice in designing their research plans. Navigating through the Pentecostal landscape, they might discover that as scholars they need a road map of essentialist and normative tracks and pitfalls. Such a map is sketched here, looking at essentialist and normative elements in the study of Pentecostalism from three perspectives: believers, outsiders, and academia. These three perspectives are discussed in the remaining sections of this chapter. Though the first two, analyzed in the next two sections, are certainly important to scholarly practice, and set the stage, most attention is given to the third perspective. Essentialist and normative tendencies in academic work are discussed in two separate sections. In the conclusion the results are summarized in a short checklist, intended for researchers' use.

ESSENTIALIST AND NORMATIVE ELEMENTS IN PENTECOSTALISM

Although the problem set forth in this chapter is primarily academic and methodological, the preliminary question must be raised as to what role adherents of Pentecostalism play in the occurrence of essentialist and normative elements in their religion.[19] In studying the slum community of Pentecostals, Susan will come across essentialist and normative elements that she has to deal with in a responsible way. Do the members of this church community confirm the essentialist and stereotypical view on Pentecostalism as a bounded and autonomous religion? Besides, what would be their expectations with regard to Susan's "high and dry" and "soaked to the skin" poles of the spectrum of participant observation? How much normative behavior is simply expected from the average researcher? And which normative behavior do the Pentecostals show with regard to the researcher who has come to study them?

As suggested in the introduction to this book, it is not easy to make generally valid statements on Pentecostalism.[20] When looking for essentialist and normative elements within Pentecostalism the same difficulty presents itself. If we were to compare specific Pentecostal settings, the forms that essentialist and normative aspects take would show a strong variation. Essentialist or normative elements that are celebrated in one church may be criticized in another. One example is the reaction to the so-called Toronto blessing.[21] To a large degree the position taken by scholars with regard to essentialist and normative tendencies depends on the view Pentecostals have of their religion, more specifically, on their possible need to give their particular brand of Pentecostalism a clear and exclusive identity.

Moreover, the history of Pentecostalism shows the dynamism of the movement, with periods of strong change, commonly labeled "waves,"[22] bringing new expressions of the familiar message. The taxonomy of Pentecostalism reflects this history.[23] The current global spread has increased the awareness among believers that they are part of a worldwide movement. They thereby apply an implicit universal definition of Pentecostalism, which includes essentialist elements.

In looking for conditions that may produce an essentialist and normative image of Pentecostalism, attention should be given to the joint impact of power mechanisms and signification processes. Usually the leadership of an expanding religion like Pentecostalism seeks to gain influence in people's lives and in society. Influencing people's behavior is a way to exercise power, even if the leadership prefers not to use that word, reserving it for the power of God, Jesus, or the Holy Spirit. Thus the effort to convert people is a way to exert power, and people also continue to be influenced in their behavior after their conversion.

There are at least three ways in which the combination of power and meaning construction may nourish essentialist and normative tendencies.[24] The first might stem from the strategic need of a church's leadership to establish a *clear identity*. This identity reinforces the church as an organization to which the members fully dedicate themselves because their own identity is thought to depend in large part on the identity of their church. The competition in the religious market demands a strong identity, as a trademark that sells well. As soon as potential converts have more options available, churches engage in the politics of difference. Recruitment strategies tend to reckon with the demands that converts make, though they do not make concessions with regard to what is considered sacred in a church's identity. When there is an awareness of the techniques of marketing and public relations, the leadership of a church may tend to put an idealized picture of their church in the window. Especially when the leadership has a strong awareness of the church's need for public visibility, for example, in mass media, essentialist and normative tendencies will make themselves felt.[25]

Second, the need for an essentialist and normative identity may find its justification in theological convictions of an *orthodox* nature. This again may be more of a concern of the church's leaders than of their flock, but at least in the official version of a church's identity it can be emphasized as a form of theological essentialism, setting the norm. Usually this cannot be separated from the organizational needs just mentioned, because orthodoxy always involves social and theological boundary keeping, excluding members who deviate from the prevailing definition of orthodoxy. Orthodoxy has been viewed as a marker of fundamentalism.[26] In the study of religion the label "fundamentalism" seems to represent the ultimate form of religious essentialism, though definitions of fundamentalism differ in this respect. Yet the question then is to what degree Pentecostal churches can be termed fundamentalist. Depending on the definitions of fundamentalism and

Pentecostalism, it seems safe to say that not all Pentecostals fall into that category.[27] The presumed fundamentalist nature of Pentecostalism should make one conscious of the arbitrary nature of definitions, of both Pentecostalism and fundamentalism. On the religious market, that is, in contexts of competition, non-Pentecostal factions may have strategic reasons for imposing the essentialist label "fundamentalist" ' on a Pentecostal group.

Third, next to orthodoxy, *orthopraxy* must be mentioned. This may refer to essentialist views on moral issues, as maintained by the church's authorities, again linked to mechanisms of exclusion and sanction. Many Pentecostal churches are known for their strict positions on moral issues.[28] Another form of orthopraxy regards the important role of experiences in Pentecostal rituals, more specifically, those connected with the gifts of the Spirit. Though there may be much room for experiments with experiences, a system of codes controls the boundaries of what is acceptable. When believers give witness of their experiences, such as in telling their conversion story,[29] this control may become visible, people adhering to variations of the scripts and formulations deemed acceptable in their church. There may, however, be attempts to change this system of codes, prompted by changes in the praxis of faith. Thus the introduction of flags, banners, and dance can be seen as a tentative way to redefine "essential" worship practice. These innovations occasioned conflicts in churches about the permissibility of new ways to experience the Spirit.

There is, however, a flipside to this threefold trend toward essentialism and normative emphasis. When looking at global Pentecostalism and the processes by which it has spread through a large variety of countries and cultures, its gift to adapt itself to local circumstances is remarkable.[30] This capacity has certainly contributed to its success. Again, power mechanisms and ways of offering meaningful solutions to people go hand in hand. As a consequence, and in contrast to the essentialist and normative tendencies just mentioned, in transnational Pentecostalism a countermovement may occur when elements from the contextualized version of Pentecostalism, as practiced in the country of origin, lose their importance in favor of new elements that are seen as more relevant in the new context. For the Pentecostal message to be relevant to the potential converts, local needs and problem areas must be taken into consideration. For example, in condemning traditional spirits or magic, concrete local adaptation is necessary for the message to be understood. What is considered essential may therefore change in the process of proliferating the Pentecostal message. Though they are supposed to maintain a level of orthodoxy and orthopraxy, missionaries find creative solutions to give new forms to essentialist tendencies. Obviously, this is the ideal picture. In practice, adaptation may be cumbersome, or the quest for a new localized identity may end in total failure.

ESSENTIALIST AND NORMATIVE APPROACHES
BY OUTSIDERS

Not only do internal sources exhibit essentialist and normative tendencies, making them typical of Pentecostalism, but outsiders produce stereotypes too, as part of mainline churches' discourse or of secular public perception of Pentecostals and their churches. Researchers may be influenced by these external sources. Susan's Episcopalian background and the views of her parents may have colored her image of Pentecostalism, at least initially. In selecting a site for her fieldwork, Susan will have become aware of the public view in Brazil on Pentecostals.

Mainline churches have been the most important outsider source of essentialist and normative images regarding Pentecostal believers. Obviously the rise and expansion of Pentecostal churches were threats to their hegemony. All the pejorative epithets that were common whenever religious movements appeared to attract people from the established churches have also been applied to Pentecostal churches. They were labeled fanatic, schismatic, heretic, and sectarian. Demonizing occurred on both sides, sometimes in the most literal sense. Some established churches have used the labels "orthodox" and "fundamentalist" as a negative qualification to warn against Pentecostals. In many cases the established churches presented themselves as the rule, the Pentecostal churches being deviations. Sometimes a class difference was at the background of the stereotypical images of mainline origin, as when Pentecostal churches were viewed as churches of the poor and the uneducated. Similarly mainline clergy condemned the lack of theological education of the Pentecostal leadership.

However, more recently, antiessentialist tendencies can be observed in the position of mainline churches. When the Charismatic renewal movements emerged, the Pentecostal modality became part and parcel of mainline churches, though often only after considerable strife. Yet a modus of communication and coexistence has emerged. Besides, that several Pentecostal churches have increasingly adopted mainline church characteristics made the differences less obvious. Wherever mainline churches have gradually moved to a more conservative position, because of the exodus of members that were influenced by secularizing tendencies, the gap between mainline and Pentecostal churches may have narrowed, although it is also possible that increased conservatism reinforces exclusivity claims.

In a number of cases the antiessentialist stance has led to an official dialogue among churches at the national level.[31] When the Dutch Pentecostal churches celebrated their centenary in 2007, the secretary general of the main Protestant church was one of the speakers, apologizing for the conflicts and polemics of the past. Also, at the level of the Vatican and the World Council of Churches a dialogue with Pentecostals has been stimulated.[32] Usually this dialogue is one of minorities, because many Pentecostal churches prefer to avoid this type of contact, just as they remain at a prudent distance from fellow Pentecostal churches. Similarly not all sectors of mainline churches accept this dialogue. Whenever dialogue is practiced, essentialist elements may play a role, especially with regard to the views that partners in dialogue may initially have of the other party. However, when dialogue lasts it is probable that essentialist and normative identities lose their impact.

Moving now to secular public opinion, here too essentialist and normative views on Pentecostal churches may be expressed, especially when these churches obtain clear public visibility. The general audience's attribution of essentialist features to Pentecostalism is then a consequence of people's experience with one of the ways in which Pentecostals make themselves visible. The foremost way in which Pentecostals draw attention is by their recruitment methods. This may take the form of simply preaching in city parks and squares but also of billboards and stadium campaigns with a well-known visiting missionary. Sometimes Pentecostals build eye-catching churches. The larger churches in particular tend to mark their presence by constructing huge halls at central locations in a city. The consistent use of a logo also contributes to an essentialist public image of a particular church. Where Pentecostal churches are active as "electronic" churches, their television and radio programs contribute to the public construction of their identity.[33] Because of their frequent appearance on television, their leaders may become public personalities. Secular mass media may produce their own images of what Pentecostalism is about, for example, by publicizing scandals of a financial or moral nature.

Another form of public presence with essentialist and normative aspects is Pentecostal participation in national politics, as Susan will soon discover in her Brazilian fieldwork.[34] Politicians may seek support from large churches because their membership represents an important part of the electorate. In some cases Pentecostal churches themselves have discovered their potential at election time, putting forward their own candidates for political representation. This is often motivated by the strong moral critique with which Pentecostals tend to approach modern society. Issues such as abortion, divorce, euthanasia, and prostitution have in some political arenas become typical Pentecostal topics, commonly put forward by Pentecostal politicians. With regard to essentialist and normative elements, the focus on these moral issues has led public opinion to see Pentecostals as conservative moral crusaders.

A special case of essentialist and normative tendencies can be observed in the Latin American situation. In the 1970s and 1980s a demonizing view of communism, propagated by both religious and secular sources in the United States, led Latin American national leaders to view Pentecostal expansion as a response to Marxist tendencies, presumed to be at work in for example theologies of liberation, as developed at the time in the Roman Catholic Church and also in some of the mainline Protestant churches.[35] Policy makers, some of them Pentecostals, considered Pentecostalism a welcome weapon to combat "communism." Interestingly, in Marxist terms Pentecostalism and class have been viewed as connected in a rather essentialist way, as when Pentecostals are supposed to be poor urban migrants, struggling to survive in the new environment and being kept silent and without class consciousness by the Pentecostal opium they were thought to consume. In a variation, Pentecostals have been said to have access to religious means of production, in compensation for the denial of such access to economic means of production.[36]

In contrast to the essentialist view of Pentecostals as belonging to the lower class, it may come as a surprise that global Pentecostalism includes affluent middle-class churches, in Latin America also.[37] Another example is the popularity of Pentecostalism among the new African urban educated middle class, attracting people from mainline middle-class churches or stimulating Charismatic renewal in these churches.[38] Pentecostal churches have been described as promoting social mobility, allowing people to move upward on the class ladder, through a sober way of life and hard and honest labor.[39] The Pentecostal adherent as the honest model worker is another essentialist image surrounding Pentecostalism.

ESSENTIALISM IN THE STUDY OF PENTECOSTALISM

So far the possible essentialist and normative influences on scholars studying Pentecostalism have been traced to Pentecostalism itself and to external public views on this modality of Christianity. Now the role of academia with regard to essentialist and normative approaches must be explored. The question before us here is how a researcher can adequately deal with stereotypical and simplifying tendencies in the study of Pentecostalism. If the "essence" of Pentecostalism can be defined, what are the pros and cons of such a perspective? To what degree can Pentecostals be identified by an essentialist image of their religion?

This is where Susan had to make some of her elementary decisions, already when designing her research project. Having chosen a localized concrete setting, her hidden presupposition is that the community she is to study is a specimen of the general category "Pentecostalism." The universal is expected to present itself in a concrete local form. The global image she has formed of Pentecostals stems in part from views held by both Pentecostals and outsiders. Her knowledge of the scholarly literature has also contributed to her expectations. With regard to Brazil, gender, and poverty, she leaves for the field with a set of presuppositions of a relatively essentialist nature.

Let us first look at the rather obvious essentialist expression that can be found in the scholars' generalizing category of Pentecostalism. It is presented as a transnational global subculture by itself, independent of and yet common to the many different local brands of Pentecostalism. In the discourse of scholars the assumed characteristics of the field they study easily become integrated in essentialist views on Pentecostalism. Searching for what is common, despite all variations and changes, scholars have often chosen the gifts of the Holy Spirit, the charismata, as the central defining characteristic of Pentecostal believers' faith and practice. This characteristic has therefore been used as defining the "essence" of Pentecostalism.[40]

As is clear from the preceding chapter, there is some arbitrariness in the art of defining. In formulating a definition of Pentecostalism the "essential" characteristic of the gifts of the Holy Spirit is selected because it occurs so frequently. Yet, by choosing it, the field is at the same time bounded. Other "essential" characteristics might be added, but there is much more discussion on their value as general defining characteristics of Pentecostalism than with the focus on the charismata. Thus the characteristics of historical origin, dramatic conversion, acceptance of Jesus as savior, a literal reading of the Bible, strict moral behavior, emphasis on experience, organizational form, recruitment, or the absolute claim on the adherents' life can all be suggested as defining features of Pentecostalism.[41] Any change in the defining "essential" criteria obviously changes the extension of the field.

Pentecostalism would thus be depicted as an autonomous and bounded entity, with its own history, having from the start in Azusa Street and elsewhere its idiosyncratic characteristics that make it different from other forms of Christianity or from any other religion. An essentialist view on Pentecostalism will present this type of Christianity as exclusively different, distinguishing it in particular from mainline Protestant churches. Its presumed essence, in whatever form, strengthens its more or less stable identity through time.

Essentialism is not only a consequence of the rise of Pentecostalism as a separate expression of Christianity. The politics of difference that engaged both mainline and Pentecostal churches appear to have reinforced essentialist—and in this case also normative—tendencies in scholarly work, even among authors who did not identify with a mainline church. The clearest example can be found in decades of discussion among sociologists of religion on church-sect typologies.[42] The mainline church, being the dominant type of religious organization, served as the starting point, pushing other forms into the category of deviations. The negative and sometimes pejorative mainline qualification of Pentecostal communities coincided with the connotations that in the typologies were attributed to the term *sect*. Gradually the typologies included other forms and terms, such as *modality* and *cult*. Some authors made their model more dynamic, suggesting transformations of, for example, a sect into a modality and even a church. The link between the transition from sect to church and increasing prosperity included class mobility in the church/sect typology. The current popularity of those Pentecostal churches that preach the so-called prosperity gospel adds a new dimension to this aspect.

It would be an interesting mental exercise to turn the perspective around and rethink the typology of religious organizations as if the dominant scholarly perspective would have been that of the so-called sect, for example, a Pentecostal church. The selection of distinguishing characteristics probably would have led to a different result from that when the mainline church was the starting point. Though in both cases the counterpart would be viewed primarily as the contrast to what the reference type represented, the result would have been radically different.

In the current context the term *sect* has lost much of its significance. Despite the scientific objectivity with which it was coined at the time, it is now history, in the sense that it mirrors an era and a specific subculture. The history of Pentecostalism and the sensational global expansion of recent decades have produced a variety of church forms. The so-called sects are increasingly presenting churchlike characteristics. Some of the larger Pentecostal churches explicitly call themselves churches, especially those that operate globally. To distinguish them as a type of organization, some use the label "neo-Pentecostal."[43] The definition of *neo-Pentecostal* is not unequivocal, depending on such different defining characteristics as the preaching of the prosperity gospel, the use of professional marketing and PR techniques, the use of media, and international expansion.

In fact, all typologies and labels, including those that are limited to the dynamics and variation in Pentecostal forms, represent an application of essentialism. Phases have been distinguished in the history of Pentecostalism, each period producing its own type of churches, characterized by a particular form of expansion. Types that have been distinguished range from the one-leader house church to the multinational megachurch and from the lone believer preaching in the street or in trains to the entrepreneurial television preachers and their merchandising firms. The rise of Charismatic renewal movements in mainline churches has added another form to these typologies of Pentecostal groups.[44]

Essentialist elements in the study of Pentecostalism are not limited to the definition of the domain or to the typologies that have been developed. Susan's case is illustrative of the way in which general theoretical and ideological notions may color scholars' discourse on Pentecostalism in an essentialist way. Susan's views on gender and poverty influence her choices and her approach. Depending on the theme, the methodology, and the theoretical framework that a researcher chooses, awareness of essentialist tendencies is important.

NORMATIVE ELEMENTS IN THE STUDY OF PENTECOSTALISM

Susan's case includes some of the possible normative aspects that must be dealt with in research. Thus she must navigate the Scylla and Charybdis of the positivist and constructivist solutions to the problem of subjectivity that her teachers propose. Since she has a preference for qualitative methods, she has to be well aware of the pitfalls that surround her. Besides, she has her personal views on gender and poverty to deal with. From her Episcopalian background she brings some theological questions and a curiosity about Pentecostal practice. She is also aware of her position as a young, white, rather wealthy woman, representative of North American culture.

The problem of normative leanings is of course not Susan's alone, or only that of students of Pentecostalism. The demand for objectivity and value-free research has to be reconciled with the circumstance that the researcher is not a camera or a recorder but a human being with her own personality, history, and preferences. The options put before students of Pentecostalism with regard to normative tendencies are not their privilege. They correspond with basic dilemmas in the social sciences and humanities faced by any other scholar in these disciplines. Yet in the case of Pentecostal studies they take a specific form.

The dilemma of positivism versus constructivism summarizes other choices, such as that between objectivity and subjectivity, the universal versus the idiosyncratic, social determinism versus voluntarism, and a value-free versus a value-oriented approach.[45] In recent decades the discussions in the social sciences and humanities on these dilemmas had consequences for the view on normative elements. The appreciation of these elements has moved from outright condemnation to a more nuanced view. The traditional objectivist positivist perspective has been joined by a subjectivist constructivist paradigm in which the role of both the researcher and the persons she studies is acknowledged, not just as a liability but also as an asset. For the study of Pentecostalism, this would mean that researcher and Pentecostal believer are viewed in relationship with each other, both involved in the activity of generating reliable knowledge.[46] Whereas the positivist researcher tends to keep distance from the people she studies and tends to measure impact and change through the production and analysis of statistics, the constructivist researcher seeks involvement with the people she studies and collects narratives about processes that take place in their lives. Subjectivity can thus be shown to be a blessing in disguise. The condition for reliable knowledge is that it is open to intersubjective control.

In reflecting on the study of Pentecostalism, the comparison between positivism and constructivism can be extended. The positivist perspective draws attention to regularity, rules, and possibly laws. This scholarly point of view is similar to that of the Pentecostal leadership, since they see it as their task to organize the church, imposing rules and seeking control. At the other extreme, constructivism defends a view of multiple realities, constructed in a dialogical manner and sustained by a provisional consensus. This perspective is close to that of the membership, living in multiple realities, often using the church for their own purposes, negotiating a solution to their day-to-day worries and problems in all areas of life.

Whereas in the positivist approach a scholar is supposed to find regularity since it is always there, in the constructivist approach the image of the reality is constantly changed because of the ongoing interaction between researchers and researched. In the latter view, regularity is much more problematic. Whereas in its more strict forms the positivist approach considers dynamics the exception to the rule-led nature of reality, the latter views dynamics as the rule.

A positivist model can be recognized in the study of Pentecostalism by the social determinist search for regularities in the rise and expansion of this type of Christianity. People sharing the same circumstances are supposed to show the same religious behavior. The allusion to the massive attraction of poor people is an example, just as is the presumed social mobility. Another example, based on the same model of scientific work, is the correlation between exposure to globalization on the one hand and adherence to a Pentecostal church on the other, especially a church of the type that has global presence. Interestingly, marketing-conscious Pentecostal churches use these ideas and survey results in their "selling" of their "product."

When a constructivist model is followed, the immense diversity of forms in Pentecostalism, and the even greater diversity of individual versions and applications, would be made visible. This approach is likely to suggest, in a nonessentialist way, that a clear boundary is lacking between what is Pentecostal and what is not. It would even consider the possibility that the partners in the research, the researcher as well as the researched, may change opinions and perhaps worldviews in the course of the contact. Among social science field-workers, a common issue in the methodological debate is how to deal with efforts at conversion by Pentecostal members, especially when the method used is participant observation.

The choice of either a positivist or a constructivist paradigm has consequences for the diverse ways in which Pentecostalism is described, characterized, explained, and perceived.[47] Much depends on the theme that is being studied. A normative approach may be rejected, just as it may be recommended. Objective and subjective perspectives on Pentecostalism, including approaches that deny its existence as a clearly bounded phenomenon, may apply. When we add to this the interests of the various stakeholders in the field of Pentecostalism, each with their own agenda and a plethora of cultural and subcultural preferences, an extra dimension is added to this variety.

Applying these views on normative elements to the study of Pentecostalism, it is worthwhile to make an inventory of subjective elements that may have influence. An obvious criterion in distinguishing positions is the researchers' religious background. Admittedly, personal views on religion, whether in favor or against, do not necessarily tell something about the approach a scholar takes in academic work. A common distinction is that between methodological theism, atheism, and agnosticism, the adjective *methodological* indicating the scholarly nature of the position taken. Each of these three positions proposes an answer to the question of how a scholar may appraise the truth claims of a religion, suggesting acceptance, rejection, and abstention respectively.[48] Even so, the religious background must be taken into account when normative elements are being discussed. Four positions can be distinguished.

First, affiliation with a Pentecostal church may play a role. The number of scholars studying Pentecostalism who themselves are Pentecostals is increasing. On several continents organizations of Pentecostal scholars and theological schools exist. The dramatic expansion of Pentecostalism in the Southern Hemisphere has increased the number of scholars from the rank-and-file of Pentecostal churches there. Methodologically, Pentecostal scholars must find a way to combine the participant's and the more distant scientific observer's point of reference. Their considerations therefore must include an appreciation of normative influences. They may face the task of viewing phenomena that are utterly normal to the common Pentecostal adherent as puzzling, and the other way around. They may tend to overlook what is common knowledge. On the other hand, they may have the immense advantage of inside knowledge. Church membership may give social scientists as well as scholars from the humanities a head start with regard to Pentecostal theological themes and practices. This may be an advantage in interdisciplinary work.

Second, researchers from mainline Christian churches, like Susan, are also faced with normative opinions that may influence their views on Pentecostalism. They may work in theological university departments and schools that are in some way linked to mainline churches. The views prevailing in these churches may be colored by the competition that can be experienced in the relationship with Pentecostal churches,[49] just as they may be motivated by the willingness to cooperate in some way with Pentecostals or to engage in dialogue. When Pentecostal and mainline churches are operating in the same market, with similar target groups, the competition may have consequences for the position occupied by scholars—theologians and nontheologians alike—from mainline churches who are studying Pentecostal churches. In a climate of competition, differences between Pentecostal and mainline churches may be overemphasized. Thus mainline theologians may present the central place of the charismata in the Pentecostal experience as problematic. Practical theological considerations on church strategies may also cause differences in viewpoint. The so-called prosperity gospel and its financial consequences for believers may meet with criticism from scholars with a mainline church background. These scholars will tend to develop their own critical essentialist image of Pentecostalism, legitimating their equally essentialist view of their own non-Pentecostal position.

Third, those scholars who participate in a Charismatic renewal movement in a mainline church constitute a special case. They have their own view of the Pentecostal message and practice, identifying with the Pentecostal heritage but seeking the renewal of their own mainline churches. In these movements too, scholarly interest exists, sometimes expressed in special chairs in theology departments.

Fourth, nonreligious scholars will have to find a way to offer a fair representation of a faith and practice that they do not share and may even criticize. Especially in the social sciences, from their beginnings, religion has been considered problematic, especially when compared to science. The contrast between religion and science has colored the scientific study of religion from the start, science putting itself in the roles of both prosecutor and judge. Classic authors such as Marx, Durkheim, and Freud studied religion mainly because they were surprised that it was so resilient. This aspect inspired their explanations. At a later stage, secularization theory went through the stage of predicting the end of religion and then of explaining why it did not disappear. In the case of the study of Pentecostalism by nonreligious scholars, the echoes of this past may be heard. Especially Pentecostalism's breathtaking global expansion, contradicting the presumed disappearance of religion, has challenged explanatory work, at the neglect of other aspects of this form of Christianity.

In the discussion of factors that draw attention to normative approaches, the multidisciplinary nature of research on Pentecostalism must be mentioned. The conscious choice between a monodisciplinary, a multidisciplinary, or an interdisciplinary framework is important. In view of this book's plea for interdisciplinary work, the question of the role of disciplines in the study of Pentecostalism is of extra importance. Who are the researchers in an interdisciplinary setting, and how do they operate, also with regard to each other? Scholars from different disciplines—and even within disciplines—have their own theoretical, thematic, and methodological preferences, based not only on their objective considerations, but also on their subjective choices regarding the basic dilemmas just mentioned. Scholars differ in the position they take in general scientific questions. As was already suggested, any researcher must make choices of an ontological, epistemological, and methodological nature.[50] Thus scholars' views on methodological theism, atheism, and agnosticism must be reckoned with, just as the influence of their religious backgrounds is to be taken into account. The chapters in part 2 and 3 of this volume illustrate the available disciplinary positions. The choice for either quantitative or qualitative methods or a combination is also relevant.

In actual practice interdisciplinary work is still in its initial stages. The conditions for joint research need improvement. Scholars engaging in this approach should have knowledge not only of their own discipline but also of at least one of the other disciplines, including the theoretical, thematic, and methodological issues. They should also be able to present the state of their art to colleagues from other disciplines. Research teams composed of scholars from different disciplines should explore the practice of an interdisciplinary approach. An inventory of the available options, such as I have elaborated, should assist future debates on interdisciplinary work. To an increasing degree university departments are offering courses designed in an interdisciplinary manner, employing lecturers from different disciplines. Students trained in this way are well prepared for interdisciplinary research. Academic associations, networks, and journals for the study of Pentecostalism should serve as common ground for joint action by scholars, going beyond the usual disciplinary subdivision. Funding agencies could play a stimulating role in giving priority to projects with an interdisciplinary design. Publishers could have a role as well. It is a good sign that this multidisciplinary book, with its interdisciplinary ambitions, is published in a series called "The Anthropology of Christianity."

CONCLUSION

Essentialist and normative elements cannot be avoided in the study of Pentecostalism. Though they have an initial connotation of frustrating "correct" scholarly research, these approaches have the potential to facilitate the understanding and analysis of Pentecostalism. Essentialism can help to discover core characteristics, as is the intention of Weber's method of ideal type. Normative elements can be useful when employed in a controlled manner.

The results of this explorative chapter may be summarized in a checklist that might help researchers such as Susan to move through this minefield and be aware of her position and preferences. The list may be consulted when research proposals and applications are being written. Whatever the choices made, some explicit consciousness on the part of the researcher is necessary and useful with regard to

- the cultural, subcultural, and religious characteristics of the context from which one originates and the context in which one does research;
- the category or categories of stakeholders one belongs to;
- the scientific paradigm and the explanatory theories chosen;
- the positivist or constructivist or combined emphasis;
- the methodological preferences regarding quantitative and qualitative approaches;
- the discipline from which the research is done;
- the mono-, multi-, or interdisciplinary position that is chosen;
- the possible identification with and inspiration by mainline, Charismatic, or Pentecostal theological and ecclesiological discourses or by a nonreligious position;
- the influence of ideologies regarding the ideal society;
- the position concerning essentialist and normative elements';

- the possible consequences of one's work for the politics of difference and vice versa;
- the possible consequences for interfaith dialogue; and
- the attitude concerning the unity as well as the diversity in the Pentecostal field.

NOTES

I gratefully acknowledge comments on earlier drafts by two anonymous reviewers; by my colleagues in the Department of Social and Cultural Anthropology, Vrije Universiteit Amsterdam; and by my coeditors.

1. In presenting Susan's case I was inspired by the approach Claudia Strauss and Naomi Quinn chose in "A Cognitive/Cultural Anthropology," in *Assessing Cultural Anthropology,* ed. Robert Borofsky (New York: McGraw-Hill, 1994), 284–300.

2. See chapter 4, this volume; Judith Butler, *Gender Trouble* (London: Routledge, 1990); Henrietta L. Moore, *Feminism and Anthropology* (Cambridge: Polity Press, 1988); Henrietta L. Moore, "Whatever Happened to Women and Men? Gender and Other Crises in Anthropology," in *Anthropological Theory Today,* ed. Henrietta L. Moore (Cambridge: Polity Press, 1999), 151–71.

3. Salvatore Cucchiari, "Between Shame and Sanctification: Patriarchy and Its Transformation in Sicilian Pentecostalism," *American Ethnologist* 17:4 (1990): 687–707.

4. André Droogers, "Paradoxical Views on a Paradoxical Religion: Models for the Explanation of Pentecostal Expansion in Brazil and Chile," in *More than Opium: An Anthropological Approach to Latin American and Caribbean Pentecostal Praxis,* ed. Barbara Boudewijnse et al. (Lanham, MD: Scarecrow Press, 1998), 1–34.

5. Russell T. McCutcheon, *Manufacturing Religion* (New York: OUP, 1997); Russell T. McCutcheon, *The Discipline of Religion* (London: Routledge, 2003).

6. "Essentialism" sometimes refers to what can be considered as universally human. In this chapter, however, I limit myself to the more relevant restricted meaning of essentialism, as an overemphasis on a specific cultural or religious identity. On this form of essentialism, see Conrad Phillip Kottak, *Cultural Anthropology* (Boston: McGraw-Hill, 2008), 382.

7. This definition of power is based on Max Weber's approach: Max Weber, *Economy and Society* (New York: Bedminster, 1968), 53.

8. Frederik Barth, ed., *Ethnic Groups and Boundaries* (Boston: Little, Brown, 1969).

9. Max Weber, *The Protestant Ethic and the Spirit of Capitalism* (London: George Allan & Unwin, 1976), 98; see also Dirk Käsler, *Max Weber: An Introduction to His Life and Work* (Cambridge: Polity Press), 180–84.

10. H. Russell Bernard, *Research Methods in Anthropology* (Lanham, MD: AltaMira, 2006), 20; Barney G. Glaser and Anselm L. Strauss, *The Discovery of Grounded Theory* (Chicago: Aldine and Atherton, 1967); Egon C. Guba, "The Alternative Paradigm Dialog," in *The Paradigm Dialog,* ed. Egon C. Guba (Newbury Park, CA: Sage, 1990), 17–27.

11. Guba, "The Alternative Paradigm Dialog," 19–23.

12. Guba, "The Alternative Paradigm Dialog," 25–27.

13. Bernard, *Research Methods,* 347–49; Robert A. Georges and Michael O. Jones, *People Studying People* (Berkeley: UCP, 1980); James P. Spradley, *Participant Observation* (New York: Holt, Rinehart and Winston, 1980).

14. Isadore Newman and Carolyn R. Benz, *Qualitative-Quantitative Research Methodology* (Carbondale and Edwardsville: Southern Illinois University Press, 1998); Abbas Tashakkori and Charles Teddlie, *Mixed Methodology* (Thousand Oaks, CA: Sage, 1998).

15. See also chapter 8, this volume.

16. Guba, "The Alternative Paradigm Dialog," 18.

17. Zygmunt Bauman, *Hermeneutics and Social Science* (London: Hutchinson, 1978); Guba, "The Alternative Paradigm Dialog"; Danièle Hervieu-Léger, *Religion as a Chain of Memory* (New Brunswick, NJ: Rutgers University Press, 2000); William Outhwaite, *New Philosophies of Social Science* (London: Macmillan, 1987).

18. See, e.g., Michael Welker, ed., *The Work of the Spirit* (Grand Rapids: Eerdmans, 2006), ix–x.

19. See, e.g., Paul Gifford, *African Christianity* (London: Hurst, 1998).

20. Allan Anderson, *An Introduction to Pentecostalism* (Cambridge: CUP, 2004), 9–15; Donald W. Dayton, *Theological Roots of Pentecostalism* (Metuchen: Scarecrow Press, 1987); David Martin, *Pentecostalism* (Oxford: Blackwell, 2002), 23–27.

21. Frank D. Macchia, "The 'Toronto Blessing': No Laughing Matter," *JPT* 8 (1996): 3–6; Margaret M. Poloma, *Main Street Mystics* (Walnut Creek, CA: AltaMira, 2003).

22. Walter J. Hollenweger, *Pentecostalism* (Peabody: Hendrickson, 1997); Margaret Poloma, "The Future of American Pentecostal Identity: The Assemblies of God at a Crossroad," in *The Work of the Spirit,* ed. Michael Welker (Grand Rapids: Eerdmans, 2006), 147–65; Peter Wagner, *The Third Wave of the Holy Spirit* (Ann Arbor: Vine Books, 1988).

23. See chapter 1, this volume.

24. André Droogers, "The Power Dimensions of the Christian Community: An Anthropological Model," *Religion* 33:3 (2003): 263–80.

25. Birgit Meyer and Annelies Moors, eds., *Religion, Media and the Public Sphere* (Bloomington: IUP, 2006).

26. Nancy Ammerman, "North American Protestant Fundamentalism," in *Fundamentalisms Observed,* ed. Martin E. Marty and R. Scott Appleby (Chicago: University of Chicago Press, 1991), 1–65; James Barr, *Fundamentalism* (London: SCM, 1977); Pablo A. Dieris, "Protestant Fundamentalism," in Marty and Appleby, *Fundamentalisms Observed,* 142–96; Harriet A. Harris, *Fundamentalism and Evangelicals* (Oxford: OUP, 1998).

27. Martin Percy, *Words, Wonders and Power* (London: S.P.C.K., 1996); Russell P. Spittler, "Are Pentecostals and Charismatics Fundamentalists? A Review of American Uses of These Categories," in *Charismatic Christianity as a Global Culture,* ed. Karla Poewe (Columbia: University of South Carolina Press, 1994), 103–16.

28. See Henri Gooren, "Pentecostal Conversion Careers in Latin America," in *Global Christianity: Contested Claims,* ed. Frans Wijsen and Robert Schreiter (Amsterdam: Rodopi, 2007), 157–76.

29. See chapter 5, this volume.

30. See chapter 6, this volume; Martin, *Pentecostalism,* 136–38; see also Harvey Cox, *Fire from Heaven* (Reading: Addison-Wesley, 1995); Murray W. Dempster et al., eds., *The Globalization of Pentecostalism: A Religion Made to Travel* (Oxford: Regnum,1999); André Droogers, "Globalization and Pentecostal Success," in *Between Babel and Pentecost,* ed. André Corten and Ruth Marshall-Fratani (London: Hurst, 2001), 41–61; *Charismatic Christianity as a Global Culture,* ed. Karla Poewe (Columbia: University of South Carolina Press, 1994); Poloma, "The Future of American Pentecostal Identity," 153.

31. Paul van der Laan, "Guidelines for a Challenging Dialogue with Pentecostals: Lessons from the Netherlands," in *Fruitful in This Land,* ed. André Droogers et al. (Zoetermeer: Boekencentrum, 2006), 100–114.

32. See chapter 14, this volume; see also Huibert van Beek, "Pentecostals-Ecumenicals Dialogue," in Droogers et al., *Fruitful in This Land,* 81–92; Cheryl Bridges Johns, "What Can the Mainline Learn from Pentecostals about Pentecost?" in Droogers et al., *Fruitful in this Land,* 93–99; Frank D. Macchia, "The Kingdom and the Power: Spiritual Baptism in Pentecostal and Ecumenical Perspective," in *The Work of the Spirit,* 109–25; *On Becoming a Christian,* Report of the Fifth Phase of the International

Dialogue between Some Classical Pentecostal Churches and Leaders and the Catholic Church (1998–2006), www.stucom.nl/document/0203uk.pdf; Michael Welker, "The Spirit in Philosophical, Theological and Interdisciplinary Perspectives," in *The Work of the Spirit*, 221–32; David Westerlund, ed., *Global Pentecostalism* (London: Tauris, 2009).

33. Stewart M. Hoover and Knut Lundby, eds., *Rethinking Media, Religion, and Culture* (Thousand Oaks, CA: Sage, 1997); Meyer and Moors, *Religion, Media and the Public Sphere*.

34. Paul Freston, *Evangelicals and Politics in Asia, Africa and Latin America* (Cambridge: CUP, 2001); Paul Freston, ed., *Evangelical Christianity and Democracy in Latin America* (Oxford: OUP, 2008).

35. David Stoll, *Is Latin America Turning Protestant?* (Berkeley: UCP, 1990), 34.

36. Francisco Cartaxo Rolim, *Pentecostais no Brasil* (Petrópolis: Vozes, 1985); Francisco Cartaxo Rolim, "Popular Religion and Pentecostalism," in *Popular Religion, Liberation, and Contextual Theology*, ed. Jacques van Nieuwenhove and Berma Klein Goldewijk (Kampen: Kok, 1991), 126–37.

37. Henri Gooren, *Rich among the Poor* (Amsterdam: Thela, 1999); Judith Hoffnagel, *The Believers* (Ann Arbor: University Microfilms International, 1978); David Martin, *Tongues of Fire* (Cambridge: Blackwell, 1990), 205–32; Martin, *Pentecostalism*, 114, 115.

38. Gifford, *African Christianity*; Paul Gifford, *Ghana's New Christianity: Pentecostalism in a Globalising African Economy* (London: Hurst, 2003).

39. Peter Berger, "Max Weber Is Alive and Well, and Living in Guatemala: The Protestant Ethic Today," www.economyandsociety.org/events/Berger_paper.pdf; Droogers (1998).

40. Vinson Synan, "The Role of Tongues as Initial Evidence," in *Spirit and Renewal*, ed. Mark W. Wilson (Sheffield: SAP, 1994), 67–82.

41. Daniel E. Albrecht, "Pentecostal Spirituality: Looking through the Lens of Ritual," *Pneuma* 14:2 (1992): 107–26; Anderson, *Introduction*, 9–15; Henri Gooren, "Reassessing Conventional Approaches to Conversion: Toward a New Synthesis," *JSSR* 46:3 (2007): 337–53; chapter 5, this volume; Hollenweger, *Pentecostalism*.

42. Irving Hexham and Karla Poewe, *New Religions as Global Cultures: Making the Human Sacred* (Boulder, CO: Westview Press, 1997); Stephen J. Hunt, *Religion in Western Society* (Houndmills: Palgrave, 2002); Roland Robertson, *The Sociological Interpretation of Religion* (Oxford: Basil Blackwell, 1970); J. Milton Yinger, *The Scientific Study of Religion* (London: Macmillan, 1970).

43. Anderson, *Introduction*, 9–15; Simon Coleman, *The Globalisation of Charismatic Christianity* (Cambridge: CUP, 2000); Peter Hocken, *The Challenges of the Pentecostal, Charismatic and Messianic Jewish Movements* (Farnham: Ashgate, 2009); Martin, *Pentecostalism*, 16–17; Meredith B. McGuire, *Pentecostal Catholics* (Philadelphia: Temple University Press, 1982); Richard Quebedeaux, *The New Charismatics* (Garden City, NY: Doubleday, 1976); Richard Quebedeaux, *The New Charismatics II* (San Francisco: Harper & Row, 1983).

44. Anderson, *Introduction*, 144–65; Margaret Poloma, *The Charismatic Movement* (Farmington Hills, MI: Twayne, 1982).

45. Guba, "The Alternative Paradigm Dialog."

46. Guba, "The Alternative Paradigm Dialog," 25.

47. For examples, see chap. 1, this volume.

48. For a fourth possibility, "methodological ludism," see André Droogers, "As Close as a Scholar Can Get: Exploring a One-Field Approach to the Study of Religion," in *Religion: Beyond a Concept*, ed. Hent de Vries (New York: Fordham University Press, 2008), 448–63, 908–10.

49. The same attitudes of either cooperation or competition may prevail as far as Pentecostal scholars are concerned.

50. Guba, "The Alternative Paradigm Dialog."

3

The Cultural Turn

Michael Bergunder

"Cultural studies" and similar designations mark a diverse field of related theoretical approaches, sometimes labeled "cultural turn," that have deeply influenced the humanities and social sciences in the past three decades.[1] In general, studies on Pentecostal and Charismatic movements have not taken up these approaches in their research design, despite notable exceptions[2] and occasional reference in anthropological studies,[3] as well as in reflections by Pentecostal and Charismatic theologians themselves.[4] Nevertheless, it is worth taking a closer look at these approaches, because some of the pressing issues in the current research on Pentecostalism are reflected therein.

The term *cultural studies* can refer to different schools with different theoretical approaches.[5] As it is not possible to cover such a wide range here, this chapter is confined to one of the major sections of cultural studies, based on a poststructuralist epistemology.[6] Moreover, the focus is not on theoretical questions but on its implication for actual scholarly research. Three specific cases that mark current controversies in the study of Pentecostalism have been chosen. The discussion of each case starts with an explanation of the specific research problem, then some theoretical considerations will be given to help develop a fresh approach, and finally it will be shown how these theoretical considerations can be applied concretely in the practical research regarding the issue in question.

As there are often basic misunderstandings about the poststructuralist approach, some introductory clarification might be necessary before we go into the case studies. Cultural studies are "concerned with the role of cultural practices in the construction of contexts of human life as milieus of power."[7] However, this does not mean that these constructions are arbitrary or fictitious, as in some constructivist approaches. They are real and have real effects, though as historical products they do not exist as necessities but are contingent.[8] In this sense, the poststructuralist approach is strictly historical. Being an heir of the "linguistic turn," its focus is on the discursiveness and linguistics of historical phenomena.[9] Moreover, this approach strives toward a deprivileging of the so-called high culture and an opening up of the corpus of sources.[10] It also has be aware of the global dimension of culture. In her classical critique, Gauri Viswanathan has shown that the notion of "culture" in cultural studies is often still bound to national concepts of culture, which neglect the global impact of colonialism.[11] She argues, for instance, that many aspects of English culture were the result of the colonial encounter, first developed in Imperial India and (re)exported from there to England. Within the past thirty years, so-called postcolonial theory, also mainly based on poststructuralist epistemology, has made considerable contributions to the understanding of modern global history from the nineteenth century on.[12] This aspect must be explicitly recognized for a comprehensive understanding of all cultural phenomena. The poststructuralist approach is not relativistic, in the sense that it regards different cultures as autonomous from each other. We know about the other and other cultures only insofar as we are in a discursive interaction with them. Yet, within this interaction, all participants are transformed and become interlinked. There is no place in this concept for the idea of cultures in the plural that are founded, a priori, on truth systems that are categorically and essentially different. Differences between cultures are negotiated differences within hegemonic discourses.

Cultural studies and the poststructuralist approach give rise to specific guiding questions for concrete research agendas that are of interest for the study of Pentecostalism. They provide a certain theoretical perspective for the exploration of cultural phenomena, but they do not propose their own methodology. As Fredric Jameson has pointed out, all efforts to establish specific methods in cultural studies have been unsuccessful.[13] The established disciplinary methods, such as fieldwork, philology, and historical methods, remain effective, though critically scrutinized for their actual heuristic value and range. As such, the questions raised are not entirely new, but they are posed from an explicit theoretical perspective. The arguments below focus on the connection between theory and concrete research agendas. This is a balancing act, as theory always becomes compromised in any practical application and vice versa.

RESEARCH TOPIC: WHAT IS THE SUBJECT OF PENTECOSTAL STUDIES?

The current academic research on Pentecostalism tends to use a very broad understanding. It is inspired by the statistics of David Barrett, who considers a great variety of churches, organizations, and ministries as representative of Pentecostalism.[14] This broad and inclusive understanding of Pentecostalism is, at present, the received view in academia and also prevails in Pentecostal circles.[15]

However, it exists up to the present without an appropriate theoretical justification. The most serious problem lies in the fact that a broad understanding of Pentecostalism refers neither to a common dogmatic basis nor to a common institutional framework (international umbrella organizations like the Pentecostal World Conference only cover parts of it). Pentecostalism's unity cannot be described in the way traditional church history has dealt with Eastern Orthodoxy, Roman Catholicism, German Lutheranism, and so on. It is certainly not a way out of the dilemma to insist on the diversity of global Pentecostalism and its many different streams, because this argument becomes circular: it only returns to the question of why we speak of global Pentecostalism as a single phenomenon in the first place. The question, then, that has to be answered again, is "whether it makes analytic sense to lump all these churches together."[16] Indeed, there are also reasons that speak against a broad definition of Pentecostalism as a single global phenomenon.[17]

In this unsatisfactory situation, a closer look into cultural studies–oriented approaches brings in new perspectives that might be helpful to substantiate the broad understanding of Pentecostalism theoretically and develop further its conceptualization. The definition of a research subject in cultural studies takes place in the prevailing discursive practice of a society. In this sense, "Pentecostalism" could be regarded as a certain discourse related to religion and scholarship. Discourse should not be misinterpreted as something purely intellectual but as a concept that is used to overcome the conventional but unsatisfactory dichotomization of language and practice. Based on a poststructuralist epistemology, discourse is understood as a social practice and thereby has a material character. It is not a linguistic phenomenon in itself but a practice that permeates "the entire material density of the multifarious institutions, rituals and practices through which a discursive formation is structured."[18] A common misunderstanding of discourse theory relates to its ontological critique that language cannot represent something that lies outside itself and that there is no transcendental signifier, as Derrida has put it. This is often misinterpreted, as if a world outside of language is denied. However, this notion misses the point completely, as Laclau and Mouffe have emphasized.[19] Hence, a discursive definition of Pentecostalism does not infer a retraction to a level beyond reality and materiality, and its greatest advantage is that it can to a large extent act formally and avoid the pitfalls of other normative and analytical definitions. It is not an analytical concept, arbitrarily chosen by scholars; nor does it side with theologically normative definitions by Pentecostals themselves.

In order to be translated into a methodical application, for the concrete empirical identification of Pentecostalism, this discursive approach requires practical specification. This could be done in several ways. One possibility would be to draw methodological links to the area of network analysis, which is at present very popular;[20] Pentecostalism has already been characterized as a network structure. Joel Robbins, for instance, speaks of "a far-flung network of people held together by their publications and other media productions, conferences, revival meetings, and constant travel."[21] The image of a network is especially graphic and addresses crucial issues of discourse analysis. The talk of a network also has the advantage of a certain proximity to sociological theory formations,[22] which most researchers are familiar with. However, according to discourse theory, Pentecostalism conceptualized as a discursive network cannot be anything else than that which is discursively articulated and reproduced. Hence the fundamental epistemological differences between discourse theory and sociological approaches should not be overlooked.[23]

Here, a network is understood as a constant and contested discursive process of negotiation. Based on discourse theory, the meaning of linguistic signs comes no more from within themselves but rather occurs through the difference from other signs. This difference continues theoretically as an unending game, which is open and cannot form any firm differential relations, since due to the differentiality of referring the signs possess no center.[24] However, if Pentecostalism should be understood as a discursive network, then this network requires some fixing of limits. How to conceptualize such a fixation is a much-debated issue in cultural studies. The theoretical implications cannot be discussed here, but it is clear that, within a poststructuralist framework, any fixation of limits has to be regarded as highly unstable because of the differentiality of any referring.[25] Therefore, there can be no fixation of the network that is not contested and contingent, and any fixation can be considered only as a discursive articulation and not as something that refers to an entity behind its representation. Furthermore, it is presumed that within this network the power of representation is in no way uniformly distributed. The intensity of the relations within the network is likewise unequally distributed, because the parameters are fluid and the circumscription and limits of the network are in no way self-evident. As its limits are only relative, such a network can only be meaningfully described when it is registered in the totality of cultural discourses. How a Pentecostal network is embedded in other discursive networks (e.g., Evangelicalism, Protestantism, Christianity, religion, conservative politics) must always be explored.

Pentecostalism, as the subject of research for Pentecostal studies, is understood neither as a nominalistic nor as an idealistic category but as a contingent discursive network. The fluidity of the network does not mean that it can be mapped arbitrarily, because the contentiousness of its frontiers is part of the Pentecostal discourse itself and not of the free musings of the researcher. However, the researcher has to recognize these frontiers and reflect conflicting claims of inclusion and exclusion. This also means that, within the Pentecostal network, competing, alternative, complementary, or subdivisional fixations, which are often hybrid, could be articulated (e.g., Oneness Pentecostalism, Positive Confession movement,[26] interdenominational churches, Charismatic movement, Hispanic Pentecostalism). It is one of the strengths of the cultural studies approach that it does not consider conflicting claims a nuisance but rather a scholarly opportunity. The process of definition is opened up for criticism and for different interpretations of the same historical sources.

Pentecostalism understood as a network could be formally identified without any need for a preconceived normative or analytical definition (such as Evangelicalism plus speaking in tongues as initial evidence of Spirit baptism;[27] or "a movement concerned primarily with the *experience* of the working of the Holy Spirit and the *practice* of spiritual gifts")[28] that unavoidably causes division among researchers and also among Pentecostals in their understanding of the phenomenon.

This does not mean that it is impossible to say anything about common doctrines or shared practices within the range of a Pentecostal network. Research in Pentecostal and Charismatic movements, understood in such a way, will qualify theological discussions and spiritual practices with and by the formal reconstruction of the Pentecostal network. Possible common features of Pentecostalism show themselves as articulations of the network; their demonstration is not a precondition for the definition process. A common identity might not necessarily be a theological conviction but anything discursively articulated. Nonetheless, it does not preclude the possibility of identifying doctrines and practices that form a distinctive Pentecostal identity, be it speaking in tongues, intuitive and experiential Spirit-centered devotion, oral liturgy, firm biblical orientation, narrative theology and testimonies, strong lay participation, healing, or whatever. In any case, this is something that is entirely dependent on its articulation and mutual affirmation within the network, and it is theoretically subject to constant change and transformation. Theology and practices in a network have to be retrieved as they show themselves in discursive articulation and not in respect to historical and theological "traditions," "roots," or "essences." Interestingly, this culturalist view meets with a self-understanding in Pentecostal theology. Everett Wilson also disputes the existence of an essentializing theological agenda in Pentecostalism, because "every generation is the first generation":[29] "By almost any standard, Pentecostalism presently is not what Charles Fox Parham or any of his successors has pronounced it to be, but rather what contemporary Brazilians, Koreans and Africans demonstrate that it actually is."[30]

This perspective on Pentecostalism as a network also has the consequence that academic research can refer to Pentecostalism as its subject only when it actually (re)constructs such a network. No church, movement, or ministry can be considered Pentecostal as long as it is not shown whether and how it is embedded in the

Pentecostal network. This caution is necessary because, as a consequence, studies of certain denominations cannot be taken as prototypical results on Pentecostalism in general, unless their part and weight in the Pentecostal network is comprehensively demonstrated. Otherwise, certain features of a particular church or movement are projected as typical Pentecostal characteristics. A study of the Church of God in the United States or the Brazilian Assemblies of God is not a study of Pentecostalism in itself. Any such representative claims have to be strongly rejected.

In reconstructing Pentecostalism as a research subject in this way, attention must also be given to the historical dimension. So far, we have counted as Pentecostalism that which has a share in a current discursive network. This strictly *synchronous* network needs to be supplemented by a *diachronous* perspective in order to be able to speak of a history of Pentecostalism. This second, diachronous criterion means that we can only speak of Pentecostalism in history when the synchronous Pentecostal network stands in a diachronous, direct, continuous historical relationship to previous synchronous networks, that is, in a historically verifiable line of reception and tradition. This leads to the issue of historiography.

HISTORIOGRAPHY: ARE THERE HISTORICAL "ORIGINS" OF PENTECOSTALISM?

The representation of the past is a powerful resource for identity positioning in the present.[31] It was Walter Hollenweger who realized that the identity of Pentecostalism could be articulated in reference to its supposed origins and who initiated today's historiographical debates in Pentecostalism. In a critical revision of the historical sources, he insisted on the "black roots of Pentecostalism" at Azusa Street, where, in Bartleman's now-famous statement, "the 'color line' was washed away by the blood."[32] Hollenweger and several of his Ph.D. students established their case firmly, and argued successfully, that the origins of Pentecostalism were not to be found in white middle-class America but in the subaltern margins of U.S. society and beyond established racial segregations.[33] This perspective led to some historical debate, like that at the Brighton Conference on World Evangelization in 1991.[34] Hollenweger consciously used the discussion on historical origins for discursive identity politics: "In the end, we have to see that the decision between Parham and Seymour is not a historical but a theological one."[35]

By the centenary of the Azusa Street revival, Hollenweger's interpretation of Pentecostal origins had become the dominant view within American Pentecostalism and beyond. This is also the case in academia,[36] though there are still portrayals of the early American Pentecostal movement that emphasize Parham and the Topeka revival.[37] However, historiography on Pentecostal origins continues and takes new twists as the awareness of the global dimension of Pentecostalism grows.

The establishment of the Azusa Street paradigm implied that Pentecostalism's origins were to be found in the United States, as Cecil Robeck has pointed out: "without wishing to be triumphalistic, the evidence gathered in all serious quests for origins of the modern pentecostal movement appears inevitably to point to North America."[38]

Especially among scholars who focus their research on the non-Western Pentecostal movement, there is a certain uneasiness with such an American-centered history. It does not seem to do justice to the multifaceted and global nature of the Pentecostal phenomenon, and worldwide Pentecostalism is interpreted as the result of Pentecostal missionary work from North America.[39]

Allan Anderson complains that "the 'made in the USA' assumption is one of the great disservices done to worldwide Pentecostalism."[40] He supports Hollenweger's emphasis on the black roots of Pentecostalism but pushes beyond this paradigm: "Without minimizing the importance of Azusa Street, due recognition must be given to places in the world where pentecostal revival broke out independently of this event and in some cases predated it."[41] He explicitly mentions the Korean Pentecost, with its prelude in 1903, the 1905–7 Mukti revival in India, and the 1909 revival in Chile.[42]

The rationale for this decentering of Pentecostal origins is a critique of Eurocentrism and implicit notions of Western (North American) dominance in the research on Pentecostalism.[43] To counter this situation, Anderson demands a new narrative of Pentecostal beginnings that privileges "multiple origins." His fresh look into Pentecostal origins is not meant as a mere historical exercise but as identity politics: "The early years of Pentecostalism represent more than its infancy. This period was the decisive heart of the movement, the formative time when precedents were set down for posterity—whatever happened later was because of the founders who blazed the way."[44]

Cultural and postcolonial studies are traditionally strongly connected with emancipation movements.[45] Their overall theoretical approach presents a critique of any kind of essentializing notions of history and society, and they also acknowledge the strong reality of hegemonic discursive formations with the power to marginalize people groups. The question arises whether it is possible to change hegemonic discourse in favor of the marginalized and subalterns, since the Foucauldian "speaking subjects" are subject to the rules and exclusion mechanisms of ruling discourses.[46] Although ruling discourses have a considerable transformatory potential and are in no way monolithic or invariant, resistance is only possible within a discursive formation, whether by inversion or mimicry.[47] Against this background, it has been argued that, for the sake of resistance, essentializing counterclaims have to be made for strategic reasons. Ernest Laclau and Chantal Mouffe, for example, combine their analysis of discursive identity politics with the application of political mobilization strategies that change the hegemonic discourse of society.[48] Under the title, "Deconstructing Historiography," Gayatri Spivak has written about the critical historiography of the Indian "Subaltern Studies" project and has characterized it "as *strategically* adhering to the essentialist notion of [subaltern] consciousness . . . within a historiographic practice that draws many of its strengths from that very critique."[49] She reads their writing of history from the subaltern perspective "as a *strategic* use of positivist essentialism in a scrupulously visible political interest."[50]

Spivak's argument for a "strategic essentialism" seems to me to be very similar to the historiographical projects of Pentecostal origins proposed by Hollenweger and Anderson. The cultural studies approach discusses this kind of emancipatory historiography with sympathy but is also critical of its shortcomings. In a later article, "Can the Subaltern Speak?" Gayatri Spivak was more cautious. She saw that the historiographical representation of the subaltern agency is in danger of recovering a subject position that the subaltern was never permitted to have, and, in this way, its representation means a hegemonic realienation by the intellectual elite.[51] The ambivalent reflections about strategic essentialism are thus illuminating for a sharper analysis of similar discussions within the research on Pentecostalism.

However, I would plead that scholarship should try to refrain from a conscious and strategic essentialism, though it has to recognize and reflect that research is always embedded in a context. The epistemological interest of cultural studies does not necessarily seek guidance for political action but is basically historical. It could be described, along the lines of Foucault, as a "permanent critique of our historical being."[52] If we apply this concretely to the examination of Pentecostalism, the main concern would be to work out its historical genealogies and contingencies. Of course, this is intrinsically connected to criticism of ideological agendas, which will always have potential political implications, but the critical ethos remains the main guiding principle for research.

On the other hand, Pentecostal identity politics relating to historical origins require more attention in scholarly research, as they are important articulations that help establish the Pentecostal network. Historians mostly use hagiographic Pentecostal histories only as a quarry for mining "real" historical data, whereas the complexities of identity production and representation contained in such accounts remain ignored. New ways to deal with this problem are proposed, for example, by Jörg Haustein's work on Ethiopian Pentecostalism. He offers a historical-critical reading of the available sources, not in an attempt to reconstruct mere historical "facts," but in order to recover the intentionality and political thrust of the sources and thus the dynamics of Pentecostal history production in Ethiopia.[53]

How then to deal critically with the history of Pentecostalism and especially the question of historical "origins"? The articulation of a Pentecostal network for the present time is largely undisputed, but what is the case with the historical dimension? Do we have a subject, Pentecostalism, which can be convincingly traced back through an unbroken line of reception and tradition? If we try to go back in the reconstruction of Pentecostalism, it ought to be possible to identify a previous synchronous network in the past that, by exhibiting similarities and historical connections with the present synchronous network, can thus be assigned to Pentecostalism. In order to make a judgment on this matter, the immediate and direct predecessors of all parts of the present synchronous Pentecostal network need to be meticulously reconstructed. If this is done, these predecessors must likewise be examined for their own synchronous connections. This reconstruction remains an assessment, since on the one hand each previous synchronous network does not contain all parts of the one that follows and on the other there will be additional parts that are not part of the following one. Moreover, the character of synchronous connections might differ in the previous networks from those that follow. Where an argument can be convincingly made that a previous synchronous network is strikingly similar to the one following, then this predecessor could be considered as belonging to the same discursive network. In this way it goes back step by step. It will always be a story of continuity and discontinuity, open to different assessment. A history of reception and tradition could theoretically be retraced as far back as desired, as there will never only be discontinuity. However, it must be accurately and accordingly weighed and discussed at every point backward. On each historical step backward, reception, continuity, and fracture need to be extensively discussed. With every one of these steps back in history, the predecessors will necessarily differ more from the present synchronous network. If a point is reached where the dissimilarity can be assessed as striking, then one could call this the "origins."

For this abstract historical application of the network concept to be of practical use in historical research, it means that certain time periods (a certain few years) have to be grouped together and identified as "synchronous" in order to be able to trace back previous synchronous networks. The concrete grouping will depend on its representation in the respective sources. It should be especially noted that diachronous reconstruction takes the present as its starting point and goes back from the present to the past.[54] This might seem confusing, as it goes against established chronology, but it gives credit to one of the crucial concerns of historicizing in cultural studies approaches.[55] In this way, a teleologizing of historical reconstructions is effectively prevented, and the "Chimera of the origin" is successfully "driven out."[56] However, this does not necessarily mean that any history of Pentecostalism has to be written in reverse chronology, even if it is based on such a diachronous reconstruction of the network.

This approach has some serious practical implications. As the critical diachronous (re)construction of the Pentecostal network inverts the old-fashioned historical chronology, the main historical interest is focused not on the supposed origins of Pentecostalism but on the historical discontinuity and continuity with the present synchronous network. Evidence from research suggests that the current global Pentecostal network came together only in the past two or three decades. An indicator for this is the observed progressive conflation of "classical" Pentecostalism and "Neo-" Pentecostalism, and often also Charismatic movements in the mainline churches, in many regions of the world.[57] This assumption also agrees with statistical evidence that the remarkable growth of global Pentecostalism did not take place before the 1970s and parallels its expansion into a broad inclusive network.[58] "Classical" Pentecostals themselves are still trying to make theological sense of this development. Pentecostal scholars affiliated with Regent University, for instance, describe global Pentecostalism in the broad sense as a "renewal movement" and ascribe to it certain theological characteristics that are acceptable to classical Pentecostals but go beyond it at the same time.[59] In addition, the whole scholarly debate about a broad understanding of Pentecostalism that arose only in the 1970s should be seen in this context. In this sense, the present synchronous Pentecostal network owes its development to what is often called the second and third waves and their subsequent conflation with "classical"Pentecostalism. From this point of view, the historical-critical focus for the "origins" of present global Pentecostalism would be the 1970s and 1980s.

However, usually, the origins of Pentecostalism are traced back to the first decade of the twentieth century, usually accompanied by strong identity claims, as we have seen above. Within the critical approach applied here, it is of course possible to go farther back than the 1970 and 1980s in a diachronous (re)construction. Yet it is never the "origin" of Pentecostalism that is discovered in this exercise, only a synchronous network at a certain time, which is assessed to stand mainly in historical discontinuity with the time before.

The advantage of this perspective is that it follows formal principles and is able to analyze the historical context without the teleological lenses of later Pentecostalism. By this means, it elicits an alternative and fresh look at events such as the Azusa Street and Mukti revivals and supports the view that they were part of a global network of evangelical missions, as has been argued by several scholars recently.[60] From this point of view, the "origin" of Pentecostalism is not in one specific revival but in the gradual development of a global missionary network,[61] and in this way Pentecostalism "was transnational from the outset."[62] It is then possible to see, in the many revivals of the 1900s, events that led to Pentecostalism, but it would be historical hijacking to claim them all as Pentecostalism. This would be a reprint of the "providential" approach and would obscure the complicated trajectory of historical development.[63]

The revival chronicler Edwin Orr speaks of a global "Fifth General Awakening" between 1900 and 1910 that was characterized by many different revivals, including Keswick, the evangelistic campaigns of Reuben Archer Torrey and Charles Alexander, the Welsh revival, the Khasi Hills revival, the Mukti Mission, the Azusa Street revival, and the Korean revival:

> It was the most extensive Evangelical Awakening of all time, reviving Anglican, Baptist, Congregational, Disciple, Lutheran, Methodist, Presbyterian and Reformed churches and other evangelical bodies throughout Europe and North America, Australasia and South Africa, and their daughter churches and missionary causes throughout Asia, Africa and Latin America, winning more than five million folk to an evangelical faith in the two years of greatest impact in each country.[64]

During that time, the global evangelical missionary movement that was connected through a dense network of extensive correspondence and personal contacts was very much focussed on revival matters: "What was remarkable was that missionaries and national believers in obscure places in India, the Far East, Africa and Latin America seemed to move at the same time to pray for phenomenal revival in their fields and world wide."[65]

Orr is of the opinion that during this "Fifth General Awakening," Pentecostalism was not a crucial factor but rather a later by-product: "Indirectly it [the Fifth General Awakening] produced Pentecostalism."[66] Frederick Henke, a contemporary theologian of established Protestantism, also saw Azusa Street simply as a small part of this greater revival: "This speaking in tongues is but one of a series of such phenomena as 'tongues of fire', 'rushing of a mighty wind', 'interpretation of tongues', jerking, writhing, and falling to the ground, which are occurring in connection with a world-wide religious revival."[67]

It is important to note that in most of the larger revivals of international impact during this decade speaking in tongues as a specified manifestation played no theological role at all, even if the phenomenon might have happened during emotional revival outbursts; Azusa Street and Mukti were the exceptions rather than the rule. Special mention must be made of the 1907 Korean revival that was called the "Korean Pentecost" but contained no theological reflection on speaking in tongues.[68] Nevertheless, the Korean revival and its Chinese offshoots in 1908 also developed in clear relation to the general expectations of revival found in evangelical missionary circles. Western missionaries to Korea had earlier visited Wales and Khasi in India and hoped for similar events in their mission fields.[69] This revival had a deep impact on Korean church history and shows what different trajectories the revivals in the first decade of the twentieth century could take.

However, where speaking in tongues was given credit, the interpretation of the phenomenon varied extensively. Speaking in tongues, interpreted as "missionary tongues" (xenoglossic tongues as the tool for dramatic endtime revival) and as "initial evidence" of Spirit baptism, was forcefully emphasized by the Azusa Street revival and from there successfully channeled through missionary networks.[70]

There were many in these missionary circles who were sympathetic to speaking in tongues but did not agree with a narrow interpretation. For other contemporaries, speaking in tongues was considered merely a special spiritual and emotional expression of revival times. The Christian and Missionary Alliance, probably the most important evangelical mission of the holiness movement at the time, is a case in point. It did not object to speaking in tongues and accepted it as a "special manifestation of the Holy Ghost."[71] It was allowed and practiced in the Alliance, and its president, A.B. Simpson, apparently desired it.[72] What was criticized by representatives of this mission organization with decades of experience in foreign countries was the idea of "missionary tongues" as a substitute for learning foreign languages and also the exclusivism of the initial evidence doctrine.[73] As late as 1910, Simpson could officially report in an editorial:

> The statement is made that the Alliance and its leaders are opposed to the manifestation of the Gift of Tongues in this age. This is wholly false. Our attitude has been often stated and is consistent and explicit. We fully recognize all the gifts of the Spirit, including 'divers kind of tongues' as belonging to the Church in every age. And many of our most wise and honored workers both in the homeland and in the mission field have had this experience. But we are opposed to the teaching that this special gift is for all or is the evidence of the Baptism of the Holy Ghost.[74]

Speaking in tongues as such was apparently not the issue, and leading members, like Robert Jaffray and John Salmon, spoke in tongues and did not need to leave the Christian and Missionary Alliance, even after the formal break with Pentecostalism in 1912.[75]

The Mukti Mission fits also into this perspective—the "multiple origins" discussion, as to whether it was the first Pentecostal revival even before Azusa Street, misses the point.[76] Pandita Ramabai and her Western missionary colleagues were firmly embedded in the global evangelical missionary network and its strong revival expectations, which they found answered in the revival that started at Mukti in 1905 and where speaking in tongues occurred. The conceptualization of speaking in tongues in the Mukti revival differed among its participants. Incoming missionaries from Azusa Street and related places in the United States propagated missionary tongues and initial evidence, but the Mukti staff apparently did not; they simply viewed these as possible exceptional manifestations of the revival. Although the American missionaries at Mukti, Minnie Abrams and Albert Norton,[77] and Pandita Ramabai herself agreed increasingly on the importance of tongues in the revival, probably under the influence of the Azusa Street teachings, they never went further than accepting it as "one of the signs of the baptism of the Holy Spirit" and were not convinced that it is "the only and necessary sign."[78] However, at a time of revival this was not felt to be a dividing issue. Minnie Abrams wrote to Alexander Boddy in England in 1908:

All may and should receive this sign [of tongues speech], yet we dare not say that no one is Spirit-baptized who has not received this sign. Yet we see the same gifts and graces and power for service in those who hold these different beliefs, and, so far as I know, we are as yet working in love and unity for the spread of this mighty work of the Holy Spirit.[79]

Ramabai, Norton, and Abrams represented the view found in circles of the Christian and Missionary Alliance, which which they had close contacts. However, there was also at least one close supporter of the Mukti Mission, Rachael Nader, who apparently did not give any weight to speaking in tongues during the revival there.[80]

Much has been made of the fact that the U.S. missionary Willis Collins Hoover first heard about the revival at Mukti through a tract by his friend, the U.S. missionary to India, Minnie Abrams.[81] A standard detail in early Pentecostal historiography,[82] this is indeed information of interest showing how decentered the evangelical missionary network at the time was. However, by 1909 Hoover was also in close correspondence with several individuals in the United States and Great Britain about Pentecostal issues, and he himself proposed a rather U.S.-centered historiography of the whole revival.[83] In 1909 he stated that the present "Pentecostal movement" had its origin in 1906 in Los Angeles,[84] and in 1928 he looked back at its history with the following words: "From 1900 in the United States, there began in several areas these same manifestations. It has extended all over the world, so that in India, China, Africa, England, Norway, Germany, etc., there are many Pentecostal churches."[85] On the other hand, this historical view did not hinder Hoover from rejecting the initial evidence doctrine.

It seems that by about 1909 global revival enthusiasm had gradually declined, and many felt that the time of awakening was over. The Azusa Street interpretation of speaking in tongues could not keep to its initial promises, and the Azusa Street revival itself lost momentum.[86] As William Faupel has stressed, by the end of 1908 it had become clear that Pentecostal expectations were not realized:[87] "The delay of the parousia and inability to speak in known tongues forced most Pentecostals to reassess their mission."[88]

Unlike many others who accepted the vanishing of spiritual gifts with the end of the revival, many of those who had believed strongly in the importance of tongues did not accept failure. The idea of missionary tongues, prominent especially in Azusa Street,[89] was discarded, and speaking in tongues transformed from a revival phenomenon into an everyday spiritual practice. With the end of the general revival, and accompanied by a dramatic change of theological tenets, a distinct global synchronous Pentecostal network established itself within a few years. I would argue that it was only here that Pentecostalism emerged and not before. It seems that those circles that placed a special emphasis on speaking in tongues came together. Especially in the United States, many retained and emphasized the initial evidence doctrine from Azusa Street,[90] after they had stripped it from its former most important component, "missionary tongues." However, other groups that emphasized speaking in tongues but never adopted an initial evidence doctrine also became an accepted part of this global Pentecostal network, for example, the earliest groups in Chile and Germany and the Elim Pentecostal Church founded in Great Britain in 1915.[91] Clear indications of the development of a distinct synchronous Pentecostal network are also the foundation of its own institutional organizations and denominations, such as, in 1909, the Iglesia Metodista Pentecostal in Chile, the Pentecostal Missionary Union in Great Britain, and the Christlicher Gemeinschafsverband GmbH Mühlheim/Ruhr in Germany. In the United States by 1909 several Holiness churches had become established Pentecostal churches, for example, the Church of God in Christ (after it had won its lawsuit) and the Church of God, which had opened its administrative office that year, eventually followed by the Assemblies of God in 1914, this latter the result of an open break with the Christian and Missionary Alliance in 1912.[92]

It is noteworthy that in his recent book Allan Anderson no longer focuses only on "multiple origins" and actually refrains from his former strategic essentialism: "It is best to see both the Mukti and Azusa Street revivals (as well as the 1909 Chilean revival) as formative events contributing towards the emergence of Pentecostalism."[93] The Korean revival, formerly put forward as an important example, is no longer highlighted.[94] The examples of Mukti and of the Christian and Missionary Alliance show also that not all participants in the revivals where speaking in tongues occurred felt compelled to join the Pentecostal network afterward. Pandita Ramabai and the Christian and Missionary Alliance did not. A discussion on origins that claims Mukti as a Pentecostal revival would emphasize the views of white American missionaries and Azusa Street–related groups that interpreted the Mukti revival as support for their claims and interpretations. It would deny persons like Pandita Ramabai their own voices, monopolizing them for Pentecostalism, though Ramabai chose not to follow that way and eventually left her mission organization to join the Christian and Missionary Alliance. Along this and similar lines of argument, a historical analysis based on a cultural studies approach enables a fresh and critical look at Pentecostal historiography.

RESEARCH PERSPECTIVES: WHAT IS THE RELATIONSHIP BETWEEN THE RESEARCHER AND THE RESEARCHED?

One of the most controversial frontiers of present-day Pentecostalism is the group called African Instituted/Independent Churches (AICs). Do they belong to the present synchronous network of Pentecostalism? Looking at the situation on the ground, it seems clear that normally AICs and Pentecostal/Charismatic movements in Africa consider each other archenemies.[95] However, in research on African Pentecostalism the similarities have been repeatedly emphasized. It was probably Hollenweger who first included the AICs in a survey of Pentecostalism. In his groundbreaking study, *The Pentecostals,* he reserved a whole chapter to them, naming them "independent African Pentecostal churches" or "Zionists."[96] He pointed to the close historical relations with early Pentecostal missions and the many similarities in spiritual practices. He engaged in a conscious remapping of the field and quoted from his correspondence with Pentecostal representatives who strenuously denied that African Zionist churches could be called Pentecostal and who had urged him to "delete the whole section on independent Pentecostals from [his] book."[97] Hollenweger tried to dilute this disagreement when he referred to other Pentecostal voices, like David du Plessis, who had acknowledged points of relationship.[98] This line of argument was forcefully followed by Allan Anderson in several of his earlier publications.[99] In later publications, Anderson has become more cautious in his claims, explicitly reacting to the charge of Hans-Jürgen Becken that his inclusive definition is also a representative claim by a (white) "Pentecostal minister."[100] However, the inclusive perspective is still present in his influential *Introduction to Pentecostalism* (2004).[101] It should be noted that Anderson is not the only Western scholar who has proposed an inclusive understanding of Pentecostalism with regard to AICs. Harvey Cox can also be mentioned here.[102]

This side of the debate is supplemented by David Barrett's powerful representation of AICs as Pentecostals. Barrett's early research interest was in the AICs and their relationship to wider Christianity. One of his achievements was to give the AICs due place in the description of African Christianity.[103] He successfully proposed an ecumenical approach to them and carefully recorded and supported the growing interactions of AICs with Orthodox churches and the World Council of Churches. When Barrett developed his *World Christian Encyclopedia* and started to map world Christianity, he created "Non-white indigenous Christianity"[104] as a typological category where the AICs found their place.[105] When his statistics found their way into the *Dictionary of Pentecostal and Charismatic Movements,* he split the AICs into "Non-White indigenous quasipentecostals" and "indigenous revivalist pentecostals."[106] Both were cited as subcategories of "First Wave Pentecostalism." For the new edition of the *Dictionary,* he changed the arrangement so that all AICs are part of the new subcategory "African indigenous pentecostal/ charismatics," which comes under "Neocharismatics"/"Non-White indigenous pentecostals/charismatics."[107]

Now, this massive scholarly representation of AICs as part of Pentecostalism has had repercussions on the self-understanding of Pentecostals and AICs, but this is rarely analyzed. However, in a cultural studies approach, it is assumed that the academic observer stands generally in an interrelationship with the research subject. Academic and other perspectives are not understood as entirely independent. Some of the reasons for this assumption were already discussed with regard to the concept of Pentecostalism as a synchronous network. However, this approach does not support what is sometimes called the "postmodern view," wherein all perspectives are considered equally valid in academia, since as any perspective, including the scholarly, is loaded with implicit worldviews, the researcher might arbitrarily choose one—even a religious one. This is sometimes brought forward by Pentecostal theologians looking for adequate academic self-articulation. David Moore, for example, proposes:

> At the dawn of the twenty-first century, the dominance of Enlightenment-influenced epistemologies is fading and appreciation for the validity of differing worldviews is growing. This new openness, though often criticized, seems to be an open door through which Renewal historians can insert an informed, providential historiography.[108]

The cultural studies approach as understood here sees itself in the tradition of the Enlightenment, as I already hinted at with reference to Foucault, and does not support an "anything goes" strategy but a *critical* reflection and above all historicizing of hegemonic discourses. It understands science as a critical task and not an affirmative one. However, critique also means the deconstruction of reductionist materialist approaches that, in the name of enlightenment, declare miracles and spiritual healing to be nothing more than crude superstition. The cultural studies approach, with its realistic view on discourse, also understands itself as an alternative to these kinds of positivistic reductionism.

The question of how academic representation influences cultural transformation processes was intensively discussed in the so-called Orientalism debate associated with Edward Said, which deals with the lasting impact of Western scientific representations of the "Orient" in the context of Western colonialism.[109] From this point of view, it can be assumed that the results of academic research on Pentecostalism have affected and continue to affect Pentecostal discourse, and the powerful dominance of Western scholarship representing movements in Africa, Asia, and Latin America is here taken into account. The history of academic research into Pentecostalism is part of the history of Pentecostalism itself. However, this does not make academic research into Pentecostalism a religious enterprise. Neither the academic nor the religious perspective needs to be relativized—though both perspectives can easily interplay, as when Pentecostals do research as social scientists or when theologians combine religious and academic perspectives.

However, the connectedness needs to be made explicit and critically discussed. With regard to my example of the AICs, this would mean that we have to have a closer look at how, for instance, Barrett's categories and representation of Pentecostalism including the AICs get widely reified beyond academia. Every recent book on global Pentecostalism has a reference to Barrett's statistics,[110] and today leading North American Pentecostal theologians have also sympathetically received Barrett's inclusivism, especially regarding the AICs. This is, for example, the case with Amos Yong and Cecil Robeck.[111] In the *New International Encyclopedia of Pentecostal/Charismatic Christianity*, edited by Stanley Burgess, who is another prominent North American Pentecostal theologian, the "African Initiated Churches" have their own entry, though their affiliation with Pentecostalism is left open.[112] One would then have to look at whether and how this positive reception of a broad understanding of Pentecostalism by Pentecostal theologians has trickled down to the popular religious press and the congregations of North American Pentecostalism. However, here the focus is on another and even more fascinating aspect of these dynamics, and that is how Western scholarly discussion about the relationship between Pentecostals and AICs has had an impact on the AICs themselves. The so-called Organization of African Instituted Churches (OAIC) is a case in point. Because the relationship with mission churches remained strained, even after the decolonization of Africa, many AICs sought alternative ways to establish ecumenical connections. As Ethiopianist ideas were common in AICs, a strong link to the Coptic and Ethiopian churches developed over the years.[113] As a result, in 1978 the OAIC was founded with the help of the Coptic church at Cairo, which brought AICs back into the larger framework of world Christianity. In the 1990s the relationship with the Coptic church loosened, but instead the ties to the WCC and its partner organizations intensified, which also included financial support. This new orientation to the Protestant WCC was accompanied by a new theological positioning within the OAIC. AICs began to think about their identity with positive reference to the Pentecostal movement and in line with the categories of Western scholarship. In a general sense this had not happened before, although, for instance, a representative from the Nigerian Christ Apostolic Church had already taken part in the second OAIC conference in 1982.[114] The Christ Apostolic Church is perhaps one of the few AIC churches that already in the 1980s claimed a distinct Pentecostal identity for itself as "Aladura Pentecostal."[115]

At the third General Assembly of 1997, which was combined with a WCC-AIC consultation, Njeru Wambugu, acting general secretary of the OAIC, suggested in an opening address "three categories of AICs":

> [1] the Ethiopian and nationalist churches which parted ways with the missions for mainly political reasons, [2] the Holy Spirit churches with a particular emphasis on culture and spiritual gifts, and [3] the Pentecostals. The latter consist of the African Pentecostals which are close to the Holy Spirit churches and Newer Pentecostals influenced by North American groups and visiting mass evangelists.[116]

In a further development, the OAIC understood "African Pentecostals" as a constitutive part of the AICs. To some extent, this development might be understood as the direct appropriation of the inclusive Western scholarly definition of

Pentecostalism. The OAIC and several churches in different parts of Africa work together with individual Western missionaries with a special concern for AICs. These missionaries are connected with each other through a small newsletter, the *Review of AICs*. In the *Review* the publications of Anderson and his definition proposals receive a great deal of attention.[117] It is certainly not far-fetched to assume that through these missionaries the inclusive definition was made known to the AICs themselves. At least in one case this has definitely happened in relation to the OAIC. John Padwick, a missionary for the Christian Missionary Society, has worked with the OAIC from its beginning and played a crucial part in its organization and theological formation. Padwick has lived and worked in Kenya since 1970 and coauthored a book with David Barrett on the AICs.[118] In 2003 he finished a Ph.D. on AICs in Kenya under the supervision of Allan Anderson at the University of Birmingham.[119] There, Padwick suggests, with explicit but also critical reference to Anderson, a threefold typology of AICs, with third type being "African Pentecostal Churches," which in style look to the West and Western Pentecostalism and have their centers more in urban society than in African rural traditions where the other AICs are deeply rooted. This threefold typology has become the received view of the OAIC in recent years. In the official report on the dialogue between the OAIC and the World Alliance of Reformed Churches in 2002 (where John Padwick was also one of the "drafters" and "editors") we read:

> 6. OAIC groups its members into three categories:
>   - Nationalist churches (also known as Ethiopian and African Churches) . . .
>   - Spiritual churches (also known as Zionist, Apostolic, and Aladura Churches) . . .
>   - African Pentecostal churches. These are African founded pentecostal style churches that have arisen since the mid-1960s. Though the stimulus to their foundation has frequently been the evangelistic missions and training conventions associated with Western pentecostals (and as a result, there is some dispute whether these churches are fully African), a number of them (those that give a positive value to African culture) have found a home in OAIC. There are tensions between these churches and the spiritual churches which relate more to styles of worship than to essential differences over doctrine.[120]

By this point the threefold typology had become the official self-understanding of the OAIC. It is also given on the OAIC official Web site under the heading "What Are African Independent Churches?" and repeated in other OAIC documents.[121] Though this does not go as far as Anderson's inclusive efforts, the OAIC now officially declares that the difference between other AICs and Pentecostals is not "theological" but a matter of "style" only and that both belong to the same type of AIC Christianity. In this way then the discussion has reached a full circle and shows the dynamics of how Western scholarly discussions of definitions relate back to identity positioning in global Pentecostalism.

OUTLOOK

The specific perspectives of cultural and postcolonial studies are in many ways of interest for research into global Pentecostalism, and not only with regard to the three issues discussed here as examples. Other topics to be explored could include, among others, identity and migration or popular culture.[122] However, their actual relevance to the study of Pentecostal and Charismatic movements has yet to be explored.

NOTES

I am particularly indebted to Allan Anderson, Kenneth Fleming, and Jörg Haustein for their comments on earlier drafts of this chapter.

1. Victoria Bonnell and Lynn Hunt, eds., *Beyond the Cultural Turn* (Berkeley: UCP, 1999).

2. André Corten, *Pentecostalism in Brazil* (London: Macmillan 1999); André Corten and Ruth Marshall-Fratani, eds., *Between Babel and Pentecost* (Bloomington: IUP 2001).

3. Simon Coleman, *The Globalisation of Charismatic Christianity* (Cambridge: CUP 2000); Joel Robbins, "On the Paradoxes of Global Pentecostalism," *Religion* 33 (2003): 221–31; André Droogers et al., eds., *Playful Religion* (Delft: Eburon, 2006); Birgit Meyer, "Impossible Representations," in *Religion, Media, and the Public Sphere,* ed. Birgit Meyer and Annelies Moors (Bloomington: IUP, 2006), 290–312.

4. Timothy Cargal, "Beyond the Fundamentalist-Modernist Controversy," *Pneuma* 15 (1993): 163–87; Jackie David Johns, "Pentecostalism and the Postmodern Worldview," *JPT* 7 (1995): 73–96.

5. Jessica Munns and Gita Rajan, eds., *A Cultural Studies Reader* (London: Longman, 1995); Roger Bromley et al., eds., *Cultural Studies* (Lüneburg: Klampen, 1999).

6. Jacques Derrida, *L'Écriture et la différence* (Paris: du Seuil 1967), Michel Foucault, *L'ordre du discours* (Paris: Gallimard 1971), Ernesto Laclau, "Why Do Empty Signifiers Matter to Politics," in *The Lesser Evil and the Greater Good,* ed. Jeffrey Weeks (London: Rivers Oram, 1994), 167–78.

7. Lawrence Grossberg, "Cultural Studies," in *Bringing It All Back Home,* ed. Lawrence Grossberg (Durham: Duke University Press, 1997), 257.

8. Grossberg, "Cultural Studies," 258–59.

9. Philipp Sarasin, *Geschichtswissenschaft und Diskursanalyse* (Frankfurt: Suhrkamp, 2003).

10. Lawrence Grossberg, ed., *Dancing in Spite of Myself* (Durham: Duke University Press, 1997); Hartmut Böhme et al., eds., *Orientierung Kulturwissenschaft* (Reinbeck: Rowohlt, 2000).

11. Gauri Viswanathan, "Raymond Williams and British Colonialism," *Yale Journal of Criticism* 4:2 (1991): 47–66; Grossberg, "Cultural Studies," 269 n. 19.

12. Patrick Williams and Laura Chrisman, eds., *Colonial Discourse and Post-Colonial Theory* (New York: CoUP 1994); Bart Moore-Gilbert, *Postcolonial Theory* (London: Verso, 1997); Robert Young, *Postcolonialism* (London: Blackwell, 2001).

13. Fredric Jameson, "On 'Cultural Studies,'" *Social Text* 34 (1993): 17–52.

14. David Barrett, "Art. Statistics, Global," in *DPCM*, 810–30; David Barrett and T. M. Johnson, "Global Statistics," in *NIDPCM*, 283–302.

15. Dale T. Irvin, "Pentecostal Historiography and Global Christianity," *Pneuma* 27 (2005): 35–50.

16. Joel Robbins, "The Globalization of Pentecostal and Charismatic Christianity," *Annual Review of Anthropology* 33 (2004): 122.

17. Gary McGee, "Pentecostal Missiology," *Pneuma* 16 (1994): 277.

18. Ernesto Laclau and Chantal Mouffe, *Hegemonie und radikale Demokratie* (Wien: Passagen, 1991), 160.

19. Laclau and Mouffe, *Hegemonie*, 158; Sarasin, *Geschichtswissenschaft*, 100–121.

20. Roman Loimeier, ed., *Die islamische Welt als Netzwerk* (Würzburg: Ergon, 2000); Bettina Hollstein and Florian Straus, eds., *Qualitative Netzwerkanalyse* (Wiesbaden: VS, 2006).

21. Robbins, "Globalization," 125.

22. Hubert Knoblauch, *Kommunikationskultur* (Berlin: de Gruyter, 1995), 308–10; Michael Schwab-Trapp, "Diskurs als soziologisches Konzept," in *Handbuch Sozialwissenschaftliche Diskursanalyse: Band I*, ed. Reiner Keller et al. (Opladen: Leske/Budrich, 2001), 270–71.

23. Stephan Moebius, *Die soziale Konstituierung des Anderen* (Frankfurt: Campus, 2003); Sérgio Costa, *Vom Nordatlantik zum "Black Atlantic"* (Bielefeld: Transcript, 2007); Reiner Keller, *Wissenssoziologische Diskursanalyse* (Wiesbaden: VS, 2008).

24. Derrida, *L'Écriture*.

25. Laclau and Mouffe, *Hegemonie*; Ernesto Laclau, "Was haben leere Signifikanten mit Politik zu tun?" *Mesotes* 4 (1994): 157–65; Homi Bhabha, *The Location of Culture* (London: Routledge 1994).

26. Coleman, *Globalisation*, 27–47.

27. Klaude Kendrick, "Vereinigte Staaten von Amerika," in *Die Pfingstkirchen*, ed. Walter Hollenweger (Stuttgart: EvangelischesVerlagswerk, 1971), 34.

28. Anderson, *Introduction*, 14.

29. Everett Wilson, "They Crossed the Red Sea, Didn't They?" in *The Globalization of Pentecostalism*, ed. Marray Dempster et al. (Oxford: Regnum, 1999),106.

30. Wilson, "They Crossed the Red Sea," 109.

31. George Clement Bond and Angela Gilliam, eds., *Social Construction of the Past* (London: Routledge, 1994); Daud Ali, ed., *Invoking the Past* (New Delhi: OUP, 1999).

32. Frank Bartleman, *Azusa Street* (Plainfield: Bridge, 1980), 54.

33. Walter Hollenweger, "After Twenty Years' Research on Pentecostalism," *IMR* 75 (1986): 3–12; Douglas Nelson, "For Such a Time as This" (Ph.D. diss., University of Birmingham, 1981); Iain MacRobert, *The Black Roots and White Racism of Early Pentecostalism in the USA* (Basingstoke: Macmillan, 1988); Iain MacRobert, "The Black Roots of Pentecostalism," in *Pentecost, Mission and Ecumenism*, ed. Jan Jongeneel et al. (Frankfurt: Lang, 1992), 73–84.

34. Cecil Robeck, "Pentecostal Origins from a Global Perspective," in *All Together in One Place*, ed. Harold Hunter and Peter Hocken (Sheffield: SAP, 1993), 166–80; James Goff, *Fields White unto Harvest* (Fayetteville: University of Arkansas Press, 1988); Japie Lapoorta, "A Response to Cecil Robeck," in Hunter and Hocken, *All Together*, 181–85.

35. Walter Hollenweger, *Charismatisch-pfingstliches Christentum* (Göttingen: Vandenhoeck, 1997), 35.

36. Harold Hunter and Cecil Robeck, eds., *The Azusa Street Revival and Its Legacy* (Cleveland: Pathway, 2006); Cecil Robeck, *The Azusa Street Mission & Revival* (Nashville: Nelson, 2006).

37. Goff, *Fields*; Grant Wacker, *Heaven Below* (Cambridge, MA: HUP, 2001), 5–6.

38. Robeck, "Pentecostal Origins from a Global Perspective,"170. Nichol called the United States the "birthplace of twentieth-century Pentecostalism": John Thomas Nichol, *Pentecostalism* (New York: Harper, 1966), 25.

39. Anthea Butler, "Constructing Different Memories," in Hunter and Robeck, *Azusa Street*, 193–201.

40. Allan Anderson, "Revising Pentecostal History in Global Perspective," in *Asian and Pentecostal*, ed. Allan Anderson and Edmond Tang (Baguio City: Regnum, 2005), 152; Anderson, *Introduction*, 166–83.

41. Anderson, "Revising Pentecostal History," 154; Allan Anderson, "Signs and Blunders," *Journal of Asian Mission* 2:2 (2000): 201.

42. Anderson, "Revising Pentecostal History," 154–58.

43. Anderson, "Signs," 193–195.

44. Allan Anderson, *Spreading Fires* (London: SCM, 2007), 5.

45. Bhabha, *The Location of Culture*, 19–39.

46. Michel Foucault, *Die Ordnung des Diskurses* (Frankfurt: Fischer 1991), 25.

47. For an example of resistance by inversion, see Michael Bergunder, "Anti-Brahmanical and Hindu Nationalist Reconstructions of the Indian Prehistory," *Historiographia Linguistica* 31 (2004): 59–104; for mimicry, see Bhabha, *Location of Culture*, 85–92.

48. Laclau and Mouffe, *Hegemonie*.

49. Gayatri Chakravorty Spivak, "Subaltern Studies," *Subaltern Studies* 4 (1985): 344.

50. Spivak, "Subaltern Studies," 342.

51. Gayatri Chakravorty Spivak, "Can the Subaltern Speak?" in *Colonial Discourse and Post-Colonial Theory*, ed. Patrick Williams and Laura Chrisman (New York: CoUP, 1994), 66–111.

52. Michel Foucault, "Was ist Aufklärung?" in *Ethos der Moderne*, ed. Eva Erdmann et al. (Frankfurt: Campus, 1990), 45; Ulrich Brieler, *Die Unerbittlichkeit der Historizität* (Köln: Böhlau, 1998), 599–628; Andrea Hemminger, *Kritik und Geschichte* (Berlin: Philo, 2004).

53. Jörg Haustein, "Writing Religious History: The Historiography of Ethiopian Pentecostalism" (Ph.D. diss., University of Heidelberg, 2009).

54. This important aspect is missing in my earlier writings on the theoretical problems of Pentecostal history, whose findings I otherwise still consider valid; see Michael Bergunder, "The Pentecostal Movement and Basic Ecclesial Communities in Latin America," *IMR* 91 (2002): 163–86; Bergunder, "Constructing Indian Pentecostalism," in Anderson and Tang, *Asian and Pentecostal*, 177–213; Michael Bergunder, *The South Indian Pentecostal Movement in the Twentieth Century* (Grand Rapids: Eerdmans, 2008).

55. Michel de Certeau, *Das Schreiben der Geschichte* (Frankfurt: Campus, 1991).

56. Michel Foucault, "Nietzsche, die Genealogie und die Historie," in *Von der Subversion des Wissens*, ed. Michel Foucault (Frankfurt: Fischer, 1987), 73.

57. Coleman, *Globalszation*, 23–24; Bergunder, *South Indian Pentecostal Movement*.

58. Barrett and Johnson, "Statistics."

59. Stanley York, "Art. Renewal, Church," in *Encyclopedia of Pentecostal and Charismatic Christianity*, ed. Stanley Burgess (New York: Routledge, 2006), 407–9.

60. Bergunder, "Constructing Indian Pentecostalism"; David Maxwell, *African Gifts of the Spirit* (Oxford: Currey 2006),17–37; Anderson, *Spreading Fire*.

61. Bergunder, "Constructing Indian Pentecostalism," 186; Anderson, *Spreading Fire, 7*.

62. Maxwell, *African Gifts of the Spirit*,18.

63. Bergunder, *South Indian Pentecostal Movement*, 7–8.

64. Edwin Orr, *Evangelical Awakenings in Southern Asia* (Minneapolis: Bethany, 1976), 99.

65. Orr, *Evangelical Awakenings*, 100.

66. Orr, *Evangelical Awakenings*, 99; William Faupel, *The Everlasting Gospel* (Sheffield: SAP, 1996),190.

67. Frederick Henke, "The Gift of Tongues and Related Phenomena at the Present Day," *American Journal of Theology* 13 (1909): 193.

68. Anderson, *Spreading Fire*, 30.

69. Myung Keun Choi, *Changes in Korean Society between 1884–1910* (Frankfurt: Lang, 1997), 261–87; Charles Yrigoyen, *The Global Impact of the Wesleyan Traditions* (Lanham, MD: Scarecrow, 2000).

70. Bergunder, *South Indian Pentecostal Movement,* 5–11.

71. Charles Nienkirchen, "A. B. Simpson: Forerunner and Critic of the Pentecostal Movement," in *The Birth of a Vision,* ed. David Hartzfeld and Charles Nienkirchen (Camp Hill: Christian Publications, 1995), 141–43.

72. Nienkirchen, "Simpson," 148–49.

73. Nienkirchen, "Simpson," 143.

74. Quoted in Robert Niklaus et al., *All for Jesus* (Camp Hill: Christian Publications, 1986), 114–15.

75. Charles Nienkirchen, "Christian and Missionary Alliance," in *NIDPCM,* 524.

76. For the discussion on Mukti and the origins of Pentecostalism, see Bergunder, "Constructing Indian Pentecostalism"; Anderson, *Spreading Fire.*

77. For Norton, see Wacker, *Heaven Below,* 285 n. 43.

78. Anderson, *Spreading Fire,* 84–87.

79. *Confidence,* no. 6 (September 1908): 14.

80. Rachael Nalder, in *Latter Rain Evangel,* November 1908.

81. Hollenweger, *Christentum,* 141; Anderson, *Spreading Fire,* 202.

82. The story is first reported in Willis Collins Hoover, *History of the Pentecostal Revival in Chile* (Santiago: Eben-Ezer, 2000), 9; Stanley Howard Frodsham, *With Signs Following* (Springfield: GPH, 1946), 175; Donald Gee, *Wind and Flame* (Croyden: Assemblies of God, 1967), 57.

83. Hoover, *History,* 9, 178–83.

84. Hoover, *History,* 154.

85. Hoover, *History,* 164.

86. Robeck, *Azusa Street,* 281–312.

87. Faupel, *Everlasting Gospel,* 228.

88. Faupel, *Everlasting Gospel,* 308.

89. Bergunder, *South Indian Pentecostal Movement,* 6.

90. Wacker, *Heaven Below,* 41–42.

91. Walter Hollenweger, *The Pentecostals* (Peabody: Hendrickson, 1988), 335; Elim Pentecostal Church, ed., *Discussion Papers Presented to a Theological Conference, the Hayes Conference Centre, Swanwick, Derbyshire, October 1991* (Cheltenham, 1991).

92. Carl Brumback, *A Sound from Heaven* (Springfield: GPH, 1971), 92.

93. Anderson, *Spreading Fire,* 83.

94. Anderson, *Spreading Fire,* 140–41.

95. Ogbe Kalu, *African Pentecostalism* (New York: OUP, 2008), 65–83.

96. Hollenweger, *Pentecostals,* 149–175.

97. Hollenweger, *Pentecostals,* 171 n. 12.

98. Hollenweger, *Pentecostals,* 150, 171–72 n.12.

99. See the following works by Allan Anderson: *Moya* (Pretoria: Unisa, 1991); *Bazalwane* (Pretoria: Unisa, 1992); "African Pentecostalism and the Ancestor Cult," *Missionalia* 21 (1993): 26–39; "Challenges and Prospects," *Missionalia* 23 (1995): 283–95; "The Hermeneutical Processes of Pentecostal-Type African Initiated Churches in South Africa," *Missionalia* 24 (1996): 171–85; "African Pentecostals in Mission," *Svensk Missionstidskrift* 87 (1999): 389–404.

100. Hans-Jürgen Becken, "Beware of the Ancestor Cult!" *Missionalia* 21 (1993): 334–35; Allan Anderson, *Zion and Pentecost* (Pretoria: Unisa, 2000), 9, 11.

101. Anderson, *Introduction,* 103–22.

102. Harvey Cox, *Fire from Heaven* (London: Cassell, 1996), 243, 246.

103. David Barrett, *Schism and Renewal in Africa* (Nairobi: OUP, 1968); David Barrett and John Padwick, *Rise Up and Walk!* (Nairobi: OUP, 1989).

104. David Barrett, *World Christian Encyclopedia* (Nairobi: OUP, 1982), 60–62.

105. Barrett, *Encyclopedia*, 62.

106. *DPCM*, 822–23.

107. *NIDPCM*, 286.

108. David Moore, "Art. Historiography," in Burgess, *Encyclopedia*, 242.

109. Edward Said, *Orientalism* (New York: Vintage, 1994); Dipesh Chakrabarty, *Provincializing Europe* (Princeton: Princeton University Press, 2000).

110. David Barrett et al., *World Christian Encyclopedia* (Oxford: OUP, 2001), I:4 (table 1-1); Anderson, *Introduction*, 1, 11–12; Burgess, *Encyclopedia*, 89–90; Donald Miller and Tetsunao Yamamori, *Global Pentecostalism: The New Face of Christian Social Engagement* (Berkeley: UCP, 2007), 18–19; for an older critical view, see McGee, "Pentecostal Missiology."'

111. Amos Yong, *Discerning the Spirit(s)* (Sheffield: SAP, 2000),192–97; Amos Yong, *The Spirit Poured Out on All Flesh* (Grand Rapids: Baker, 2005),18–19; Cecil Robeck, "Making Sense of Pentecostalism in a Global Context," paper presented at the 28th Annual Meeting of the SPS, Springfield, 1999, 18–26.

112. Burgess, *Encyclopedia*, 15–17.

113. Barrett and Padwick, *Rise Up and Walk!*; Michael Bergunder, "Die Afrikanischen Unabhängigen Kirchen und die Ökumene," *Ökumenische Rundschau* 47 (1998): 504–16.

114. Organization of African Independent Churches, ed., *OAIC 2nd Conference, 6th–13th November 1982, Nairobi. Welcome to Kenya* (Nairobi, 1982); OAIC, ed., *2nd Conference Nairobi, Kenya, 1982: Conference Papers* (Nairobi, 1983).

115. Christopher Olubunmi Oshun, "Christ Apostolic Church" (Ph.D diss., University of Exeter, 1981), 24; and "The Pentecostal Perspective of The Christ Apostolic Church," *ORITA Ibadan Journal of Religious Studies* 15:2 (1983): 105–14, esp. p. 105. I thank Anna Quaas for bringing these references to my attention.

116. Hubert van Beek, ed., *WCC-AIC Consultation and OAIC Assembly, Limuru, Kenya, 24–30 August 1997: Summary Report* (Geneva: WCC, 1997) (quotations are from van Beek's report and not from Wambugu's paper, which was not available to the author); OAIC, ed., *Report to the 3rd General Assembly* (Nairobi, 1997). See also Olu Atansuyi's representation of AICs during the WCC-AIC consultation in 1996. Atansuyi is from the Nigerian Cherubim and Seraphim and speaks of "Pentecostalism" in his church. However, he does not connect in any way AICs and Pentecostal churches (see Hubert van Beek, ed., *Consultation with African Instituted Churches* [Geneva: WCC, 1996], 51–52).

117. See, e. g., the announcement by Anderson of his book *Zion and Pentecost* in vol. 11, 3, pp. 75–76; and the review by Stan Nussbaum in vol. 12, 2, pp. 50–52.

118. Barrett and Padwick, *Rise Up and Walk!*

119. John Padwick, "Spirit, Desire and the World" (Ph.D. diss., University of Birmingham, 2003).

120. *Christianity in the African Context: The Report on the Dialogue between the OAIC and World Alliance of Reformed Churches.* Adopted in Mbagathi, near Nairobi, Kenya, February 9–14, 2002.

121. www.oaic.org; accessed April 17, 2008. See also the undated paper "Facilitating AICs to Articulate Their theologies in the Global Context" (Version 9) at the same Web site.

122. Stuart Hall, "Cultural Identity and Diaspora," in *Colonial Discourse and Post-Colonial Theory*, ed. Patrick Williams and Laura Chrisman (New York: CoUP, 1994), 392–403. Some first ideas with regard to Pentecostalism are presented by Claudia Währisch-Oblau, *The Missionary Self-Perception of Pentecostal, Charismatic Church Leaders* (Leiden: Brill, 2009).

4

Gender and Power

Elizabeth Brusco

The goal of this chapter is to comment on the scholarship on gender in the Pentecostal movement and to provide some case contextualization from my own ethnographic field research with Pentecostals in Colombia. Since I began to explore the gendered nature of Pentecostal conversion in the beginning of the 1980s, there has been, not exactly an explosion, but at least some steady growth in scholarly interest in the area, across a range of disciplines. My own discipline, anthropology, and area specialty in Latin America bias my perspective, but I believe that some of the most significant publications on the topic of women in the movement have come out of these areas.[1] But the issue of gender in Pentecostalism begs for interdisciplinary perspectives, and anthropology, sociology, social work, history, political science, Latin American and other area studies, religious studies, and theology are all engaging the topic. The fine article by Joel Robbins in *Annual Reviews of Anthropology* in 2004 gives a comprehensive recent review of the literature on the globalization of Pentecostal and Charismatic Christianity.[2] Bernice Martin's critical review of literature on gender in Pentecostalism in the *Blackwell Companion to the Sociology of Religion* is another key resource on the subject.[3]

CHALLENGES OF TRACKING GENDER IN THE ELUSIVE RESEARCH OBJECT "PENTECOSTALISM"

Before I go any further, let me clarify a few terms. I recently tried to trace the trends in academic publications on women and Pentecostalism by decades since the 1970s. One approach I used was to conduct article database searches using some of the major academic on-line search engines: among them, Anthrosource, which indexes the major anthropology journals; American Theological Library Association (ATLA), for religion and theology sources; Gender Studies Databases; Dissertation Abstracts; and WorldCat, which indexes books in the majority of academic libraries in the world. To keep it simple and, I hoped, comparable, I searched using the terms "Pentecostal*" and "women or gender." The broad trend was readily evident: for example, on WorldCat for the 1970s there were 4 hits; for the 1980s, 29, for the 1990s, 54; and so far in the first decade of the twenty-first century, 63 books and theses on gender or women in Pentecostalism have been collected in libraries. However, it instantly became clear to me from what was missing from these lists that if I were to do this kind of search effectively, I would need to repeat the searches using a whole range of terms: pentecostal, fundamentalist, Protestants, Evangelicals, Charismatics, conservative Christians, specific denominational names like Assemblies of God, and even confusing new acronyms like P/c, which appears to stand, not for "politically correct" in this case, but for "Pentecostals and Charismatics."[4] And to reveal the often-hidden women, I would need to add keywords such as marriage, family, household, kinship, sex roles, and motherhood. Time constraints did not allow me to complete this task, but the attempt was instructive in the elusiveness of the research object "Pentecostalism." Terminological inconsistencies in this review reflect the organization of the literature itself. Take, for example, the five volumes of the Fundamentalism Project conducted under the auspices of the American Academy of Arts and Sciences. The editors of that series, Martin Marty and R. Scott Appleby, acknowledge that many of the contributors were uncomfortable with the term *fundamentalism* when applied to the movements on which they reported, including some who made significant contributions on Pentecostalism. Despite this fact, the editors give some compelling reasons to retain the term as a coordinating description entailing certain unifying factors or "family resemblances" of this hypothetical family.[5]

PENTECOSTALISM AND COLOMBIAN *EVANGÉLICOS*

In this volume, "Pentecostalism" is the hypothetical family, and the nature of its family resemblances are well explored in the definitional treatment by Allan Anderson (see chapter 1). My approach to the topic, both in this review and in my field research in Colombia, is primarily ethnographic and secondarily discursive. I have consistently used the term *evangelical* or better yet the native category *"evangélico"* to designate the groups and individuals who have been the focus of my research in Colombia. Perhaps the most compelling rationale for adopting this term is that *evangélico* is what they call themselves. Within the considerable array of denominations, missions, and splinter groups that may argue over issues of doctrine and styles of worship and whose historical development has followed substantially different trajectories, similar positions on certain basic issues contribute to a common identity as *evangélicos*. The nature of this *evangélico* identity in Colombia is not accurately glossed by any of the religious categories commonly found in the United States. Certainly the terms *Pentecostal* or *Charismatic* are either irrelevant in the Colombian context or used in a substantially different way from that in the United States. In the religious landscape of Colombia, the term *Pentecostal* usually evokes a single denomination, the "Jésus Sólo" Iglesia Pentecostal Unida, or IPU. The IPU's rejection of the Trinity isolates them from fellowship with the rest of the evangelical movement in Colombia. And despite their custody of the descriptor "pentecostal," they are by no means the only emergent religious group in Colombia whose adherents are "concerned primarily with the experience of the working of the Holy Spirit and the practice of spiritual gifts."[6] This spiritual focus may be of greater importance for some *evangélicos* in Colombia than others, and there are a number of unifying factors among *evangélicos* specific to the Colombian context. These include a rejection of and often considerable antagonism to Catholicism; a focus on the Bible as both the key text and powerful master symbol for *creyentes* (believers), the status of a marginalized and persecuted minority within Colombian society; greater or lesser degrees of asceticism, including behavioral proscriptions against drinking, secular dancing, extramarital sex; and so forth. Finally, most significant to my own study and analysis of *evangélicos* in Colombia and, I believe, to an understanding of the worldwide appeal of Pentecostalism, there is an aggressive focus on the family, on marital and parental roles and responsibilities, that results in a discernible shift in the domestic life of converts.

KEEPING THE WOMEN UP FRONT IN PENTECOSTAL STUDIES

Which brings us back to the starting point and main theme of this chapter, which is to consider the scholarship on gender and Pentecostalism. In the study of a religious movement that undeniably involves more than the average amount of gender politics, what would it take to keep the women up front? This question has many implications but can be taken quite literally, as it stems from my first experience with Latin American Pentecostalism in the Church of Juan 3:16 in New York City. In the first Pentecostal service I ever attended, scores of identically dressed women, wearing dark blue skirts, white blouses, and gold sashes across their chests, ran almost the entire service from the floor of the theater-like building while four men dressed in business suits sat on the stage in ornate chairs. Every so often, one of the men would rise to lead a prayer or give a short sermon, but by and large the praying, testimonies, preaching and teaching, speaking in tongues, laying on of hands, and general conduct of the service was taken care of by the women, who never ascended to the stage. In fact, it is easier to answer the question, why aren't the women up front *literally* in the Pentecostal church than to figure out why women aren't up front *analytically* in the academic treatment of Pentecostalism as a worldwide religious movement.

What would it take to keep the women up front?

Identifying Male Bias in the Ethnographic Reporting on Pentecostalism

Twenty-eight years ago, at the end of the 1970s, when I began my work on women in the Pentecostal movement in Colombia, research on the subject was sparse. To find the women, one had to learn to read between the lines. Take, for example, James Sexton's 1978 publication on the evangelical movement and modernization among Maya in Guatemala. In the Assemblies of God (the largest congregation in Panajachel, the community he studied), Sexton noted that 63 percent of the voting members were female. He then proceeded to interview almost exclusively male heads of households. His bias is telling in the language of his conclusion: "Protestants . . . more often work in nonagricultural occupations, they are more often legally married, *their wives* are measurably more educated than Catholic wives," and so forth.[7] So we have Protestants, and then we have their wives. To his credit, he does suggest that more research is needed on the differential appeal of Protestantism to men versus women.

But what would the conclusions be, I thought at the time I read Sexton's article, if instead of considering *Protestants* and their *wives,* we considered *Protestants* and their *husbands?* Not only what would the conclusions be, but what would the questions be? What if we put the women up front?

For a newly awakened feminist graduate student in the 1970s, identifying male bias in scholarship was both a necessity and something of an obsession. Certainly women had often been systematically ignored as subjects when it came to understanding social, political, economic, and cultural systems. The devaluation of women's social and cultural roles by scholars of religion is evident in the application of "the marginality thesis" to explain women's attraction to Pentecostalism. In this model, women are drawn to Pentecostalism for the same reason other "marginal" people are: because it simply affords them an opportunity for expression and status not available to them in mainstream society. Marginality explanations, however, assume a center, and the "decentering" that has gone on over the past decades as a result of feminist and postmodern challenges to established scholarly assumptions seriously erodes the explanatory power of such logic.

Pentecostalism as an Agent of Women's Oppression

However, giving women the prominence in the scholarship on Pentecostalism to which they should be entitled (if for no other reason than their sheer numbers within the movement) has not been a straightforward feminist success story, of "making women visible" and overcoming male bias. A feminist arguing that women in conservative Christian groups might be serving their own interests faced some imposing ancestors. Elizabeth Cady Stanton, often cited as the founding genius of the women's rights movement in nineteenth-century America, said, "The Bible and the Church have been the biggest stumbling blocks in the way of women's emancipation."[8] No less forcefully, Mary Daly, a prominent radical feminist theologian of the Second Wave stated in her 1968 book, *The Church and the Second Sex,* "A woman's asking for equality in the church would be comparable to a black person's demanding equality in the Ku Klux Klan.[9]

The reason they said these things, of course, is because there is biblical support for women's subordination to men in the family and in society in general. Or, at least there are scriptural references for those who are seeking divine support for the subordination of women. (e.g., the Letter of the Apostle Paul to the Ephesians Chapter 5, verses 22–33: "Wives, be subject to your husband as to the Lord, for the husband is the head of the wife as Christ is the head of the church") In writing this chapter, I discovered a remarkable Web site, put up by a conservative Baptist church in my home state of Washington. It includes a very useful compendium of the accomplishments of Pentecostal women through the history of the movement, which is in itself impressive, but at the same time condemns these very women and the men who supported them as being "unscriptural" for usurping male authority.[10]

The 16-million-member Southern Baptist Convention amended its statement of beliefs in 1998 to add this phrase: "a woman should submit herself graciously to her husband's leadership and a husband should provide for, protect, and lead his family." Helen Hardacre, professor of religious studies at Harvard University, called fundamentalism "the ultimate patriarchal mandate." She states, "It is little wonder, then, that men are attracted to fundamentalist creeds, but the persuasive power of such creeds for women is much more difficult to comprehend."[11] Now certainly Southern Baptists are not Pentecostal (or at least not all of them), nor is fundamentalism a synonym for Pentecostalism. Yet I would argue that this discourse about the biblical justification for patriarchal dominance is relevant and, in fact, inescapable in contemporary scholarship on gender in Pentecostalism, which is why I include it here.

The "Pentecostal Gender Paradox"

This brings us to what Bernice Martin has recently called "the Pentecostal Gender Paradox."[12] In fact, the word *paradox* in the discussion of women in Pentecostalism has cropped up repeatedly over the past few years.[13] Implicit in the paradox are the questions: Why do women convert to Pentecostalism in greater numbers than men, when Pentecostal doctrine and practice are so evidently oppressive to women? Why are women often the first to convert and bring husbands and sons in later rather than the other way around? These questions are more easily resolved locally than globally. The paradox and the question of women's roles in Pentecostal movements have been effectively addressed in an increasing number of specific ethnographies and case studies since the 1980s, some of which I noted above. And recent feminist scholarship has overcome some of its blind spots of the past by recognizing "the embeddedness of human experience": that each place is "uniquely constituted and produced by local inhabitants, their everyday negotiations, and their ongoing struggles to shape their lives."[14] As feminist scholarship developed and began to use a tool kit of methodologies for "writing women's worlds,"[15] such as life history, personal narrative, and testimony, the problem of the "double-disappearance of dominance and othering" affecting research on Pentecostal women was addressed.[16] These new, more grounded approaches are immensely significant for improving understandings of what conservative religious movements "do" for women in any particular instance. However, when we get beyond the particular, beyond the monograph to the theoretical treatise or comprehensive analysis, it becomes much harder to keep the women up front.

Let me mention two recent publications, both of which will, without a doubt, be influential on the future development of scholarship on Pentecostalism for years to come. First, Allan Anderson's 2004 book, *An Introduction to Pentecostalism*, focuses our attention on the Pentecostal experience in the majority world and laudably underscores its complexity (what he calls "contextualization")[17] and the backflow influence of world Pentecostal expression on the overall theology and development of the movement.

Yet only two and half pages near the end of the book are dedicated directly to a discussion of women and Pentecostalism. Here Anderson notes that women "form the great majority of the church worldwide," but his brief discussion is concerned primarily with women in ministry rather than the way the experience of conversion and Pentecostal practice are gendered.[18] Citing Cheryl Johns's work on Pentecostalism as a pedagogy of the oppressed,[19] he implicitly recognizes the potential for challenge to the gender status quo. The fact that Spirit baptism and the call of God are the only qualifications for ministry, Johns pointed out, "preempted social norms and accepted patterns of ministry."[20] Yet he concludes this brief section on women with Johns' rather depressing observation that in the U.S. at least, Pentecostalism has been co-opted, has failed to address gender and other forms of cultural oppression, and is now characterized by "a male clergy and a high degree of institutionalism."[21]

Published in 2007, Miller and Yamamori's *Global Pentecostalism: The New Face of Christian Social Engagement* also makes an important contribution to our understanding of the movement on a worldwide scale.[22] They coin the term *progressive Pentecostalism* and detail the social ministries of Pentecostal churches, from emergency relief programs to education, counseling, medical assistance, economic development, and even policy change. Again, if you want to find the women here, look in the back of the book. Miller and Yamamori dedicate two pages to "The Role of Women." They note that women are "typically the majority of most congregations"[23] and summarize briefly three attempts they know of to explain the appeal of Pentecostalism to women. The one they prefer reads like this (and again, as in Sexton's case, the language is telling): For rural women migrating to urban areas, the Pentecostal church is "a liberating institution," providing "an escape from domestic chores" and a "relatively egalitarian location in which they can exercise their 'gifts.'"[24] Why they would feel that explanation is sufficient to explain the most rapidly expanding religious movement in the world today is unclear, but it is a variation on the old marginality hypothesis. Even less satisfying is their treatment of what they call "the patriarchal bargain." This is that "women will trade prestige and authority within religious settings for husbands that become 'domesticated' as a result of conversion"—that is, "men become less abusive at home, give up extramarital affairs, and spend more time raising children."[25] It is unfortunate that they do not elaborate on this scenario or cite any of the many studies exploring the impact of conversion on the home. It would be nice to know what "prestige and authority" women are allegedly giving up to join Pentecostal groups? Furthermore, a transformation of the male role (including getting men to be less abusive, contribute to child care, and remain faithful in a relationship) has been the hardest challenge facing Western feminists—and if Pentecostal conversion accomplishes this, isn't it worthy of more than a brief note?

Throughout Miller and Yamamori's book the description and analysis of the movement is from the top down. Their concentration on church hierarchy, which privileges the voices of those in formal leadership roles, camouflages the importance of women in Pentecostal churches. The first fact Miller and Yamamori point to in their brief section on women's roles is that only one of the many congregations they visited around the world was headed by a woman (in Singapore). Yet they note that many of the most exceptional Pentecostal social programs they studied were founded by women.[26] Rather than embed this fact in a systematic analysis of gender that would shed light on the question of women's attraction to Pentecostalism, they pointedly detach these "social entrepreneurs," as they call them, from their gender, instead crediting each individual's "creativity and drive."[27] In other words, in their estimation it is not women who are responsible for these social programs but simply exceptional people.

Even more important, the authority of personal charisma, the inspirational versus institutional quality of leadership, the priesthood of all believers, and the parallel and complementary nature of male and female organizational structures within Pentecostal churches are overlooked by the authors. Both books would have been helped by a recognition of gender as a culturally constituted institution in society, like kinship or religion, that systematically articulates with other institutions. From that standpoint, women in a religious movement such as Pentecostalism (which undeniably has significant gendered attributes one way or another) deserve more than a couple of pages of consideration.

GENDER IN PENTECOSTALISM: AN EXAMPLE
FROM COLOMBIA

Let me take a moment to examine how each of the Pentecostal characteristics mentioned above intersects with gender dynamics, using case material from my research in Colombia. All of these points build on each other. First, that spiritual authority in Pentecostal churches is accessed through manifestation of charismatic gifts, such as speaking in tongues, healing, or prophecy, means that women and men basically have equal access to this authority. Moreover, the playing ground is not quite level, in this instance in women's favor, as many studies have should that cross-culturally women have a higher propensity for entering into trance or dissociative states than men do. On the other hand, receptivity to the diffuse power represented by the Holy Spirit is uncharacteristic for Colombian males: The image of male converts with their arms and faces upraised, inviting in the Holy Spirit, is extraordinary, in that it stands in stark contrast to the impenetrable pose of machismo. For women, this "spiritual permeability" is not dissonant with acceptable feminine roles. But I would argue that for women receiving these charismatic gifts is deeply empowering on many levels and that others who witness them in individual women (including their husbands and male partners) cannot help but be impressed. A woman's conversion and display of charismatic gifts may not always be received positively in her household (many men feel threatened and are hostile and try to prohibit their wives' involvement in the church), but in some cases, especially if a man is sick or otherwise debilitated, a woman's newfound authority gives her influence over her husband that she formerly did not have and can result in his following her into the church.

Second, leadership roles in Pentecostal churches (especially in the fast-growing popular churches outside of the denominational structure) are often the result of inspiration rather than allocation by formal institutional mechanisms. The eventual development of seminaries and official bureaucracies may seem like inevitable steps in the evolution of new religious movements, and women may tend to be excluded or at least discriminated against as the movement becomes more structured and hierarchical. However, it is important to recognize the highly schismatic nature of Pentecostal churches in settings such as Colombia, which results in the tempering or moderation of formal leadership positions over the development cycle of particular churches. And clearly, within such fluid systems, women have greater opportunity to occupy leadership positions, or perhaps to put it more accurately, to take on leadership roles at specific points in time. Through our own cultural lenses (as Westerners, from industrialized, highly bureaucratic states favoring male leaders with titles and formal positions) such women's leadership may be hard to see (e.g., the women running the service from the floor of the theater in La Iglesia Juan 3:16 in New York City). And in fact, in societies such as Colombia where a woman's overt dominance or direction over males might be intolerable, there may be good reason to keep it somewhat obscure. I return to this issue below when I take up "the Pentecostal paradox."

Both of the points above relate directly to the third issue of importance when considering how the specific characteristics of Pentecostalism intersect with gender: the priesthood of all believers. However, this characteristic of Pentecostalism takes on heightened importance in Colombia, where the Catholic hierarchy has had tremendous dominance over both the spiritual and social dimensions of society. In 1887 the Colombian government signed a formal treaty with the Vatican. David Levine, the foremost historian of Latin American religious history, describes this arrangement as "a model of the traditional ideal of Christendom—complete Church-State integration."[28] The educational system was run by the Catholic Church, and a Catholic baptismal certificate was necessary in order to enroll in school. *Evangélicos* often found themselves forced to baptize their children in the Catholic Church for this reason. There was no civil birth registry, nor were civil marriages recognized during most of Colombia's history. Strikingly, even death was regulated by the Catholic clergy, and anyone who strayed from the flock, including *evangélicos,* could not be buried in the church cemetery. The vertical power relations of the Catholic clergy and the laity were echoed in patron-client ties between hacienda owners and the peasants who worked their land. Needless to say, a societal configuration such as this reinforces radical inequality and results in a strong desire on the part of the underclass for any avenues for combating their oppression. Hence the fact that Colombia has the oldest and longest-lasting leftist insurgency in Latin America, with highly durable groups such as the Fuerzas Armadas Revolucionarias de Colombia (FARC) founded in the 1960s and still a thorn in the side of the Colombian military. The Pentecostal "priesthood of all believers" also subverts the established lines of power in Colombia, not by attempting to topple the government, but by promoting nonmediated access to the divine and multiple rather than unitary lines of authority. A tangible example of this relates to the Bible. Emphasis on individual Bible reading in Pentecostal churches is a primary and definitive characteristic. Before Vatican II, Bibles were all but unavailable to the Colombian populace. I heard stories of new converts hand-copying large portions of the Bible by candlelight at night after a full day's work in the fields. When I inquired why, in the past, the Catholic Church had been so antagonistic to the laity owning and reading the Bible, I was told that the Catholic clergy believed the uneducated rural folk could not be counted on to interpret the Scriptures correctly. Moreover, people in the countryside had been known to use pages of the Bible to work witchcraft, or to create magical talismans or amulets. Now, the purchase of a Bible is the first major commitment by those considering conversion. The "discovery" of the Bible or the truths in the Bible figure prominently in the testimonies of believers. And although this breaking of the monopoly on scriptural interpretation affects both male and female converts, again it can be seen to directly empower women. The reflective, introspective, and analytical quality of Pentecostal practice in Colombia is a radical departure for women from passive acceptance of their lot in life. The account of one of my informants from the Four-Square Gospel church in Bogotá illustrates several of the points above. I include it here as an evocative first-person account of both the feminine ethos of Pentecostalism in Colombia and the personal transformatory potential conversion holds for Colombian women:

> In order to prepare a sermon you start by praying. Then you go to the Bible. You don't sit and write it all at once, the inspiration comes to you bit by bit, as you're cooking, doing things around the house and all the Holy Spirit guides you in terms of what to write down. You have to have love and discipline. When I prepared a sermon for a service at my church, I spent all week in prayer, and the Holy Spirit gave me the message little by little. The Holy Spirit helps you get over your nervousness, helps you to forget the people in front of you. (Author's interview with "Marina," July 1983, Bogotá)

The last piece of this puzzle, the parallel and complementary nature of male and female organizational structures within Pentecostal churches occupies a noticeable blind spot for many scholars evaluating the position of women within Pentecostalism. For example, in his review of Latin American movements for the Fundamentalism Project, Pablo Deiros, a professor of mission history at Fuller Theological Seminary, focuses primarily on the persuasive abilities of the male authority figure, be he the local pastor or the mass evangelist, and hence misses the diverse contributions of women who make up the majority of the congregations.[29] The core of evangelizing efforts in Colombia are the *cultos a domicilio* (services in the home). Every church, in addition to frequent services and special meetings held in the temple, has a list of these home services, which are held at varying times and in a range of locations during the week. It is usually the case that members (almost always women) volunteer their homes for these meetings and take on the responsibility of leading the prayer, Bible reading, and hymn singing. This technique of evangelization is a brilliant use of the primary resources available to the church: the commitment of female members, their interpersonal skills in a traditional context, and their personal networks of kin and friends. A female preacher stresses the compatibility of evangelization with the traditional role of Colombian women: "The Bible says to go out to the whole world and preach the gospel. Those of us who have homes and children, it's very difficult for us to go all over the world. But we can give the message to our neighbors, to our families, to our friends, our block—we have a lot of people to give it to." I believe that in fact the *cultos a domicilio* are much more important in both conversion and sustaining new converts than the much more visible "crusades"—mass open-air rallies, usually led by a famous preacher, that are associated with worldwide Pentecostal expansion. Big crusades in fact have not had much success in Colombia. Whereas the *cultos a domicilio* are personal, intimate, and private, the open-air rallies are impersonal, anonymous, and public. There is no basis for a Colombian woman's involvement in such activity, and the concept is likely to seem foreign to her.

But it is not only the *cultos a domocilio* wherein we see the parallel gender structure in Pentecostal churches in Colombia. Most successful evangelical churches in Colombia have active women's organizations. Cornelia Flora found that eight of thirteen Pentecostal churches in the area she studied had "active and aggressive" women's organizations, the leaders of which were often the wives of the pastors.[30] All of the evangelical churches I studied had women's organizations, and it was often the case that the *confraternidad de damas* took on the lion's share of responsibility for the church, including evangelization campaigns, fund-raising, social welfare work, and furnishing, maintaining, and decorating the church. Special weekly services for women are held by many churches and are often as well attended as the Sunday services. In churches that do not allow women to be pastors (some do), the role of the pastor's wife is strikingly important, and in many ways her influence can be equal to that of her husband. She is in a sense (and sometimes formally) co-pastor. Men without wives willing to take on an active leadership role in the church are rarely successful in Colombian Pentecostal churches.

GENDER AND THE PENTECOSTAL EXPLOSION

To return now to a consideration of gender in the current scholarship on global Pentecostalism, I would argue that if we want to know why there is an *explosion* of Pentecostalism around the world we need to take seriously the question of why *women* convert. And we need to follow that question with another one: How does women's presence in the church transform it? Does it further a "feminine ethos" in Pentecostal worship? Are the social ministries developed by Pentecostal congregations often likely to be addressed specifically to women's needs?

At the beginning of the second wave of feminism, the poet Adrienne Rich spoke about "a fundamental perceptual difficulty for which sexism is too facile a term."[31] As Anderson notes, the prominence (or lack of prominence) of women in Pentecostalism often depended on who told the stories."[32] Was William Seymour in front at Azuza Street a century ago? Or Lucy Farrow? And here I need to add to my list of acknowledgments Jan-Åke Alvarsson who raised my awareness of Farrow's importance and has honored her by setting up an invited lecture series at Uppsala University in her name.

Bernice Martin, in her recent review, writes about "blinkering paradigms" that need to be overcome in the study of women in Pentecostalism.[33] At the level of macrotheory, neither Weberian variations on the Protestant Ethic nor Marxist arguments about the way religion mystifies class relations are helpful in parting the cloud covering women in Pentecostalism. I would argue that we need to reject once and for all the victimization hypothesis and put to rest the notion that Pentecostal women are victims of false consciousness. It is also high time to get beyond the marginality explanation. If we allow women both value and agency, we can begin to see conversion as stemming in part from a linked set of processes that renegotiate gender and family relationships and personal identity, especially in climates of crisis.

What would it take to keep the women up front? Some have suggested that the potential of Pentecostalism to improve women's lives is precisely because women are *not* up front.

Bernice Martin puts it this way: It seems to be that a substantive shift toward greater equality will be tolerated so long as women are not seen to be publicly exercising formal authority over men.[34] In his influential work on women and popular religion in Brazil, John Burdick considers the question whether women's participation in Pentecostal churches in Latin America might actually challenge patriarchy more effectively than Latin American feminist movements.[35] His study of religion in Rio de Janeiro led him to reflect on "the Gramscian position that hegemonic and counterhegemonic beliefs coexist simultaneously within the subaltern's contradictory consciousness." "The problem," Burdick states, "is the assumption that we can always distinguish which is which."[36]

Patriarchy versus Machismo

I would add that an uncritical use of the term *patriarchy* in many analyses of gender in Pentecostalism obscures the culturally specific dynamic of the sex/gender system in any locale. For example, I have written about the difference between "patriarchy" and "machismo" in Colombia. Both are forms of male dominance but with radically different implications for women.[37] Although machismo has ramifications for the domestic realm, it does not stipulate the content of any key relationships within the family, except by default. Its striking characteristic is that it is a *non*domestic (one might almost say *anti*domestic) role. "La mujer es de la casa y el hombre de la calle" (The woman is of the house and the man is of the street) is a statement made in Colombia and elsewhere in Latin America.

Machismo often entails domestic abdication, that is, the lack of involvement of men in their families and homes. This abdication can run the gamut from the man whose work and social life both take place outside of the home to men who abandon their wives and children. One study identified Colombia as having the highest percentage of female-headed households among seven South American countries examined: 31 percent. There are complex reasons (both historical and contemporary) for the high rate of abandonment (by husbands, both formal and consensual), which is partly responsible for this situation. In Colombia, people fleeing from violence is one. According to the United Nations, Colombia has the largest displaced population in the world after the Democratic Republic of the Congo and Sudan. The vast majority are women and their children. By 2001 there were over 34,000 displaced female-headed households in Colombia,[38] and 60 percent of displaced women have no sources of income. Women often engage in informal sector labor to feed their families. Even in the formal sector, and despite new laws stemming from the 1991 Colombian constitution prohibiting gender discrimination in employment, women are still barred from working in many industries (e.g., in jobs perceived to be dangerous), and there remains a differential of 30 percent between the salaries of men and women.

The culturally specific dynamic of the sex/gender system in Colombia must be taken into account in building explanations of why people choose to convert to Pentecostalism. Machismo, as an aspect of masculine behavior and identity in Colombia, is best understood as a transitional role reflecting the enormous social change, including proletarianization and political and economic insecurity, in Latin American society. Historical changes in the mode of production matter, too, as the peasant household of the past, which formed a domestic economy from production to consumption, has largely been replaced by a cash economy and female dependency on a male wage earner. When men and women begin to occupy separate spheres, their values diverge. Men consume their paychecks in the public world of the bars and spend their earnings on things that mark their status in a male world. Women are left hoping to be able to capture a portion of what is left to support the household, the children, and themselves. For the poorest sectors of Colombian society, for both men and women, this situation can turn desperate. Yet even for middle-class women, or what in Colombia is referred to as the *"clase profesional,"* a woman's loss of access to a portion of her husband's earnings can be devastating for her and her children.

Women's Motivations for Conversion

Why do women convert? Why do they join evangelical churches in Colombia? For many reasons, as evidenced in personal testimonies: for healing, for spiritual fulfillment, and because the evangelical churches provide an accepting and supporting community of fellow believers for those dislocated by violence. But I have argued that importantly for Colombian women, the evangelical churches effectively address the problems resulting from machismo. The churches provide a template for rearticulating men and women, redirecting men back into the family and revaluing the domestic realm. In this context, the perils of patriarchy are far from consideration.

Pentecostalism and Forms of Women's Collective Action

Let me say a word about women's collective action here. One concern that emerged from the second wave of the women's movement in the United States was whether feminism was global. Feminists wanted to know whether women everywhere experience inequality and oppression. In anthropological language the question was, is women's subordination universal? The particular nature of women's responses to oppression were also deemed important. For instance, our sisters in Argentina who took to the streets to protest inflation, banging pots and pans to let the powers that be know they couldn't put food on the table—were they feminists? Or at least incipient feminists?

The British sociologist Maxine Molyneux came up with a useful distinction between practical and strategic forms of women's movements.[39] Women sometimes mobilize because of a societal development (e.g., inflation) that keeps them from fulfilling their traditional roles. This is Molyneux's "practical form" of women's collective action. The "strategic form," on the other hand, *challenges* these traditional roles, like Western feminism does. They target basic inequalities in the sex/gender system, so such movements have more far-reaching consequences for social change and ideological transformation. In Gramscian terms they would be considered counterhegemonic.

Although to many feminists and not a few Pentecostals, it makes for very strange bedfellows indeed, my analysis of Colombian Pentecostalism concludes that it entails gender role transformation in a strategic way that stacks up rather well alongside Western feminism. It was gratifying, therefore, to read Bernice Martin's recent comment, "If there is a 'women's movement' among the poor of the developing world, Pentecostalism has a good claim to the title."[40] Lorentzen and Mira wondered if they had stumbled onto a feminist Utopia in their Pentecostal field site in San Francisco. Despite the fact that it is not a religion that self-consciously aims at dismantling patriarchy, they say, it does seem to result in "increased participation of men in the home, public roles for women, challenges to conceptual dualisms, harsh criticisms of U.S. consumerism and hyperindividualism, and help with child care."[41] Will the miracle *stay* in the home, they ask, or will it lead to larger social transformations? It is curious that they end with that question. Of all the gains that have been made by the women's movement in the past decades, the hardest areas to change have been those associated with home and family. A transformation of the home *is* a major social transformation.

The anthropologist Lila Abu-Lughod, in a thought-provoking piece published in the *American Anthropologist* shortly after September 11, 2001, outlines the ethnocentrism inherent in the notion that Muslim women in Afghanistan need to be "saved" from their oppression by American military intervention. She writes that it is wrong to see history "simplistically in terms of a putative opposition between Islam and the West," as well as "strategically dangerous to accept this cultural opposition between Islam and the West, between fundamentalism and feminism."[42] She asks that we be aware of differences and respectful of other paths toward social change. And although drawn from a substantially different cultural context, she raises some important questions pertinent to the current discussion. Perhaps "liberation" in the sense that the Western women's movement has used this word is not something for which all women everywhere strive. "Might other desires be more meaningful for different groups of people?" Abu-Lughod asks. "Living in close families? Living in a godly way? Living without war?" She notes that no woman she has met in twenty years of fieldwork in Egypt has ever expressed envy for American women, whom they see as "bereft of community, vulnerable to sexual violence and social anomie, driven by individual success rather than morality, or strangely disrespectful of God."[43] Abu-Lughod's points are important, both that we recognize our own ethnocentrism when considering women's lives elsewhere and that we do not resign ourselves only to a radical cultural relativism, accepting anything that happens to women anywhere because it is simply "their culture." But a recognition that there are other paths toward change, other approaches to a good life, and other value systems seems like a critical starting point in understanding the growth of Pentecostalism on the global scale.

CONCLUSION

In a recent analysis of patriarchal gender politics in fundamentalist movements, Riesebrodt and Chong provide a useful typological distinction between what they call "legalistic-literalist" fundamentalism and "Charismatic" fundamentalism, the former being politically active and the latter less so, at least overtly.[44] They argue that the two forms have very different motivations and ramifications when it comes to gender. In the Americas, they see Charismatic fundamentalism as "a self-organization of women actively attempting to reshape the patriarchal family in their own interest."[45] Legalistic-literalist fundamentalism is the opposite: "a self-organization of men who compensate for loss of authority and status by increasing their control over women." Acknowledging that women do convert to legalistic movements and men to Charismatic ones, they recognize that the dichotomy is imperfect. The outcome of participation in fundamentalist religions ultimately depends not so much on the "type" of fundamentalism as on "existing authority structures."[46] This conclusion seems to beg the question of how these religious movements effect the transformations that they do. Such an understanding can only be achieved by breaking down unexamined categories such as "the patriarchal family" and recognizing women's agency even within systems where male dominance seems overwhelming. To expand on Burdick's statement quoted earlier, we should hesitate to assume that certain beliefs are hegemonic until we have explored their particular expressions in context.

Finally, does Pentecostalism at all times and in all places have the same gender dynamic? I wouldn't expect it to, and that is why contextualization is so important. Throughout Latin America, however, we see common characteristics of gender systems, household and family structures, migration patterns, and political economic formations that have an impact on the gendered Pentecostal experience. These include sex segregation, especially in the context of rural-urban migration, a reduction in emphasis on the wider kin group in favor of the nuclear family, disarticulation of men and women in households due to a transition from agriculture to wage labor, increasing female dependency on male wage earners, a devaluation of the private realm, and a tendency toward domestic abdication and family abandonment on the part of men. Women suffer from a lack of correspondence between their own and male values, and when both husbands and wives convert to Pentecostalism, things improve. There is some evidence that this pattern may extend beyond Latin America. The authors of a recent study on Pentecostalism and gender in Mozambique noted that the increasing economic inequality between men and women in that country resulting from neoliberal reforms coincides with the flood of women into Pentecostal churches and that when their husbands also convert tensions in the household are ameliorated.[47]

When I have presented these conclusions from my research to *evangélicos* in Colombia, I have often been asked, "But why would *men* convert?" Behind this question is an assumption that the behaviors and standards of machismo are somehow desirable or advantageous for men. In fact, it is a very difficult and perilous kind of masculine role, often accompanied by pain and violence. It cannot be assumed that the majority of men are cut out for this lifestyle, and certainly for many an alternative is welcome. Furthermore, men often state in their testimonies that they were led to convert as the result of having been healed of an illness. *Machista* culture, with its premium on individual independence and physical prowess, makes no provisions for illness, and in fact physical disability is anathema to it. When a man gets sick he must withdraw from his usual activities and return home so that his wife (or other female relative) can nurse him. He becomes dependent on his wife and family in a way that would be unthinkable if he were well. He is also physically suffering, and his fear of what is going to happen to him and his dependence on his wife and family combine to render him uncharacteristically receptive to their counsel. If his wife has already converted she is armed with the logic of the church to argue that his illness is the result of his *vicios* (vices) and that only by giving them up will he be well again. The spectacular aspects of evangelical worship (e.g., speaking in tongues and other displays of ecstatic worship) provide further fuel to convince him of the power of the new religion.

I am heartened by the directions that the analysis of women in Pentecostalism has taken over the past three decades. I look forward to an increasing number of contextualized case studies that will help us to understand the particularity of the Pentecostal experience for women. And I hope to see those understandings built into the very foundations of our analysis of the movement on the global scale. Finally, I. M. Lewis has noted that "once they have shown what for secular ends is done in the name of religion, some anthropologists naively suppose that nothing more remains to be said." This means that we leave relatively unexplained "the characteristic mystical aspects which distinguish the religious from the secular" and fail completely to "account for the rich diversity of religious concepts and beliefs."[48] My approach to the topic of Pentecostalism tends to focus on mundane affairs, individual strategies and interests. This is in no way meant to slight the passionate emotion and the fervent faith that are the "true" meaning of Pentecostalism for the followers of that path.[49]

NOTES

1. Elizabeth Brusco, *The Reformation of Machismo: Gender and Evangelical Conversion in Colombia* (Austin: University of Texas Press, 1995); John Burdick, *Blessed Anastácia: Women, Race, and Popular Christianity in Brazil* (New York: Routledge, 1998); R. Andrew Chesnut, *Born Again in Brazil: The Pentecostal Boom and the Pathogens of Poverty* (New Brunswick: Rutgers University Press, 1997); María das Dores Campos Machado, "Family, Sexuality, and Family Planning: A Comparative Study of Pentecostals and Charismatic Catholics in Rio de Janeiro," in *More than Opium: An Anthropological Approach to Latin American and Caribbean Pentecostal Praxis,* ed. Barbara Boudewijnse, André Droogers, and Frans Kamsteeg (Lanham, MD: Scarecrow Press, 1998), 169–202; Carol Drogus, "Private Power or Public Power: Pentecostalism, Base Communities, and Gender," in *Power, Politics, and Pentecostals in Latin America,* ed. Edward I. Cleary and Hannah W. Stewart-Gambino (Boulder, CO: Westview Press, 1997), 55–75; Leslie Gill, "'Like a Veil to Cover Them': Women and the Pentecostal Movement in La Paz," *American Ethnologist* 17 (1990): 708–21; Cecilia Loreta Mariz and María das Dores Campos Machado, "Pentecostalism and Women in Brazil," in Cleary and Stewart-Gambino, *Power, Politics, and Pentecostals,* 41–54; Anna L. Peterson, "'The Only Way I Can Walk': Women, Christianity, and Everyday Life in El Salvador," in *Christianity, Social Change, and Globalization in the Americas,* ed. Anna L. Peterson, Manuel A. Vásquez, and Philip J. Williams (New Brunswick: Rutgers University Press, 2001), 25–44; Hanneke Slootweg, "Pentecostal Women in Chile," in Boudewijnse, Droogers, and Kamsteeg, *More than Opium,* 53–73; to name a few.

2. Joel Robbins, "The Globalization of Pentecostal and Charismatic Christianity," *Annual Reviews in Anthropology* 33 (2004): 117–43. Robbins helpfully divides Pentecostal outcomes into "World-Breaking" (focused on dualism, asceticism, and ontological preservation) and "World-Making" ones, focused on institutionalization and the localization of religious authority.

3. Bernice Martin, "The Pentecostal Gender Paradox: A Cautionary Tale for the Sociology of Religion," in *The Blackwell Companion to the Sociology of Religion*, ed. Richard K. Fenn (Oxford: Blackwell, 2001), 52–66.

4. Robbins, "Globalization," 117.

5. Martin E. Marty and R. Scott Appleby, "Introduction: The Fundamentalism Project: A User's Guide," in *Fundamentalisms Observed*, ed. Martin E. Marty and R. Scott Appleby (Chicago: University of Chicago Press, 1991), vii–xiii, 816.

6. Robert Mapes Anderson, *Vision of the Disinherited* (Peabody: Hendrickson, 1979), 4.

7. James Sexton, "Protestantism and Modernization in Two Guatemalan Towns," *American Ethnologist* 5 (1978): 280–302, 297 (my emphasis).

8. Elizabeth Cady Stanton, *The Woman's Bible* (New York: Arno Press, 1974 [1895]).

9. Mary Daly, *The Church and the Second Sex* (New York: Harper & Row, 1968).

10. Pastor Mike Paulson, Touchet Baptist Church, "Paul's Third Charge to Timothy," www .touchet1611.org/PentecostalWomen.html; accessed 14 September 2008.

11. Helen Hardacre, "The Impact of Fundamentalisms on Women, the Family, and Interpersonal Relations," in *Fundamentalisms and Society*, ed. Martin E. Marty and R. Scott Appleby (Chicago: University of Chicago Press, 1993), 129–50, 141.

12. Martin, "Pentecostal Gender Paradox," 52–66, 52.

13. Lois Ann Lorentzen and Rosalina Mira, "El Milagro Está en Casa: Gender and Private/Public Empowerment in a Migrant Pentecostal Church," *Latin American Perspectives* 32 (2005): 57–71, 57; Robbins, "Globalization,"119.

14. Altha J. Cravey, "Local/Global: A View from Geography," in *Gender's Place: Feminist Anthropologies of Latin America*, ed. Rosario Montoya, LessieJo Frazier, and Janise Hurtig (New York: Palgrave Macmillan, 2002), 281–87, 281–82.

15. Lila Abu-Lughod, *Writing Women's Worlds: Bedouin Stories* (Berkeley: UCP, 1993).

16. Lorentzen and Mira, "El Milagro," 67.

17. Allan Anderson, *An Introduction to Pentecostalism: Global Charismatic Christianity* (Cambridge: CUP, 2004), 283.

18. Anderson, *Introduction*.

19. Cheryl B. Johns, "Pentecostal Formation," cited in Walter J. Hollenweger, *Pentecostalism: Origins and Developments Worldwide* (Peabody: Hendrickson, 1997), 79–80.

20. Johns, "Pentecostal Formation," cited in Anderson, *Introduction*, 275.

21. Johns, "Pentecostal Formation," 276.

22. Donald E. Miller and Tetsunao Yamamori, *Global Pentecostalism: The New Face of Christian Social Engagement* (Berkeley: UCP, 2007).

23. Miller and Yamamori, *Global Pentecostalism*, 209.

24. Miller and Yamamori, *Global Pentecostalism*, 210.

25. Miller and Yamamori, *Global Pentecostalism*, 209.

26. Miller and Yamamori, *Global Pentecostalism*, 208.

27. Miller and Yamamori, *Global Pentecostalism*, 209.

28. Daniel Levine, *Religion and Politics in Latin America: The Catholic Church in Venezuela and Colombia* (Princeton: Princeton University Press, 1981), 70.

29. Pablo A. Deiros, "Protestant Fundamentalism in Latin America," in Marty and Appleby, *Fundamentalisms Observed*, 142–96.

30. Cornelia Butler Flora, *Pentecostalism in Colombia: Baptism by Fire and Spirit* (Cranbury: Associated University Presses, 1976).

31. Adrienne Rich, *Of Woman Born* (New York: Norton, 1976).

32. Anderson, *Introduction*, 274.

33. Martin, "Pentecostal Gender Paradox," 64.

34. Martin, "Pentecostal Gender Paradox," 54.

35. Burdick, *Blessed Anastácia.*

36. Burdick, *Blessed Anastácia,* 201.

37. Brusco, *Reformation of Machismo,* 77.

38. PROFAMILIA, "Sexual and Reproductive Health in Underserved Conditions: A Survey of the Situation of Displaced Women in Colombia," PROFAMILIA, Bogotá, October 2001.

39. Maxine Molyneux, "Mobilization without Emancipation? Women's Interests, State, and Revolution," in *Transition and Development,* ed. Richard Fagen, Carmen Diana Deere, and José Luis Caraggio (New York: Monthly Review Press, 1986), 280–302, 284.

40. Martin, "Pentecostal Gender Paradox," 56.

41. Lorentzen and Mira, "El Milagro," 69.

42. Lila Abu-Lughod, "Do Muslim Women Really Need Saving? Anthropological Reflections on Cultural Relativism and Its Others," *American Anthropologist* 104 (2002): 783–90, 788.

43. Abu-Lughod, "Do Muslim Women Really Need Saving?" 778.

44. Martin Riesebrodt and Kelly H. Chong, "Fundamentalisms and Patriarchal Gender Politics," *Journal of Women's History* 10:4 (1999): 55–77.

45. Riesebrodt and Chong, "Fundamentalisms," 56.

46. Riesebrodt and Chong, "Fundamentalisms," 57.

47. James Pfeiffer, Kenneth Gimbel-Sherr, and Orvalho Joaquim Augusto, "The Holy Spirit in the Household: Pentecostalism, Gender, and Neoliberalism in Mozambique," *American Anthropologist* 109 (2007): 688–700. This fine analysis by three male researchers is an important illustration of how the importance of gender to understanding pentecostal conversion is not and should not be solely the purview and responsibility of women. Earlier studies—Salvatore Cucchiari, "Adapted for Heaven: Conversion and Culture in Western Sicily," *American Ethnologist* 14 (1988): 417–442; Burdick, *Blessed Anastácia;* and Chesnut, *Born Again*—also illustrate this point. In addition, David Stoll has recognized the importance of gender in his groundbreaking book, *Is Latin America Turning Protestant?* (Berkeley: UCP, 1990).

48. I.M. Lewis, *Ecstatic Religion: An Anthropological Study of Spirit Possession and Shamanism* (Harmondsworth: Penguin, 1971), 36.

49. Marie Freedman Marquardt, "From Shame to Confidence: Gender, Religious Conversion, and Civic Engagement of Mexicans in the U.S. South," *Latin American Perspectives* 32:1 (2005): 27–56, echoes this concern. Marquardt observes, "While the content of the conversions themselves was 'irreducibly religious' [citing Cucchiari, "Adapted for Heaven," 418], the possibilities for entering into conversion and the results of conversion were, in both cases, structured by gender" (p. 31).

5

Conversion Narratives

Henri Gooren

The emphasis in this chapter is on *how* people tell the story of their conversion. I follow a historical and phenomenological approach to the conversion narrative, analyzing it as a social construction and not necessarily as a factual description of the main events in an individual's life. A comprehensive conversion experience changes one's self-image. This transformation, which is a process taking longer than just one day or one week, is gradually reflected in the most important indicator of conversion: *biographical reconstruction.*[1] People who undergo a conversion experience literally reconstruct their lives, giving new meanings to old events and putting different emphases in the bigger "plot" of their life stories.[2] To analyze the success of Pentecostalism worldwide, it is imperative to understand the Pentecostal conversion experience. Evangelical and Pentecostal conversion stories all over the world contain standardized elements. The typical formula seems to be as follows: I was living in sin, but now I'm saved; I was lost, but now I'm found. Most conversion narratives are variations on the theme, You have to go through hell in order to get to heaven.[3] My main questions here are, What makes Pentecostal conversion stories unique? What factors are typically involved in Pentecostal conversion, judging from the conversion narratives? Are there differences between male and female Pentecostal conversion stories in the Americas? I earlier pointed out that there are many similarities between Pentecostal converts in North and Latin America—and even between Pentecostal and Charismatic Catholic converts.[4] The main differentiation I analyze below is based on *gender,* which to my knowledge has up to now not been examined systematically in Pentecostal conversion stories. I present them here in chronological order, the oldest stories going back directly to the Azusa Street revival in Los Angeles (1906–9) and the most

93

recent ones recorded in the United States, Guatemala, and Argentina in the 1990s.[5] The studies I quote from here are either from excellent ethnographies, most of them collected by anthropologists, or from narrative analyses based on written documents by converts (men and women from the United States).

Most ethnographers transcribed the complete conversion stories of their informants.[6] Some reported that they collected conversion stories, but they did not actually write them out or used only tiny fragments of them.[7] This omission is regrettable if one wants to identify degrees of Pentecostal participation over the course of people's entire lifetimes—in short, their pentecostal conversion careers. We earlier defined the *conversion career* as "the member's passage, within his or her social and cultural context, through levels, types, and phases of church participation."[8] The conversion career approach represents a systematic attempt to analyze shifts in levels of individual religious participation. Four important elements of this approach are the conceptualization of dissatisfaction with a former religion, a five-level typology of religious participation, a life-cycle approach, and a systematic analysis of the many factors influencing changes in religious participation. An essential element of the conversion career approach is developing a typology of religious activity that includes more dimensions than just disaffiliation and conversion. Elsewhere I distilled five primary levels of individual religious participation.[9] *Pre-affiliation* describes the worldview and social context of potential members of a group. *Affiliation* refers to formal church membership, which is not necessarily a central aspect of one's identity. *Conversion,* used here in the limited sense, refers to a (radical) personal change of worldview and identity. *Confession* is core membership, describing a high level of participation inside the new religious group and a strong missionary attitude toward nonmembers. Finally, *disaffiliation* refers to a lack of involvement in an organized religious group.

The conversion career approach also distinguishes five main groups of factors influencing conversion: personality factors; social factors; institutional factors, dealing with the religious organization; cultural factors (including political and economic factors); and contingency factors. The latter involve situation events, random meetings with missionaries, acutely felt crises, stressful situation, and other contingencies that bring individuals into the orbit of various religious groups. Pentecostals would call this Providence, of course, or divine intervention. I use the conversion career approach in this chapter as a tool to analyze the Pentecostal conversion narrative. After tracing the origin and development of the conversion concept in Christianity, I analyze the core rituals involved in the Pentecostal conversion process, following the supposed order of classical Pentecostalism: first, accepting Christ as one's personal Savior; second, baptism by full immersion; third, sanctification (or holiness); and fourth, speaking, singing, and praying in unknown tongues. For each core ritual, special attention is given to male and female conversion stories from the United States and various countries in Latin America to see how the core rituals are integrated in the stories of people's lives. The conclusion also addresses the gender component in Pentecostal conversion stories.

CONVERSION IN CHRISTIANITY

The conversion concept in Christianity is heavily influenced by the classical example of biblical conversion: Saint Paul on the road to Damascus, as described in the Book of Acts (9: 1–22).[10] The Pauline conversion is spectacular, once-in-a-lifetime, fraught with miracles, and brought on by surrendering to a higher authority.[11] Many of its principal elements—especially the bright light and the need to surrender to God's authority—still turn up in the conversion stories of believers all over the world, as becomes clear below in the stories from North and Latin America. The Pauline conversion concept also illustrates the importance of the religious organization in developing, framing, legitimizing, and, finally, shaping conversion among its affiliates.[12]

I argued elsewhere that the Puritan conversion ideal of the seventeenth century was the stern forerunner of the contemporary individualized conversion concept in evangelical and Pentecostal churches.[13] The Puritan concept of salvation is gloomy: "it invariably assures unbelievers that all their efforts to reach God are vain and sinful, but that nevertheless they had better keep trying and that perhaps God will choose arbitrarily to lift them out of these strivings if they persist."[14] In other words: even after going through hell on earth, the Puritans could never be fully certain that they would go to heaven. I showed that the modern individual concept of conversion in evangelical Christianity can be traced back to the Second Awakening in the United States.[15] Flinn describes the 1805 Cane Ridge Revival in Kentucky as an important triggering event, where emotional phenomena like barking, dancing, and falling in the Spirit started: "The 'falling' phenomenon later came to be known as 'being slain in the Spirit.'"[16] The tent revivals and mass rallies of the 1820s were followed by a less emotional Third Awakening in the 1880s and continued into the twentieth century, for example, in the Billy Graham crusades.

The conversions that took place during the Second and subsequent awakenings conformed to the now-generalized evangelical conversion model of repentance, accepting Jesus Christ as one's personal Savior and baptism by full immersion. This model was consolidated by the Holiness movement, which dominated the Third Awakening. During emotional mass rallies, people who felt the influence of the Holy Spirit in their bodies began to shout, dance, or cry. Accepting Jesus Christ as one's personal Savior was supposed to be the start of a more general sanctification process, allowing *holiness,* or "sanctification," to heal all aspects of the born-again convert's life (see below for more details).

ACCEPTING CHRIST AS ONE'S SAVIOR:
BUILDING TESTIMONY

Ever since the Holiness movement of the nineteenth century, Evangelicals and Pentecostals have drawn on a limited number of standardized formulas to describe their conversion. The most common one is "accepting Christ as one's personal Lord" or "accepting Christ as one's personal Savior." People also spoke repeatedly of "surrendering," "yielding," or "giving" themselves or their lives to Christ. In the Harvard historian Virginia Brereton's words, "Male as well as female narrators have used this formulation, but it is particularly striking in connection to women, who are normally seen as 'yielding' or 'surrendering' themselves sexually. Also common, narrators have spoken of having 'asked' or 'invited' or 'received' Jesus Christ (or the 'Lord Jesus') into their lives or (sometimes their hearts). They have also recalled 'finding,' 'meeting,' 'coming to know,' or 'turning to' Jesus Christ, or they describe themselves as having been 'converted,' 'saved,' 'born again' or 'become a Christian.'"[17] Some early Pentecostal converts, men and women, went far in their rebellion and struggle to repent: "Much to her mother's shock and dismay, Aimee Semple McPherson announced at a Salvation Army service that 'there was no God, nothing in the Bible.' But her apostasy was short-lived; her conversion came that very night."[18]

Starting with Pentecostalism at the beginning of the twentieth century, Brereton notes a general change in the language of the convert. People start talking about having a *personal* relationship with Christ or about Christ as their personal Savior. They would even say, "Jesus died for me, *personally*"; others referred to their "personal knowledge of Jesus Christ" or to knowing him *"personally."*[19] In the twentieth century, Christ the Savior gradually became a "friend" or a "companion": "He is addressed more colloquially and informally than in the past. Narrators often speak to and about him simply as 'Jesus.'"[20] Brereton notes that another crucial difference is that later in the twentieth century conversion is almost always described in the active voice: people *accept* Christ as their Savior rather than being *accepted by* him.[21] People are seldom forced to yield or surrender, like Saint Paul was on the road to Damascus. Afterward, they feel reasonably assured of their salvation. This is a far cry from the continued agony of the Puritan converts.

Many female conversion stories were motivated by a fear of dying and going to hell—perhaps more than in the case of men, who rarely mention this fear in their conversion stories (they might still experience it, of course, and prefer not to express it because of gender stereotypes allowing men less room to do so). Consider the conversion narrative of Ana, who was a teenager when a contingency factor caused her to convert from Catholicism to a Pentecostal church in Guatemala City.

> At fifteen I converted to the gospel, when I came here to the capital. . . . It was because of the 1976 earthquake. I always believed that the Catholic religion was a good one. And I always thought that all was well, if you were searching for God. But during the 1976 earthquake, I saw so many people die and I was so close to them. . . . I told myself: How is it possible that I don't even know where I'll go if I die?! Right? So I thought of searching for something different. I went to the evangelical church and I heard two messages and it was enough to convince me that if I received Jesus Christ in my heart today, I'd know where I'd go. And I made a decision. Only later did I know the whole gospel, what it implied. That is: I made a decision in ignorance, convinced only that if I'd die I'd go to heaven.[22]

Fear of dying and going to hell is still an important motivation for converts. Baptism is the core ritual that ensures Evangelicals and Pentecostals of their salvation.

BAPTISM BY FULL IMMERSION

The core transition ritual of baptism by full immersion in water has been an important element in most forms of Pentecostalism since its early beginnings.[23] One of the earliest and most devastating Pentecostal schisms, in fact, was based on the baptism formula. "Jesus Name" or Oneness Pentecostalism, starting in 1913, "adopted a non-Trinitarian view of the Godhead and taught that water baptism must be done in the name of Jesus Christ, the redemptive name of God revealed in the New Testament."[24] Some early Pentecostals also used the water baptism as a metaphor to describe the overwhelming experience of receiving the Holy Spirit for the first time (see below). However, most converts these days rarely go into detail about their feelings leading up to the date of their baptism by full immersion. It does not appear to be a central element of the Pentecostal conversion experience any longer. Baptism is almost always mentioned, often with a specific date, but not given as much importance as the day people accepted Christ as their personal Savior, the day the sanctification of their lifestyle supposedly started, or the specific day they first praised in tongues (see below).

SANCTIFICATION: BRINGING HOLINESS INTO ONE'S LIFE

Holiness is an older idea dating back at least to John Wesley's Methodism, based on Leviticus 20:7: "Sanctify yourselves therefore, and be ye holy." It has been advocated with a new urgency since the mid-1850s in the United States, with preachers stressing the role of the Holy Spirit: "Holiness preachers taught the faithful that the 'second blessing'—a crisis experience of sanctification (i.e., a perfection of motives and desires), separable from conversion—would instantaneously eradicate their sinful dispositions and elevate them to a new plateau of

Christian living."[25] Brereton highlights the element of surrender in Holiness, which proved to attract more women than men: "Advocates of holiness or sanctification taught that Christians could achieve or at least approach 'sinless perfection'; holiness was variously regarded as an experience (one entered into holiness or was sanctified in a short span of time, usually moments or hours), a way of life, and a doctrine. . . . [E]ntering into holiness or being sanctified meant letting God take over one's entire life, in all its dimensions. This 'surrendered' attitude often entailed living what was called 'the life of faith.' . . . The sanctified woman was to give up all effort and struggle and let God act in her life. . . . [T]he believer was not merely 'surrendered' but *'wholly'* or *'completely'* or *'totally'* surrendered."[26]

Many Holiness elements can still be discerned in the gendered Pentecostal conversion stories presented here. The U.S. anthropologist Susan Harding stressed the importance of language in the conversion process: "at the center of the language of fundamentalism is a bundle of strategies—symbolic, narrative, poetic, and rhetorical—for confronting individuals, singly and in groups."[27] This is the conversion story of the Baptist Reverend Cantrell, who was forty-six at the time of the interview.

> So I joined that particular church after about a month of visiting there. But I was first saved and then I followed Christ to baptism, which I hadn't been baptized before. . . . And then after this my life began to grow and materialize into something that was real, something that I could really identify with. The emptiness that was there before was now being replaced by something that had meaning and purpose in it. And I began to sense the need of telling others about what had happened to me. And basically I think perhaps the change could be detected in my life, as the Bible declares, that when a person is saved, the old man, the old person, or the character that they were passes away, and then they become a new creation in Christ Jesus. That is to say, they might be a character that may be drinking and cutting up and carrying on and a variety of other things that are ill toward God. All of these things began to dissolve away. I found that I had no desire for these things, but I began to abhor them. I actually began to hate them. And this was in accordance with the Scriptures as I found out later.[28]

Many familiar elements are visible in the Reverend Cantrell's conversion story: the importance of primary religious socialization (Methodism), the typical early conversion age of fifteen, the friend who invited him to another church, the realization that something was missing in his life, and the quick acceptance of the need to repent (one month, four visits). Important additions are the equally quick change in his life following his conversion and the urgent need to give testimony of this—typical for the confession level. The hate expressed for drinking and other things of his former sinful lifestyle is also highly symbolic. The biblical expression "new creation in Christ Jesus" (2 Cor. 5:17) showed up in various Pentecostal conversion stories I heard in Guatemala and Nicaragua.

PRAISING IN TONGUES: SPEAKING,
PRAYING, AND SINGING

Praising in tongues—that is, speaking, praying, or singing in unknown tongues—was the main marker for the typical early Pentecostal conversion experience. Pentecostalism was to provide the concept of conversion that would eventually become dominant in the Americas and in much of the (non-Western) world since at least the 1980s.[29]

Pentecostal churches derived their name from the second chapter of Acts in the New Testament, in which the Spirit came over the apostles in "tongues, as of fire."[30] Some Holiness pastors already adopted the new idea of the Spirit as a force capable of changing individual lives in the late 1890s. Frank K. Flinn writes, "Significantly, the key founders of the pentecostal movement, Charles F. Parham and William J. Seymour, both came from a Methodist Holiness tradition. . . . The first recorded evidence of pentecostal conversion took place when Agnes Ozman began speaking in tongues at Charles F. Parham's Bible school in Topeka, Kansas, on New Year's Day, 1901."[31] Early Pentecostalism thus had strong Wesleyan roots and continued its emphasis on sanctification: "Sanctification was therein understood to be an instantaneous operation of heart purification following regeneration but preceding Spirit baptism."[32] Early Pentecostal conversions thus involved three stages: conversion, sanctification, and Spirit baptism. Later Pentecostal churches, lacking roots in Wesleyanism, viewed sanctification as an ongoing process throughout the Christian's life and thus only recognized two stages: conversion and Spirit baptism.

This second, or Spirit, baptism referred to being "filled" with the Holy Spirit, becoming "immersed" in the Holy Spirit. The use of water metaphors by converts was always very common. One Pentecostal man from India described it as follows: "Talking about a baptism, it was just like I was being plunged into a great sea of water, only the water was God, the water was the Holy Spirit."[33] Although it was likened to people's first baptism when they accepted Christ and became Christians, baptism in the Holy Spirit was viewed by Pentecostals from the beginning as "an experience that presupposes conversion."[34] Not all true believers received this extraordinary form of empowerment from the Holy Spirit, but all who received it by definition were powerful born-again Christians. Pentecostals considered the basic requirements for receiving the Holy Spirit to be faith, prayer, obedience to Christ, and—just as in the case of Holiness—surrender.

The most extreme form of surrender was praising in tongues, as a form of "self-transcending speech glorifying God."[35] The initial evidence for early Pentecostals that people had received the Spirit was praising in tongues. Their surrender to God was so complete that they no longer needed language. These converts no longer needed to form the words that came out of their own mouths. The tongues phenomenon was again based on Acts (10:45–46; 19:6): "Speaking in tongues was the unmistakable evidence to the Jewish believers that the Caesarians had experienced Spirit baptism."[36] Praising in tongues took many different forms during the Azusa Street revival in Los Angeles (1906–9): speaking in tongues, interpreting tongues, praying in tongues, and singing in tongues. Many of these forms of tongue praise are still important for Pentecostal believers across the Americas, as I explain below. A major innovation of the Charismatic movement since the 1960s has been making praising in tongues a sign of commitment and belief but not necessarily the *evidence* of a successful conversion. Many Pentecostal churches went through a similar process of toning down the importance of praising in tongues after the mid-twentieth century.[37]

The Pentecostal conversion concept thus drew from the nineteenth-century Holiness model but expanded it theologically. Flinn writes, "Most varieties of Pentecostalism have placed unusual emphasis on the second baptism in the Spirit which bestows the nine gifts of the Spirit listed in 1 Corinthians 12 and 14, including speaking in tongues *(glossolalia)* and healing of physical ailments. The nine gifts are: wisdom, prophecy, knowledge, discernment of spirits, faith, speaking in tongues, healing, interpretation of tongues, and the working of miracles."[38] However, "pentecostal conversions are typically more intense than those experienced by evangelicals."[39] The evangelistic fervor was usually stronger in Pentecostalism, because of the eschatological urgency: Jesus will return soon, so accept him today! Many—but certainly not all—of these elements turn up in the conversion stories in the Americas.

In the Catholic Charismatic Renewal (CCR), just like in Protestant Pentecostalism, a "sure sign"[40] of receiving the baptism of the Holy Spirit was the ability to praise in tongues. Hence the key experience for many converts to the CCR was learning to speak in tongues. This is the conversion story of Jill Newsome:

> When I heard it, all I knew is that I wanted it and I wanted to be able to praise God in that way. . . . I received the gift of tongues and I had a really hard time with the gift of tongues. . . .
>
> So when I first got the gift of tongues, I only had one word. And I didn't want anyone to hear it because I wasn't sure if this was really the gift or not. . . . I went home and started practicing with them—it is a new experience, and you want to try it out. . . . And as I kept praying in tongues I began to get attacked. . . . [M]y word was "mono-mono." . . .
>
> I was going "Oh my God what is this? Maybe I didn't really get the gift of tongues." All of this started going through my head. So I went to my sister and I go "Are you sure I got the gift of tongues? Listen to what I have" and I started speaking in tongues so that she could hear it. And she said that it was beautiful. . . . She goes "it's so peaceful." And it just reassured me and I just kept praising God.[41]

As Neitz points out, "one powerful form of evidence is the evidence that comes from other people's interpretations. . . . When one respects, trusts, and likes the other people in the group, the probability of their beliefs seeming reasonable increases." The prime importance of social relations and social networks in the conversion process is clear in this case. It is unfortunate, however, that Neitz does not provide more basic information on her informant Jill (age, background, how long in prayer group, etc.).

FEMALE CONVERSION STORIES: "INTERPENETRATED BY THE BLISS OF LIGHT"

Brereton skillfully describes and analyzes female conversion stories in the United States, including various Pentecostal ones. She vividly describes a powerful conversion experience involving Spirit baptism that happened during the original Azusa Street revival to Kathleen Scott, a teenager. An unknown man came into the Upper Room while Scott was there: "The moment he entered, Kathleen, moved by the Spirit, arose and pointed to the man as he stood at the head of the stairway, and spoke in a language other than her own for several minutes. At the beginning of the service immediately following Scott's outburst, the man testified to her powers:

> 'I am a Jew, and I came to this city to investigate this speaking in tongues. No person in this city knows my first or my last name, as I am here under an assumed name. . . . This girl, as I entered the room, started speaking in the Hebrew language. She told me my first name and my last name, and she told me why I was in the city and what my occupation was in life, and then she called upon me to repent. She told me things about my life which it would be impossible for any person in this city to know.' "[42]

This episode shows that already from its early beginnings, Pentecostalism offered opportunities for active participation by women (even teenage girls). Pentecostalism also stimulated converted women to "conquer the shyness that frequently troubles women unused to speaking in public."[43] The most famous woman to receive the Spirit regularly, to preach actively, and finally to start her own church, the Foursquare Gospel Church, in the 1920s was Aimee Semple McPherson.[44]

Agnes Sanford wrote an entire book about her powerful conversion experience, *The Healing Gifts of the Spirit* (1966). She describes what happened to her one day as she was on a lake:

> I prayed for God's life to reach me through the rays of the sun. And even though I did not know the Holy Spirit, the Spirit of God entered in a way so defying understanding that I have never tried to explain it. Nor could I explain it now. I can only say that for a split second I lived consciously and awarely in the bliss of eternity. I saw nothing and heard nothing, but I was so enwrapped and interpenetrated by the bliss of light that I thought, "If this doesn't stop I shall die!" And again I thought: "But I don't want it to stop!" It ceased, and I have no way of measuring the time of

it, for I was living beyond time. But the holy fire burned within my head for some fourteen days. I did not know then that it was the baptism of the Holy Ghost. . . . But no experience ever equaled in bliss this baptism of pure light and power that came to me from God.[45]

Brereton did not provide information on the events preceding this extraordinary religious experience on the lake or its aftermath. But Agnes Sanford never became an active member of a Pentecostal church, although she was a Charismatic and had a healing ministry for some time.[46]

DANCING IN THE SPIRIT: "CARRIED AWAY TO A PLACE OF WONDROUS BEAUTY"

Many women reported that they could not stop themselves from dancing, especially when they were filled by the Holy Spirit for the first time. This phenomenon is reported especially often by female Pentecostal converts throughout Latin America. I have also witnessed it myself during my fieldwork in Guatemala (1994–95) and Nicaragua (2005–6). The first book on Pentecostalism in Latin America already contained excerpts from thirty-four conversion stories from random leaders and members in different churches in Brazil and Chile.[47] Willems skillfully combined secondary materials, ethnographic methods (participant observation and interviews), and surveys in three states of Brazil and three provinces of Chile. The informant's initials, age, occupation, marital status, and religious background were always mentioned.[48] The only missing information was the age at which the actual conversion took place. Almost forty years later this material is still very rich, and the parallels with conversion stories that were collected decades later are remarkably strong. In fact, many of the stories—down to almost verbatim phrasings—that Willems recorded in the 1960s are identical to recently collected conversion stories.

Take, for instance, the Pentecostal conversion story of E.C.G., an eighteen-year-old single woman from Chile.

> Grandmother used to take me to a pentecostal temple, but I had no energy to resist temptations. Afterwards I returned to church to repent but I always fell back into sin. One day I heard the voice of the Lord who told me that all my sins had been forgiven. My heart filled with *gozo* and I was seized by the Holy Spirit. I danced and heard soft voices singing exquisite melodies. I felt carried away to another place of wondrous beauty. When I recovered I found myself kneeling and praying in front of the altar. Immediately all temptations and anxieties ceased. I gave up painting my lips and curling my hair. . . . When I was fourteen years old I had ear surgery and became almost deaf. After my conversion I took part in a *cadena de oración* (continuous prayer meeting of seven days). During one of these meetings an *hermano* laid hands on my head and gradually my hearing went back to normal.[49]

Willems already concluded in this early study that all those who joined a Pentecostal church shared a strong desire to change their lives.[50] If a conversion took place, it was often connected to miraculous healings. This has proven to be a recurring theme in studies of Pentecostalism in Latin America—as well as in the United States. It applies to both women and men.

MALE CONVERSION STORIES: "CAN A MAN LOVE THE LORD AND NOT BE A SISSY?"

Brereton pointed out that the social and psychological costs of converting to Pentecostalism are almost always higher for men: "Perhaps most damaging to their image of themselves, in converting men had to renounce the activities that tended to identify them as manly men: lusty drinking, gambling, smoking, womanizing. In the world etc."[51] In other words, "Can a man love the Lord and not be a sissy?"[52]

The "manly" activities mentioned here form an integral part of a cultural complex designated *machismo* in Latin America. Scholars have credited Pentecostalism with empowering women to correct their husbands and reorient them to become more integrated with their families. Some scholars think Pentecostalism stimulated more egalitarian gender roles; others point to the patriarchal elements in Christianity in general and Pentecostalism in particular.[53] I shall consider two examples from Latin America and one from the United States.

The Argentine anthropologist Daniel Míguez analyzed Pentecostal identity in a Buenos Aires suburb in the mid-1990s. He collected many conversion stories, including this one. Víctor was already attracted to evangelical television programs before his actual conversion, which happened after a dream.

> I was always looking for God, and . . . I had a very real dream . . . I kept getting smaller. And I knew I was going to disappear, I felt I was disappearing . . . The only thing I could think of . . . was to say: Lord, take care of me . . . The desire to find God was so great that I read all the Bible . . . Now the Church holds these house meetings . . . Once there was a meeting near my home and a neighbour . . . invited me . . . Seven years ago I went forward here at church and I made my vow of faith . . . I received Christ in my heart, that's where all our life starts . . . I studied, if there was a need to visit people I visited, then I was designated as leader . . . First I was Visitor . . . I traveled on my bicycle . . . Then I was made Area Leader.[54]

Víctor's conversion career can be sketched chronologically. As a child, he respected his evangelical neighbors. During his adolescence, he liked to watch evangelical TV programs, because he was "always looking for God." This is the pre-affiliation stage of the conversion career. Then he had a supernatural experience in a dream, which seems to have confronted him with his mortality and insignificance. A neighbor invited him to a house meeting of a local Pentecostal church (a clear institutional factor), where he "received Christ in his heart." He became very active in the church, first as a visitor, then as an area leader. To use the terminology of the conversion career: he went from affiliation to conversion to confession in a relatively short time.

The Spanish anthropologist Manuela Cantón also noted that conversion stories are more or less standardized and fulfilled three different functions.[55] According to her, the conversion testimonies are simultaneously socializing, didactic, and proselytizing. The narratives then form the basis of the informant's "new spirituality." It thus comes as no surprise that Cantón's book contains various detailed conversion stories. It also gives due attention to the time before conversion, or the pre-affiliation period. Cantón's informants mention the importance of their dissatisfaction with Catholicism, their extreme suffering, family and alcohol problems, illness, and general dissatisfaction with their lives.[56] Over half of the informants report that the first contact with the church happened through a spouse, relative, friend, neighbor, or acquaintance.[57] Cantón's study thus confirms the importance of institutional, contingency, and social factors in recruitment.

The following conversion story is told by Carlos, who was forty-six at that time.[58] He became an alcoholic at fourteen or fifteen and started using marijuana after he joined the army at eighteen. When he had no money to buy drugs, he engaged in armed robbery on the streets of Antigua and Guatemala City. He said he was in prison forty times, and his resentment against society grew stronger each time he was there. He went to a beautiful old colonial Catholic church in Antigua Guatemala and said:

> Lord, I believe that you are the son of God; if you exist, change my life; take away this burden from my soul. Lord, I can't take it anymore! . . . And you know what happened? Nothing happened, absolutely nothing happened! Witchcraft couldn't change my life; human science couldn't change my life; strong literature like Lenin and Marx couldn't change my life. Something was happening in my life; I didn't understand all of it. . . . For the first time I went to an evangelical congregation . . . I went with long hair and a ring in my ear . . . but something stronger than myself touched my heart, it lifted me up and I walked to the platform. . . . I threw myself down on the floor and I started to cry. I started to see my life one by one, step by step, everything that was my earlier life (he is crying). And I told Him: "Lord, forgive me, if you are more powerful, if you are stronger than the drugs, change me please, take away what I'm feeling in my heart." . . . [N]obody could change my life, only His holy and powerful gospel.

Carlos's dramatic conversion career went from adolescent alcoholism and drug use to crime and a long prison life—a contingency crisis brought on by a combination of social and personality factors. Carlos was violent and full of resentment against society, conforming to stereotypical gender roles in Guatemala. He looked for solutions in various places—not all religious. Ultimately, his conversion experience took place in a Pentecostal church, where he started to cry. He was crying again as he told his conversion story to a female Spanish anthropologist. He was obviously unconcerned about appearing a sissy.

I end with a final North American case. The U.S. anthropologist Peter Stromberg presented a highly detailed interview with George, who was in his early sixties.[59]

> George's father, who died when George was 26 years old, was a committed Christian and a firm person. By this I mean he had strong opinions on things and shared them with his son. George emphasizes that he and his father had many disagreements, but insists they did not fight with one another. Rather, for the most part George tried to bow to his father's wishes, for he admired the older man tremendously. . . . After college, George married his high school sweetheart, but after three children and seven years of marriage he struck up an affair with a coworker. He eventually left home and decided to divorce his wife. The relationship with the coworker also broke up, and thereafter George embarked upon a period in which he dated many different women. However, on a visit to his family, George was shocked when the youngest of his children did not recognize him. He was troubled, and seeing this, his ex-wife recommended he go and speak to a minister. George did so, and the minister asked him "where he stood with God." George answered that he did not believe in God, to which the minister responded that perhaps he should give that position some thought. George left the pastor's office with a Christian book and, after some days of debating with himself the existence of God, decided to pray to God and ask his forgiveness. Upon doing so he was flooded with a profound feeling of forgiveness; he refers to this as a "road-to-Damascus type of experience" (comparing his conversion to the Biblical description of the conversion of Saul of Tarsus). Having thus been converted to Christianity, George decided that he should put his life in order.[60]

This is a part of George's conversion story.[61]

> Oh. I really . . . I mean I know hell on earth. I *really* know hell on earth. Two things especially stand out in my mind. One time I came home and our daughter didn't know me. I was just a stranger . . . Oh I tell you, boy, that *really* shook me up. . . .
>
> And then another time or maybe the same visit—I don't know—my son said . . . who was five, six said: "Daddy aren't you ever coming home?" . . . Talk about a shake up. Oh brother. . . .
>
> And finally on noon on the third day I was . . . thinking about it and then all of a sudden I just felt I should pray. And I . . . My prayer went like this: "Dear God, if you exist, let me know that you exist and that you can forgive me."

George's conversion story is an example of how informants themselves use the Pauline conversion experience as a model of—but also as a model *for*[62]—their own conversion experience. For George, "hell on earth" was represented by feeling alienated from his children. Hence George's conversion story again confirms the importance of social factors in the conversion process and the need to go through hell in order to get to heaven.

CONCLUSION: CONVERSION, GENDER, AND BIOGRAPHY

The main questions addressed in this chapter were, What makes Pentecostal conversion stories unique? What factors are typically involved in Pentecostal conversion, judging from the conversion narratives? Are there differences between male and female Pentecostal conversion stories in the Americas? The studies described here show that most authors have focused on what they considered "conversion" to Pentecostalism among adolescents and young married adults in major urban centers of North and Latin America. The main factors they reported affecting the conversion process were social networks, institutional factors (evangelization methods and churches' conversion requirements), and contingency events such as meeting a missionary or looking for healing from illness.

In closing, I will tentatively try to compare the Pentecostal conversion continuum to the five-level conversion careers typology of religious activity. I don't aim for 100 percent correspondence; I merely want to systematically bring out some salient facts, which I will later relate to male and female Pentecostal conversion experiences. The pentecostal *pre-affiliation* stage seems to be marked by crisis and repentance. Again, the point here is not whether all converts actually went through a crisis,[63] or to try to delineate in detail the nature of the crisis,[64] but to note that the crisis was a wakeup call for the future convert: a sign that something was wrong; a sign that Jesus cared about them, too. Most converts had previous knowledge about Pentecostalism picked up from relatives, friends, neighbors, or the mass media. Once people were sufficiently socialized into the Pentecostal worldview, they felt the need to accept Jesus Christ as their personal Savior and express this in the public sphere—typically a Pentecostal church. This forms the start of their Pentecostal church *affiliation,* which is usually symbolized by their baptism by full immersion. However, the actual baptism ritual was rarely an important element of people's conversion narratives.

Conversion, used here in the limited sense of the conversion career approach, involves a change of identity and a change of worldview. Both are expressed in biographical reconstruction, that is, reshaping one's life story in accordance with Pentecostal conventions. Sanctification is a main theme here: many converts described how easy it was to maintain a new and far more disciplined lifestyle, free of alcohol abuse and adultery. They talked about finding God in their lives and about feeling at peace. They longed to read the Bible, and it was now far easier to understand than before their conversion. They typically credited the Holy Spirit for that achievement, not their Bible study. Only a select minority of Pentecostals reached the stage called *confession* in the conversion career typology of religious activity—a high level of participation inside the new religious group and a strong missionary attitude toward nonmembers. These were the main church leaders (pastors, deacons, assistants, band members, missionaries, etc.), who are usually men, and other core members, both men and women. It is tempting to think that all those people will occasionally praise in tongues, but the evidence does not always corroborate this. Many of them have spoken in tongues in the past, and most of them will pray in tongues regularly. But this is certainly not true of all of them.

According to their narratives, many converts to Pentecostalism had experienced haunting dreams and visions before converting or right after the moment they accepted Jesus Christ as their Savior. Almost all Pentecostal converts were "seized by the Holy Spirit," "healed by the Holy Spirit," or just "filled by the Holy Spirit" at some point in their conversion careers—usually in the beginning. Some of them had experienced "dancing in the Spirit" as well. Many Pentecostal converts—women and men—heard the voice of God and described "a sense of warmth" and feelings of incredible joy, often leading them to cry.

Brereton makes an interesting case for considering the Pentecostal conversion process (i.e., conversion career) as consisting of increasing steps of surrendering control. She concludes:

> Pentecostals view the experience of receiving the Spirit as the final step in a progressive surrender that may well have been going on since before their conversion; the baptism in the Spirit represents the extreme in "yieldedness" to God. When they receive the Spirit, Pentecostals allow the Holy Spirit to supersede their intellects and wills; they let the Spirit take control of their tongues, their power of speech, which they consider a central part of their beings. They pray the prayer that the Holy Spirit puts in their mouths, that is, they "pray in the Spirit."[65]

Nevertheless, we saw that the subject remains in control when describing these experiences. Many female conversion stories were motivated by a fear of dying and going to hell, but men rarely mentioned this fear in their conversion stories. This suggests that traditional gender patterns perhaps took control here, with men showing their traditional reluctance to express fear.

It is equally tempting to suggest that women, because of their gendered socialization, would find it easier to yield, to surrender, to let go of control, than men. On the other hand, in the Guatemalan case Pentecostal men described some powerful and emotional conversion experiences.

A more open interpretation suggests that Pentecostalism offers its converts an alternative repertoire of scenarios or *schemas* to guide their daily behavior.[66] The Spirit can force a change in social expectations associated with traditional gendered behavior. Under the influence of the Holy Spirit, strong men routinely broke down crying and demure women found themselves taking control of difficult situations. Pentecostalism has certainly had its share of strong and even rebellious Pentecostal women, with Aimee Semple McPherson presenting the archetype here. However, all over Central America I have met these women who "walked with the Spirit." They did not always have a formal leadership position in their churches, but they were recognized as informal leaders. Their biographies had hardened and seasoned them, and the continued empowerment by the Holy Spirit kept them going.

The potential for a transformation of traditional gender patterns is certainly available in Pentecostalism all across the Americas. However, just as in the case of Pentecostalism'ss potential for political transformation, the main factors that will allow it to transform not only individuals but also societies are social, institutional, and cultural. These factors change over time—just like individuals often do, but much more slowly.

Peace's remark that "pentecostal conversions are typically more intense than those experienced by evangelicals"[67] seems to be true only for those people who are involved in their Pentecostal churches at the above-mentioned levels of conversion and confession. It is typically here that we also find the strong evangelistic fervor that many see as typical of Pentecostalism, because of its eschatological urgency. However, I have argued elsewhere that many informants in Latin America, male and female, did not really *convert* to a Pentecostal church in the strict sense of experiencing a change in their worldviews and identities. Most people merely *joined* the Pentecostal church for a while, which would be called affiliation in the conversion career typology.[68] Making this distinction between conversion and affiliation makes it easier to analyze the significant desertion rates in Pentecostal churches throughout Latin America. It also helps to explain the high mobility of some believers, who move easily from one church to another. Hence in a context of growing religious competition on most continents, especially North America and South America, it is all the more important that researchers of Pentecostalism (and other religions) in the future

1. delineate in detail the various levels of religious participation they utilize in their studies of religion;
2. systematize the variables influencing the various levels of conversion and disaffiliation;
3. recognize the importance of subjective religious experience in the conversion process;
4. plan their research to systematically gauge the influence of gender on conversion for both male and female informants;
5. try to accomplish an even spread of informants from *all* levels of religious activity and *all* phases of the life cycle adolescents, married people, midlife persons, and old age; and
6. endeavor to collect the most complete data possible at various locations in order to fill in the full comparative model of the conversion career.

NOTES

1. David A. Snow and Richard Machalek, "The Convert as a Social Type," in *Sociological Theory*, ed. Randall Collins (San Francisco: Jossey-Bass, 1983), 259–89. David A. Snow and Richard Machalek, "The Sociology of Conversion," *Annual Review of Sociology* 10 (1984): 167–90. Lewis R. Rambo, *Understanding Religious Conversion* (New Haven: Yale University Press, 1993).

2. See Henri Gooren, *Religious Conversion and Disaffiliation: Tracing Patterns of Change in Faith Practices* (New York: Palgrave Macmillan, forthcoming), for an elaboration of my narrative approach to conversion.

3. See Virginia Lieson Brereton, *From Sin to Salvation: Stories of Women's Conversions, 1800 to the Present* (Bloomington: IUP, 1991).

4. Henri Gooren, "Conversion Careers in Latin America: Entering and Leaving Church among Pentecostals, Catholics, and Mormons," in *Conversion of a Continent: Contemporary Religious Change in Latin America*, ed. Timothy J. Steigenga and Edward L. Cleary (New Brunswick: Rutgers University Press, 2007), 52–71. Gooren, *Religious Conversion and Disaffiliation*.

5. I limit myself here to my own region of expertise: Latin America and the United States. My apologies to Canadian readers, who will note that no conversion stories from their country are quoted.

6. See, e.g., Janneke Brouwer, "Nieuwe Scheppingen in Christus: Bekeringsverhalen van Protestante Evangélicos en Katholieke Carismáticos in Masaya, Nicaragua" (M.A. thesis, Utrecht University, 2000). John Burdick, *Looking for God in Brazil* (Berkeley: UCP, 1993). Manuela Cantón Delgado, *Bautizados en fuego: Protestantes, discursos de conversión y política en Guatemala (1989–1993)* (Antigua Guatemala: CIRMA, 1998). Susan Friend Harding, *The Book of Jerry Falwell: Fundamentalist Language and Politics* (Princeton: Princeton University Press, 2000); Rowan Ireland, *Kingdoms Come: Religion and Politics in Brazil* (Pittsburgh: University of Pittsburgh Press, 1991); Daniel Míguez, " 'To Help You Find God': The Making of a Pentecostal Identity in a Buenos Aires Suburb" (Ph.D. diss., VU University, Amsterdam, 1997).

7. See, e.g., Elizabeth E. Brusco, *The Reformation of Machismo: Evangelical Conversion and Gender in Colombia* (Austin: University of Texas Press, 1995); Christian Lalive d'Épinay, *Haven of the Masses: A Study of the Pentecostal Movement in Chile* (London: Lutterworth, 1969); Cecília Loreto Mariz, *Coping with Poverty : Pentecostal Churches and Christian Base Communities in Brazil* (Philadelphia: Temple University Press, 1994).

8. André Droogers, Henri Gooren, and Anton Houtepen, "Conversion Careers and Culture Politics in Pentecostalism: A Comparative Study in Four Continents" (Proposal submitted to the Netherlands Organization for Scientific Research [NWO], 2003, 5–6). See also Henri Gooren, "Towards a New Model of Conversion Careers: The Impact of Personality and Situational Factors," *Exchange* 34 (2005): 149–66; Henri Gooren, "The Religious Market Model and Conversion: Towards a New Approach," *Exchange* 35 (2006): 39–60; Henri Gooren, "Towards a New Model of Religious Conversion Careers: The Impact of Social and Institutional Factors," in *Paradigms, Poetics and Politics of Conversion*, ed. Wout J. van Bekkum, Jan N. Bremmer, and Arie Molendijk (Leuven: Peeters, 2006), 25–40; Gooren, "Conversion Careers in Latin America." My use of conversion career is somewhat different from James Richardson, who coined the term in *Conversion Careers: In and out of the New Religions* (Beverly Hills, CA: Sage, 1978).

9. Gooren, "Conversion Careers in Latin America," 53–54; Gooren, *Religious Conversion and Disaffiliation*, chapter 2.

10. Hawkins correctly points out that Saint Paul and Saint Augustine both represent the archetypical versions of the crisis conversion experience. Anne Hunsaker Hawkins, *Archetypes of Conversion: The Autobiographies of Augustine, Bunyan, and Merton* (London: Associated University Presses, 1985), 21, 45.

11. James Richardson identified Pauline surrender as the origin of the "passive convert" approach to conversion in his "The Active vs. Passive Convert: Paradigm Conflict in Conversion/Recruitment Research," *JSSR* 24 (1985): 163–79.

12. Cf. Rambo, *Understanding Religious Conversion.*

13. Gooren, *Religious Conversion and Disaffiliation;* Patricia Caldwell, *The Puritan Conversion Narrative: The Beginnings of American Expression* (Cambridge: CUP, 1985).

14. Richard C. Lovelace, "The Anatomy of Puritan Piety: English Puritan Devotional Literature, 1600–1640," in *Christian Spirituality: Post-Reformation and Modern,* ed. Louis Dupré and Don E. Saliers (London: SCM, 1989), 304.

15. Gooren, *Religious Conversion and Disaffiliation.*

16. Frank K. Flinn, "Conversion: Up from Evangelicalism or the Pentecostal and Charismatic Experience," in *Religious Conversion: Contemporary Practices and Controversies,* ed. Christopher Lamb and M. Darroll Bryant (London: Cassell, 1999), 62–63.

17. Brereton, *From Sin to Salvation,* 55.

18. Brereton, *From Sin to Salvation,* 123.

19. Brereton, *From Sin to Salvation,* 57.

20. Brereton, *From Sin to Salvation,* 58.

21. Brereton, *From Sin to Salvation,* 56.

22. Henri Gooren, *Rich among the Poor: Church, Firm, and Household among Small-Scale Entrepreneurs in Guatemala City* (Amsterdam: Thela, 1999), 154.

23. J. R. Williams, "Baptism in the Holy Spirit," in *NIDPCM,* 360–61.

24. G. B. McGee, "Initial Evidence," in *NIDPCM,* 787.

25. McGee, "Initial Evidence," 785.

26. Brereton, *From Sin to Salvation,* 61, 65; emphasis in original.

27. Susan F. Harding, "Convicted by the Holy Spirit: The Rhetoric of Fundamental Baptist Conversion," *American Ethnologist* 14 (1987): 167.

28. Harding, "Convicted by the Holy Spirit," 171–73.

29. Some consider the Christian revival that started in the 1980s the Fourth Awakening (Flinn, "Conversion," 64).

30. "When the day of Pentecost had fully come, they [the Apostles] were all with one accord in one place. And suddenly there came a sound from heaven, as of a rushing mighty wind, and it filled the whole house where they were sitting. Then there appeared to them divided tongues, as of fire, and one sat upon each of them. And they were all filled with the Holy Spirit and began to speak with other tongues, as the Spirit gave them utterance" (Acts 2: 1–4).

31. Flinn, "Conversion," 66. Note that Flinn treats the fact that Agnes Ozman spoke in tongues as evidence of her conversion.

32. Williams, "Baptism in the Holy Spirit," 358.

33. K. Ranaghan and D. Ranaghan, quoted in Williams, "Baptism in the Holy Spirit," 355.

34. Williams, "Baptism in the Holy Spirit," 356.

35. Williams, "Baptism in the Holy Spirit," 359.

36. Williams, "Baptism in the Holy Spirit," 358.

37. See McGee, "Initial Evidence," for a detailed historical overview of changing Pentecostal ideas on the subject.

38. Flinn, "Conversion," 65.

39. Richard V. Peace, "Conflicting Understandings of Christian Conversion: A Missiological Challenge," *IBMR* 28 (2004): 9.

40. Mary Jo Neitz, *Charisma and Community: A Study of Religious Commitment within the Charismatic Renewal* (New Brunswick: Transaction, 1987), 85.

41. Neitz, *Charisma and Community,* 85–86.

42. Quoted in Brereton, *From Sin to Salvation,* 95.

43. Brereton, *From Sin to Salvation,* 96.

44. Brereton, *From Sin to Salvation,* 95–96.

45. Brereton, *From Sin to Salvation,* 70, based on Agnes Sanford, *The Healing Gifts of the Spirit* (New York: Lippincott, 1966).

46. Allan Anderson, e-mail communication to author, April 8, 2008.

47. Emilio Willems, *Followers of the New Faith: Culture Change and the Rise of Protestantism in Brazil and Chile* (Nashville: Vanderbilt University Press, 1967), 125–31.

48. Willems, *Followers of the New Faith,* vi–vii, 125–31.

49. Willems, *Followers of the New Faith,* 127.

50. Willems, *Followers of the New Faith,* 130–31.

51. Brereton, *From Sin to Salvation,* 99.

52. Brereton, *From Sin to Salvation,* 100.

53. For more information on the relationship between Pentecostalism and machismo, see Brusco, *Reformation of Machismo;* Lesley Gill, "Like a Veil to Cover Them: Women and the Pentecostal Movement in La Paz," *American Ethnologist* 17 (1990): 708–21; Mariz, *Coping with Poverty;* Cecília Loreto Mariz and María das Dores Campos Machado, "Pentecostalism and Women in Brazil," in *Power, Politics, and Pentecostals in Latin America,* ed. Edward L. Cleary and Hannah W. Stewart-Gambino (Boulder, CO: Westview Press, 1997); David Martin, *Pentecostalism: The World Their Parish* (Oxford: Blackwell, 2002), 75–76; Donald E. Miller and Tetsunao Yamamori, *Global Pentecostalism: The New Face of Christian Social Engagement* (Berkeley: UCP, 2007), 208–10; David Smilde, *Reason to Believe: Cultural Agency in Latin American Evangelicalism* (Berkeley: UCP, 2007); Timothy J. Steigenga, *The Politics of the Spirit: The Political Implications of Pentecostalized Religion in Costa Rica and Guatemala* (Lanham, MD: Lexington Books, 2001).

54. Miguez, "To Help You Find God," 103–6. Miguez acknowledges the problems of "representivity and generalization" in ethnographic research (p. 28). He randomly interviewed members and leaders in the Pentecostal Centro Cristiano in a representative suburb of Buenos Aires, Argentina.

55. Cantón, *Bautizados en fuego,* 134.

56. Cantón, *Bautizados en fuego,* 148–60. Her twenty-three key informants, selected at random, come from seventeen different congregations in various Guatemalan towns and cities. Eight are Pentecostals and one is a charismatic Catholic (p. 136).

57. Cantón, *Bautizados en fuego,* 168.

58. Cantón, *Bautizados en fuego,* 189–96; translation mine.

59. Peter G. Stromberg, "Ideological Language in the Transformation of Identity," *American Anthropologist* 92 (1990): 48–51; Peter G. Stromberg, *Language and Self-Transformation: A Study of the Christian Conversion Narrative* (Cambridge: CUP, 1993), 112–18.

60. Stromberg, "Ideological Language," 48–49.

61. Stromberg, *Language and Self-Transformation,* 114–15.

62. See Clifford Geertz, *The Interpretation of Cultures* (New York: Basic Books, 1973), 93–94.

63. Using a control group of nonconventists who also went through severe crisis experiences, Heirich showed that converts tended to exaggerate their pre-affiliation sinfulness in order to increase the power and value of their current conversions (Max Heirich, "Change of Heart: A Test of Some Widely Held Theories about Religious Conversion," *American Journal of Sociology* 83:3 [1978]: 653–80). This forms part of the biographical reconstruction mentioned above (Rambo, *Understanding Religious Conversion;* Snow and Machalek, "The Convert as a Social Type"; Snow and Machalek, "The Sociology of Conversion").

64. See Rambo, *Understanding Religious Conversion*, 46–48, for a systematic analysis of the crisis experience in conversion.

65. Brereton, *From Sin to Salvation*, 70.

66. Claudia Strauss and Naomi Quinn, "A Cognitive/Cultural Anthropology," in *Assessing Cultural Anthropology*, ed. Robert Borofsky (New York: McGraw-Hill, 1994), 284–300.

67. Peace, "Conflicting Understandings," 9.

68. See Gooren: "Towards a New Model of Conversion Careers"; "Toward a New Model of Religious Conversion Careers"; "Conversion Careers in Latin America"; *Religious Conversion and Disaffiliation*. The last two works are based on a more extensive review and analysis of conversion stories in the literature than the one presented here.

6

Pentecostalism and Globalization

Birgit Meyer

The title of this chapter couples two big terms around each of which a huge scholarly field has evolved over the past two decades. In brief, the concept of globalization signals a departure from the metanarrative of modernization, according to which 'development' would eventually render the second (socialist) and third worlds more or less similar to the first world, the modern West.[1] Globalization, with its vocabulary of flux and mix, diversity, fragmentation, multiple identities, postmodernity, and hybridity, registers a growing skepticism vis-á-vis such teleological narratives. Pertaining to the intensified encroachment of capitalism on the everyday lives of people all over the globe, globalization entails a "glocalizing" dynamics. Far from bringing about a well-integrated system in which the spheres of the social, the political, the economic, the cultural, and the religious, all play their distinct role, globalization is rife with disjunctures.[2] Given that even a quick glance at Pentecostal self-descriptions highlights that many churches and movements present themselves as "global" or "international," and also feature these terms in their names, it is not surprising that *globalization* stands central in the study of Pentecostalism—a term I use as a shorthand to refer to a broad variety of churches, as outlined by Allan Anderson in chapter 1. Of special interest for the study of globalization are the more recently founded Pentecostal-Charismatic churches, which are organized as global megachurches addressing masses of believers, make prolific use of media technologies to spread the message, and endorse the prosperity gospel.

The nature of the "fit" between Pentecostalism and globalization has occupied many scholars.[3] Two recent overview articles, by André Droogers and Joel Robbins,[4] testify to the theoretical and empirical achievements made in this field.

113

Taking these well-documented pieces as a starting point, this chapter spotlights a number of issues that I consider important in studying Pentecostalism as a global religion. First, I focus on the relation between globalization and religion in general and Pentecostalism in particular. I plead to move beyond a narrow use of Max Weber's famous thesis about the link between Protestantism and the rise of capitalism, so as to get a better grasp of the distinct features of Pentecostal-Charismatic churches in our time. Second, instead of treating Pentecostalism and globalization as two separate entities, I approach Pentecostalism as a globalizing, religious project. Therefore three key foci in the study of Pentecostalism that are of immediate importance to globalization are explored: its imaginary of the world, the emphasis on outreach and spread, and the concern with rupture. Third, I launch some concepts that may help us deepen our understanding of Pentecostalism in our current age.

GLOBALIZATION AND RELIGION: THE WEBER THESIS AND BEYOND

Many scholars note a consonance of Pentecostal Christianity with the advance of neoliberal capitalism. In recent research—especially in the sociology of religion—Weber's famous thesis about the relation between Protestantism and the rise of capitalism forms an important point of reference.[5] As is well known, Weber posited a causal relation between the Protestant ethic, geared toward innerworldly ascesis, and the rise of capitalism. He pointed out that Protestantism instigated a process of disenchantment that culminated in the decline of religion. Protestantism, having played the role of midwife in the birth of the spirit of capitalism, is no longer needed to sustain this spirit. Modern people are stuck in the "iron cage" (a better translation for the original German expression *stahlhartes Gehäuse* might be "casing of steel") of modernity, longing for the return of God or gods and new prophets who cannot, however, claim enduring credibility because of the irreversibility of the process of disenchantment, which ensures that reenchantment can only be an illusion.

While the link between Pentecostalism and neoliberal capitalism certainly demands our attention, when invoking Weber we need to be aware of the differences that exist between the period analyzed by him and the contemporary era. While Weber's analysis was driven by the quest to discern what caused the rise of modern capitalism that uniquely occurred in Western societies, global capitalism is now well in place. That Pentecostal-Charismatic churches, albeit to varying degrees, prove exceptionally well suited to formulate an appealing message and modes of participation in its wake need not imply that the relation between these churches and capitalism is the same as Weber had in mind. This can be highlighted by considering three issues.

First, instead of secularization and disenchantment, we face religionization and reenchantment, suggesting an inversion of the Weber thesis, as Droogers also has noted.[6] Indeed, one of the most salient issues in the discussion about the limits of modernization as a viable concept that has informed the turn to "globalization" concerns the presence of religion in public settings and its entanglement with politics and the economy. Secularization theory is no longer found suitable to explain the (future) role and place of religion in contemporary societies in our "postsecular" era. The spread of democracy has facilitated the rise of religions, including Pentecostalism, due to the retreat of the state from the public sphere and the deregulation of hitherto state-controlled mass media. In many settings, religions appear to be of prime importance not only on the level of private experience and inner belief but also with regard to the sphere of politics and public affairs, thus thwarting a typically modernist vision of society as differentiated into separate compartments, one of them being religion.[7] In order to grasp the current situation, the modernist distinction between religion, politics, and the economic sphere (or "the market") needs to be transcended in favor of conceptualizations that take the public presence of religion and its diffusion into other spheres into account. This applies in particular to Pentecostalism, which is often characterized as global religion par excellence. It is not only the case that religions assume a public presence instead of remaining a matter of private belief; contrary to the Calvinism depicted by Weber, current Pentecostals also endorse a view of the world as a site of war between God and the devil, thus instigating enchantment rather than disenchantment. For instance, for scholars working in Africa it is difficult to overlook the problematic implications of African Pentecostal assertions of the existence of witchcraft as a real threat by real people (often but not necessarily family members) and a vision of politics as a field of a cosmological struggle.[8]

Second, scholars need to register the variety of modes through which Pentecostals relate to the economy. While conversion to Pentecostalism may be conducive to a capitalist work ethic and overall lifestyle in certain settings, as suggested by Weber,[9] in others the effects may be quite different. In his critical analysis of Pentecostal-Charismatic churches in Ghana, for instance, Paul Gifford noted that their consumerist ethos and affirmation of beliefs in spirits may be an impediment to "development."[10] Other authors, too, question the assumption of "born-again" conversion yielding an orderly ethos that is instrumental for modernization. For instance, Rafael Sanchez's depiction of born-again squatters in Caracas, Venezuela, for whom seizing houses is the flipside of being seized by the Holy Spirit, and Daniel Smith's study of born-again corruption in Nigeria thwart assumptions about the mind-set and lifestyle of Pentecostals and question the validity of the Weber thesis as a blueprint.[11] It is high time for scholars of Pentecostalism to also pay attention to such examples. We need to resist taking for granted the relation between Pentecostalism and capitalism and acknowledge that a variety of attitudes exist: from an engaged concern with health and poverty to an inclination toward corruption and self-enrichment.

Third, instead of keeping people in a "casing of steel" that requires discipline and hard work, capitalism appears to owe its appeal to a large extent to the promise of pleasure via the consumption of goods that become central to the construction of identity. This has been pointed out elaborately by Colin Campbell in his critique of Weber's undue emphasis on ascesis at the expense of consumption.[12] Indeed, rather than stress "innerworldly ascesis" and distance from the world, many of the newer Pentecostal-Charismatic churches embrace the prosperity gospel, according to which material goods may be blessings from God.[13] In order to grasp the specific ethos implied by this appreciation of material goods, attention needs to be paid to consumption as a religious practice. It would, however, be mistaken to understand this in terms of a sheer materialism that is opposed to genuine religious spirituality. Instead we should question the inclination of scholars of religion to regard material religion, including the so-called worship of idols as well as the incorporation of commodities, as inferior to an ideal religious "spirituality." My point here is that our contemporary view of Protestantism as rejecting materiality—and conversely our view of materiality as indexing a lower form of religion—may in part be attributed to Weber's sketch of Protestantism as disenchanted and situated beyond and above a (Catholic) reliance on objects, which affirms Protestant self-descriptions as anti-idolatric. Given the obvious importance of material things in the Pentecostal setting, this view needs revision. The study of Pentecostal churches offers highly suitable cases to develop more adequate ideas about the relation between religion and materiality in our time.

These three issues indicate that current Pentecostalism operates in new constellations that require alternative, empirically grounded theories and concepts that can help us grasp religion in our time. Globalization, as indicated above, signals a new historical moment at which the substance, place, and role of religion is changing. The Weber thesis, provided it is not simply used as a model for which confirmation is sought, is useful for discerning the distinctive aspects of Pentecostalism's current centrality that require new approaches. The study of Pentecostalism, as a global, postmodern religion, is of great theoretical interest, as it can help us gain a vision of what religion entails in our time.

PENTECOSTALISM AS GLOBAL RELIGION

Certain reservations about a decontextualized application of the Weber thesis to contemporary Pentecostalism notwithstanding, it is clear that the study of Pentecostalism has profited tremendously from a Weberian methodology. Resisting a reductive approach to religion, this methodology grounds scholarly analysis on Pentecostals' own views and practices. Obviously, such an approach resonates well with anthropological modes of research and knowledge production and is conducive to multidisciplinary cooperation with scholars in religious studies and theology. It can safely be stated that the most insightful scholarship on Pentecostalism is based on a successful translation of "internal" into "external" perspectives, taking as a point of departure what people believe and experience. The strength of this approach is that, rather than impose a neutral analytical language, it stays close to Pentecostalism's own vocabulary and does not solely explain its success by referring to nonreligious factors. This is also the approach followed here. In the next section, the notion of Pentecostalism as a global religion is explored by taking as a starting point the following key terms from pentecostal discourse:[14] *the world, global outreach* and *breaking from the past* so as to be *born again.*

The Pentecostal Imaginary of "the World"

As Arjun Appadurai has noted, the most salient aspect of globalization—at least for scholars in the social-cultural sciences—concerns its cultural dimension: the possibility for people to deploy alternative imaginaries that give rise to new kinds of public cultures.[15] This poses a challenge to the modern state, which no longer features as the privileged entity in the formation of identity and politics of belonging but faces the rise of alternative, religious, or ethnic identities that put into question its role in articulating the imagined community of the nation. Imaginaries of the world position self and others in the world conceptually, socially, and politically, mobilize people into mass movements, and determine spaces of action. It needs to be stressed that "imagining" the world is a well-structured and culturally, socially, and politically grounded project. This yields imaginaries that organize powerful ways of thinking and feeling and sustain particular modes of belonging that thrive on inclusion and exclusion.[16]

Pentecostalism plays a central role in the rise and spread of such imaginaries that are not confined to local or national settings but construe and make sense of the world "at large" and determine people's position and radius of mobility therein. Though very much aware of local specificities, Pentecostals have a sense of the world as a space that contains many unfamiliar territories,[17] yet is shaped by invisible principles that Pentecostals claim being able to uncover. The diversity in the field of Pentecostalism notwithstanding, it is safe to state, as intimated already, that Pentecostals share a view of the world as the site of a spiritual war between demonic forces and God .[18] In order to "see" what goes on behind the surface of appearance, extraordinary vision power—the spirit of discernment—is required. Hence the emphasis on pastors, prophets, and believers who have the power to "see." As this spiritual war affects every aspect of existence, it may well be found to operate in a person's body, but also in public spaces, institutions, or even whole countries. All these locations may be arenas for the struggle between opposite forces. Concomitantly, salvation is to be achieved by a process of casting out evil through the intervention of the Holy Spirit. This is a purifying force that spreads "like fire" and rids spaces—within persons, on the level of their spirit, but also the secret, hidden interiors of companies, markets, cities, or countries—of their uncanny, dangerous occupants.[19]

One intriguing aspect of this view of "the world" as torn between dualistic forces that clash on any level—from the personal to the political, from public to cosmic—concerns the fact that the Pentecostal imaginary of the world (its cosmology) and personal experience are made to reinforce each other. A person's experience of an inner struggle with, or even possession by, a demonic force affirms the truthfulness of the imaginary of the cosmic war. In the same way as prayer may be called for to deliver an afflicted person, or protect him or her against evil, prayer is also considered suitable for healing the nation. A born-again Christian can in principle use the "weapon of prayer" and invoke the power of the Holy Spirit in any setting, from the personal to the political. The experience of the body as a microcosm for the spiritual war between God and Satan and the imagination of the world as a site of this war depend on each other. This tight linkage between experience and embodiment, on the one hand, and imaginary and cosmology, on the other, ensures a deep sense of certainty about the state of the world at large, the reality of demonic assaults, and the need for protection, as well as the possibility of salvation and a new beginning. In short, the Pentecostal imaginary structures personal experience, while at the same time the latter authenticates the former as truthful and real.

Another important issue is that, in distinction to Weber's description of Calvinists and Puritans, for Pentecostals the world is not a compromising setting per se from which to turn away—as taught by Bunyan's *Pilgrim's Progress* or the lithograph the *Broad and the Narrow Path*—but one that requires action and transformation, even though this is full of difficulties and dangers. In this sense, Pentecostal cosmology is strongly oriented toward world-making. Consumer items, as the prosperity gospel also stipulates, are an inalienable part of this process. While commodities and gifts may be identified as linked to the devil and his demons, it is important to realize that they are far from bad per se; their positive or negative nature entirely depends on the spirit that is behind them.[20] In principle, anything can be imbued with the Holy Spirit and thus be part of a born-again believer's life. This is what accounts for the close connection between the spread of capitalism, consumption, and the appeal of Pentecostalism: Pentecostalism "embeds" neoliberal economic policies.[21] Likewise, the realm of politics can easily be subjected—and it seems increasingly so—to extensive prayers.[22] And even a football match is an appropriate target for the Holy Spirit. During a recent visit to Ghana at the time of the African Cup of Nations (January 2008), I was amazed to notice that Pentecostals attended church services dressed in the colors of the Ghanaian flag and prayed for the Holy Spirit to be with the Ghanaian team, and let it win. Many more examples could be made to sustain the point that Pentecostals endorse a world-embracing attitude that complicates the possibility to maintain the classical Protestant distinction between being *in* the world, yet not *of* the world.

Global Outreach and Spread

In the literature there is much emphasis on the phenomenal spread of Pentecostalism across the globe. Much reference is made to growth in terms of converts but also of separate Pentecostal organizations that reach the size of megachurches with their own media empires. That covering space is central to the logic of Pentecostalism can be well illustrated by the following vignette. When I visited Mensa Otabil's International Central Gospel Church (ICGC) at Christ Temple (Accra) in January 2008,[23] in his sermon he asserted the principle that once a church leader gets hold of a larger space, there will be more attendants: "It is not people that are the problem, space is the problem." Otabil related jubilantly how he had made his church grow by making ever larger spaces available—a strategy he also advised his followers to take in the sphere of business: "Think big! Move from the kiosk to large stores!" Here again we come across a striking parallelism between the expansion of the church and one's personal well-being: both are a matter of taking place. In the same vein, public space also is to be filled with Pentecostal signs and sounds. Believers declare their beliefs with stickers on cars, verses on buses, and references to the Bible on sign boards. Through such signs Pentecostal Christianity becomes virtually omnipresent.

Both sympathetic and critical observers regard Pentecostalism as the future form of Christianity (believed to be less and less dominated by Westerners). This is endorsed by many Pentecostals from the Global South who embrace the project of "reaching out into the world," thereby making use of modern media facilities, global infrastructures, and forms of mass organization. Expansion in space being one of the distinctive characteristics of Pentecostalism, many researchers have investigated the dynamics of the relation between the local and the global, whether by stressing the incorporation of the latter into the former ("extraversion") or, conversely, the circulation of certain locally grounded ideas and practices into broader realms. In so doing, the study of Pentecostalism reveals the intricacies of the entanglement of global flows with local settings.

Christian expansion, aiming to spread the gospel among all nations, has always been "transnational" (even before the term was coined). Building on this drive, the spread of Pentecostalism engenders a new attitude toward locality. While earlier mission churches were usually concerned with "inculturation" and instigated locally grounded appropriations of Christianity, for instance, by the vernacularization of Christian discourse, many contemporary Pentecostal-Charismatic churches now move a step further and explicitly seek to connect with broader, global networks in which English is the main language. This implies a marked shift in scale, in the course of which the local becomes a site that is enveloped in a broader scheme. The Pentecostal imaginary of the world is deployed in transnational networks that create a new space and networks of communication and circulation that impinge on and transform local sites.

Many Pentecostal-Charismatic churches make extensive use of modern mass media to assert their public presence. All this is part of an active conversion of public space into a Christian environment, much in line with the project of worldmaking. As stated, the world is the ultimate space that needs to be filled, and many churches develop global outreach programs that materialize through Web site, international crusades and prayer meetings, and new networks instigated from Africa, Latin America, or Asia. While for a long time research on Pentecostalism has focused on distinct churches, in the past couple of years there has developed a new body of research on Pentecostal expansion throughout Africa, Latin America, and, to a lesser extent, Asia and Europe. A number of researchers follow the circulation of the Pentecostal message across continents, for instance, regarding the popularity of Brazilian and Portuguese churches in lusophone Africa,[24] the spread of African Pentecostal churches to Eastern Europe,[25] and the rise of African- and Latin American–derived migrant churches in the West.[26] Of special interest here is the phenomenon of "reverse mission," which aims at reconverting Western people. Again, this points toward the incorporation of locations into the Pentecostal imaginary and illustrates the concern to work on establishing a Christian world. That the generations following the Western missionaries who spread the gospel among the "heathens" have lost faith and succumbed to a process of un-churching is read as an admonishment to stick to faith and not loose it to the corrupting influence of the world.

In the future, more work is needed that investigates new connections in Pentecostal global networks, along which ideas, media products, preachers, and believers circulate. Also required is research that is explicitly devoted to comparison, highlighting significant differences and similarities in the spread of Pentecostalism across continents. In so doing, more attention should be paid to determining which circumstances are conducive to allowing Pentecostalism to spread and which circumstances might rather form an impediment.

Breaking from the Past and Being Born Again

Alongside the emphasis placed on spatial expansion, scholars—closely following the Pentecostals among whom they do their research—have been much concerned with the question of rupture from the past and being born again. As Robbins put it, Pentecostalism expands via a simultaneous process of "world-making" and "world-breaking."[27] A born-again Christian is a person supposed to make "a complete break with the past"—as I tried to point out in an earlier publication.[28] What is cast here as "the past" may well concern coeval beliefs and practices that are however dismissed as "backward" or even "satanic." As pointed out already, many researchers have noted that Pentecostals tend to mobilize a diabolizing stance toward indigenous gods, which are recast as demons operating under the aegis of Satan. In deliverance services such forces are cast out of people's bodies, as part and parcel of a project through which they are symbolically separated from their broader relations—represented by the "witches in the village" or the gods that are worshiped on the level of the village or the clan. "Accepting Jesus Christ as my personal savior," as the saying goes, promises the possibility to become a different, new person who has left behind the powers of darkness, "by the power of the Holy Spirit." This transition is promised to happen instantaneously—in the here and now! Though much research is still needed on the consequences of becoming born again for people's personal and social identities, the relation with their partners, children, and the wider family,[29] it is clear that for many the turn to Pentecostalism implies a dissociation—or at least an attempt to do so—from earlier social and cultural affiliations. As David Martin has argued, Pentecostalism launches an alternative understanding of the person as a mobile self with a "portable identity" and concomitant "portable practice" and "transportable message," all being conducive to spatial and social mobility.[30]

At stake is a temporalizing discourse that seems to be basic to Pentecostal identity as grounded in the present and geared toward the future. As Robbins has pointed out, as scholars we urgently need to come to terms theoretically with the emphasis placed by Pentecostals on rupture and change.[31] While he is certainly right to stress the importance of moving beyond a mode of analysis that denies the possibility of profound cultural change and remains indebted to models of inculturation and syncretism, we need to be aware that rupture necessarily implies some kind of discursive continuity, if only because "being against" always entails some degree of "being with."

Taken together, the dynamics of spread and new birth—the spatial expansion and the marking of a new time—account for Pentecostalism as a distinctly global religion, with its own imaginary of the world as a whole that transcends more limited, local worldviews and promises to involve believers in a global born-again community. Pentecostalism can best be described not as an essential substance, made up of a fixed set of doctrines and practices, but as evolving around a number of core features that can be deployed in local arenas in specific ways and through which these arenas become part of a broader imaginary of the world. In other words, Pentecostalism owes its success in spreading across the world to its lack of a fixed substance and of large-scale organizational structures (very unlike the Catholic Church, and perhaps surprisingly similar to Islam)—to its liquidity—and its capacity to envelop the local into a larger scheme of things. In this sense, Pentecostalism is always in the process of becoming, a matter of movement and performance rather than a fixed religious system backed up by frozen structures of authority. An intriguing tension exists between the affirmation of Charismatic authority, which demands obedience and discipline from followers, on the one hand, and the power of the Holy Spirit, on the other. As every believer, in principle, can be filled with the Holy Spirit and assume spiritual authority, there is room—provided this spiritual authority is acknowledged and practically supported by others—for endless fission and the opening of new churches.

EXPANDING OUR VOCABULARY

The explicit emphasis on the Holy Spirit and spirituality should not blind us to the fact that Pentecostalism has a very concrete dimension. The point is to pay due attention to the ways in which Pentecostal imaginaries of the world not only exist in people's minds but also materialize through technological infrastructures, media, and modes of speaking and showing. They are embodied by persons and become tangible through things. An imaginary of the world generates a space for personal experience that vests this imaginary with reality and truth. Therefore the Pentecostal imaginary of the world, the spread of the message, and the rupture from "the past" are not merely conceptual but very material processes, involving bodies, things, and technologies. Something is experienced as actually happening. In order to grasp what I would like to call the "truth effects" of Pentecostalism, we need to move beyond the dualism of matter and spirit that has informed much of our thinking about modern religion. I propose that the notions of sensational form, media and mediation, and aesthetics and style are key to understanding the appeal of Pentecostalism as a global religion. Pentecostalism is characterized by constituting a mass movement binding individuals together via a strong emphasis on embodiment, spreads thanks to the adoption of new technologies, and espouses distinct, recognizable styles.

Sensational Form

In order to capture the materiality of Pentecostal performance—and for that matter the materiality of contemporary religion—I have recently coined the notion of sensational form.[32] In fact, my long-standing experience with Pentecostal performance in Ghana has pushed me to think about religion as evolving around sensational forms that address people by appealing to the senses and the body in distinct ways and by forming specific religious subjects. With many researchers I share the view that Pentecostal services and other events owe their appeal to the strong emphasis on inducing dramatic experiences of an encounter with the Holy Spirit and a spiritual war against the satanic (manifesting as old gods, witchcraft, and other spirits).[33] Even for a superficial observer it is impossible to overlook the constant appeal made to believers to participate with the whole body. Being called to stand up or sit, to lift one hand or two, to put forward the right or left foot, to pray (in tongues), to dance, to sing, to shake hands with neighbors and to hold their hands, and at times to read, to listen, and to be quiet indicates the high degree of bodily involvement, which generates—at times overwhelming—religious experiences.

It needs to be noted here that my understanding of religious experience differs from theories that place the genesis of religious experience in private feelings. Contrary to the view of William James, who has had a tremendous impact in the study of religious experience,[34] I do not take as a departure point the primacy of individual sensations because this would neglect the importance of religious forms in generating religious experience as well as the role of authorized structures of repetition in shaping and affirming specific religious subjectivities. The point is to understand the genesis of religious experiences and subjectivities as a process in which the personal and the social are inextricably bound up with each other.

The notion of sensational form seeks to capture the process through which the transcendental or divine is rendered approachable and sense-able by means of a shared mode of participation. Sensational forms, in my understanding, are relatively fixed, authorized modes of invoking and organizing access to the transcendental, thereby creating and sustaining links between religious practitioners in the context of particular religious organizations. These forms are transmitted and shared, they involve religious practitioners in particular practices of worship, and play a central role in inducing religious experience and forming religious subjects. In short, they are central to religious communication, both with God and among believers, and thus to the making of religious communities.

Media and Mediation

Many researchers have been struck by Pentecostalism's skillful and efficient appropriation of modern mass media, such as radio, television, film, and audiocassettes. Media are indispensable for Pentecostalism's spread as a mass movement and thus vehicles for transmitting divine presence. Traveling crusades, the circulation of books, tapes, and DVDs and the beaming of televangelist radio and television programs have been central to capturing broad audiences. Likewise, there are a host of Pentecostal posters, banners, sign boards, stickers, and sounds that index the presence and power of Pentecostal churches, creating a heavily Pentecostal environment, especially in urban space but also spreading into the countryside.[35]

This is a thriving new field of inquiry. Media not only make possible the spread of a church beyond the confines of a congregation but also feature as signs of technological mastery and up-to-dateness. The point here is that the eager adoption of new media by Pentecostal churches (often in marked contrast to mainline churches) has pushed scholars to realize that these are not necessarily foreign to religion but may be authorized as intrinsic to it. What occurs is a salient fusion of new media technologies and the transcendental that these technologies are made to mediate via particular sensational forms. In the process, media are often naturalized and taken for granted, or hailed as especially suitable technologies to convey a sense of divine presence.

The use of screens for the display of Power Point slides, but also an enlargement of the image of the pastor or others onstage, has become a constitutive element of a service. At the same time, visitors are very much aware that the cameras not only record the images that are beamed onto the many screens in the building but also cover the service as a whole, so as to broadcast an edited version of it on television and radio. In this sense these media are central to the logic of spread. Media are far more than just instruments; they are substantial ingredients through which the service is produced as a "thick" sensational form that aims at involving participants with bodies and minds. The extent to which media contribute to the making of collective religious experience can be evoked in a small example from my own research. When I attended a prayer service—Jericho Hour—organized by Action Faith Chapel in Accra in January 2008 and the electricity broke down, the importance of microphones became obvious. Everything came to a standstill, and prayers could continue only when the generator was switched on—indicating the importance of the "generator" not only in generating electricity but religious experience as well. Loudness—to such an extent that participants' bodies vibrate from the excess of sound—and also pastors' use of microphones in rhythmic sayings induce a certain trancelike atmosphere that conveys a sense of an extraordinary encounter with a divine force that is experienced to be present and that can be reached by opening up and stretching one's arms.

This is not to claim that media are simply used to make up—or even "fake"—the presence of the Holy Spirit but to indicate the inextricable entanglement of media in religious communication. Similarly, media such as the microphone, radio, television, and books, are being sanctified as suitable harbingers of divine power, without which it could not be transmitted and present. Divine power must be expressed—and from a more distant perspective, we could say is invoked—via sensational forms that make use of certain media that have been authenticated as suitable. This again points toward Pentecostals' world-embracing attitude: new technologies are taken up and incorporated in such a way that they become vehicles of the Holy Spirit, as well as the project of outreach. Therefore I agree with the argument made by the Dutch philosopher Hent de Vries,[36] who posits that no ontological difference exists between religion and technology, as any link with the transcendental depends on some kind of mediation and hence the use of media. What we find, in other words, is a synthesis of media technologies and the transcendental that they claim to mediate.

Aesthetics and Style

In recent years, the notion "aesthetics" has started to appear in research on religion, including Pentecostalism. Aesthetics, however, is a complicated notion that is being used in a variety of ways. Our commonsense understanding of aesthetics, echoing Kant, refers to the "disinterested beauty" of a work of art and privileges the mind above the body, high art above low art, and art above religion.[37] Aesthetics then becomes a question of "good taste" and can easily be mobilized in charging others with "bad taste." As Bernice Martin has also argued in her critique of David Lehman's dismissal of Brazilian Pentecostals as lacking style, such a use of aesthetics is problematic.[38] Currently there is a trend toward a broader understanding of the term. Recognizing the need to account for the affective power that images, sounds, texts, and other cultural forms wield over their beholders, scholars seek to develop more integrated understandings of sensing and knowing. Obviously, this inquiry no longer locates aesthetics in the domain of the high arts alone (as opposed to popular arts and religion) but rather in everyday life. This implies moving toward a recognition of the more encompassing Aristotelian notion of *aisthesis:* our corporeal capability on the basis of a power given in our "psyche" to perceive objects in the world via our five different sensorial modes, thus in a kind of analytical way, and at the same time as a specific constellation of sensations as a whole. *Aisthesis* then refers to our total sensorial experience of the world and to our sensitive knowledge of it.[39]

Such a broad understanding of aesthetics, which obviously can be conjoined with phenomenological approaches following Merleau-Ponty, is of great use for identifying the sensory modes through which Pentecostal sensational forms address, appeal to, and tune and form believers. On one level, attention needs to be paid to the ways in which God, the Holy Spirit, but also the devil are rendered present and tangible in personal experience. What is striking here is the strong Pentecostal emphasis on the sense of touch. Believers are made to be touched by God—by the performance of the preacher, the words s/he utters, the gestures, the images used, and above all the music—and this is found to have a strong physical and material effect. Indeed, the sense of touch stands central in Pentecostal worship and identity. Intriguingly, touch is not limited to God but also employed by Satan. A telling example here is a sticker I noticed on the dashboard of a taxi in Accra: "I am an untouchable Christian." Being touched by God implies being inhabited by the Holy Spirit, and this, as the driver explained when I asked him about the sticker, renders people *untouchable* to demonic forces. In order to deploy how a sense of being touched by, as well as untouchable for, spirit forces occurs, it is of great importance to pay close attention to the particularities of Pentecostal performance: to the attribution of power to words and utterances (rather than just seeking to understand their meaning), the importance of music and sound, the role of things that affect people in a divine manner (olive oil, holy water, stones as modes of transporting Holy Spirit power) or tie them to the devil (e.g., via material objects that are dismissed as idols).

Style is a core aspect of aesthetics. An emphasis on style liberates us researchers from a focus on the level of concepts (and meaning)—for a long time one of the prime concerns of the anthropology of religion—and opens up a broader field of inquiry that alerts us to the importance of appearance and modes of doing things without assigning them to "mere" outward and hence secondary matters.[40] Recently in the study of Pentecostalism there has been more attention paid to style, especially with regard to music, as one of the central features through which Pentecostalism travels.[41] Attention to style allows researchers to take seriously the actual appearance of religion—in the built environment, in mass-mediated audio-visual images, and in the bodies of religious practitioners—without reducing appearance to a mere outward expression. Taking into account the actual emphasis placed on appearance by religious people is a suitable point of entry into an approach to religion from a material, sensory angle.

Significantly, it is commonly acknowledged that appearance is a prime concern for those participating in Pentecostal churches. A person's appearance—the type of clothes, the car, the house—is seen as an indication of an interior spiritual state. As, in consonance with the prosperity gospel, wealth is regarded as a sign of blessing from the Lord, there is much emphasis on what might be viewed as "mere outward things" from a more orthodox Christian perspective. Of course, not all people attracted to these churches are healthy and rich, but the guiding idea is that participation may work in favor of this aim, by calling the Holy Spirit into the materiality of being. Many people attending these churches, or watching the television programs, live under difficult conditions, replete with experiences of poverty and misery. I still remember vividly how, in the first service I attended in the ICGC in 1992, Otabil asked all participants to shake hands with each other and say, "You are beautiful!" I was intrigued by this message, because it places so much emphasis on appearance. Many of the young people attracted to this kind of church told me that they could not attend church in the same dress every Sunday. Mutual dress exchange systems came into being so as to avoid embarrassment and shame. Other people backed out because they found that it was too expensive to model themselves in line with the ideal Christian appearance. Such, at first thought perhaps marginal things indicate the tremendous relevance of a shared style in this kind of megachurch. Participation works very much by sharing certain patterns of consumption and ways of doing and sensing things together, even if by sheer mimicry. In this way people feel like somebody, although they may find it very difficult to bring their lives fully in line with the blessed state of the ideal born-again believer.

CONCLUSION

My concern in this chapter has been to examine the "fit" between Pentecostalism and globalization by (1) arguing that as scholars we are well advised to study contemporary Pentecostalism from a standpoint that transcends a typically modernist perspective on Protestantism (as derived from Weber's *Protestant Ethic*); (2) exploring—in the tradition of a Weberian methodology—key terms of Pentecostal discourse that are central to its global identity and appeal; and (3) presenting some new notions and concepts so as to further our understanding of the appeal of contemporary Pentecostalism. Throughout this chapter I have opted to take into account the materiality and tangibility of Pentecostalism's spread, its impact on the body and the senses, and the ways in which it generates distinct styles that make Pentecostal identity become apparent. The concern to take into account Pentecostalism's materiality and tangibility is driven by my dissatisfaction with an apparent mismatch between theories of contemporary religion that reiterate, explicitly or implicitly, a basic distinction between spirit and matter (understanding religion as beyond the latter), on the one hand, and the reality of global Pentecostalism that appears to undermine the very possibility to maintain such a distinction, on the other. The phenomenon of global Pentecostalism calls for creative conceptual work and an extended vocabulary. It has been the purpose of this chapter to contribute to this endeavor.

NOTES

I would like to thank André Droogers, Stephen Hunt, and Jojada Verrips for their helpful comments on earlier versions of this chapter and Erik van Ommering for his practical assistance.

1. It also marks a departure from critical word system theories that would explain the relation between center and periphery in terms of sustained dependency and "underdevelopment" or denial of development. Significantly, the notion of globalization gained momentum in the 1990s, in the aftermath of the cold war and the breakdown of socialism as an alternative to capitalism.

2. Arjun Appadurai, *Modernity at Large: Cultural Dimensions of Globalization* (Minneapolis: University of Minnesota Press, 1996), 27–47.

3. See André Corten and Ruth Marshall-Fratani, eds., *Between Babel and Pentecost: Transnational Pentecostalism in Latin America and Africa* (Bloomington: IUP, 2001); Murray W. Dempster, Byron D. Klaus, and Douglas Peterson, *The Globalization of Pentecostalism: A Religion Made to Travel* (Oxford: Regnum, 1999); Stephen Hunt, "'Winning Ways': Globalisation and the Impact of the Health and Wealth Gospel," *Journal of Contemporary Religion* 15 (2000): 331–47; David Martin, *Pentecostalism: The World Their Parish* (Oxford: Blackwell, 2002); Sturla J. Stålsett, ed., *Spirits of Globalization: The Growth of Pentecostalism and Experiential Spiritualities in a Global Age* (London: SCM, 2006). In addition to studies of Pentecostalism as a global religion, there is an intriguing body of work on the notion of global Christianity. For a critical discussion, see Robert Wuthnow, *Boundless Faith: The Global Outreach of American Churches* (Berkeley: UCP, 2009).

4. André Droogers, "Globalisation and Pentecostal Success," in Corten and Marshall-Fratani, *Between Babel and Pentecost,* 41–61; Joel Robbins, "The Globalization of Pentecostal and Charismatic Christianity," *Annual Review of Anthropology* 33 (2004): 117–43.

5. Max Weber, *The Protestant Ethic and the Spirit of Capitalism,* trans. and ed. Talcott Parsons (New York: Scribners, 1920). One of the most prominent scholars mobilizing the Weber thesis is Peter Berger; see Peter Berger, "Max Weber Is Alive and Well, and Living in Guatemala: The Protestant Ethic Today" (paper presented at the 100th anniversary conference celebrating Max Weber's *The Protestant Ethic and the Spirit of Capitalism,* Cornell University, New York, October 2004), available at www.economyandsociety.org/events/Berger_paper.pdf; accessed 30 April 2008. See also Centre for Development and Enterprise 2008, *Under the Radar: Pentecostalism in South Africa and Its Potential Social and Economic Role* (Johannesburg: CDE, 2008), 25.

6. Droogers, "Globalisation and Pentecostal Success," 50.

7. Peter Beyer, *Religions in Global Society* (London: Routledge, 2006).

8. Birgit Meyer, "Witchcraft and Christianity," in *New Encyclopedia of Africa,* ed. John Middleton and Joseph C. Miller (Detroit: Scribners, 2008), 226–30.

9. David Martin, *Tongues of Fire: The Explosion of Protestantism in Latin America* (Oxford: Blackwell, 1990); Donald Miller and Tetsunao Yamamori, *Global Pentecostalism: The New Face of Christian Social Engagement* (Berkeley: UCP, 2007).

10. As the only exception to the rule, he mentions Mensa Otabil (see below). Paul Gifford, *Ghana's New Christianity: Pentecostalism in a Globalising African Economy* (London: Hurst, 2004).

11. Rafael Sanchez, "Seized by the Spirit: The Mystical Foundation of Squatting Among Pentecostals in Caracas (Venezuela) Today," *Public Culture* 20 (2008): 267–305; Danial Jordan Smith, *A Culture of Corruption: Everyday Deception and Popular Discontent in Nigeria* (Princeton: Princeton University Press, 2007), 218–19.

12. Colin Campbell, *The Romantic Ethic and the Spirit of Modern Consumerism* (Oxford: Blackwell, 1987). See also Jean Comaroff and John Comaroff, eds., *Millenial Capitalism and the Culture of Neoliberalism,* Special Issue, *Public Culture* 12:2 (2000); Birgit Meyer, "Pentecostalism and Neo-liberal Capitalism: Faith, Prosperity and Vision in African Pentecostal-Charismatic Churches," *Journal for the Study of Religion* 20:2 (2007): 5–28.

13. Simon Coleman, ed., *The Faith Movement: A Global Religious Culture,* Special Issue of *Culture and Religion* 3:2 (2002); David Maxwell, "'Delivered from the Spirit of Poverty?' Pentecostalism, Prosperity and Modernity in Zimbabwe," *JRA* 28 (1998): 350–73.

14. A. Corten and V. Molina, "Transnationalisation et pentecôtisme: La Force Instituante du Sens," *Anthropologica* 49 :11 (2007): 67–79.

15. Appadurai, *Modernity at Large,* 6–7.

16. Benedict Anderson, *Imagined Communities: Reflections on the Origins and Spread of Nationalism,* rev. ed. (London: Verso, 1991); Charles Taylor, *Modern Social Imaginaries* (Durham: Duke University Press, 2004).

17. On "space," see Richard Eves, "Waiting for the Day: Globalisation and Apocalypticism in Central New Ireland, Papua New Guinea," *Oceania* 71:2 (2000): 73–91.

18. Harry Englund, "Cosmopolitanism and the Devil in Malawi," *Ethnos* 69 (2004): 293–316; Harry Englund, "Witchcraft and the Limits of Mass Mediation in Malawi," *Journal of the Royal Anthropological Institute,* n.s., 13 (2007): 295–311; Yannick Fer, "Pentecôtisme et Modernité Urbaine: Entre Déterritorialisation des Identités et Réinvestissement Symbolique de l'Espace Urbain," *Social Compass* 54 (2007): 201–10; Birgit Meyer, *Translating the Devil: Religion and Modernity among the Ewe in Ghana* (Edinburgh: Edinburgh University Press, 1999).

19. Allan Anderson, "Spreading Fires: The Globalization of Pentecostalism in the Twentieth Century," *IBMR* 31:1 (2007): 8–14.

20. Päivi Hasu, "World Bank and Heavenly Bank in Poverty and Prosperity: The Case of Tanzanian Faith Gospel," *Review of African Political Economy* 33 (2006): 679–92; Birgit Meyer, "Commodities and the Power of Prayer: Pentecostalist Attitudes towards Consumption in Contemporary Ghana," in

Globalization and Identity: Dialectics of Flow and Closure, ed. Birgit Meyer and Peter Geschiere, Special Issue of *Development and Change* 29 (1998): 751–77; Rijk van Dijk, "The Pentecostal Gift: Ghanaian Charismatic Churches and the Moral Innocence of the Global Economy," in *Modernity on a Shoestring: Dimensions of Globalization, Consumption and Development in Africa and Beyond,* ed. Richard Fardon, Wim van Binsbergen, and Rijk van Dijk (Leiden: EIDOS, 1999), 71–90.

21. Isabelle Barker, "Engendering Charismatic Economies: Pentecostalism, Global Political Economy, and the Crisis of Social Reproduction" (paper presented at the Annual Meeting of the American Political Science Association, Washington, D.C., 2005).

22. Martijn Osterbaan, "Divine Mediations: Pentecostalism, Politics and Mass Media in a Favela in Rio de Janeiro" (Ph.D. diss., University of Amsterdam, 2006); Roger Sansi Roca, "Dinheiro Vivo: Money and Religion in Brazil," *Critique of Antropology* 27 (2007): 319–39.

23. For more information on this church, see Paul Gifford, "Ghana's New Christianity"; Marleen de Witte, "Spirit Media: Charismatics, Traditionalists, and Mediation Practices in Ghana" (Ph.D. diss., University of Amsterdam, 2008).

24. See Paul Freston, "The Universal Church of the Kingdom of God: A Brazilian Church Finds Success in Southern Africa." *JRA* 35 (2005): 33–65. In the Department of Social and Cultural Anthropology (VU University, Amsterdam), Linda van de Kamp and Regien Smit conduct research on transnational Pentecostalism in Mozambique and Angola; at the London School of Economics, Ilana van Wijk studies the popularity of the Brazilian Igreja Universal in Durban, South Africa..

25. J. Kwabena Asamoah-Gyadu, "An African Pentecostal on Mission in Eastern Europe: The Church of the 'Embassy of God' in the Ukraine," *Pneuma* 27 (2005): 297–321.

26. Afe Adogame and Cordula Weissköppel, eds., *Religion in the Context of African Migration* (Bayreuth: Breitinger, 2005); Marion Aubrée, "The Religious in Movement: The Spread of a Neo-Pentecostal Brazilian Church among Immigrant Populations in Western Europe," *Anthropologie et Sociétés* 27 (2003): 65–84; Hunt, " 'Winning Ways,' " 331–47; Rijk van Dijk, "The Soul Is the Stranger: Ghanaian Pentecostalism and the Diasporic Contestation of 'Flow' and 'Individuality,' " *Culture and Religion* 3 (2002): 49–67. See also Gertrud Hüwelmeier and Kristine Krause, *Travelling Spirits: Migrants, Markets and Mobilities* (London: Routledge, 2009).

27. Robbins, "The Globalization of Pentecostalism," 127–31; Dan Jorgensen, "Third Wave Evangelism and the Politics of the Global in Papua New Guinea: Spiritual Warfare and the Recreation of Place in Telefolmin," *Oceania* 75 (2005):444–61.

28. Birgit Meyer, " 'Make a Complete Break with the Past': Memory and Post-colonial Modernity in Ghanaian Pentecostalist Discourse," *JRA* 27 (1998): 316–49.

29. James Pfeiffer, Kenneth Gimbel-Sherr, and Orvalho Joaquim Augusto, "The Holy Spirit in the Household: Pentecostalism, Gender, and Neoliberalism in Mozambique," *American Anthropologist* 109 (2007): 688–700.

30. Martin, *Pentecostalism,* 24; Thomas J. Csordas, "Introduction: Modalities of Transnational Transcendence," in *Transnational Transcendence: Essays on Religion and Globalization,* ed. Thomas J. Csordas (Berkeley: UCP, 2009), 4 ff.

31. Joel Robbins, "Continuity Thinking and the Problem of Christian Culture," *Current Anthropology* 48 (2007): 5–38.

32. Birgit Meyer, "Religious Sensations: Why Media, Aesthetics and Power Matter in the Study of Contemporary Religion" (Inaugural Lecture, VU University, Amsterdam, 6 October 2006).

33. E.g., Thomas J. Csordas, "Asymptote of the Ineffable: Embodiment, Alterity, and the Theory of Religion," *Current Anthropology* 45 (2004): 163–84.

34. William James, *The Varieties of Religious Experience* (Harmondsworth: Penguin, [1902] 1998).

35. Important examples are the work of Katharine Wiegele on radio and her book on the Catholic-Charismatic El Shaddai movement in the Philippines (*Investing in Miracles: El Shaddai and the Trans-*

formation of Popular Catholicism in the Philippines [Honolulu: University of Hawaii Press, 2005]), the works by Patricia Birman and David Lehman ("Religion and the Media in a Battle for Ideological Hegemony: The Universal Church of the Kingdom of God and the TV Globo in Brazil," *Bulletin of Latin American Research* 18 [1999]: 145–64); Martijn Oosterbaan (see n. 24) and Erik Kramer ("Making Global Faith Universal: Media and a Brazilian Prosperity Movement," *Culture and Religion* 3 [2002]: 21–47); the work by Rosalind Hackett ("Charismatic/Pentecostal Appropriation of Media Technologies in Nigeria and Ghana," *JRA* 28 [1998]: 1–19); and J. Kwabena Asamoah-Gyadu's work on Nigerian and Ghanaian Pentecostal-Charismatics ("Pentecostal Media Images and Religious Globalization in Sub-Saharan Africa," in *Belief in Media: Cultural Perspectives on Media and Christianity,* ed. Peter Horsfield, Mary E. Hess, and Adán M. Medrano [Aldershot: Ashgate, 2004], 65–80); or the detailed analysis by Marleen de Witte ("Altar Media's *Living Word*: Televised Christianity in Ghana," *JRA* 33 [1993]: 172–202) of how the church-owned media studio produces televised performances of Mensa Otabil.

36. Hent de Vries, "In Media Res: Global Religion, Public Spheres, and the Task of Contemporary Religious Studies," in *Religion and Media,* ed. Hent de Vries and Samuel Weber (Stanford: Stanford University Press, 2001), 4–42.

37. Birgit Meyer and Jojada Verrips, "Aesthetics," in *Key Words in Religion, Media and Culture,* ed. David Morgan (London: Routledge, 2008). See also Birgit Meyer, ed., *Aesthetic Formations: Media, Religion and the Senses* (New York: Palgrave, 2009).

38. Bernice Martin, "The Aesthetics of Latin American Pentecostalism: The Sociology of Religion and the Problem of Taste," in *Materializing Religion: Expression, Performance and Ritual,* ed. Elizabeth Arweck and William Keenan (Aldershot: Ashgate, 2007), 138–60. Martin offers a highly intriguing discussion of Weber's genealogy of aesthetics and the role of Protestantism and disenchantment in separating aesthetics from religion, which still belonged together in medieval times. While there certainly is some ground to say that this separation occurred, we still need to realize the basic inadequacy of this separation and the highly reduced understanding of aesthetics on which it depends (see below). In my understanding, as scholars we are well advised to rediscover the nexus of aesthetics and religion, in particular, Pentecostalism, in our time.

39. Jojada Verrips, "Aisthesis and An-aesthesia," *Ethnologia Europea* 35 (2006): 27–33.

40. Birgit Meyer, "'Praise the Lord': Popular Cinema and Pentecostalite Style in Ghana's New Public Sphere," *American Ethnologist* 31 (2004): 92–110.

41. Timothy Rommen, *'Mek Some Noise': Gospel Music and the Ethics of Style in Trinidad* (Berkeley: UCP, 2007).

Social Sciences and Humanities

7

Psychology of Religion

Stefan Huber and Odilo W. Huber

The psychology of religion investigates religious beliefs, experiences, and behavior in relation to psychological concepts and theories. It analyzes the psychological representation and functioning of religious content in the individual. This perspective is useful for revealing and describing aspects of religion that may not be captured otherwise, but obviously it is only one of a universe of perspectives that may be taken with respect to religion, each contributing in a different way to the investigation of the field—but, concurrently, each perspective submitted to specific restrictions.

As an academic discipline, psychology is characterized by heterogeneity of approaches and fields of research that have been developed in the context of different theoretical frameworks, each based on a set of distinct assumptions on the nature of "psyche" and the function and goals of psychology. Examples are psychodynamic, behavioristic, humanistic, or, beginning in the second half of the twentieth century a variety of cognitive and, recently, evolutionary approaches. These approaches have been used to provide models for a broad range of fields of research, for example, biological bases of experiences and behavior, motivation, cognition, and perception.

In the present chapter we give an overview of psychological research on the religious beliefs, experiences, and behavior of Pentecostals. The approaches in this research on Pentecostals reflect the heterogeneity of the general field of the psychology of religion. Given space constraints, we cannot analyze all aspects of these heterogeneous approaches but base our analysis on the distinction between two psychological perspectives on religiosity that implicitly underlie a variety of the approaches mentioned above. Our attempt serves to structure the field by revealing basic research questions characterizing these perspectives. In this way we want to provide access to the central results and approaches and enable the development of new research questions.

In the first perspective, the religiosity of Pentecostals is conceptualized only in terms of general psychological structures and processes. It is regarded primarily as an epiphenomenon of these structures. This perspective leads to questions about exogenous psychological causes and consequences of religious beliefs, experiences, and behaviors of Pentecostals. Endogenous structures and dynamics of these beliefs are not considered. Pentecostalism is seen as a black box pushed and pulled by external psychological causes and consequences. This type of research is very common in the psychology of religion. Examples are investigations concerning the correlations of Pentecostalism with general psychological constructs such as suggestibility, regression, and neuroticism on the one hand and emotional stability, adjustment, and satisfaction of life on the other.

In contrast, the second perspective both investigates and respects endogenous structures and dynamics of Pentecostal religiosity. This type of research considers personal religion as a topic of its own. It asks for psychological structures and dynamics of personal religious systems that are derived from the content of this system itself. The most influential model of endogenous religious structures was introduced by Charles Glock.[1] He differentiates between five core dimensions of religiosity: religious intellectuality, religious ideology, private religious practice, religious experience, and public religious practice. Based on these dimensions, we try to open the "black box" of Pentecostal religiosity in the second part of this chapter. The basic assumption of this research strategy is that the psychology of Pentecostal religiosity depends primarily on endogenous structures and dynamics of contents of this religiosity itself.

Methodologically, the basis of our review is relevant psychological literature concerning the religiosity of Pentecostals. We identified relevant literature in two ways: first, we considered former reviews on the topic; and second, we conducted literature research in order to identify recent relevant psychological literature that has not been considered by the former reviews,[2] because it is more recent or is beyond the limited scope of the former reviews, which concernedmainly glossolalia.[3] Our own literature research was conducted in the database PsychLit, which covers all major psychological journals and other publications. We searched for peer-reviewed journal articles with the keyword "Pentecostal" in the period from 1987 up to 2006. This research yielded sixty-two articles.

EXOGENOUS CAUSES AND CONSEQUENCES

In 1976 Kilian McDonnell reviewed extensively psychological research on Pentecostalism in the period 1919–75.[4] In 1988 Steven A. Gritzmacher and colleagues published a review of the literature on the psychological characteristics of Pentecostals and extended previous literature reviews on Pentecostalism by including studies from the period 1976–85.[5] Recently William Kay reviewed psychological research concerning glossolalia from its beginnings in 1910 up to 2006.[6] All three reviews focus on the general psychological causes and consequences of Pentecostal religiosity. In this section we mainly follow these authors in summarizing the research from the standpoint of the first perspective. McDonnell, Gritzmacher and colleagues, and Kay agree in distinguishing clearly between two periods in psychological research of Pentecostalism, a primarily "hostile" period from the beginning in 1910 up to the 1960s, followed by a more "friendly" period beginning in the 1960s and continuing to the present.

In the primarily "hostile" period, research was based on the underlying hypothesis that Pentecostalism is an expression or direct consequence of abnormal psychological processes and mental disorders. Consequently, research employed mainly a psychopathological framework using concepts such as schizophrenia, hysteria, regression, emotional instability, immaturity, neuroticism, or dogmatism. McDonnell emphasizes that most of the respondents were members of the lower social classes and that most of the research was methodologically insufficient, for instance, practicing observation without a controlled methodology. However, all three reviews agree on the conclusion that most of the elicited data did not foster the general underlying hypothesis that the experiences and behaviors of Pentecostals are caused by or correlated with psychopathology. The persistence of the hostile perspective over more than four decades, despite the fact that data did not clearly support the hypotheses, emphasizes that a specifically chosen set of presuppositions for scientific research with respect to controversial issues can be placed in ideological frameworks.

In the more recent, "friendly" period, research has focused more on normal personality characteristics and concepts indicating psychological stability. McDonnell emphasizes that the respondents were mainly middle- and upper-class Pentecostals. Methodologically, the research in this period is much more sophisticated. Kay stresses that recent research is theologically better informed and more interdisciplinary. The data support the general hypothesis that the experiences and behaviors of Pentecostals are adaptive. Its results overturned most of the findings of the first period.

In sum, psychological research has progressed from viewing Pentecostalism from a perspective of abnormal psychology using concepts of psychopathology and social deprivation to a perspective of normal psychology investigating non-pathological, normal personality characteristics associated with Pentecostalism. This change of perspective reveals that scientific psychology is not as objective and unbiased as sometimes supposed. On the contrary, it depends strongly on value judgments of individual psychologists as well as of the scientific community, determining the selection of specific topics, the specific groups studied, the theoretical concepts, and the methodology applied. Obviously, the scientific community has changed its value judgment concerning Pentecostalism. Because the scientific system is dependent on other social systems, this change may reflect the change in value judgments of the society as a whole.

In the following, in order to make the logic and approaches salient, we first present one illustrative and typical example of each period in detail. Then we list research linked to key psychological concepts that were used for the explanation of Pentecostal religiosity.

Probably the most influential book in the "hostile" period was George Barton Cutten's *Speaking with Tongues: Historically and Psychologically Considered,* published in 1927.[7] Cutten (1874–1962) was president of Colgate University in New York from 1922 to 1942, and he was a Baptist minister with a dispensationalist theology. But he was not only a theologian; he was a psychologist too, publishing many popular books concerning the psychology of religion and Christianity, as well as the psychology of moral questions.

Cutten characterized speaking in tongues as a "childish reaction," emphasizing the lack of education of most of the Pentecostals of his time: "Those who speak with tongues are almost without exception devout, but ignorant and illiterate people."[8] He suggests that their verbal capacity and their ability to reason were limited. Psychologically, Cutten referred to a psychodynamic framework. In his frame of reference glossolalia consists of subconscious emotional elements arising when somebody speaks in tongues. Cutten interpreted this process as a psychopathological form of regression, as subconscious impulses becoming predominant in the subjects who speak in tongues. The predominance of the subconscious is seen as similar to mental disorders such as schizophrenia or psychosis. In this line of interpretation, glossolalia can be characterized as "a state of personal disintegration."[9] Furthermore, from a psychodynamic perspective, the content of speaking in tongues may be explained by previous encounters with foreign languages stored in the subconscious.

It is noteworthy that the use of a psychodynamic frame of reference is not necessarily linked with a psychopathological interpretation of glossolalia. Cutten interpreted glossolalia as a psychopathological form of regression. In contrast, other more recent psychoanalysts interpret glossolalia as a healthy regression in the service of the ego, or a healthy emotional coping mechanism.[10]

A typical example of the "friendly" period is the 1995 study, *The Personality Characteristics of Pentecostal Ministry Candidates,* by Leslie Francis and William Kay.[11] Both authors are theologians and psychologists and well-known researchers in the field of the psychology of religion in general, Pentecostalism in particular. Francis has published a wealth of articles about the relationship between personality and religion, using especially the Francis Scale of Attitude toward

Christianity, one of the most common religiosity scales. In their study Francis and Kay investigated the personality characteristics of 259 male and 105 female Pentecostal ministry candidates using the theoretical framework of Hans-Jürgen Eysenck's model of personality, differentiating between three basic dimensions of personality. The dimension of extraversion (vs. introversion) reflects one's sociability. The dimension of neuroticism reflects one's emotional stability (and vulnerability to neurotic personality disorders). The dimension of psychoticism reflects one's impulsivity (and vulnerability to psychoses such as schizophrenia). According to Eysenck's theory, all types of personalities can be deduced from the interplay of these dimensions. For instance, the so-called melancholic type is emotionally unstable, that is, high in neuroticism, and not very sociable, that is, low in extraversion. Eysenck's model may be applied to describe all four personality types first proposed by the Greek physician Hippocrates. Defined in the terminology of the dimensions of neuroticism (N) and extraversion (E), the choleric type is high N and high E, the melancholic type is high N and low E, the sanguine type is low N and high E, and the phlegmatic type is low N and low E.

Methodologically, Francis and Kay's study is based on the Eysenck Personality Questionnaire (EPQ) in comparing ministry candidates with population norms. Concerning extraversion, the ministry candidates did not differ from population norms. The largest difference occurred with respect to neuroticism. Pentecostal ministry candidates scored much lower than the population norms for the neuroticism scale. This indicates that they were emotionally much more stable than the general population. This result contradicts strongly psychodynamic speculations concerning psychopathological causes and consequences of Pentecostal religiosity in general and glossolalia in particular. It is noteworthy that in female ministry candidates the difference from the population norms is larger than in male ministry candidates. With respect to psychoticism only the male ministry candidates differ from population norms. They scored significantly lower than the general population, indicating that male Pentecostal ministry candidates can better control their impulses and are less vulnerable to psychoses. This finding contradicts speculations on inner psychodynamic links between glossolalia and psychotic phenomena such as schizophrenia.

Because a large proportion of the psychological research on the religiosity of Pentecostals focuses on glossolalia, some reviews are exclusively concerned with research on glossolalia.[12] This may be due to the fact that glossolalia is the most distinctive and for some authors even strange and deviant—and concurrently overtly and easily observable—feature of Pentecostal religiosity. In the scientific community this characteristic seems to have dominated the research on Pentecostal religiosity, and Pentecostal religiosity has been equated with and reduced to the single phenomenon of glossolalia. This concentration on a single aspect of religiosity severely restricts the perspective taken and subsequently limits possible research questions and research results.

As was the case with research on other aspects of Pentecostalism, the psychological research on glossolalia can be classified according to two periods, a friendly one and a hostile one.[13] In the hostile period glossolalia was primarily analyzed with respect to abnormal personality characteristics and social deprivation. Cutten's study may serve as an example.[14] In contrast, in the friendly period research focuses on correlates of glossolalia associated with a psychologically healthy personality. Two general psychological explanations for glossolalia dominated scientific discourse—the trance hypothesis and the learning hypothesis.

The trance hypothesis suggests thatthe phenomenon of glossolalia originates in an extraordinary state of consciousness.[15] Following Goodman, glossolalia is based on two mechanisms. Neurologically, Goodman suggests subcortical overstimulation caused by "driving." Examples of driving techniques are rhythmic clapping, ecstatic singing and praying, and twitching movements. She proposes that when subcortical structures are overstimulated by means of driving a state of trance occurs, characterized by the control of these subcortical structures over normally consciously controlled cortical functions, specifically in the speech area. Glossolalia is thus conceptualized as a pseudolinguistic manifestation of the rhythmic discharge of subcortical neural structures. Complementary to these basic neurophysiological processes, Goodman proposes a cultural factor: social expectations. In this model these expectations mediate the effect of driving on glossolalia.

The learning hypothesis, in contrast, interprets glossolalia mainly as socially learned behavior. In this view glossolalia is a personal competence that may be activated at any time by the subject once it has been acquired through a learning process. This hypothesis has been empirically tested by Spanos in two experiments. Spanos and Hewitt demonstrated that glossolalia is not exclusively dependent on extraordinary states of consciousness (such as trance) but also may be performed in states of normal consciousness or alertness. Spanos and colleagues showed that glossolalia may be acquired by training.[16] Some authors, however, argue that the learning hypothesis does not account completely for the whole phenomenon of glossolalia. They suggest that glossolalia is initially socially learned behavior that may in part involve trance states.[17]

A new methodological approach in the investigation of glossolalia employs neuroimaging techniques. Neuroimaging studies compare brain activity in a control condition with that of the target condition, with the goal of identifying specific differential changes in cerebral activity in the target state. Andrew Newberg conducted the first functional neuroimaging study on glossolalia and chose as a control condition spiritual singing.[18] The subjects displayed distinctive patterns in neural activity connected with glossolalia. The study found an extreme decrease in activity in the frontal lobe, which is generally concerned with control of neural activity in other parts of the cortex. It is seen as the locus of the mental central executive and as the neural correlate of the control of the self. Decreased activity was also found in the caudate, an inhibitory structure that has a role in the control of facial-gestual expression and posture, for example, in the ability to stand still. In contrast, in the parietal lobes Newberg found increased neural activity. The parietal lobes are the cortical brain structures that process the sensory information originating in the body, for example, from the receptors on the skin or in the muscles and joints. It generates a sense of the self as part of the environment. Newberg also found increased activity in subcortical structures responsible for the generation of emotions. These findings are globally consistent with the trance hypothesis.

Interestingly, in contrast to studies on the state of glossolalia, Newberg found in earlier studies on the state of meditation enhanced activity in the frontal lobe.[19] This finding may allow the conclusion that meditation, exerting a calm and controlled feeling of the self, is a qualitatively different state of mind from glossolalia, which exerts a feeling of being controlled by some spirit. Newberg's study on glossolalia, however, may not falsify a role for learning in the acquisition of the behavior because the subjects had practiced glossolalia on a daily basis for at least five years, so that it was executed on a highly trained and automatic level. In effect, a possible mediating effect of learning as suggested by some authors could not be confirmed by the study. An investigation of this hypothesis employing novices in glossolalia would be desirable.

Below we list research linked to key concepts and correlates that were used for the psychological description and explanation of Pentecostal religiosity. We group the concepts according to their correlation with Pentecostal religiosity, that is, their impact or dependence on Pentecostal religiosity. Many of these concepts, however, are important in different psychological models. Schizophrenia, for instance, may be analyzed using a psychodynamic model or a personality model, like Eysenck's. We thus list the concepts in the respective groups in alphabetical order.

For the following concepts, empirical results show either that there is no correlation or that the results are ambiguous, indicating different directions of association.

- *Adjustment:* Pentecostals are neither clearly less well adjusted nor clearly better adjusted than the general population.[20]
- *Anxiety:* Pentecostals experience as much anxiety as the general population.[21]
- *Suggestibility:* Pentecostals are reported to be more suggestible in the presence of a spiritual leader;[22] however, the study seems to suffer from methodological problems.[23] Thus further research is needed to retest the hypothesis.

For the following concepts, most empirical results indicate a positive association with Pentecostal religiosity; that is, Pentecostals have higher values in the measures of the respective concepts than other groups.

- *Anxiety:* Pentecostals are more engaged in socially approved behavior.[24]
- *Dependency:* Pentecostals exhibit great dependency on spiritual leaders.[25]
- *Emotional release:* Pentecostals' emotionally and physically expressive religious activities such as glossolalia have led some observers to remark on similarities to hysteria.[26]
- *Emotional stability:* A positive relationship between emotional stability and charismatic experience is reported in several studies by Francis and colleagues.[27]
- *Extraversion:* Some recent studies found a positive relationship between extraversion and charismatic experience.[28]
- *Regression:* In psychodynamic frameworks, glossolalia is often interpreted as regression. It can be interpreted as a psychopathological form of regression with similarities to schizophrenia,[29] as well as a healthy form of regression.[30]
- *Self-control:* Pentecostals maintain high levels of self-control,[31] and they have an internal locus of control.[32]
- *Submissiveness:* This is a characteristic trait of Pentecostals.[33]

The following concepts are negatively associated with Pentecostal religiosity; that is, Pentecostals have lower values in the measures of the respective concepts.

- *Depression:* Pentecostals experience less depression than the general population.[34]
- *Hostility:* Pentecostals show fewer manifestations of hostility.[35]
- *Psychoticism:* A recent study found a negative relationship between psychoticism and charismatic experience.[36]
- *Self-esteem:* Pentecostals show lower self-esteem than the general population.[37] Gritzmacher and colleagues point out that low self-esteem can also be considered as humility or depreciative self-presentation.[38] Hence the psychology of self-esteem probably has to be reconsidered in the context of the religious culture of Pentecostalism.

ENDOGENOUS STRUCTURES AND DYNAMICS

Here, changing our perspective, we do not ask for exogenous psychological causes and consequences of Pentecostal religiosity but focus on their endogenous structures and dynamics in the psyche. In a future step, the differentiated elements of the endogenous structure of Pentecostal religiosity may be linked separately to exogenous psychological causes and consequences. The widening of the perspec-

	Religiosity	
Exogenous Causes	**Endogenous Model**	**Exogenous Consequences**
Adjustment *Anxiety* *Dependency* *Depression* *Emotional release* *Emotional stability* *Extraversion* *Hostility* *Psychoticism* *Regression* *Self-control* *Self-esteem* *Submissiveness* *Suggestibility*	**Intellect** **Ideology** **Public practice** **Experience** **Private practice**	*Adjustment* *Anxiety* *Dependency* *Depression* *Emotional release* *Emotional stability* *Extraversion* *Hostility* *Psychoticism* *Regression* *Self-control* *Self-esteem* *Submissiveness* *Suggestibility*

FIGURE 1. Model of religiosity: endogenous and exogenous components.

tive here allows us to depict a much more differentiated picture of Pentecostal religiosity, with higher explanatory power. This is illustrated in figure 1. It becomes obvious that the elements of the endogenous structures that we explain below are not differentiated by the first perspective, and thus neither their inner relations nor their relation to exogenous psychological causes and consequences may be identified.

The right and left columns of the diagram depict examples of exogenous psychological causes and consequences of Pentecostal religiosity. The list of concepts is not exhaustive. Henceforth these concepts are mostly related to Pentecostal religiosity as a whole because it was regarded as a "black box" by the majority of researchers. In the broad central part of the diagram the black box is opened. The multidimensional model of religiosity defined in the 1960s by Glock and Stark serves as our frame of reference for the discussion of endogenous religious structures.[39] Beginning in the 1990s this originally sociological model was transformed into an interdisciplinary model by Huber, who considered psychological as well as theological dimensions.[40] In 2007 the transformed interdisciplinary model served as the theoretical basis of an intercultural and interreligious survey by the Bertelsmann Foundation investigating representative samples in twenty-one nations on all continents (Australia, Austria, Brazil, France, Germany, Guatemala, India, Indonesia, Israel, Italy, Morocco, Nigeria, Poland, Russia, South Korea, Spain, Switzerland, Thailand, Turkey, the United Kingdom, the United States).[41]

A substantial share of the respondents of this global study are members of Pentecostal churches.

The endogenous model of Pentecostal religiosity distinguishes five core dimensions of religiosity: religious intellectuality, religious ideology, religious experience, private religious practice, and public religious practice. The explicit distinction between these dimensions is necessary because empirical research revealed that to a high degree they are independent of each other.[42] This means that in the individual, the personal relevance of each of the five dimensions may not be deduced from the personal relevance of one single dimension or any combination of the remaining four dimensions. Thus for a comprehensive picture of endogenous structures and the dynamics of personal religiosity, it is necessary to consider all five core dimensions.

Sociologically, the five core dimensions describe distinct social expectations with regard to religious people. In interaction with these social expectations, the individual develops specific psychic structures and dynamics with respect to the five dimensions. The more a person is involved in such interactions, the higher and richer the distinctive endogenous psychic structures of his or her personal religiosity will emerge in the psychological modes of perception, cognition, and action. This process of the transformation of social expectations and interactions into psychic structures allows us to discuss psychological studies about Pentecostal religiosity in relation to the five core dimensions.

This discussion is based on relevant psychological literature of the past twenty years as identified by our literature search. We analyze what we already know about endogenous structures in the psychic representation of the five dimensions and the dynamics of their interplay by Pentecostals. Each core dimension is discussed separately following the same outline. First, the sociological expectation as defined by Stark and Glock is described. Second, the corresponding psychological representation within the personal religious system is discussed and identified. Third, articles are classified according to the dimensions considered in the research. And fourth, selected examples of research investigating the respective psychological representation are presented in order to illustrate the approach and logic of research addressing that specific dimension.

The Intellectual Dimension

The intellectual dimension is related to the social expectation that religious persons have some knowledge about their faith in particular and about religion in general. They should be able to explain their faith and discuss religious questions.

Glock restricted this dimension primarily to the aspect of religious knowledge. He distinguishes only between different types of knowledge.[43] Examples are knowledge about the Bible (or other holy scriptures), knowledge about the history of religion (or the church), interfaith knowledge, and knowledge about critical literature on religion.

Psychologically, however, Glock's perspective is too static. We assume that the individual's religious knowledge constitutes a personal frame of reference that structures his or her religious experiences and behaviors. Because experience and behavior are dynamic, the static aspect of knowledge does not cover the processes' full richness. In a more dynamic sense, the intellectual dimension is related to "religious literacy." Psychologically, religious literacy comprises at least two competences:

- The competence to play with religious symbols and to actively construct a subjective personal theology.
- The competence to transfer the vocabulary and grammar of religion to specific situations in daily life.

In this more dynamic perspective, we can expect that each kind of knowledge influences personal religiosity in a specific way. For instance, let us imagine a person who daily studies the Bible. Over the years he or she will acquire a profound and well-differentiated knowledge about biblical books, stories, persons, ethical prescriptions, types of religious experiences, and, last but not least, the role of God in interaction with human beings. Beyond that, the daily practice of Bible reading will also foster the competence to recognize the content of one biblical story in another. As a first consequence, the reader will discover more and more nuances in biblical content. This competence will enable the person to recognize biblical content in his or her daily life. As a second consequence, the person will develop a personal theory about the role of God in the interaction with human beings, enriching his or her capacities for religious experiences.

What do we know about the intellectual dimension of Pentecostals? What do we know about the different types of their religious knowledge? What do we know about their personal frames of reference? How do these personal frames of reference influence religious experiences, religious ideology, and religious practice? In the sixty-two peer-reviewed articles, the role of the intellectual dimension is only a marginal one. In our literature research, we found four articles with substantial data concerning the intellectual dimension: three of them deal with subjective theologies and implicit personality theories,[44] and the fourth deals with the intensity of the intellectual dimension and its relevance for religious experiences.[45]

One of the two articles about subjective theologies, by Hagan, published in 2006, investigates making theological sense of migrants.[46] Using qualitative methods, Hagan discovers the theological bases for pastoral care and social justice actions for migrants in the context of the current immigration policy of the U.S. government. Her findings suggest that the frames of reference of Catholic religious workers are structured by a communitarian social theology, which leads to social justice activities on migration issues. The frames of reference of mainline Protestant workers are similar to those of Catholic workers. In contrast, Pentecostal and evangelical workers maintain an individualistic frame of reference. As a consequence, they shy away from immigration politics, focusing instead on the needs and salvation of individual members of their ministries.

The 1989 article by Poloma and Pendleton deals with the intensity of the intellectual dimension and its relevance for religious experiences.[47] They used quantitative survey data on 1,275 Assemblies of God adherents from sixteen congregations in six states in the United States to explore the significance of Pentecostal religious experiences (e.g., glossolalia, prophecy, divine healing) for the vitality of their denominations. In detail they analyzed the interrelation of the ideological dimension (orthodoxy, moral attitudes) and the intellectual dimension (Bible reading and reading religious literature) with religious experience. Their intriguing result was that charismatic religious experiences are correlated much more with the intellectual dimension than with the ideological dimension. The higher the frequency of Bible reading and of reading religious literature, the higher the frequencies of charismatic experiences such as praying in tongues, prophecies in church services, and being slain in the Spirit. Methodologically, it has to be mentioned that Poloma and Pendleton did not separate the intellectual dimension from the devotional dimension (prayer). In their three-item index the intellectual dimension is represented by two items, whereas the devotional dimension is represented by only one. This makes salient the importance of the separate measurement of the dimensions proposed in the multidimensional model, because unambiguous interpretations are difficult to achieve.

From our perspective, these results should stimulate further research concerning the intellectual dimension in Pentecostals. We suggest as examples for future research thequestions, What kinds of religious knowledge do Pentecostals have? What styles of religious problem solving do Pentecostals have? How does the religious quest operate in Pentecostals?

The Ideological Dimension

The ideological dimension is constituted by the social expectation that the religious person will hold to certain beliefs. The semantic universe of religious beliefs is nearly infinite. Good examples of the large variety of religious beliefs are those related to God. Individuals may believe in a personal or an impersonal God. God can be conceptualized as law, which is valid throughout all eternity, or as some kind of energy flowing through everything, or as a higher power that determines everything, or as a value that is the greatest value of all, or as some kind of personal reality communicating with human beings. In addition, individuals may for example believe in a primarily merciful and forgiving God or a primarily punishing God.

Glock proposed a general distinction between three types of beliefs to order the semantic universe of religion.[48] We suggest that a comprehensive investigation of religious ideology should regard all three types of beliefs, which are as follows:

- Beliefs about the existence and the nature of God.
- Beliefs about the will of God and the divine destination of human beings and, respectively, the role of human beings in light of this will.
- Beliefs about the correct behavior of human beings in relation to God and in relation to fellow human beings.

From a psychological perspective, an additional distinction concerning religious beliefs seems to be necessary. In particular, the differentiation between the general belief in the existence in a transcendent or supernatural reality and specific beliefs concerning the nature of that reality is desirable.

The general belief in the existence of a transcendent or supernatural reality is psychologically fundamental for the relevance of the ideological dimension. If a person does not hold this general belief, specific beliefs about the nature of the transcendent reality may not become relevant. Thus the general belief is the psychological prerequisite for the individual's ability to access a religious frame of reference. The more plausible the existence of a transcendent reality is for an individual, the easier it is for that individual to refer to specific religious beliefs.

The fundamental question of the individual's general belief, however, allows no prediction on the specific beliefs that are relevant for an individual's frame of reference, which specifically directs his or her experience and behavior. For instance, it can be assumed that the belief in a merciful and forgiving God leads a person into a different direction from the belief in a wrathful and punishing God. In the semantic universe of religion, there are a multitude of beliefs that may be salient or relevant in the individual's religious frame of reference. Thus, after having considered the fundamental question of the individual's general belief, it is desirable to pose questions on his or her specific beliefs concerning the nature of the transcendent or supernatural reality as systematically as possible. Only if we follow this strategy are we able to investigate which behavioral direction religious ideology leads a person into.

Pentecostals, as generally acknowledged, hold a very strong general belief in the existence of a supernatural reality. Hence research concerning this fundamental aspect of religious belief systems cannot be expected to be fruitful in samples of Pentecostals. But what do we know about their endogenous structures of religious ideology? For instance, do they believe in a primarily merciful and forgiving or a primarily punishing God? Or do they believe in both, a merciful God for themselves and a punishing God for others? The analysis of doctrinal statements (e.g., concerning hell) embedded in the constitutional texts of Pentecostal churches, often more than one hundred years old, may provide a starting point. It is, however, indispensable to analyze the representation on the psychological level in order to identify effective beliefs on the level of the individual. This is only one example; there are many more facets of religious ideology that are worthy of investigation, for example, beliefs about ethical issues like marital and sexual behavior.[49]

In our literature research we found five articles since 1987 that are focused on aspects of the ideological dimension.[50] One example is the 2005 study of Eurelings-Bontekoe and colleagues.[51] They compared 208 members of a Reformed church and of a Pentecostal church concerning the association between personality, attachment, psychological distress, church denomination, and the God concept. The results showed that the Reformed church members hold a more negative concept of God than the Pentecostal church members do. Independently of personality, attachment, and psychological distress, Reformed church members see God in particular as a punitive judge. These differences suggest that religious culture has a strong influence on this type of God concept. It is noteworthy that in the study the experiential dimension was more important than the ideological dimension: negative feelings toward God were associated with a high level of harm avoidance, insecure attachment, and a high level of psychological distress.

Another example is the study by Poloma and Pendleton mentioned above.[52] Among other variables they investigated were two aspects of religious ideology, orthodox beliefs (e.g., the necessity of tongues as initial evidence of Spirit baptism) and moral attitudes (e.g., regarding attending movies, alcohol, and social dancing). Both aspects of religious ideology were highly intercorrelated ($r = .51$), but their correlations with other dimensions were small (e.g., $r = .19/.20$ with the intellectual dimension, $r = .19/.21$ with the experiential dimension). These results highlight the relative autonomy of the ideological dimension. This means that the ideological dimension contains structures and dynamics that are independent of the other dimensions of the model and thus may not be sufficiently predicted by them. Because of the high importance of this dimension for behavior and attitude, the identification of the specific dynamics within the ideological dimension is an important enterprise. Thus in future more investigations on ideology are necessary.

Both studies described above are examples of quantitative research. A good example of a qualitative approach is the 2004 study by Youngblood and Winn.[53] They apply ethnographic methods to investigate the worldview and communication codes of the members of an African American Pentecostal church in the U.S. South. Two complex codes structuring the worldview and the communication of the church members were identified: a racist code of exclusion reflecting their interactions with people outside their church community; and a code of belonging representing their experiences inside their church community. Both codes express systems of values and beliefs. "However," the authors write, "the values and beliefs inscribed in the code of belonging embrace a positive view of personhood and a value for Black community social relations."[54] The code of belonging provides a powerful corrective to the racist communication of the dominant white society by providing a spiritual community that stands in opposition to racism.

The Experiential Dimension

The experiential dimension is related to the social expectation that the religious person has some kind of direct contact with an ultimate reality. According to Rodney Stark, "The essential element characterizing religious experience . . . is *some sense of contact with a supernatural agency.*"[55] From this point of view Stark distinguishes four types of religious experiences: confirming, responsive, ecstatic, and revelational experiences. The responsive type is subdivided into three modes, the salvational, the miraculous, and the sanctioning. Finally, Stark differentiates between divine and diabolic contents that can fill these categories. In our view this typology could be a fruitful tool in investigating endogenous structures and the dynamics of religious experiences. Until now, only a small fraction of this typology has been investigated empirically. Hence there is still a wide field of research to be done.

What do we know about the religious experiences of Pentecostals so far? A lot, of course. But most of the research up to now has focuses on glossolalia[56] and on spiritual healing or faith healing.[57] This research, with respect to exogenous causes and consequences in the specific experiences of glossolalia and faith healing, has provided important insights. The research perspective taken, however, allows us no conclusions on the endogenous structures and dynamics of the experiential dimension, which are indispensable for a deeper understanding of the religious experiences of Pentecostals. Thus we need systematic investigations into the full range of their religious experiences. On the one hand, we need research concerning the variety of the content of religious experiences of Pentecostals; on the other, we need analyses of the interrelations between the dimension of religious experience and the other dimensions of personal religion.

A detailed phenomenological description of the meaning of a specific kind of religious experience of Pentecostals was given by Williamson, Pollio, and Hood, who investigated the anointing among religious serpent handlers.[58] Their aim was to investigate the meaning of this experience from within its religious context. Conducting eleven phenomenological interviews, they found that serpents were taken up in some cases by faith but most often by so-called anointing. The deeper hermeneutical analysis of anointing revealed that can be described as an embodied experience involving an awareness of five themes: (1) "God moving on me," (2) a feeling of empowerment, (3) "indescribable" good feelings, (4) a sense being "not there" in the immediate context, and (5) a "contagious flow." The major context of the anointing is the experience of one's own body, which serves "to ground each of the themes in corporeal existence as well as to provide a context within which they are understood."[59] In the first-person perspective of anointed worshipers the theme "'God moving on me'" was central to the experience of anointing and directly related to all other themes experienced.[60] The authors gave the following dense description of the process of anointing:

> The experience begins primarily with feeling the moving of God on the person, which is experienced in terms of various body sensations, a sense that God is taking control of the person, and the hearing of God's directive voice. With this experience, there is a profound sense of empowerment that infuses a feeling of protection from all harm, combined with a feeling of being sufficiently empowered to do the will of God at the present moment. This experience is such that the person feels drawn away in varying degrees and no longer feels fully present to the immediate surroundings, date, or time; yet the person feels a flow that radiates through contact with others as they come into awareness. Indescribably good feelings—variously approximated as a high, joy, peace, love, and victory—are felt from the onset of the anointing and continue to linger after the experience lifts.[61]

A good example of an investigation into religious causes and dynamics concerning the experience of healing is Poloma and Hoelter's 1998 study on the "Toronto blessing."[62] In a multidimensional analysis, they investigated the effects of ritual participation (the times the respondent reported being prayed for by someone), bodily experiences of the Spirit (bending, birthing, being drunk in the Spirit, jerking, rolling, thrashing, and shaking), and emotional experiences (positive religious emotions, e.g., happiness, satisfaction, joy, love, love for God, gratitude, peace, being cleansed, being humbled, forgiveness toward self, strength, and compassion) on four types of healing in a sample of 918 attendees at the Toronto Airport Christian Fellowship. The four healing variables are spiritual healing (experiences of God's forgiveness and of deliverance from Satan), inner healing (experience of an inner or spiritual healing), mental healing (experience of healing from clinically diagnosed mental health problems), and physical healing (experience of healing of a physical health problem). A series of regression analyses reveal a specific structure in the process of healing. Spiritual healing was influenced by ritual participation, bodily experiences of the Spirit, and positive religious emotions. The model explained that in 13 percent of the variance, the most influential variable was the experience of positive emotions. Inner healing was influenced by bodily experiences of the Spirit, positive religious emotions, and spiritual healing. The model also explained that in 23 percent of the variance, the distinctively most influential variable was the experience of spiritual healing. Mental healing and physical healing were influenced only by spiritual healing, with an explained variance of 4 percent and 3 percent, respectively. In their summary the authors conclude that their model supports the notion that the relationship with the divine "must be in 'right order' before other forms of healing ordinarily can take place."[63] Unfortunately, Poloma and Hoelter did not integrate the intellectual dimension into their model. In Poloma and Pendleton's earlier study, it was shown that that charismatic religious experiences are strongly influenced by the intensity of the intellectual dimension of religiosity.[64] Hence it could be expected that the integration of this dimension would deepen the results of the Toronto study. In future, therefore, multidimensional investigations of the religious causes and dynamics of the experience of healing should cover all core dimensions of religiosity as systematically as possible.

The Private Religious Practice Dimension

Originally, Glock defined only one dimension for all kinds of religious practice.[65] Later, in the refined multidimensional model, Stark and Glock split this global dimension into two relative autonomous dimensions: private religious practice and public religious practice.[66]

The most typical example of private practice is personal prayer. Hence Glock referred to this dimension also as the devotional dimension. The overall intensity of this dimension reveals a person's actual use of a transcendent frame of reference, because prayer is one of the most obvious constructions of a transcendent reality. The more a person prays, the more he or she opens the full potential of a transcendent frame of reference.

Pentecostals, as generally acknowledged, have an intense and rich prayer life. Hence research concerning the psychological effects of the intensity of the devotional dimension may not be expected to be fruitful in samples of Pentecostals due to the lack of variance. In contrast, we expect that Pentecostal prayer life encompasses a rich and wide variety of forms and content of prayer. Hence research concerning the psychological representations and effects of diverse forms and contents of prayer should be fruitful. For instance, the personal relevance and representation of, for example, petition, thanks, praise, lamentation, and accusation could be investigated. We suggest that we will find various different profiles of prayer, characterizing typical configurations of contents in the individual. On that basis the psychological dynamics of these profiles of prayer could be investigated, and we could compare the distribution of profiles of prayer in Pentecostals with those prevalent in other Christian denominations. This approach would allow us to extend and deepen our knowledge of the distinctiveness of Pentecostal religiosity.

Although glossolalia has been broadly investigated in psychological studies of Pentecostalism, the review of this research leaves open the question of whether Pentecostals only pray in tongues. Other forms and contents of prayer have rarely been investigated. In the sixty-two peer-reviewed articles, we found only one article that focuses on other forms of prayer, by Decker, which suggests four-step model of "praying through."[67] This article, however, presents only theoretical considerations, indicating a general lack of empirical work on Pentecostal prayer practices besides glossolalia. Such investigations are an enterprise that is clearly indispensable.

The Public Religious Practice Dimension

The four dimensions discussed above are characterized by the fact that they may be practiced individually. In contrast, public religious practice involves the integration of a person's religiosity into a social network. Thus this dimension is an important complement to the other, more private dimensions of religiosity. It reflects the social expectation that the religious person belongs to a specific group of believers.

In Christianity the most typical public practice is church attendance. Psychologically, the general intensity of this practice reveals the social validation and stabilization of the individual's religiosity and his or her perception of transcendence. The more frequently a person attends church, the more his or her religious framework is socially validated. Social validation of religiosity is crucial, because in general the experience of transcendence is possible only in the mode of belief. Hence the individual needs the testimonies of other believers for the validation of his or her religious experiences.

Most Pentecostals are deeply committed to their congregations. Hence research concerning the general intensity of the ritual dimension does not need to be recommended. But just as with respect to the devotional dimension, research concerning endogenous structures and dynamics of Pentecostal rituals seems to be promising. In the recent literature only a few articles consider this topic. Four articles refer to the role of ministry.[68] A fifth article investigates the role of music in the church service.[69] In an inventive research design, Miller and Strongman asked ninety-five members of a Pentecostal church about their moods "at three different times: directly before the Sunday morning church service, after the musical portion (approximately 45 minutes into the service), and after the entire service was finished." The mood scale ranged from "(1) tremendously depressed, to (10) very elated and in very high spirits."[70] Directly before the service, the mood was already on a level above average (M = 7.15). Nevertheless, the mood significantly increased (M = 8.05) after the music and worship part of the service. After that, the mood remained on a high level without significant changes (M = 8.15). This result underlines the psychological importance of Pentecostal worship practice. Comparative studies with non-Pentecostal congregations should enhance our knowledge about the endogenous dynamics of Sunday services.

CONCLUSION

Our overview of psychological research on Pentecostal religiosity is structured by the distinction between two research perspectives. The first perspective analyses exogenous psychological causes and consequences of Pentecostalism. Pentecostalism in this perspective is regarded as a black box connected with these causes and consequences and thus solely as an epiphenomenon of general psychological processes. The theoretical bases are general psychological categories, which are applied to the religious experiences and behavior of Pentecostals. In this perspective two phases may be distinguished. In early research a psychopathological framework prevailed using mainly psychodynamic concepts such as schizophrenia, hysteria, and regression. Research beginning in the 1960s focused more on normal personality characteristics and concepts indicating psychological stability.

In contrast, the second perspective both investigates and respects the endogenous psychological structures and dynamics of pentecostal religiosity, as derived from the content of this system itself. In our review of the literature based on the distinction of the five core dimensions of religiosity, it became obvious that there is a wide and promising field for future psychological research on the religiosity of Pentecostals.

The study of the endogenous dynamics and structures of the religiosity of Pentecostals, however, is not an enterprise that refers only to itself. We expect that the knowledge to be gained in future research will allow researchers to target questions in a new way. Once we know more about the interplay of the elements of endogenous psychological structures and the dynamics of Pentecostal religiosity, exogenous psychological causes and consequences may be linked to specific elements of the personal religious system, leading to a much more detailed and richer picture.

NOTES

1. Charles Glock, "On the Study of Religious Commitment," in *Review of Recent Research Bearing on Religious and Character Formation,* Research supplement to *Religious Education* 57 (July–August 1962) (New York: Religious Research Association, 1962), 98–110; R. Stark and Charles Glock, *American Piety: The Nature of Religious Commitment* (Berkeley: UCP, 1968).

2. Kilian McDonnell, *Charismatic Renewal and the Churches* (New York: Seabury, 1976); Steven A. Gritzmacher, Brian Bolton, and Richard H. Dana, "Psychological Characteristics of Pentecostals: A Literature Review and Psychodynamic Synthesis," *JP&T* 16 (1988): 233–45.

3. William K. Kay, "The Mind, Behaviour and Glossolalia—A Psychological Perspective," in *Speaking in Tongues: Multi-Disciplinary Perspectives,* ed. Mark J. Cartledge (Milton Keynes: Paternoster, 2006), 174–205.

4. McDonnell, *Charismatic Renewal and the Churches.*

5. Gritzmacher, Bolton, and Dana, "Psychological Characteristics of Pentecostals."

6. Kay, "The Mind, Behaviour and Glossolalia."

7. George B. Cutten, *Speaking with Tongues: Historically and Psychologically Considered* (New Haven: Yale University Press, [1927] 2006).

8. Cutten, *Speaking with Tongues,* 168.

9. Cutten, *Speaking with Tongues,* 160.

10. Ezra E. H. Griffith, Thelouzs English, and Violet Mayfield, "Possession, Prayer, and Testimony: Therapeutic Aspects of the Wednesday Night Meeting in a Black Church," *Psychiatry* 43 (1980): 120–28;

Morton T. Kelsey, *Tongue Speaking: An Experiment in Spiritual Experience* (Garden City, NY: Doubleday, 1964); Ari Kiev, "The Study of Folk Psychiatry," in *Magic, Faith, and Healing: Studies in Primitive Psychiatry,* ed. Ari Kiev (Glencoe, IL: Free Press, 1964),3–35; James N. Lapsley and John H. Simpson, "Speaking in Tongues: Infantile Babble or Song of the Self? (Part II)," *Pastoral Psychology* 15 (1964): 16–24; E. Mansell Pattison, "Behavioral Science Research on the Nature of Glossolalia," *Journal of the American Scientific Affiliation* 20 (1968): 73–86; John Wilson and Harvey K. Clow, "Themes of Power and Control in a Pentecostal Assembly," *JSSR* 20 (1981): 241–50.

11. Leslie J. Francis and William K. Kay, "The Personality Characteristics of Pentecostal Ministry Candidates," *Personality and Individual Differences* 8 (1995): 581–94.

12. Kay, "The Mind, Behaviour and Glossolalia"; H. Newton Malony and A. Adams Lovekin, *Glossolalia: Behavioral Science Perspectives on Speaking in Tongues* (New York: OUP, 1985); Watson E. Mills ed., *Speaking in Tongues: A Guide to Research in Glossolalia* (Grand Rapids: Eerdmans, 1986).

13. Kay, "The Mind, Behaviour and Glossolalia."

14. Cutten, *Speaking with Tongues.*

15. Felicitas D. Goodman, "Phonetic Analysis of Glossolalia in Four Cultural Settings," *JSSR* 8 (1969): 227–39; Felicitas D. Goodman, "Altered Mental State vs. 'Style Of Discourse': Reply to Samarin," *JSSR* 11 (1972): 297–99; Felicitas D. Goodman, *Speaking in Tongues: A Cross-Cultural Study of Glossolalia* (Chicago: University of Chicago Press, 1972); Felicitas D. Goodman, "Glossolalia and Hallucination in Pentecostal Congregations," *Psychiatria Clinica* 6 (1973): 97–103; Felicitas D. Goodman, "Body Posture and the Religious Altered State of Consciousness: An Experimental Investigation," *Journal of Humanistic Psychology* 26 (1986): 81–118; John P. Kildahl, *The Psychology of Speaking in Tongues* (New York: Harper & Row, 1972).

16. Nicolas P. Spanos and Erin C. Hewitt, "Glossolalia: A Test of the 'Trance' and Psychopathology Hypothesis," *Journal of Abnormal Psychology* 88 (1979): 427–34; Nicolas P. Spanos, Wendy P., Cross, Mark Lepage, and Marjorie Coristine, "Glossolalia as Learned Behaviour: An Experimental Demonstration," *Journal of Abnormal Psychology* 95 (1986): 21–23.

17. Virginia H. Hine, "Pentecostal Glossolalia: Toward a Functional Interpretation," *JSSR* 8 (1969): 211–26; William J. Samarin, "Glossolalia as Learned Behaviour," *Canadian Journal of Theology* 15 (1969): 60–64; William J. Samarin, "Sociolinguistic vs. Neurophysiological Explanations for Glossolalia: Comment on Goodman's Paper," *JSSR* 11 (1972): 293–96; William J. Samarin, *Tongues of Men and Angels* (New York: Macmillan, 1972); William J. Samarin, "Glossolalia as Regressive Speech," *Language and Speech* 16 (1973): 77–89.

18. Andrew B. Newberg et al., "The Measurement of Regional Cerebral Blood Flow during Glossolalia: A Preliminary SPECT Study," *Psychiatry Research: Neuroimaging* 148 (2006): 67–71.

19. Andrew B. Newberg et al., "The Measurement of Regional Cerebral Blood Flow during the Complex Cognitive Task of Meditation: A Preliminary SPECT Study," *Psychiatry Research: Neuroimaging* 106 (2001): 113–22; Andrew Newberg et al., "Cerebral Blood Flow during Meditative Prayer: Preliminary Findings and Methodological Issues," *Perceptual and Motor Skills* 97 (2003): 625–30.

20. Jesse E. Coulson and Ray W. Johnson, "Glossolalia and Internal-External Locus of Control," *JP&T* 5 (1977): 312–317; Nancy L. Niesz and Earl J. Kronenberger, "Self-Actualization in Glossolalic and Non-Glossolalic Pentecostals," *Sociological Analysis* 39 (1978): 250–56; Robert B. Simmonds, James T. Richardson, and Mary W. Harder, "A Jesus Movement Group: An Adjective Check List assessment," *JSSR* 15 (1976): 323–37; L.M. Vivier, "Glossolalia" (Ph.D. diss., University of Witwatersrand, Johannesburg, 1960); William W. Wood, *Culture and Personality Aspects of the Pentecostal Holiness Religion* (Paris: Mouton, 1965).

21. Ari Kiev, "Psychotherapeutic Aspects of Pentecostal Sects among West Indian Immigrants to England," *British Journal of Sociology* 15 (1964): 129–38; A. Adams Lovekin and H. Newton Malony, "Religious Glossolalia: A Longitudinal Study of Personality Changes," *JSSR* 16 (1977): 382–93; Pattison,

"Behavioral Science Research"; Daniel S. Smith and J. Roland Fleck, "Personality Correlates of Conventional and Unconventional Glossolalia," *Journal of Social Psychology* 88 (1981): 427–34.

22. Kildahl, *The Psychology of Speaking in Tongues*; John P. Kildahl, "Psychological Observations," in *The Charismatic Movement*, ed. Michael P. Hamilton (Grand Rapids: Eerdmans, 1975), 124–42.

23. Kay, "The Mind, Behaviour and Glossolalia," 187–88.

24. Marion Dearman, "Christ and Conformity: A Study of Pentecostal Values," *JSSR* 13 (1974): 437–53.

25. Kildahl, *The Psychology of Speaking in Tongues*; Kildahl, "Psychological Observations."

26. Emma Gonsalves, "A Psychological Interpretation of the Religious Behaviour of Pentecostals and charismatics," *Journal of Dharma* 7 (1982): 408–29; Griffith, English, and Mayfield, "Possession, Prayer, and Testimony," 120–28; E. Mansell Pattison, "Speaking in Tongues and about Tongues," *Christian Standard,* 15 February 1964, 3–5; Pattison, "Behavioral Science Research,"73–86; Simmonds, "A Jesus Movement Group," 323–37.

27. Leslie J. Francis and Susan H. Jones, "Personality and Charismatic Experience among Adult Christians," *Pastoral Psychology* 45 (1997): 421–28; Leslie J. Francis and Mandy Robbins, "Personality and Glossolalia: A Study among Male Anglican clergy," *Pastoral Psychology* 51 (2003): 391–96; Leslie J. Francis and T. Hugh Thomas, "Are Charismatic Ministers Less Stable? A Study among Male Anglican Clergy," *Review of Religious Research* 39 (1997): 61–69; Francis and Kay, "The Personality Characteristics."

28. Francis and Jones, "Personality and Charismatic Experience"; Francis and Robbins, "Personality and Glossolalia"; Mandy Robbins, James Hair, and Leslie J. Francis, "Personality and Attraction to the Charismatic Movement: A Study among Anglican Clergy," *JBV* 20 (1999): 239–46.

29. Anton T. Boisen, "Economic Distress and Religious Experience: A Study of the Holy Rollers," *Psychiatry* 2 (1939): 185–94; Cutten, *Speaking with Tongues*.

30. Griffith, English, and Mayfield, "Possession, Prayer, and Testimony"; Kelsey, *Tongue Speaking*; Kiev, "Psychotherapeutic Aspects"; Elvira Koić, Pavo Filaković, Sanea Nađ and Ivan Čelić, "Glossolalia," *Collegium Antropologicum* 29 (2005): 307–13; Lapsley and Simpson, "Speaking in Tongues"; Pattison, "Behavioral Science Research"; Klement Preus, "Tongues: An Evaluation from a Scientific Perspective," *Concordia Theological Quarterly* 46 (1982): 277–93; Karl G. Rey, *Gotteserlebnisse im Schnellverfahren: Suggestion als Gefahr und Charisma* (Munich: Kösel, 1985); Wilson and Clow, "Themes of Power."

31. Wilson and Clow, "Themes of Power."

32. Coulson and Johnson, "Glossolalia."

33. Kildahl, *The Psychology of Speaking in Tongues*; Kildahl, "Psychological Observations"; Simmonds, "A Jesus Movement Group"; Vivier, "Glossolalia."

34. Kildahl, *The Psychology of Speaking in Tongues*; Lovekin and Malony, "Religious Glossolalia"; Robert C. Ness and Ronald M. Wintrob, "The Emotional Impact of Fundamentalist Religious Participation: An Empirical Study of Intragroup Variation," *American Journal of Orthopsychiatry* 50 (1980): 302–15; Spanos and Hewitt, "Glossolalia"; A. Tellegen et al., "Personality Characteristics of Members of a Serpent-Handling Religious Cult," in *MMPI: Research Developments and Clinical Applications,* ed. James N. Butcher (New York: McGraw-Hill, 1969), 221–24.

35. Lovekin and Malony "Religious Glossolalia"; Ness and Wintrob, "The Emotional Impact"; Christopher R. Stones, "Fundamentalism and Conservatism among Jesus People in South Africa," *Journal of Psychology* 98 (1978): 225–29.

36. Francis and Kay, "The Personality Characteristics."

37. Simmonds, "A Jesus Movement Group"; Tellegen et al., "Personality Characteristics"; Vivier, "Glossolalia."

38. Gritzmacher, Bolton, and Dana, "Psychological Characteristics."

39. Glock, "On the Study of Religious Commitment"; Stark, *American Piety.*

40. Stefan Huber, *Dimensionen der Religiosität* (Bern: Verlag Hans Huber, 1996); Stefan Huber, *Zentralität und Inhalt: Ein neues multidimensionales Messmodell der Religiosität* (Opladen: Leske + Budrich, 2003); Stefan Huber, "Are Religious Beliefs Relevant in Daily Life?" in *Religion Inside and Outside Traditional Institutions,* ed. Heinz Streib (Leiden: Brill, 2007), 211–30; Stefan Huber, "Der Religiositäts-Struktur-Test (R-S-T). Systematik und operationale Konstrukte," in *Individualisierung und die pluralen Ausprägungsformen des Religiösen,* ed. Wilhelm Gräb und Lars Charbonnier (Münster: Lit-Verlag, 2008), 109–43.

41. Stefan Huber, "Aufbau und Prinzip des Religionsmonitor," in *Bertelsmann Religionsmonitor 2008,* ed. Bertelsmann Stiftung (Gütersloh: Gütersloher Verlagshaus, 2007), 19–29; Stefan Huber, "Religion Monitor 2008: Structuring Principles, Operational Constructs, Interpretive Strategies," in *What the World Believes: Analysis and Commentary on the Religion Monitor 2008,* ed. Bertelsmann Stiftung (Gütersloh: Verlag Bertelsmann Stiftung, 2009), 17–51. Stefan Huber and Volkhard Krech, "The Religious Field between Globalization and Regionalization—Comparative Perspectives," in Bertelsmann Stiftung, *What the World Believes,* 53–93.

42. Huber, *Zentralität und Inhalt.*

43. Glock, *On the Study of Religious Commitment.*

44. Donald L. Clark, "An Implicit Theory of Personality, Illness, and Cure Found in the Writings of Neo-Pentecostal Faith Healers," *JP&T* 12 (1984): 279–85; Jacqueline Hagan, "Making Theological Sense of the Migration Journey from Latin America: Catholic, Protestant, and Interfaith Perspectives," *American Behavioural Scientist* 49 (2006): 1554–73; Pamela D. Trice and Jeffrey P. Bjork, "Pentecostal Perspectives on Causes and Cures of Depression," *Professional Psychology: Research and Practice* 37 (2006): 283–94.

45. Margareth Poloma and Brian F. Pendleton, "Religious Experiences, Evangelism, and Institutional Growth within the Assemblies of God," *JSSR* 28 (1989): 415–31.

46. Hagan, "Making Theological Sense."

47. Poloma and Pendleton, "Religious Experiences."

48. Glock, *On the Study of Religious Commitment.*

49. William K. Kay, *Pentecostals in Britain* (Carlisle: Paternoster, 2000).

50. C. Rodrigues Brandao, "Religious Identity as a Symbolic Strategy: Brazilian Dimensions," *Social Science Information / sur les sciences sociales* 25 (1986): 229–57; Elizabeth H. M. Eurelings-Bontekoe, Janneke Hekman-Van Steeg, and Margot J. Verschuur, "The Association between Personality, Attachment, Psychological Distress, Church Denomination and the God Concept among a Non-Clinical Sample,"*MHRC* 8 (2005): 141–54; Christine A. Kray, "The Pentecostal Re-Formation of Self: Opting for Orthodoxy in Yucatan," *Ethos* 29 (2001): 395–429; Poloma and Pendleton, "Religious Experiences"; John D. Youngblood and J. Emmett Winn, "Shout Glory: Competing Communication Codes Experienced by the Members of the African American Pentecostal Genuine Deliverance Holiness Church," *Journal of Communication* 54 (2004): 355–70.

51. Eurelings-Bontekoe et al., "The Association between Personality, Attachment."

52. Poloma and Pendleton, "Religious Experiences."

53. Youngblood and Winn, "Shout Glory," 355–70.

54. Youngblood and Winn, "Shout Glory," 365.

55. Rodney Stark, "A Taxonomy of Religious Experience," *JSSR* 5 (1965): 98; original emphasis.

56. E.g., Nils G. Holm, "Sunden's Role Theory and Glossolalia," *JSSR* 26 (1987): 383–89; Nils G. Holm, "Pentecostalism: Conversion and Charismata," *IJPR* 1 (1991): 135–51; Ralph W. Hood Jr., "Holm's Use of Role Theory: Empirical and Hermeneutical Considerations of Sacred Text as a Source of Role Adoption," *IJPR*1 (1991): 153–59; Poloma and Pendleton, "Religious Experiences"; Russell F. Proctor, "The Rhetorical Functions of Christian Glossolalia," *JPC* 9 (1990): 27–34; Andrew Singleton, "The

Importance of Narrative in Negotiating Otherworldly Experiences: The Case of Speaking in Tongues," *Narrative Inquiry* 12 (2002): 351–73.

57. E.g. John R. Belcher, "Religious Education and Pastoral Counselling: The Classical Pentecostal Experience," *Pastoral Psychology* 53 (2002): 97–106; Deborah C. Glik, "Symbolic, Ritual and Social Dynamics of Spiritual Healing," *Social Science and Medicine* 27 (1988): 1197–1206; Karin Horwatt, "The Shamanic Complex in the Pentecostal Church," *Ethos* 16 (1988): 128–45; James Pfeiffer, "Commodity Fetichismo, the Holy Spirit, and the Turn to Pentecostal and African Independent Churches in Central Mozambique," *Culture, Medicine and Psychiatry* 29 (2005): 255–83; Margaret M. Poloma and Lynette F. Hoelter, "The 'Toronto Blessing': A Holistic Model of Healing," *JSSR* 37 (1988): 257–72.

58. W. Paul Williamson, Howard R. Pollio, and Ralph W. Hood Jr., "A Phenomenological Analysis of the Anointing among Religious Serpent Handlers," *IJPR* 10 (2000): 221–40.

59. Williamson, Pollio, and Hood, "A Phenomenological Analysis," 228.

60. Williamson, Pollio, and Hood, "A Phenomenological Analysis," 229.

61. Williamson, Pollio, and Hood, "A Phenomenological Analysis," 235–36.

62. Poloma and Hoelter, "'Toronto Blessing.'"

63. Poloma and Hoelter, "'Toronto Blessing,'" 269.

64. Poloma and Pendleton, "Religious Experiences."

65. Glock, *On the Study of Religious Commitment.*

66. Stark, *American Piety.*

67. Edward E. Decker, "'Praying Through': A Pentecostal Approach to Pastoral Care," *JPC* 20 (2001): 370–77.

68. Leslie J. Francis and Douglas W. Turton, "Are Charismatic Clergy More Satisfied with Their Ministry? A Study among Male Parochial Clergy in the Church of England," *MHRC* 5 (2002): 135–42; William K. Kay, "Job Satisfaction in Pentecostal Ministers," *AJPS* 3 (2002): 83–97; William K. Kay, "Role Conflict and British Pentecostal Ministers," *JP&T* 28 (2000): 119–24; Francis and Kay, "The Personality Characteristics."

69. Mandy M. Miller and Kenneth T. Strongman, "The Emotional Effects of Music on Religious Experience: A Study of the Pentecostal-Charismatic Style of Music and Worship," *Psychology of Music* 30 (2002): 8–27.

70. Miller and Strongman, "Emotional Effects of Music," 11.

8

Anthropology of Religion

Joel Robbins

Mark Noll, discussing the early-twentieth-century emergence of Pentecostalism, refers to it as a development that "as is now well known, has had world historical significance."[1] It is fair to say that Noll is right on both counts: Pentecostalism has changed and is changing the global landscape in world historical ways, and more and more people are coming to know that it is doing so. In reference to the first point, about global influence, it is hard today to dispute the claim that Pentecostalism, broadly understood throughout this chapter to include both Pentecostal and Charismatic groups, has been and continues to be a major presence around the world. Even the *Economist,* a source not known for hyperbole, has recently plumbed for the figure of 500 million Pentecostals worldwide, a number that just a few years ago seemed like a very high-end estimate but has recently achieved the status of reasonable best current guess.[2] And as important as the number of converts Pentecostalism has made is the fact that it routinely transforms in profound ways the groups in which it becomes a force. Pentecostalism's effect among converts is most often akin, say, not to rearranging the cultural furniture but to moving that furniture to an altogether new house, one where even old familiar pieces look different than they did before. This point—that Pentecostalism is a powerful driver of radical cultural change—is what makes its importance world historical in scope.

Noll's second claim, that the global import of the Pentecostal explosion has become well known, also rings true, at least within the social sciences and humanities. In the past twenty years or so—perhaps we can take the 1990 publication of David Martin's hugely influential *Tongues of Fire* as a starting point—the growth in the literature on Pentecostalism has been staggering. During that time, Pentecostalism has found a place on the agenda of all manner of scholars, from sociologists, anthropologists, historians, and political scientists to economists, scholars of religious studies, and theologians. Moreover, and this is my real starting point in this chapter, the developing discourse on Pentecostalism has been marked by a pervasive and remarkably easygoing interdisciplinarity, one in which scholars from all these fields more regularly read and use one another's work. It is almost as if there is a sense among scholars that to survive a storm as intense as the rise of Pentecostalism, we need to have all hands on deck. Given this sense, those who study Pentecostalism have shown little tendency to retreat into narrow circles of cooperation, or to reject out of hand the findings of those whose disciplinary background is different from their own.

The thoroughly interdisciplinary character of Pentecostal studies is important for me here because it makes the task I have been assigned, that of discussing the contributions of anthropology to the Pentecostal studies mix, a more challenging but also more intriguing one than it would be in an area where disciplinary contributions and traditions of research were more distinct. Two recent cases in point from the anthropological literature indicate the obstacles one faces trying to figure out what would count as a specifically disciplinary contribution to the study of Pentecostalism. Birgit Meyer's major review of the rise of Pentecostalism in Africa and my review of the literature on the globalization of Pentecostalism appeared in 2004 in the same volume of the *Annual Review of Anthropology*.[3] Even a quick glance at these two pieces is enough to demonstrate that neither of them dwells exclusively or even prejudicially on anthropological work. Meyer draws much from historians like Maxwell and Ranger and sociologists like David Martin, and I likewise take as many cues from historians like Maxwell, sociologists like Smilde and David and Bernice Martin, and many others from various fields as I do from my anthropological colleagues. Given that these two review articles appeared in a widely circulated, gate-keeping annual, they can be taken to mark the arrival of Pentecostal studies into the mainstream of anthropology. At the same time, however, their eclectic, disciplinarily tangled bibliographies suggest that some hard work awaits anyone who wants to pull from them a few wholly anthropological threads.

In spite of the challenges of finding a distinctly anthropological voice in the Pentecostal studies chorus, the task of doing so is quite worthwhile. With the growth in the literature on Pentecostalism showing no signs of slowing, this is a good time to step back and examine the strengths of each of the disciplines that is contributing to it. In what follows I try to do this for anthropology under three broad rubrics. The first I will call Pentecostalism and cultural process. In the section devoted to this topic, I take up what anthropology has taught us about the cultural dynamics that have attended the spread of Pentecostalism. My second rubric is the study of Pentecostalism as lived religion. Here I examine such topics as ritual, morality, embodiment, media, and the use of language that constitute the subject matter of studies of Pentecostalism as a feature of everyday life. The third and final organizing rubric takes up the much mulled over topic of the relationship of Pentecostalism to modernity, focusing on anthropological work on the ways Pentecostalism fosters individualism, changing gender norms, and the transformation of economic and political ideas. In these three sections I hope to lay out in a reasonably orderly way some of the debates that have most consumed anthropologists and to give a sense of some of the original insights they have offered.

Before beginning, a word is in order about two qualities of the upcoming discussion. First, I have not set myself the impossible task of citing only anthropologists in what follows. What I have done, however, is tried to keep to issues anthropologists have found themselves preoccupied with. Second, given the recent publication of the two densely referenced review essays I just mentioned, I have forgone the urge to be exhaustive in my citations here. Instead, I have tried to highlight some of the most important sustained ethnographic and analytical projects in the anthropological literature on Pentecostalism, discussing them in a bit more depth than would be possible in a piece dedicated to referencing as much as possible of what has been written.

PENTECOSTALISM AND CULTURAL PROCESS

Anthropology is the discipline generally credited with having developed the modern notion of culture. With the rise of cultural studies and the vogue for cultural analysis across the social sciences and humanities, it is often observed that over the past several decades anthropology has lost any monopoly on the concept of culture it might once have had. Yet it remains true that the average anthropologist pays more attention to culture than does the average scholar from other disciplines and that anthropologists in general are more aware than others of the comparative dimensions of cultural research and of the features that make the cultures each of them study distinctive. It thus makes sense to begin a discussion of the anthropology of Pentecostalism by considering what anthropologists have identified as some of the distinctive features of Pentecostal culture.

In their study of Pentecostals in Northern Ireland, Buckley and Kenney observe that "the identity of Pentecostalists consists not only of being a Christian, but also of having become one."[4] On the basis of this strong emphasis on becoming—on conversion to something one did not subscribe to before—Pentecostalism routinely sets in motion processes of cultural change wherever it takes root among a large number of people. One of the most notable findings in the anthropological literature on Pentecostalism is that the processes of cultural change it generates are similar across the world; despite the wide variety of local settings in which the religion lodges itself, the kinds of transformations it sets in train look in many ways to be almost the same.

At the most general level, the primary kind of change Pentecostalism promotes is one of radical discontinuity with what has come before.[5] Pentecostal converts do not imagine that what is required of them is some kind of gradual transformation or development, the kind of change that preserves the best of what currently exists as it moves with careful, steady steps toward something new, or the kind that evolves through numerous stages. Instead, they focus on reforming their lives by effecting a series of ruptures with the ways in which they have lived up to the time of their conversion.

The ruptures in question take place in a number of different dimensions of converts' lives. One of these is personal. In a widely cited paper that has greatly influenced the way anthropologists approach Pentecostal processes of change, Meyer reports that the Ghanaian Pentecostals with whom she worked enjoined one another to "make a complete break with the past."[6] Injunctions of this type are found among Pentecostal groups in various parts of the world, though their precise meanings can differ in subtle ways. For the Ghanaians whom Meyer studied, for example, a primary concern is breaking with one's kin, whose traditional practices open one to demonic possession.[7] In Latin America, by contrast, one finds that converts stress the need for people, in particular, men, to leave behind personal practices such as drinking and adultery that are associated with the acquisition of male prestige.[8] In yet other cases in Latin America, Africa, and elsewhere, there is an emphasis on the need for people to open a chasm between themselves and the society around them more generally, leaving behind in particular their identification with secular social roles connected with class and ethnicity (and in some respects gender as well).[9] While in each of these cases the line separating the convert's new life from his or her old one is drawn in a different place, all of them share an emphasis on the need to draw such lines—a need for converts to fashion themselves as new kinds of people, different from what they had been before.

Along with requiring that converts embrace discontinuity in their personal lives and senses of themselves, Pentecostalism frequently calls for discontinuity in the cultural realm as well. As Dombrowski has put it in his study of native North American Pentecostals, Pentecostalism is frequently a culture "against culture."[10] What is at issue in the cultural dimension is not just a change in personal behavior but also a disavowal of the importance of traditional beliefs and values—a break, as Droogers puts it, with the "dominant culture."[11] This often takes the form of a rejection of a traditional ritual life aimed at ancestors and other kinds of spirits—a ritual life that in many places did much of the work of setting the moral tone of daily life. Another form this cultural rupture can take is the overthrow of local traditions of historical narrative in favor of a new historical sensibility in which groups situate themselves within the universal Christian rendering of the past. Ancestral figures and local culture heroes fade from the scene as people come to rethink their past in terms of a move from darkness to light. Finally, this kind of rupture can be inscribed on the cultured landscape as practices of spiritual warfare aim to erase the vestiges of tradition carried by nature spirits and other spirits of place.[12]

Meyer's work has also been pivotal in the development of the literature on Pentecostal cultural disjunction.[13] Her key point in this regard has been that Pentecostalism does not lead converts to doubt the existence or power of traditional spiritual beings but rather to demonize them by defining them as wholly evil. Many discourses of change that circulate widely in contemporary global culture, discourses concerning modernization, development, and many forms of Christianity, proclaim that the spirits that populate people's traditions are illusory. But this is not the tack Pentecostalism takes. Instead, as I have put it elsewhere, Pentecostalism preserves traditional spiritual ontologies at the same time that it demonizes them. This allows it, as Meyer has noted, to make of demonization—its brand of cultural critique—a constant practice rather than one that does the job of eradicating the spirits of the past at conversion and then fades away.[14] In constantly recalling the past under the sign of demonization, Pentecostal efforts to create discontinuity foster their own practices of remembering and continuity, albeit ones that are different from those anthropologists generally associate with the reproduction of tradition. This means that even as anthropologists have been alert to the emphasis on discontinuity within Pentecostal culture, they have been challenged by studying Pentecostals to develop new ways of thinking about processes of cultural continuity as well.

A final kind of discontinuity Pentecostalism sometimes promotes is that related to active millenarianism. Many Pentecostal groups await the second coming as an imminent event.[15] It is interesting to note in passing that of all those features of Pentecostalism taken as definitional of this kind of faith—the belief that Jesus offers salvation, that Jesus heals, that Jesus baptizes with the Holy Spirit, and that Jesus is coming again—the millenarian one is most variable in its presence.[16] Although the first three features are in evidence almost everywhere Pentecostalism is found, many Pentecostal groups are not actively millenarian. Explaining why active millenarianism is present in some cases and not others, given that the ideas underpinning it are always present among Pentecostals, is an open research question of great interest. Given that their discipline has a large and distinguished literature on millenarianism, one hopes that anthropologists will look into this topic further in the future. Here, however, I only want to make the point that Pentecostal millenarianism, where it does appear, constitutes another promotion of rupture, though this time with the collective present, not with the personal or cultural past.

While the Pentecostal stress on rupture across these three dimensions—the personal, the cultural, and the eschatological—exists on the ideological level in the form of a host of cultural models of radical change, it is important to note that it also appears regularly at the level of action. This is so because Pentecostals routinely enact the importance of rupture in ritual practices that aim to make disjuncture a constant theme in the practice of everyday life. I have elsewhere called these rites "rituals of rupture."[17] They range from rites of deliverance that work to disconnect people from past relationships[18] to the Malawian rituals designed to "seal off" believers from the wider society that van Dijk discusses.[19] So too do all of the rituals of praying, waiting, and purifying that make up the millenarian practice of preparing for and aiming to bring about a future that will be disjoint from the present.[20] And, of course, conversion rituals such as baptism are also rituals of rupture,[21] as is tongue speaking when it is understood as a second baptism in classical Pentecostalism and some Charismatic churches, in which it serves as what Gerlach and Hine call a "bridge-burning act" that sets people who experience it apart from those with whom they associated in the past.[22] Finally, and perhaps most prominently today, the rituals of spiritual warfare I alluded to above also qualify as rituals of rupture in their efforts to radically change the landscapes on which they are undertaken.

The thoroughgoing emphasis on rupture in Pentecostal thought and practice renders it culturally distinctive. Anthropologists have, as I have just discussed, done a good job of describing the ways Pentecostals imagine and ritualize discontinuity, but they have struggled somewhat in trying to find a way to characterize Pentecostal culture overall. I have already mentioned Dombrowski's suggestion that it is a culture against culture, and in the past I have framed it, as I have here, as a culture of discontinuity.[23] Meyer, making a similar point, has represented it as a culture that keeps the past alive in order to persistently define itself against that past.[24] Most recently, Coleman has characterized Pentecostal cultures as "'part-cultures,'" ones that present "worldviews . . . often in tension with the values of any given host society."[25]

What unites all of these definitional attempts is an insistence that Pentecostal culture be seen as marked by tension with whatever existed before its arrival. The existence of cultural tension, however, is not in and of itself what makes Pentecostal culture unique. Anthropologists have long argued that most cultures are marked by contradictions between different values and ideas and that these contradictions often lead to tensions. Yet at the same time they have also regularly explained how in most cultures these tensions are attenuated by having contradictory values hold in different contexts, or apply to different kinds of people. What distinguishes Pentecostal culture from others is that it does little to reduce such tensions but rather encourages and feeds off them.[26] Indeed, Pentecostals often appear to possess a duplex culture, consisting of Pentecostal ideas and values on one level and the ideas and values converts define themselves by rejecting on another. It is this kind of dual culture, one marked by tensions that give it life rather than sap it of strength, that makes Pentecostalism so culturally distinctive. This point is important because anthropologists today commonly assert that all cultures are made up of bits and pieces of varied origin—all cultures are, they now say, hybrid. But few cultures are marked by the kinds of enduring, stable tensions between parts of disparate origin that are so evident in Pentecostal cultural formations, and fewer still thrive on such tension.

Before going on to look at how people live Pentecostal lives, I want to point out that, along with its focus on discontinuity and tension, there is one additional feature that stands out when Pentecostalism is compared to other cultures, particularly when it is compared to other religious movements. This feature relates to the way Pentecostalism spreads as a culture. Anthropologists tend to imagine that major movements of cultural change, particularly those that are religious in background, will be directed by powerful Charismatic leaders. This image is at the heart of revitalization theory, one of the classic anthropological approaches to movements of radical religious change, and has greatly shaped the study of Melanesian cargo cults, one of the most exhaustively studied kinds of change movements, as well.[27] In direct contrast to this image, Pentecostal movements tend to be locally led and to produce numerous religious leaders with limited authority rather than a few extremely powerful charismatic giants. In one of the earliest anthropological studies of Pentecostalism, Gerlach and Hine characterized its social organization as decentralized, segmented, and reticulate.[28] In terms of leadership, decentralization means that Pentecostal movements can be seen as acephalous (without leaders) or polycephalous (with many leaders) but not as possessing strong central leaders. Segmentation refers to the existence of many similar local groups, each responsible for itself, while the idea of reticulation points to the diverse connections between segments. Csordas has explored the cultural logic of this sort of decentralized organization, and he lays out his main point nicely when he writes that "in principle spiritual gifts are available to all Charismatics, and this precludes their exclusive adherence to a single individual."[29] He then goes on to rethink Weber's notion of charisma to make it suitable for analyzing situations in which charisma is shot through the social order rather than the possession of only a few. I have also recently tried to look at this question, though in more Durkheimian terms focused on ritual.[30]

A question that naturally arises in the wake of this discussion of the nature of Pentecostal culture is why people would want to adopt a culture that insists so much on discontinuity and that promotes such a high level of tension, and why they would come to do so even in the absence of overarching charismatic leaders adept at constructing a centrally organized movement. The usual answer to this question among anthropologists is similar to the one given by most social scientists: the people who find Pentecostalism appealing tend to be those whose lives have already been subject to a good deal of discontinuity and tension. It is a religion of rural migrants to towns and cities, or of people who have remained rural but have been shaken out of their traditional routines by colonialism and globalization. In short, the answers that come most quickly to mind are the by now well known ones about deprivation and disorganization. I do not want to dwell on these arguments here. I find them both somewhat inescapable and also not wholly compelling.[31] Furthermore, they do not constitute an approach to which anthropologists have added much that is new. Instead of devoting more space to them here, I want simply to note their presence and to follow most anthropologists in changing the question from Why convert to Pentecostalism? to How do people live with Pentecostalism after they have converted to it? What is it like to live in a culture in which the production of discontinuity is a goal and the existence of cultural tensions is taken for granted and actively embraced? This brings me to the topic of Pentecostalism as lived religion, the subject of the next section.

PENTECOSTALISM AS LIVED RELIGION

If anthropology's greatest contribution to modern thought has been the idea of culture, its unique method of research runs a close second. Sometimes called "the ethnographic method," or "participant observation," or simply "fieldwork," this method consists of living with people and of trying to conduct one's life as much as possible on their terms. Clifford Geertz once referred to it as "deep hanging out." In the present context, this method is important for the way it leads anthropologists to study people's daily lives. To be sure, anthropologists care about people's ideas, and they attend carefully to the public symbolic order that shapes them, but they also examine how those ideas and symbols hang together in practice. When it comes to Pentecostalism, this means that anthropologists have studied what those in religious studies and history sometimes call "lived religion." They study Pentecostalism not just as something people believe but also as something people do. In this section I want to consider some of the areas of lived Pentecostalism that have been important foci of anthropological scholarship. The topics I discuss include Pentecostal approaches to ritual, the body, language, morality, and media.

In 2004 I observed that "from an anthropological perspective," the absence of studies focused on ritual "represents probably the greatest lacuna in the work done thus far."[32] A recent conference titled "Ritual Practice in Charismatic Christianity," organized by Martin Lindhardt, took its bearings from a similar premise. It is not hard to adduce at least one important reason why this lacuna might exist. As the social scientifically trained Pentecostal theologian Albrecht has noted, "Pentecostals themselves have often objected to or reject[ed] the term 'ritual' and its implied conceptualization."[33] Placing a high value on spontaneity and authenticity, Pentecostals condemn ritual as too routine, mechanical, or, as Albrecht has it, "'unspiritual.'" Furthermore, the Pentecostal tendency to introduce ritual into almost all domains of social interaction tends to rob believers' ritualized productions of that sense of set-apartness that scholars often see as central to the definition of ritual.[34] Since anthropologists like to take their cues about where to focus from the things the people they work with represent as important, and since they are accustomed to looking for rituals that announce themselves as such, it has been easy for them to find their attention directed away from this aspect of religious practice.

Yet despite both the lowly status of ritual in Pentecostal self-understanding and the extent to which Pentecostal ritual fails to announce itself as such in ways scholars can easily recognize, it is not difficult to make the argument that a very frequent recourse to ritual is a key aspect of Pentecostal social life. To begin with, if we look carefully, we will see that Pentecostal anti-ritualism is, as Pfeil has noted, itself ritualized.[35] Moreover, to an observer who does not dwell solely on Pentecostal folk theology, it is hard to miss how much of what Pentecostals do with each other easily counts as ritual in terms of its formulaic quality and its directness toward divinity—and this is true even if the forms in question allow for a good deal of spontaneous elaboration of personal content in approaching the divine. Given this, it is easy to concur with Albrecht when he goes on to say that despite their protestations to the contrary, "Pentecostals do in fact, engage in rituals, though they often call them by other names: 'worship services,' 'spiritual practices,' [and] 'Pentecostal distinctives,' for example."[36]

In light of Albrecht's points and the outcome of the recent conference, I have come to rethink somewhat my earlier claim that there is little study of ritual in the anthropological literature on Pentecostalism. It is true that there are no monographs devoted wholly to Pentecostal ritual life, and careful analyses of the symbolic structure of Pentecostal rites are relatively rare.[37] But this does not mean that the importance of ritual to Pentecostalism has not impressed itself on the anthropological record. Indeed, if one looks at that record carefully, it is hard to miss the fact that Pentecostal life is saturated with ritual to an unusual extent. From impromptu prayers to spontaneous outpourings of praise and from healing sessions to major Sunday church services, anthropologists have explored the ritual activities in which Pentecostals invest a good deal of their time.

Csordas has to date done the most to theorize the centrality of ritual in Pentecostalism.[38] He has argued that in Pentecostalism there is little acceptance of a distinction between the sacred and profane—or, putting it in the terms of the previous section, Pentecostals work to maintain a break between themselves and profane life such that they never participate in contexts they define as wholly profane. For this reason, Pentecostals see ritual as relevant in all social domains, and it comes to permeate their everyday life. Consider Pentecostal prayer in this respect. As Csordas notes, prayer is not "restricted to a particular setting, and indeed people may pray at any time or while engaged in any activity."[39] Pentecostals are also liable to deploy other ritual forms, such as song, healing, and praise, in any number of settings. Along with having recourse to ritual in all manner of circumstances, Csordas adds, Pentecostals caught up in active religious movements often engage in ritual intensification—calling for ritual to influence daily life even more thoroughly than it already does. This is an important part of what occurs in revivals and periods of heightened millennial enthusiasm.

Ritual is by nature an embodied practice, and given the ritualization of Pentecostal daily life, it is not surprising that anthropologists have found a concern for the body a second important aspect of Pentecostal lived religion. Csordas's works have again been important here, and along with the role of the body in ritual, he has attended in detail to Pentecostal bodily healing.[40] He and Luhrmann have also stressed the way in which the ritual training of the body is central to the production of the Pentecostal habitus and the ecstatic experiences that so deeply inform it.[41] Others have pointed to the way Pentecostals moralize the body, subjecting it to strict controls and taking its sufferings as signs of moral failure.[42] And finally, there is a growing awareness of the communicative role of the body in Pentecostal communities. As Albrecht has put it, Pentecostal churches are often unadorned because the worshipers themselves become, through the action of the Spirit, icons to be seen by one another. In a related vein, Hoenes has recently done important work on the role of gesture in Pentecostal churches, showing the importance of this form of bodily communication.[43]

As Austin-Broos's work shows, attention to trajectories of historical change can be very valuable in the study of Pentecostal embodiment.[44] Mellor and Shilling's work on the various "re-formations" of the body in Western history is useful in this regard.[45] They trace the transformations between what they describe as the sensuous and participatory Catholic body of the medieval period, the distanced and rational Protestant modern body, and the contemporary "baroque modern" body that combines elements of the previous two.[46] From the point of view of their historical narrative, Pentecostal embodiment clearly fits the emerging baroque modern paradigm. It both celebrates bodily participation during religious rites and subjects the body to strict moralizing controls in high modern fashion in other contexts. Mellor and Shilling also pay a good deal of attention throughout their book to the changing ways in which the mind and body are understood in relationship to one another, and this points to the need to develop the study of Pentecostal notions and practices of the body hand in hand with careful attention to Pentecostal ethnopsychology.[47]

The Pentecostal use of language is a third area in which anthropologists have made good progress in understanding lived aspects of the Pentecostal faith. Anthropologists studying Christianity more generally have remarked on how central speech is to Protestant life.[48] In Pentecostalism, as in much of Protestant-ism, speech is expected both to evidence the kind of spontaneity that points to the presence of the Spirit and to fit the broader formulaic patterns that make it recognizably sacred in character.[49] Various works have either implicitly or explic-itly looked at the ways in which Pentecostals realize both of these seemingly contradictory values in their daily practice, paying particular attention to prayer.[50] Other works have focused on the way Pentecostal language circulates and the effects its circulation is understood to have on believers. Coleman's well-known work is a key example here,[51] but some of Csordas's thinking about the Charis-matic process can be read in this way as well, as can work on media I will discuss later.[52]

Another topic that can perhaps be taken up as part of the study of Pentecostal language is glossolalia, though determining how to classify it is difficult (it can also be seen as ritual, embodied gesture, etc.). Though many anthropologists have touched on glossolalia in suggestive ways as part of their work, and Goodman and Samarin devoted early books to it,[53] I think it is fair to say that we do not yet have a fully contemporary, ethnographically based and ethnographically thorough study of glossolalia in the literature. There is room here to produce a work that would push the anthropology of Pentecostalism in new directions.

Morality is a fourth area that is of evident importance in Pentecostal daily life. Pentecostals often experience their daily lives as arenas of struggle between good and evil, or God and the devil, and they see the cultivation of Spiritually enhanced self-control as an important personal project. In some respects, this very self-conscious focus on the moral stakes of everyday living follows from the Pente-costal emphasis on discontinuity. Converts are well aware of having left a non-Pentecostal moral order behind and they fear that pressures to return to conforming to it will lead them away from their new Pentecostal moral commit-ments. I have elsewhere looked in detail at how the tensions produced by living between different moral orders in this way shapes life in the Pentecostal communi-ties studied by Austin-Broos, Kiernan, and myself.[54] Here I would like to add a further comparative point. While all Pentecostals worry about sin, and most of them tend to moralize large swathes of their daily practice, they can differ pro-foundly in the ways they conceptualize the causes of moral breach. In some places, especially in Africa, the devil is a prominent figure, drawing or pushing people into sin.[55] In other places, and my own work in Melanesia can serve as an example here, there is a far greater emphasis on the fallen nature of human beings, and believers tend to hold their own impulses and desires, rather than the devil per se, responsible for sinful behavior.[56] Anthropologists have not yet determined why one of these patterns occurs in some cases and the other in others, but this is a worthy topic for further comparative investigation, and one concerning which the interested reader will find many resources in the already existing anthropological literature.

A fifth and final feature of Pentecostal daily life that has begun to become prominent in the anthropological literature is the importance of mass media. From its birth in the early twentieth century, Pentecostalism has made extensive use of mass media both to keep the segments of its far-flung networks in contact with one another and to reach the unconverted. Among anthropologists, Coleman has attended most closely to the global aspects of the production and circulation of mass media, and he has examined the ideas about language, communication, and selfhood that underpin it.[57] On the reception end, Wiegele has produced a sensitive study of the way prosperity gospel followers in the Philippines engage the extensive media productions of their church.[58] She explores the way radio broadcasts extend sacred space, bringing the sacred into the home.[59] Meyer, in publications stemming from a research project focused on the production and reception of Ghanaian Pentecostal films, has argued that Pentecostal-themed media can also direct their sacralizing force in the other direction: not just into the home, but also throughout secular public space.[60] When they do so, they lend public culture in places like Ghana what she calls a Pentecostalite style. Wiegele too takes some note of this capture of public space, which she sees as a project of claiming it for religious purposes. Meyer offers a caution here, however, noting that those who produce and consume Pentecostalite culture are not always committed church members: public space may be dusted with religious imagery without there being a great up-tick in the level of piety throughout the broader population. Both Wiegele's and Meyer's views are surely correct. From the perspective of converts, we need to analyze the spectacular spread of Pentecostal media as among other things an important aspect of Pentecostals' more general effort to make all of life, public life included, an engagement with the sacred. From the perspective of the public more broadly, we also need to examine the way Pentecostal media can create meaningful and entertaining worlds for those who do not subscribe to the religion from which it draws its themes and imagery and can in doing so change the curve of public space.

The five areas of Pentecostal life I have discussed—ritual, embodiment, language, morality, and media—are not discrete. Ghanaian Pentecostal films are full of moralizing messages and rely on the embodied nature of Pentecostal life to make their narratives visibly gripping. Pentecostal ritual engages language and the body to produce events that are frequently focused on moral reform and that are regularly broadcast to those beyond the church walls. Given the interrelation of these areas, specialized study in each of them has enriched the anthropology of Pentecostalism as a whole and has moved the best current ethnographies ever closer to giving fully rounded portraits of Pentecostalism as a lived religion.

PENTECOSTALISM AND MODERNITY

The first section of this chapter focused on the processes of cultural change Pentecostalism frequently introduces in the societies into which is spreads. I highlighted the tendency for Pentecostalism to lead people to seek to introduce discontinuities with the past in their personal and cultural lives and with the future in their millenarian yearnings. The second section looked at how Pentecostalism shapes the everyday lives of believers. This final section builds on the previous ones to consider what kind of culture Pentecostal ideologies of discontinuity and Pentecostal lived practices produce. A major question anthropologists have asked along these lines is whether this culture is best understood as a modern one.

The question of Pentecostalism's relation to modernity is a persistent one precisely because it is not easy to answer. From some perspectives, Pentecostalism clearly looks modern. Its emphasis on discontinuity, for example, maps neatly onto modernist ideas about the need for radical change and about transformation as progress. Yet from other vantage points, it equally looks to be something other than modern. Its frank supernaturalism and commitment to ontological preservation, to take two cases in point, give it a "premodern" cast, while its wide dispersal of authority and the network quality of its social organization have led some to classify it as postmodern.[61] My goal in what follows is not to settle the issue of Pentecostalism's relationship to modernity in anything like final terms. Instead, I want to look at a few things anthropologists have discovered about the ways Pentecostal culture, especially but not exclusively as it appears outside the West, relates to what we might take in rough-and-ready terms to be some features of Western modernity. The features I consider are modern formations of individualism, gender, economy, and politics.

A number of anthropologists have observed that Pentecostalism generally introduces some form of individualism into the cultures of its converts. Like modernity itself, individualism is not a concept with a single definition, and authors use it in different ways in relation to Pentecostalism. Surveying the literature on African Pentecostalism, Meyer has seen the cutting of kinship ties in rituals of deliverance as "a symbolic creation of the modern individual subject," and many others have stressed how such efforts to disembed the individual from extended family networks make good individualist sense for urban migrants trying to succeed in the capitalist market economy.[62] In my work in Papua New Guinea among the Urapmin, a group of rural Pentecostal subsistence farmers with little market engagement, I found that individualism expressed itself most fully in an imagined economy of salvation. People understood that each person was responsible for saving himself or herself. Salvation could not be shared between friends or among family members. As one eloquent leader put it, "My wife can't break off part of her belief and give it to me." The Urapmin fully grasp the individualism of this model of salvation, and they work toward it, even as they find it difficult to square this individualism with other aspects of their lives.[63] The study of Pentecostal individualism is destined to grow in importance and sophistication in the future. Even as it does so, however, it is important to remember, as Meyer points out, that we also need to study the innovative ways Pentecostals form communities.[64] This is a point I will return to when I discuss economic issues below.

Turning to gender, it is worth noting at the outset that the question of whether or not Pentecostalism has generated among converts outside the West something that resembles Western notions of gender equality has been one of the most thoroughly debated in the literature. It has been especially important in writings on Pentecostalism in Latin America. I cannot do justice to this topic in the space available here but will simply point to a few main themes.[65]

The acknowledged classic in this field is Brusco's book, *The Reformation of Machismo*.[66] Based on research in Colombia, Brusco argues that Pentecostalism "domesticates" men, turning their attention to the home and directing them away from the alcohol consumption and adultery that are so much a part of the male prestige sphere of the street. Since women also value the home, this change in male interests and behavior is of direct benefit to them. Hence, Brusco argues, Pentecostalism in Colombia can be seen as a form of "female collective action" aimed at improving the social conditions under which women live.[67] Other anthropologists have gone beyond Brusco to note that the transformations Pentecostalism makes in women's lives are relevant not only at home. They point out that the egalitarian logic of inspiration in Pentecostal churches, in which any member may receive gifts of the Spirit, opens up a number of leadership roles to women. These are often roles such as healer, lay preacher, or evangelist that are grounded in Charismatic authority, but they also include some formal positions of leadership in church groups.[68] In its drive toward both companionate marriage and something approaching gender equality in the religious realm, Pentecostalism seems to be moving converts into accord with modern gender ideologies in their Western liberal form.

Even as there is a good deal of evidence pointing to this modernizing trajectory in the realm of gender, many scholars have noted that Pentecostals also tend to embrace traditional Pauline notions of patriarchy, in which women are expected to subordinate themselves to men. They have found this difficult to reconcile with a reading of Pentecostalism as a liberating force. A number of careful studies have helped address this issue by examining in great detail Pentecostal patriarchy in practice in both Latin America and the United States.[69] What they have found is that while patriarchal ideas are accepted by both Pentecostal men and women, taken together with the rest of Pentecostal beliefs they cohere into what Smilde nicely calls a distinct "religiously bounded patriarchy."[70] In this kind of patriarchy, women see themselves as answering ultimately to God, not to the men in their lives. It is true that they must be obedient when their husbands and other men make demands that are in keeping with their understandings of God's will, but they must equally disobey their husbands and other men who push them to behave in sinful ways. Furthermore, they are authorized to directly and publicly criticize men who themselves engage in sinful behavior. Mariz and Machado, working in Brazil, have pointed to these kinds of findings and suggested that to judge them as emancipatory or not on the basis of Western liberal political norms is a mistake.[71] Instead, they say, we should examine them for evidence of the religiously inflected models of oppression and liberation that matter to the Pentecostals we study. This assertion is nicely in keeping with the traditional goals of anthropological research, which have been to understand people as fully as possible on their own terms.

I turn now to looking at Pentecostal influence on economic thought and behavior. While there is some discussion in Pentecostal studies about the extent to which Pentecostalism may play a role in modernizing people's economic lives by instilling in them something like Weber's Protestant ethic, little of this work has been done by anthropologists.[72] For this reason, I am going to set this issue aside and focus my brief discussion here on the economic impacts of the prosperity gospel—the kind of Pentecostalism that is attracting the greatest anthropological attention at the moment. As is now widely known, the terms *prosperity gospel* and *faith gospel* refer to those forms of Charismatic Christianity in which believers expect God to give them physical health and material wealth on earth in the present, as well as a place in heaven in the future. In order to realize these benefits, prosperity gospel followers, who are often quite poor, are enjoined to tithe and then to expect a great return on their investment. As many scholars have shown, the rhetoric of prosperity gospel sermons dwells on the ways gifts of belief and money to God ensure success in life.

The first impulse anthropologists have had when confronted with the massive popularity of the prosperity gospel in the Global South has been to assume that it appeals to people because it makes a kind of mystical sense of, and promises some security in the face of, the kind of chaotic economic circumstances in which they live. It is a kind of camera obscura portrait of neoliberal capitalism as it is experienced full force in the structurally adjusted cities of the periphery of the global capitalist system—where some people get rich, but it is hard to figure out how or why, and where the vast majority of people are poor and becoming poorer. The Comaroffs offer the most convincing account along these lines, grouping the prosperity gospel with other "occult economies" and situating it in relation to the neoliberal condition in Africa and elsewhere.[73]

As compelling as is the argument that the prosperity gospel is a way of making sense of capitalism in the places where that economic system most spectacularly fails to contribute to a flourishing social life, there is room for another interpretation. Coleman, one of the first anthropologists to study a prosperity gospel church in detail, has emphasized the importance of the notion of the gift in the rhetoric and thinking of those who belong to the Swedish Word of Life Church he studied.[74] Members of the church, he argues, understand themselves to be involved in something like a complex gift exchange system of the kind first discussed by Malinowski[75] and Mauss[76] and later elaborated in great detail by Lévi-Strauss.[77] They give to God, then await a return gift—a gift that may not come directly from God but may be given by another of God's subjects who does the original giver a kindness. As Wiegele has shown in her very nicely observed study of prosperity believers in the Philippines, members of El Shaddai similarly learn to reinterpret all the good things that happen to them as gifts God has delivered, either directly or through others, in return for the tithes they make.[78]

This line of interpretation that sees the prosperity gospel as shot through with gift economy rather than commodity economy thinking has recently been pushed forward in an important paper by Haynes.[79] She begins by drawing on work on the "villagization" of urban Africa. Scholars who speak of villagization point to the development of decidedly villagelike practices of gift giving and widespread mutual support that have become prominent in some African cities in the wake of the failure of the market economy to provide for people's needs in the region. Haynes argues that the prosperity gospel churches appeal to people not because of the material success they promise—for it is clear that this almost always fails to arrive—but rather for the training they provide in how to conceptualize and operate an economy of gifts. Prosperity churches mirror and explicitly demand the very kinds of practices of gift giving and trust that young urban Africans with little experience of rural life need to learn if they are to find a place for themselves in the gift economies that are coming to prominence all around them. They thus speak directly to people's current experience, and it is this relevance, Haynes suggests, that accounts at least in part for their current popularity.

The final topic I want to touch on briefly in this section on modernity is the political impact of Pentecostalism. Here the questions scholars most often ask have to do with whether Pentecostalism leads to quietism or to support for movements of social justice, and whether or not its form of church life, which at least sometimes has an egalitarian streak, might be a spur to democratization. Such questions have been most forcefully and influentially raised by Martin, and they have been most frequently examined in Latin America, with some work appearing from Africa and elsewhere as well.[80] Much of this work is done by sociologists and political scientists, and it runs a range from strongly empirical in focus to almost wholly speculative. Since I assume these issues will be taken up extensively by others in this volume, I have decided not to dwell on them here. Instead, I want to make two linked points in relation to these questions. The first is that, as I read the literature, the results of studies of the way Pentecostalism shapes political attitudes and practices is at this point utterly inconclusive. The second is that, given this fact, there is a great need for the kind of careful studies anthropologists can provide of the details of Pentecostal political culture and of the way religious ideas imbricate with political ones within it. Burdick's well-known books on Brazil provide one example of this kind of work,[81] as does Kamsteeg's important study of Chile, which is the first detailed one we have of a Pentecostal group committed to working for social justice.[82]

It is fitting that I conclude this section on modernity with the observation that the question of whether or not Pentecostalism is a modernizing force in the political realm can only be answered inconclusively. For I think this claim can be generalized: in spite of all the work anthropologists and others have done on the relation of Pentecostalism to modernity, the nature of this relationship in general is one about which we have reached few settled conclusions. When Pentecostalism is introduced in contexts outside the West, it tends to push some things in more modern directions than they were headed before. It puts in place some individualist ideas, for example, and some ideas about gender equality and about the desirability of wide access to leadership positions in a world where the Holy Spirit can inspire anyone. At that same time, however, it also appears to head in some directions that do not look canonically modern. Its supernaturalism is one case in point, but so is its tendency toward unabashed (even if religiously bounded) patriarchy. And in its prosperity guise, its push to build new communities founded on gift exchange runs directly counter to market norms.

One could say, and I think with some justification, that this lack of neat fit between Pentecostalism and modernity is of limited import because social scientists tend to work with fuzzy, ever-shifting, and often only implicit definitions of modernity. As Droogers has argued is more generally the case in studies of Pentecostalism, it may be the diversity of our own ways of defining modernity that makes Pentecostalism look paradoxical on this score.[83] But at the very least, I think the studies we already have do warrant a slightly more powerful formulation that would go something like this: Pentecostalism was born in modernity and could not exist without it; at the same time, however, it is something other than simply modern. It clearly helps people cope with many of the disorienting aspects of modernity, but it does not necessarily lead them to single-mindedly quest to build modern lives in the way, say, market ideology does. Future work in the anthropology of Pentecostalism is thus destined to move beyond the kind of is-it-modern-or-is-it-not questions I have taken from some parts of the literature and used to organize this section and will likely take up instead a careful accounting of both the modernist impulses and something-other-than-modern counterimpulses that make of Pentecostalism something genuinely new.

One emerging area of research that is destined to feed strongly into debates about Pentecostalism and modernity in the future is that focused on the role of Pentecostalism in the lives of immigrants. As Martin has argued, Pentecostalism is a "religious 'movement' accompanying and facilitating the movement of people."[84] Anthropologists have begun to study migrant Pentecostal churches in Europe and North America, and work of this kind is poised to be a growing area of interest in the future. The work of scholars such as van Dijk has already indicated that such research will encourage new thinking about the ways in which Pentecostalism fosters changes in ideas about individualism, gender, economy, and politics that in turn transform in complex ways believers' relationship to modernity, however we choose to define that term.[85]

CONCLUSION

As I suggested at the outset, I have approached the writing of this chapter as a chance to try to disentangle the elaborately interdisciplinary discourse of Pentecostal studies to determine what contributions to it might have been made by distinctly anthropological threads. The three threads I have pulled out here are those dealing with Pentecostal cultural process, everyday life, and relation to modernity. In the first two areas anthropology has made, I think, unique contributions. It has shown that Pentecostalism, with its emphasis on discontinuity, shapes cultural process by introducing novel dynamics of cultural change. It has also laid out in increasingly rich detail the substance of Pentecostalism as lived religion, showing how ritual, embodiment, language use, moral concern, and media production and consumption work together to give Pentecostal life its distinctive shape. The third thread—that which looks at the link between Pentecostalism and modernity—has been equally fertile, but in a different way. Rather than anthropologists making their contribution on their own, as they have in some respects done in the first two areas, in this one they have tended to perform one of their key interdisciplinary roles—that of taking broad generalizations offered up by those in other fields and complicating them through close attention to comparative detail. They have, that is to say, productively nuanced rather than settled the debate about Pentecostalism and modernity.

I have scattered throughout this chapter observations concerning what I consider promising topics or approaches for future work in the anthropological study of Pentecostalism. In conclusion, then, I will just mention one interdisciplinary engagement I think anthropologists have missed. This is the one with Pentecostal theologians. As Pentecostal theology continues to grow and come into its own, I think there is great promise for dialogue here. Anthropologists know a lot about various aspects of Pentecostal folk theology. But we often examine that theology one topic at a time. Thus, for instance, someone studying embodiment will learn a good deal about Pentecostal folk theories of embodiment but will perhaps learn less about Pentecostal folk theology of media, or of morality. Pentecostal theologians may, among other things, teach us to attend more carefully to the intellectual life of the Pentecostals we study and to look for the ways their thought coheres as a whole. This is precisely the kind of new engagement that I hope an at once disciplinary and interdisciplinary volume like this one may serve to foster.

NOTES

1. Mark A. Noll, "Foreword: American Past and World Present in the Search for Evangelical Identity," in *Pilgrims on the Sawdust Trail: Evangelical Ecumenism and the Quest for Christian Identity,* ed. T. George (Grand Rapids: Baker Academic, 2004), 12.

2. "Christianity Reborn," *Economist,* December 23, 2006, 48–50.

3. Birgit Meyer, "Christianity in Africa: From African Independent to Pentecostal-Charismatic Churches," *Annual Review of Anthropology* 33 (2004): 447–74; Joel Robbins, "The Globalization of Pentecostal and Charismatic Christianity," *Annual Review of Anthropology* 33 (2004): 117–43.

4. Anthony D. Buckley and Mary Catherine Kenney, *Negotiating Identity: Rhetoric, Metaphor, and Social Drama in Northern Ireland* (Washington, DC: Smithsonian Institution Press, 1995), 137.

5. Joel Robbins, "On the Paradoxes of Global Pentecostalism and the Perils of Continuity Thinking," *Religion* 33:3 (2003): 221–31.

6. Birgit Meyer, "'Make a Complete Break with the Past': Memory and Postcolonial Modernity in Ghanaian Pentecostal Discourse," in *Memory and the Postcolony: African Anthropology and the Critique of Power,* ed. R. Werbner (London: Zed Books, 1998), 182–208.

7. Meyer, "'Make a Complete Break'"; Birgit Meyer, *Translating the Devil: Religion and Modernity among the Ewe in Ghana* (Trenton: Africa World Press, 1999).

8. Elizabeth E. Brusco, *The Reformation of Machismo: Evangelical Conversion and Gender in Colombia* (Austin: University of Texas Press, 1995); John Burdick, *Blessed Anastácia: Women, Race, and Popular Christianity in Brazil* (New York: Routledge, 1998).

9. Burdick, *Blessed Anastácia*; André Droogers, "Globalisation and Pentecostal Studies," in *Between Babel and Pentecost: Transnational Pentecostalism in Africa and Latin America,* ed. A. Corten and R. Marshall-Fratani (Bloomington: IUP, 2001), 45; Paul Freston, "Evangelicalism and Globalization: General Observations and some Latin American Dimensions," in *A Global Faith: Essays on Evangelicalism and Globalization,* ed. M. Hutchinson and O. Kalu (Sydney: Centre for the Study of Australian Christianity, 1998), 69–88; Joel Robbins, "On Reading 'World News': Apocalyptic Narrative, Negative Nationalism, and Transnational Christianity in a Papua New Guinea Society," *Social Analysis* 42:2 (1998): 103–30; Rijk van Dijk, "Pentecostalism, Cultural Memory and the State: Contested Representations of Time in Pentecostal Malawi," in Werber, *Memory and the Postcolony,* 155–81.

10. Kirk Dombrowski, *Against Culture: Development, Politics, and Religion in Indian Alaska* (Lincoln: University of Nebraska Press, 2001).

11. Droogers, "Globalisation and Pentecostal Studies," 45.

12. Jean DeBernardi, "Spiritual Warfare and Territorial Spirits: The Globalization and Localisation of a 'Practical Theology,'" *Religious Studies and Theology* 18:2 (1999): 66–96; Dan Jorgensen, "Third Wave Evangelism and the Politics of the Global in Papua New Guinea: Spiritual Warfare and the Recreation of Place in Telefolmin," *Oceania* 75:4 (2005): 444–61; Joel Robbins, "On Giving Ground: Globalization, Religion, and Territorial Detachment in a Papua New Guinea Society," in *Territoriality*

and Conflict in an Era of Globalization, ed. M. Kahler and B. Walter (Cambridge: CUP, 2006), 62–84.

13. Birgit Meyer, "Beyond Syncretism: Translation and Diabolization in the Appropriation of Protestantism in Africa," in *Syncretism/Anti-Syncretism: The Politics of Religious Synthesis,* ed. C. Stewart and R. Shaw (London: Routledge, 1994), 45–68; Meyer, *Translating the Devil.*

14. Meyer, *Translating the Devil.*

15. Joel Robbins, *Becoming Sinners: Christianity and Moral Torment in a Papua New Guinea Society* (Berkeley: UCP, 2004); Thomas J. Csordas, *The Sacred Self: A Cultural Phenomenology of Charismatic Healing* (Berkeley: UCP, 1994).

16. Donald W. Dayton, *Theological Roots of Pentecostalism* (Peabody, MA: Hendrickson, 1987).

17. Robbins, "Paradoxes," 224.

18. Meyer, "'Make a Complete Break'"; Paul Gifford, *Ghana's New Christianity: Pentecostalism in a Globalizing African Economy* (Bloomington: IUP, 2004).

19. Van Dijk, "Pentecostalism."

20. Robbins, *Becoming Sinners.*

21. Malcolm Ruel, *Belief, Ritual and the Securing of Life: Reflexive Essays on a Bantu Religion* (Leiden: Brill, 1997), 41–42.

22. Luther P. Gerlach and Virginia H. Hine, *People, Power, Change: Movements of Social Transformation* (Indianapolis: Bobbs-Merrill, 1970), 124–25.

23. Robbins, "Paradoxes"; John Burdick, *Looking for God in Brazil: The Progressive Catholic Church in Urban Brazil's Religious Arena* (Berkeley: UCP, 1993).

24. Meyer, *Translating the Devil.*

25. Simon Coleman, "Studying 'Global' Pentecostalism: Tensions, Representations and Opportunities," *PentecoStudies* 5:1 (2006): 1–17.

26. André Droogers, "Paradoxical Views on a Paradoxical Religion: Models for the Explanation of Pentecostal Expansion in Brazil and Chile," in *More than Opium: An Anthropological Approach to Latin American and Caribbean Pentecostal Practice,* ed. B. Boudewijnse, A. Droogers, and F. Kamsteeg (Lanham, MD: Scarecrow Press, 1998), 9.

27. Anthony F.C. Wallace, *Revitalizations and Mazeways: Essays on Cultural Change,* vol. 1, ed. Robert S. Grumet (Lincoln: University of Nebraska Press, 2003).

28. Gerlach and Hine, *People, Power, Change,* 34 ff.

29. Thomas J. Csordas, *Language, Charisma, and Creativity: The Ritual Life of a Religious Movement* (Berkeley: UCP, 1997), 133.

30. Joel Robbins, "Pentecostal Ritual and the Spirit of Globalization: On the Social Productivity of Ritual Forms," *Social Analysis* 53:1 (2009) 55–56.

31. Robbins, "Globalization," 123–27; Virginia H. Hine, "The Deprivation and Disorganization Theories of Social Movements," in *Religious Movements in Contemporary America,* ed. I.I. Zaretsky and M.P. Leone (Princeton: Princeton University Press, 1974), 646–61; Stephen J. Hunt, "Deprivation and Western Pentecostalism Revisited: The Case of 'Classical' Pentecostalism," *PentecoStudies* 1:1 (2002): 1–32; Stephen J. Hunt, "Deprivation and Western Pentecostalism Revisited: Neo-Pentecostalism," *PentecoStudies* 1:2 (2002): 1–29.

32. Robbins, "Globalization," 126.

33. Daniel E. Albrecht, *Rites in the Spirit: A Ritual Approach to Pentecostal/Charismatic Spirituality* (Sheffield: SAP, 1999), 21.

34. Catherine Bell, *Ritual Theory, Ritual Practice* (New York: OUP, 1992).

35. Gretchen Pfeil, "Imperfect Vessels: Emotion and Rituals of Anti-Ritual in American Pentecostal and Charismatic Devotional Life," in *Practicing the Faith: The Ritual Life of Pentecostal-Charismatic Christianity,* ed. R. Lindhardt (New York: Berghahn, forthcoming).

36. Albrecht, *Rites in the Spirit*, 21–22.

37. Though see Diane J. Austin-Broos, *Jamaica Genesis: Religion and the Politics of Moral Order* (Chicago: University Chicago Press, 1997); Csordas, *Language, Charisma, and Creativity*; J. P. Kiernan, "The Work of Zion: An Analysis of an African Zionist Ritual," *Africa* 46:4 (1976): 340–56; Meyer, *Translating the Devil*; Robbins, *Becoming Sinners*.

38. Csordas, *Language, Charisma, and Creativity*.

39. Csordas, *Language, Charisma, and Creativity*, 175.

40. Csordas, *The Sacred Self*.

41. Csordas, *Language, Charisma, and Creativity*; Tanya M. Luhrmann, "Metakinesis: How God Becomes Intimate in Contemporary U.S. Christianity," *American Anthropologist* 106:3 (2004): 518–28.

42. Austin-Broos, *Jamaica Genesis*; Paul Brodwin, *Medicine and Morality in Haiti: The Contest for Healing Power* (Cambridge: CUP, 1996).

43. Eric Hoenes del Pinal, "Gestural Ideology? Gesture, Body Movement and Language Ideology among Q'eqchi'-Maya Catholics," paper presented at the Biennial Meeting of the Society for the Anthropology of Religion, Phoenix, April 13–16, 2007.

44. Austin-Broos, *Jamaica Genesis*.

45. Philip A. Mellor and Chris Shilling, *Re-Forming the Body: Religion, Community and Modernity* (London: Sage, 1997).

46. Mellor and Shilling, *Re-Forming the Body*, 8–13; Simon Coleman, "Materializing the Self: Words and Gifts in the Construction of Charismatic Protestant Identity," in *The Anthropology of Christianity*, ed. F. Cannell (Durham: Duke University Press, 2006), 163–84.

47. Csordas, *Sacred Self*; Robbins, *Becoming Sinners*.

48. Webb Keane, *Moderns: Freedom and Fetish in the Mission Encounter Christian* (Berkeley: UCP, 2007); Joel Robbins, "God Is Nothing but Talk: Modernity, Language and Prayer in a Papua New Guinea Society," *American Anthropologist* 103:4 (2001): 901–12.

49. Csordas, *Language, Charisma, and Creativity*; Robin A. Shoaps, "'Pray Earnestly': The Textual Construction of Personal Involvement in Pentecostal Prayer and Song," *Journal of Linguistic Anthropology* 12:1 (2002): 34–71.

50. Robbins, "God Is Nothing but Talk"; Shoaps, "'Pray Earnestly.'"

51. Coleman, "Materializing the Self"; Simon Coleman, *The Globalisation of Charismatic Christianity* (Cambridge: CUP, 2000); Simon Coleman, "The Charismatic Gift," *Journal of the Royal Anthropological Institute* 10:2 (2004): 421–42.

52. Csordas, *Language, Charisma, and Creativity*.

53. Felicitas D. Goodman, *Speaking in Tongues: A Cross-Cultural Study of Glossolalia* (Chicago: University of Chicago Press, 1972); William J. Samarin, *Tongues of Men and Angels: The Religious Language of Pentecostalism* (New York: Macmillan, 1972).

54. Austin-Broos, *Jamaica Genesis*; J. P. Kiernan, "Images of Rejection in the Construction of Morality: Satan and Sorcerer as Moral Signposts in the Social Landscape of Urban Zionists," *Social Anthropology* 5:3 (1997): 243–54; Robbins, *Becoming Sinners*, 320–24.

55. Meyer, *Translating the Devil*.

56. Robbins, *Becoming Sinners*.

57. Coleman, *Globalisation*; Coleman, "Materializing the Self."

58. Katharine L. Wiegele, *Investing in Miracles: El Shaddai and the Transformation of Popular Catholicism in the Philippines* (Honolulu: University of Hawai'i Press, 2005).

59. Wiegele, *Investing in Miracles*, 50.

60. Birgit Meyer, "'Praise the Lord': Popular Cinema and Pentecostalite Style in Ghana's New Public Sphere," *American Ethnologist* 31:1 (2004): 92–110; Birgit Meyer, "Impossible Representations:

Pentecostalism, Vision, and Video Technology in Ghana," in *Religion, Media, and the Public Sphere,* ed. B. Meyer and A. Moors (Bloomington: IUP, 2006), 290–312.

61. Csordas, *Language, Charisma, and Creativity;* Bernice Martin, "From Pre- to Postmodernity in Latin America: The Case of Pentecostalism," in *Religion, Modernity and Postmodernity,* ed. P. Heelas, D. Martin, and P. Morris (Oxford: Blackwell, 1998), 102–46.

62. Meyer, "Christianity in Africa," 461.

63. Robbins, *Becoming Sinners,* chap. 8.

64. Meyer, "Christianity in Africa," 461.

65. See, for longer reviews, Bernice Martin,"The Pentecostal Gender Paradox: A Cautionary Tale for the Sociology of Religion," in *The Blackwell Companion to Sociology of Religion,* ed. R. K. Fenn (Oxford: Blackwell, 2001), 52–66; and Robbins, "Globalization."

66. Brusco, *The Reformation of Machismo.*

67. Brusco, *The Reformation of Machismo,* 138.

68. Salvatore Cucchiari, "Between Shame and Sanctification: Patriarchy and Its Transformation in Sicilian Pentecostalism," *American Ethnologist* 17:4 (1990): 687–707.

69. Burdick, *Looking for God in Brazil;* David A.Smilde, "The Fundamental Unity of the Conservative and Revolutionary Tendencies in Venezuelan Evangelicalism: The Case of Conjugal Relations," *Religion* 27:4 (1997): 343–59; Judith Stacey and Susan Elizabeth Gerard, " 'We Are Not Doormats': The Influence of Feminism on Contemporary Evangelicals in the United States," in *Uncertain Terms: Negotiating Gender in American Culture,* ed. F. Ginsburg and A. L. Tsing (Boston: Beacon Press, 1990), 98–117; Cecília Loreto Mariz and María das Dores Campos Machado, "Pentecostalism and Women in Brazil," in *Power, Politics, and Pentecostals in Latin America,* ed. E. L. Cleary and H. W. Stewart-Gambino (Boulder, CO: Westview Press, 1997), 41–54.

70. Smilde, "Fundamental Unity," 354–55.

71. Mariz and Machado, "Pentecostalism and Women in Brazil," 49–52.

72. Max Weber, *The Protestant Ethic and the Spirit of Capitalism* (New York: Scribners, 1958).

73. Jean Comaroff and John Comaroff, "Millennial Capitalism: First Thoughts on a Second Coming," *Public Culture* 12:2 (2000): 291–343; Jean Comaroff and John Comaroff, "Second Comings: Neo-Protestant Ethics and Millennial Capitalism in Africa, and Elsewhere," in *2000 Years and Beyond: Faith, Identity and the "Common Era,"* ed. P. Gifford, D. Archard, T. A. Hart, and N. Rapport (London: Routledge, 2003), 106–26.

74. Coleman, "Charismatic Gift"; Coleman, "Materializing the Self."

75. Bronislaw Malinowski, *Argonauts of the Western Pacific: An Account of Native Enterprise and Adventure in the Archipelagoes of Melanesian New Guinea* (New York: Dutton, [1922] 1961).

76. Marcel Mauss, *The Gift: The Form and Reason for Exchange in Archaic Societies,* trans. W. D. Halls (London: Routledge, [1925] 1990).

77. Claude Lévi-Strauss, *The Elementary Structures of Kinship,* trans. J. H. Bell, J. R. v. Sturmer, and R. Needham (Boston: Beacon Press, [1949] 1969).

78. Wiegele, *Investing in Miracles.*

79. Naomi Haynes, "Locating the Gift in an Emerging Urban Gift Economy: The Role of Prosperity Churches in the Villagization of the African City," paper presented at the Biennial Meeting of the Society for the Anthropology of Religion, Phoenix, April 13–16, 2007; see also Jon Bialecki, Naomi Haynes, and Joel Robbins, "The Anthropology of Christianity," *Religion Compass* 2:6 (2008): 1139–58.

80. David Martin, *Tongues of Fire: The Explosion of Protestantism in Latin America* (Oxford: Blackwell, 1990).

81. Burdick, *Looking for God;* Burdick, *Blessed Anastácia.*

82. Frans H.Kamsteeg, *Prophetic Pentecostalism in Chile: A Case Study on Religion and Development Policy* (Lanham, MD: Scarecrow Press, 1998).

83. Droogers, "Paradoxical Views," 25.

84. David Martin, *Pentecostalism: The World Their Parish* (Oxford: Blackwell, 2002), 23.

85. Rijk van Dijk, "Negotiating Marriage: Questions of Morality and Legitimacy in the Ghanaian Pentecostal Diaspora" *JRA* 34:4 (2004): 438–67; Rijk van Dijk, "The Moral Life of the Gift in Ghanaian Pentecostal Churches in the Diaspora: Questions of (In-)dividuality and (In-)alienability in Transcultural Reciprocal Relations," in *Commodification: Things, Agency, Identities (The Social Life of Things Revisited)*, ed. W. M. J. van Binsbergen and P. L. Geschiere (Münster: Lit Verlag, 2005), 201–24.

9

Sociology of Religion

Stephen Hunt

SOME PRECURSORY OBSERVATIONS

In the mid-1960s David Martin furthered the view that the prevailing sociological concept of secularization regrettably carried a strong ideological dimension—that religion was inevitably on the decline and, moreover, that this was to be welcomed. Put succinctly, humanity would eventually be liberated from the shackles of religion.[1]

The dominance of the "hard" secularization thesis in mainstream sociology clearly had implications for the subdiscipline of sociology of religion. In short, if the decline of religion was relentless, then so was the status of that specialism which sought to comprehend it as a sociocultural manifestation. In an increasingly religiousless world, the sociology of religion would be pushed to the margins of scholarly inquiry and subsequently be reduced to a Cinderella academic field.

This had not previously been the case. The sociology of religion is one of the oldest branches of the discipline of sociology. In fact, there is good reason for arguing that it is the oldest. The early so-called Founding Fathers of sociology such as Comte, Durkheim, and Weber took a particular interest in religion. The topic was also of concern to Karl Marx in his earliest philosophical works. The reason religion proved of such interest was because it appeared to be an integral part of all human societies. Often belief and practices were similar across cultures; at other times they seemed very different. Similar or different, in preindustrialized society social institutions were saturated in religious belief and ritual.

The sociology of religion, despite its contrasting and divergent approaches, has historically and primarily focused on the dialectical relationship that religion has with wider society: society is the main source of religion expression, indeed its origin, while religion influences society. Beyond this foundational assumption the

179

sociology of religion has universally been concerned with a number of major themes, including the analysis of religious practices and beliefs, the interface between religion and social structures and culture, and the historical origins and developments of religiosity.

The early sociologists had contrasting explanations for the social importance of religion. Nevertheless, most agreed that it was on the decline in modern industrial societies. This was another reason they held this notable concern with religion. It seemed that religion was a marker of wider social and economic change. Its apparent decline in Western societies was bound up with the advance of forces of modernity, rationalism, and the development of the pluralist society. This "decline of religion," therefore, was often equated with the growth of the secular societies of the West.

It is clear that today the sociological study of religion is enjoying something of a new lease on life. This can be attributed in part to Pentecostalism, a century-old movement that is now benefiting from a spectacular global rise. The sociological interest in the subject is not new, however. Earlier accounts tended to be located within the dominant paradigms of the time or, in short, the working application of "classical" sociology. This enterprise focused on certain pivotal concerns, not least the implications of the rise of modernity for religiosity. The challenge of rationalism, the decline of community, the significance of class and other social formations, and much more besides, all played an integral part in the attempt to understand Pentecostalism.

Since the early accounts of Pentecostalism, the sociological approach to the movement has moved on. Pentecostalism has evolved considerably, adapting itself to radically different global contexts. Dynamics within the movement and the emergence of numerous "streams" have added to its complexity. Despite the continuing popularity of themes and typologies rooted in classical sociology, the general current tendency is to attempt to understand Pentecostalism in the light of the cultural shift from modernity to late/postmodernity. Hence sociological commentators have come to develop fresh frameworks that give scope to understanding contemporary Pentecostalism. This seems to be especially the case in the discussion of neo-Pentecostalism, in what amounts to another (perhaps unsatisfactory) typology.

CLASSICAL PENTECOSTALISM AND MODERNITY

A fair amount of early historical sociology centered on the origins and initial emergence of Pentecostalism in the United States and Europe. To the fore was the theme of the relationship between Pentecostalism and modernization. The origins of the movement were discussed in terms of its fundamentalist inclinations and the interrelated theme of sectarian development. Here Pentecostalism seemed part of the rearguard conservative Christian reaction to modernity. This emphasis has continued. Hence Robert Mapes Anderson, in his groundbreaking Marxist reduction of the early movement, interprets it as essentially a response to liberalizing tendencies among certain strands of Evangelicalism.[2]

Anderson lists the particular innovations of modernity that confronted evangelical Christianity. These include the challenge of evolutionary theory, which, through science, eroded the supernatural and personal aspects of God; Higher Criticism, which undermined the authority of Scripture; and comparative religious studies, which relativized Christianity, depriving the faith of its unique and absolute character. Pentecostalism, in Anderson's appraisal, thus protested against the growing secular order, as well as the sterile mainstream denominations that sought to accommodate themselves within the worldview of modernity. And it did so with a particular form of sectarianism that articulated the movement's unique ecstatic and esoteric expression of Christianity.

Such views have been contested on the grounds that the movement's response to modernity has always been more complex and ambiguous than a Marxist interpretation might suggest. Moreover, debates have been opened in the sociology of religion as to what exactly is the nature of fundamentalism. For instance, Cox maintains that Pentecostals are not fundamentalists, in the usual application of the term, given the boundaries established by traditional fundamentalists with the movement. Moreover, Cox suggests that the difference is essentially phenomenological. Whereas the beliefs of the fundamentalists are enshrined in formal theological systems, those of Pentecostalism are largely embedded in a system of symbols of meaning that constitute "a full-blown religious cosmos."[3]

The orientation of Pentecostalism as a variety of fundamentalism that was essentially backward-looking has also been challenged in the light of its overall development. Andrew Walker has little doubt that Pentecostalism has proved to be the twentieth century's most successful embodiment of revivalism, ensuring the successful transmission of the Protestant religion into the modern era. Such early revivals, despite their esoteric outpourings, were not opposed to critical rationality, individualism, the capitalist ethic, and progressivism. Pentecostals around the time of World War II had been reluctant modernizers, but they became progressively modern by a slow process of cultural osmosis. Walker concludes that although Pentecostalism may be seen as fundamentalist, it would be a mistake to see it as antimodern.

DEMOGRAPHIC FEATURES
OF CLASSICAL PENTECOSTALISM

If the reaction of Pentecostalism to modernity was a dominant theme in sociological accounts, another was the interrelated concern with the movement's social composition. Pentecostalism in the United States was for a long time regarded as the "religion of the dispossessed" and socially marginalized.[4] In Robert Mapes Anderson's account of the early Pentecostals, their babble of tongues was interpreted as little more than the cries of the oppressed and downtrodden who formed a Second Coming movement. Most converts had peasant roots and were predisposed to Pentecostalism by the mystical, supernatural, even animalistic and magical notions common to those who lived off the land.

There appeared to be some justification of this view in the geographic spread of the movement. From 1906 to 1909 the American South became the first region in the world where Pentecostalism put down deep roots and significantly changed the spiritual landscape. It found fertile soil among the impoverished and where both blacks and whites struggled for subsistence on the margins of society. It was in the South that the first Pentecostal denominations in the world went on to enjoy an extraordinary appeal. Pentecostalism advanced to influence those geographic regions that were most familiar with revivalistic Christianity and often subject to troubling change and conflict; the Southwest, Midwest, and Far West.[5]

Alternatively, classical Pentecostalism has been viewed as a distinct form of religion that helped the urbanized masses overcome social disorganization. Here sociological analysis took more of a Durkheimian turn in that a sense of purpose and community was seemingly provided by the emerging Pentecostal communities.[6] This function appeared to be especially evident at the beginning of the twentieth century—the period in which immigration to the United States had reached its peak. There thus existed conditions of rootlessness that engendered the search for certainty in revivalistic religion.[7]

The link between deprivation and Pentecostalism has also been a central aspect of sociological accounts of black Pentecostalism. Certainly, deprivation in the form of social marginalization, low social status, and the effects of discrimination has dominated appraisals of black Pentecostal churches in the United States.[8] Similarly, aspects of deprivation seemed applicable to black communities in diaspora. Calley's early work showed that the Caribbean Pentecostal sects in Britain represented a deliberate attempt to create an ethnic enclave: to enhance collective solidarity and to construct a retreat from white society.[9] In terms of theology, the Afro-Caribbean Pentecostal churches have tended to be sectarian in nature and to provide compensatory aspects of religion in that the principal emphasis has been on offering a futuristic kingdom of God.

That the general inclination has been for Pentecostals to become more prosperous and socially integrated over time has frequently been explained in terms of preexisting theories of sectarian development. Niebuhr had noted that time and time again what began life as a radical sect evolved into denominational form on comfortable terms with its social and cultural environment.[10] Subsequent generations, however, not only lost the vigor of the first but also became increasingly upward mobile and prepared to mix with those of elevated standards in the secular world.

There was also evidence to suggest that the Pentecostal sect could bring prosperity through a Puritan work ethic that seemed to confirm Weber's writings on sectarian transformations.[11] For example, Gerrard characterizes the Pentecostal churches in Appalachia as composed of the upwardly mobile poor. While having little hope of advancement, they nonetheless made strenuous efforts for their congregations to lead respectable lives, eschewing welfare benefits and bringing up their children to achieve in *this* world.[12] Similar developments appeared to be observable among Afro-Caribbean churches in Britain.[13] While these congregations initially brought a sense of community and established an ethnic enclave in order to escape the ravages of discrimination in the host society, the second generation of Afro-Caribbean Pentecostals had grown more prosperous. Prosperity brought respectability, new aspirations, and greater social integration, while the black Pentecostal sect lost many of its millenarian aspirations.

DEPRIVATION THEORIES REVISITED

Those explanatory factors that have fallen back on one variety or another of deprivation theory frequently advanced by sociologists for the growth of classical Pentecostalism have, however, been challenged. Indeed, in his critique of such deprivation theories, Miller, while acknowledging Pentecostalism's distinct social roots, nonetheless interprets the movement as part of an earnest religious quest among the masses.[14] This alternative analysis points to the fact that sociological reductionist approaches have been inclined to play down the subjective experiences and worldview of the social "actor"—a tendency observed by Grant Wacker in his review of Anderson's *Vision of the Disinherited*.[15]

This would seem to be substantiated in a rather overlooked but comprehensive treatment of the subject of deprivation by Bradfield, who sought to examine various forms of deprivation as applied to Pentecostalism.[16] Bradfield took his investigation of Glock's multidimensional schemata of deprivation to an analysis of the Full Gospel Business Men's Fellowship International.[17] "Deprivation" largely took the form of spiritual "needs." Many of those changing allegiances to this Pentecostal para-church organization were individuals looking for a fresh interpretation of the New Testament: they sought changed lives that brought a sense of worth and purpose, a "right relationship with God," which created more liberty and a vibrant form of spirituality without anticlericalism, church dogma, and tradition.[18]

This recognition of the importance of spiritual seeking was supplemented by social movement theory, which brought an emphasis on *how*, rather than *why*, people subscribed to Pentecostalism and reflected wider increasing interest in theories of conversion processes.[19] Whatever the social roots of Pentecostalism, certain dynamics associated with integrative networks explained the mechanisms for allegiance. Gerlach and Hine suggest that the growth of Pentecostalism is due to several factors that explain high levels of commitment and are unrelated to deprivation of any kind.[20] They identify a seven-stage process in commitment to the movement that is related to preexisting networks: initial contact with a participant, the focus on personal needs through demonstration (of the charismata), resocialization through group interaction, decision and surrender, the commitment event (the baptism in the Holy Spirit), testament to the unique Pentecostal experience, and group support for the subsequent cognitive and behavioral patterns.

THE RISE OF NEO-PENTECOSTALISM

The emergence of mid-twentieth-century neo-Pentecostalism attracted a good deal of sociological interest. At the outset the emphasis was on the Charismatic movement as a continuation of classical Pentecostalism. Hence the core focus tended to be on its major discernible characteristics: its experientialism, embrace of the charismata, and accompanying doctrines, alongside its cultural attributes of spontaneity and the joyous and emotive form of worship. Yet there were sufficient departures from older expressions of Pentecostalism to suggest that the Charismatic movement was a unique religious manifestation in its own right. This view was to be substantiated as the movement evolved and later became transformed by way of its theology and praxis. Indeed, by the 1980s sociologists questioned whether the distinguishing features of Pentecostalism were still significant in its contemporary apparition, especially with the onset of the so-called Third Wave movement.[21]

Although a good number of the Pentecostals, either through the rewards of a Puritan work ethic or through general rising standards of living, experienced unprecedented levels of social mobility, their lower-class position can be compared to the more affluent and educated Charismatics. What precisely the attractions of the Charismatic movement are to the middle classes has been the subject of some speculation. Deprivation of one form or another remains a persistent theme.[22] For example, Anderson moves from a careful analysis of the beginnings of the Pentecostal movement, from 1906 to the 1930s, to hypothesize about neo-Pentecostals in terms of deprivation.[23] Given their social position, it was unlikely that the attractions of the Charismatic movement were rooted in absolute economic deprivation. I take up the theme of alternative forms of deprivation shortly.

If the arrival of neo-Pentecostalism, in all its guises, reopened earlier sociological debates, it also engendered fresh ones. The pure scope of the movement stimulated a broader interest by way of its organizational dynamics and relationship to modernity. Again there was speculation related to the question of whether the movement constituted a unique form of Christian fundamentalism or amounted to something entirely different. Frequently commentators asserted that, in much the same way as the earlier Pentecostal movement, neo-Pentecostalism displayed many of the elements of fundamentalism and was only separated from more traditional forms by way of its unique esoteric and ecstatic qualities.[24]

Early accounts from this perspective were often anchored in theories of secularization. Hence the movement was not infrequently viewed as marking a reaction to the "internal" secularizing tendencies in the Christian Church: its increasing worldliness and liberalizing trends. Simultaneously, the Charismatic Renewal movement, with all its Pentecostal trappings, was perceived as a response to the decline of the historical denominations, to which dwindling attendance and membership statistics bore abundant witness.

Certainly, there were clear sectarian expressions of neo-Pentecostalism outside of the mainstream churches. In his pathbreaking work, *Restoring the Kingdom*, Andrew Walker described the Restorationist, or "house church," movement as "the most significant religious formation to emerge in Great Britain for over half a century."[25] Among other themes, Walker examined the sectarian aspects discernible to one extent or another in the various streams of the movement. Restorationism, as a hybrid form of Pentecostalism, seemed more active, through its distinct dogma, in demonstrating the power of God, restoring a "lost" Church, and rebuilding the Kingdom of Christ in the End Times.

That Charismatic Renewal in the established denominations was sectarian by nature may appear implausible. Yet Harper makes a convincing argument that the Renewal movement within Roman Catholicism approached the typology of the sect.[26] Here the Renewal movement displayed its small, unbureaucratic nature with a voluntary membership that was subject to strong internal regulation. This included a rigorous form of socialization, an ambivalent attitude to the mother church, emphasis on the distinctive Pentecostal spiritual rebirth, and emphasis on constant interaction and commitment.

NEO-PENTECOSTALISM AS A NEW
RELIGIOUS MOVEMENT

Although neo-Pentecostalism displayed certain sectarian characteristics, its diversity made such a designation largely unworkable. Given that neo-Pentecostalism appeared in many respects to be different from the early expression, many sociologists preferred to designate it the New Religious Movement (NRM). In this respect, Wallis placed neo-Pentecostalism under the remit of a "world-accommodating" NRM.[27] Wallis argued that there appeared to be a link between the membership of such NRMs and various forms of deprivation. Individuals not sufficiently affluent and with no great stake in the social order would be attracted to movements that neither completely embraced nor completely rejected the world. Wallis suggested that movements such as neo-Pentecostalism helped their followers cope with their life experiences and compensate them for the difficulties thrown up by the modern world, notably, the rationalization and bureaucratization of life.[28]

There were said to be other "deficiencies" that the NRMs addressed. The inspiration of Durkheim's work was again evident. The mid-twentieth-century social order, so it was argued, could not offer a coherent moral system, and this was evident in the decline of traditional Christianity and the civil religion that was believed to underpin North American culture. According to Anthony and Robbins, NRMs in their different ways brought a sense of belonging and a system of stringent moral guidelines.[29]

By marked contrast, some commentators saw the new religions as symbolizing a rejection of modernity, similar to the counterculture revolution of the 1960s— offering an alternative lifestyle to an increasingly materialistic, rationalist, and individualistic society.[30] In the early 1970s a number of sociologists suggested that the NRMs reflected "the search for community." This seemed to be so with some expressions of the Charismatic movement in its formative years, for example, its ability to spawn "intentional communities." Certainly, this proved strong throughout Roman Catholic renewal, with the Church's tradition of communal living. It was also central to the charismatically inclined Jesus People (JP) whose origins were in California.[31]

Alternatively, by way of explaining the JP phenomenon, Tipton argued that after the counterculture period the alternative religions allowed young people a way forward.[32] Disoriented by drugs, embittered by politics, disillusioned by the apparent worthlessness of work and the transience of relationships, they found a way back through these new religions, a way to get along with conventional American society.[33] Speculating more widely, Tipton saw a mirror of these functions in the resurgence of conservative Christian churches and sects across America—Evangelical, fundamentalist, Pentecostal, alongside the growth of Charismatic Renewal in the established denominations.[34]

Whether neo-Pentecostalism deals with matters of deprivation has, however, been challenged in the same way that assumptions about classical Pentecostalism have been critiqued. In her study of Catholic groups of Charismatics, Neitz found little evidence of deprivation.[35] Perhaps more important, deprivation was not part of the conversion narrative. Often motivated by deeper commitment or service to God, Charismatics were largely engaged in problem solving related to their spiritual lives.

Neo-Pentecostalism also appeared to display certain cultural characteristics that seemed to transcend matters of deprivation. It is perhaps no coincidence that when Pentecostalism was transformed from its working-class to its middle-class style it had moved from early to late modernity: an era during which the advent of consumerism in the 1950s saw the demise of what Daniel Bell refers to as ascetic individualism and the rise of hedonistic individualism.[36]

In 1968 McDonnell was probably the first scholar to suggest the similarity between Charismatic Christianity and the secular human potential movement. In the group dynamics of the latter and in the prayer group meetings of neo-Pentecostals were to be found similar experiments in "community building," interpersonal honesty, and nonverbal forms of communication (such as hand holding and embracing) that were elements of the counterculture that had been increasingly absorbed and diluted throughout mainstream life.[37]

McGuire wrote in a similar vein in her comparative exploration of a range of healing groups. From a phenomenological perspective, McGuire analyzed healing strategies and teachings, and discovered that common to all were notions of divine, supernatural, or "hidden" cosmic powers through which healing techniques found and channeled their source.[38] Healing strategies, while following a generalized cultural preoccupation with human potential and individual fulfillment, nevertheless flowed from an especially middle-class concern with self-improvement and empowerment. This was so with Roman Catholic Charismatic healing groups.

PENTECOSTALISM AND THE POLITICAL WORLD

While neo-Pentecostalism, and, increasingly, classical Pentecostal groupings, had embraced certain aspects of contemporary culture, they also proved capable of reacting to those sociocultural changes to which they objected through political activism and moral campaigns. In recent times the Pentecostals and Charismatics have been especially prominent in the rise of the New Christian Right in the United States. Hitherto, hostility from the social order beyond its sectarian boundaries, as well as the established churches, alienated the Pentecostals from the political sphere. Instead they clung tenaciously to their otherworldliness and dogma concerning the "rapture" that was rooted in the premillenarian teaching that asserted that believers would be miraculously removed from earth before the foretold "time of tribulation."[39] Hertzke, however, argues that the Pentecostal movement from its inception was a revival forged in the popularist tradition of America's Great Awakenings of religious revival and carried considerable political potential.[40] He cites the Pentecostal Church of God, which appealed to the same people as the secular popularists, offering a spiritual rather than worldly response to the chaotic changing world.

Many traditional Pentecostals took a new direction in the latter part of the twentieth century in their embrace of the cause of the NCR in what appeared to be an increasingly secular and permissive society. When more conservative-minded Christians were prepared to move confidently into the political arena, many of the older Pentecostal denominations joined them. To a degree their greater respectability and organization allowed them to become part of the very religious and cultural mainstream that had been alien to them for so long. They were to be accompanied by the Charismatics. Jeremy Rifkin highlighted their potential by stating that Charismatics were providing the most significant challenge to the liberal and permissive society. Faith healing, speaking in tongues, and prophecy were weapons of rebellion against the spirit of the modern age.[41]

While Poloma suggested the continued limitations of a movement that placed an emphasis on paranormal religious experiences and millenarianism,[42] political scientists pointed to the inherent weakness of the NCR. Jelen concludes that despite similar agendas, religious fragmentation appeared to have an independent effect on support for specific NCR political figures (Pat Robertson's greater support among Charismatics, fundamentalists' support of Jerry Falwell), even if they held similar attitudes toward subjects such as abortion, foreign policy, social issues, gender roles, and gay rights.[43] This once again endorsed the significance of the cultural and theological differences between Pentecostals, Charismatics, Evangelicals, and fundamentalists.

ROUTINIZATION AND REVIVALISM

Not only has the broad Pentecostal movement responded to external cultural changes, endorsing some and rejecting others, it has also succumbed to its own internal dynamics. Discussions related to the routinization and the institutionalization of Pentecostalism as a movement of revivalism and sectarianism have roots in the work of Weber. This theme dovetailed with the theory of sect development, briefly overviewed above, which suggests the inevitable social mobility of adherents to sectarianism. It is one famously described by Poloma in her account of developments in the Assemblies of God (AOG).[44] The AOG, typical of many of the larger Pentecostal groupings, indicated that the movement was evolving all the traits of the very denominationalism to which it had earlier been vehemently opposed. It thus began to lose its eschatological edge, while the principal bodies increasingly firmed up their doctrines. Also evident was the decline of religious enthusiasm as the socioeconomic position of the AOG rank and file improved. the expectation that its ministers would be seminary trained, the relaxation of ethical standards such as personal attire, the acceptance of popular media and university education, the mobilization of organizational structures to promoter evangelism, and the increasing pervasiveness of highly structured liturgical order in Pentecostal worship.

The matter of the routinization of charisma has also been applied to the world of neo-Pentecostalism. It has engendered various interests. In his discussion of the evolution of many Restorationist streams to the more modernist-oriented "New Churches," Walker suggests that the sectarian dynamics within Western societies werespeeding up—that sect formations were coming and going, starting and stopping at a relentless pace.[45] This more than hinted at the increasing processes related to secularization. Evidence of this was that in a very short space of time Restorationism underwent the kind of growth, changes, splits, and eventual routinization that took the classical Pentecostal sects sixty years to undergo.

Routinization may also spur reaction, and this has tended to be in the form of revivalism. Perhaps this has proved most evident in accounts of the rise and demise of the Toronto blessing—a form of esotericism that swept through many Pentecostal and Charismatic churches in the mid-1990s. While the Toronto blessing has been viewed as an expression of pent-up psychological hope for revival in the End Times,[46] it was plausibly a revivalistic response to the routinization of neo-Pentecostalism indicating that the Charismatic movement was turning back on its self to rediscover Pentecostalism's initial impetus and with greater measure in terms of its pneumatological phenomena.[47]

Routinization may also have less obvious repercussions. One of the more neglected aspects of the study of Pentecostalism is that of gender. It is clear that a radical counterculture identity characterized the early Pentecostal movement. In the era when women were excluded from public voice, early Pentecostalism was a revival movement, and frequently during times of revival women enjoyed greater freedom. There was usually a tremendous emphasis on evangelism and mission. During a revival, with the time considered short before the End, all available personnel, whether men or women, were needed, with authority grounded more on experience than ecclesiastical qualifications.[48]

In later decades Pentecostal denominations have not generally affirmed women as pastors. Even in the few Pentecostal denominations that offer women full ordination, that office has infrequently been translated into equal access to positions of denominational leadership.[49] Poloma's explanation for changing attitudes in the AOG indicates that female leaders, preachers, and evangelists have became much less common as the church, both as a denomination and at the congregational level, grew much larger and more institutionalized. Just as important, the fundamentalist-modernist controversy engendered a fear of apostasy among Pentecostals, who began to restrict female leadership roles as revival also cooled down.[50]

GLOBAL DIVERSITY

Much of my overview of Pentecostalism so far has focused on the broad movement in the Western context. Given its global influence, we may range farther afield. Before doing so, something may be said about its differential impact across the nations of the world. While acknowledging that Europe has apparently traveled farther down the road to secularization than the United States and other parts of the world, there are different levels of growth across the continent.[51] For Martin, the key variable would appear to be the dominance or otherwise of a strong state church. This feasibly explains why Pentecostalism in Catholic countries has done less well. The more recent growth of the movement in such nations as Spain and Italy has only occurred with the declining power of the Catholic Church and the subsequent emergence of a greater religious pluralism.

Although the impact of Pentecostalism in its various expressions has proved considerable in various parts of the majority world, there is evidence that the overall picture in Europe is one of stagnation. Sweden and Norway are among the countries where Pentecostalism was introduced within very few months after the onset of the 1906 Azusa Street revival. However, after one century of Pentecostal missionary effort, less than 1 percent of the population in both countries subscribe to Pentecostalism outside of the Charismatic Renewal movement. In the United Kingdom, Germany, and the Netherlands, the levels are as low as 0.5 percent.

In explaining Pentecostalism's rise at a particular time and place, Bloch-Hoell advanced a number of broader factors that were a product of the religious culture of the United States and which led to its eulogized birthing during the Azusa Street revival.[52] These included the pervasive diversity in church life, a high level of religious activity, low-church principles reflected in personal religious experiences and nonritualized forms of worship, and fervent evangelism in the form of revival campaigns. Such variables were accompanied by prevailing religious tolerance, voluntary association in church membership, and a general climate of individualism.

Some of these variables still hold and forge what is commonly known as the American "exceptionalism" that explains the high level of religiosity in the United States when compared to Europe. Pentecostalism, including its Charismatic protégés, remains a powerful component in the growing conservative camp, along with the more conventional Evangelicals and fundamentalists. Yet there is a certain paradox to be observed here. In Europe the Pentecostal/Charismatic constituency probably remains the most vibrant form of Christianity against a background of religious decline. In the United States, however, Pentecostalism is rivaled and partially eclipsed by the growth of conservative Evangelicalism and fundamentalism.

Into this milieu in the United States, and for that matter in Europe, there has proved to be a new and especially vibrant form of Pentecostalism. This is the spectacular growth of West African churches over the past decade, or what may be termed the "New Black Churches."[53] Largely embracing the "health and wealth gospel," such churches as the Redeemed Christian Church of God have embarked on a "reversed mission" to the secularized nations of the West. Questions may be raised about whether such churches can stimulate the broad world of Pentecostalism or even have an impact on the wider social environment. Findings suggest that such churches appeal almost exclusively to West Africans in diaspora and serve many of the same functions as the earlier Afro-Caribbean sects. Their potential to reinvigorate Pentecostalism in the West would therefore appear to be muted.

The area of recent significant growth of Pentecostalism is the majority world. In 1979 Acquaviva's treatise suggested that the evidence proved that religion was declining not only in the industrialized West but also in those countries undergoing industrialization. Latin America was a case in point. In many countries on the continent, the Catholic Church was spiraling into decline.[54] This thesis, however, proved premature. In Latin America, the Catholic monopoly—its social, cultural, and political power—has been broken. Undoubtedly this has resulted from modernization, but Catholic hegemony has also been spectacularly eroded by the impact of Protestant Pentecostalism.

Latin America is not the only part of the world that has seen the prolific spread of Pentecostalism. Sub-Saharan Africa and many parts of Southeast Asia have been affected and perhaps for different reasons. The reasons for the success of Pentecostalism in a global context will not be addressed in considerable detail here. They are comprehensively overviewed in such comparative studies as those of David Martin and Harvey Cox.[55] Nonetheless, a number of observations can be made.

First, it is clear that what the Pentecostal missionaries have transported to the non-Western world is the capacity to transcend numerous cultures with an alternative worldview that embraces miracles and esotericism. Beyond this initial observation questions can be raised whether the net result of Pentecostalism is to enculturate itself or to bring cultural innovation. I shall not dwell on this debate at length since it is fully addressed by Joel Robbins in chapter 8 of this volume. Nevertheless, it might be stated that it does both simultaneously. Pentecostalism would appear to generate change but does so by enculturating itself to extant political, economic, and sociocultural environments, and it is able to do so, as Martin points out, because of its theological flexibility, emphasis on the experiential, and appeal to a sense of community during periods of rapid social and economic change.

Martin also addresses the link between modernization and the growth of Pentecostalism in the majority world and identifies a relationship between Pentecostalism and the Protestant work ethic. He shows that leaders in South America are entrepreneurs and small businessmen and that their congregations, the "evangelical poor," are imbued with a work ethic that is an integral part of the process of industrialization.[56]

By contrast, Brouwer and colleagues' quasi-Marxist reduction of global Pentecostalism considers the movement an integral part of the global impact of U.S.-style fundamentalism.[57] This analysis of globalized religion is one that sees Western countries, the United States in particular, as dominating the world's productive resources: manufacturing, banking, and commercial institutions. Such transformations amount to a "fundamentalist Americanism"—the belief peculiar to North American Christianity that simultaneously sanctifies imperialism and the gospel of success, wealth, and prosperity. For Brouwer and colleagues, the Pentecostal/Charismatic movement is part and parcel of a broader fundamentalism that appeals to those parts of the world where local cultures are disintegrating in the wake of modernizing impulses, of the erosion of traditional family structures, and, in urban areas, of large numbers of migrant peoples and the poor.

PENTECOSTALISM IN LATE/POSTMODERNITY

It is interesting to observe that the contrasting work of Martin and Brouwer et al. falls back respectively on quasi-Weberian and Marxian perspectives. This suggests the continuing appeal of classical sociological approaches (albeit with a certain degree of modification), but other accounts of contemporary Pentecostalism are more strident in adopting late/postmodernist frameworks.

One dominant theme is the contribution of religion to identity construction. While the matter of ethnic and community identity has been a strong continuing theme in the academic literature exploring the function of the black Pentecostal churches, recent academic work has stressed its complexities. Gerloff, for example, sees the significance of Pentecostalism in the context of the African diaspora as an instrument for defining black international identity in the face of oppression and powerlessness from not only the host society but also the country of origin and frequently supplemented by gender discrimination.[58] More recent studies have used similar themes to explore identity constructs in the emerging wave of New Black Pentecostal churches in the Western environment.[59]

The link between identity structures and the search for a lifestyle religiosity in a spiritual marketplace has attracted sociologists of religion exploring the rational and pluralistic nature of late modernity. Such a framework has been applied to surveys of neo-Pentecostalism. Mauss and Perrin's work highlights this development and is derived from a survey of Vineyard churches—a highly successful confederation of Charismatic congregations that are especially attractive to the baby boom generation.[60] The thrust of Mauss and Perrin's account results from a debate with the work of Kelley. They argue that Kelley was broadly correct in that "seekers" in the spiritual marketplace are looking for "the essential functions of religion," that is, "making life meaningful in ultimate terms,"[61] but that he was wrong in that successful churches necessarily demand personal commitment and self-sacrifice through a change in lifestyle. In short, there is the attraction of belonging to a successful church caught up in a significant tide of evangelism and revivalism, without a great deal of allegiance to the church itself.

Late/postmodernity would also seem to engender fresh forms of religious organization that undermine existing typologies such as "denomination" and "sect." The primary home of the Pentecostal-style spiritual marketplace would seem to be the "new paradigm," or "postdenominational" churches. Miller sees these churches as the "supply side" of the marketplace—attempting to serve the niche-related needs of religious seekers.[62] This move from uniformity to specialized services is a hallmark of the wider trend of moving from global mass marketing to focusing on local consumer needs.

The new paradigm churches are "churches"of a particular organizational expression. Their congregations typically meet in a converted warehouse, a rented school auditorium, or a leased space in a shopping mall. Many are of a Pentecostal persuasion. A few have been built around the ministries that advocate the "health and wealth" gospel. Others still, especially those originally based in California, grew from the mid-1970s where they were joined by adherents of the now-extinct Jesus People movement who had sought more casual forms of church organization as an alternative to joining already existing Pentecostal churches. Some such new paradigm churches have reached mega proportions.[63] However, it is not very helpful, suggests Miller, to use terms such as *evangelical* or *fundamentalist* to describe these new churches.[64] Even categories such as Charismatic or Pentecostal are too broad to capture their distinct character.

Miller contributes to the secularization debate by arguing that the various subscribers to traditional sociology have made the mistake of equating it with institutional decline. While new paradigm churches have some sectarian qualities, such as intensity of religious experiences, they are not cultural separatists like sects are. Rather, while enticing their members away from cultural engagement, they paradoxically appropriate many aspects of contemporary culture, transforming those aspects for their own purposes.

However, Miller points out that there is one aspect of the new paradigm churches that runs counter to wider cultural developments. He identifies a chain of command, typically found inn the local congregations, based on "charismatic" male authority figures. The desire for pastoral authority over the church membership, as interpreted from the Bible, suggests that the churches are leading the faith toward new kinds of patriarchy. The nuclear family relationship has a hierarchy of God, pastor, wife, and children that reflects traditional notions of masculinity.

Another feature of the new paradigm church, one shared by other Pentecostal para-church ministries, is the use of mass media, television and satellite communication being the most obvious. Although initially opposed to the "sin" of mass media, early Pentecostals soon recognized its value in the evangelizing endeavor. Today in the United States more than 34 million houses tune in to the so-called electronic church programs featuring popular fundamentalist and evangelical preachers of different persuasions or preachers with a Pentecostal or Charismatic orientation.

Not only have the neo-Pentecostal Evangelists taken advantage of a contemporary medium, but they have helped establish a certain kind of Charismatic culture that reflects the aspirations of the American way of life. If not overtly proclaiming the gospel of health and wealth that has become increasingly popular throughout Pentecostalism, the electronic church frequently advances an ethic of personal success that dovetails well with American culture. These are trends forcefully described in J. N. Horn's *From Rag to Riches,* which identifies the televangelist with one or another form of the prosperity gospel that tends to break down the holistic vision of human life by integrating the spiritual with the socioeconomic and political realities of the temporal.[65]

Female ministries in the electronic church provide an outlet for women's aspirations that have commonly been denied by Pentecostals and Charismatics. The arrival of the electronic church gave female evangelists a fresh opening. A sizable number of women have embarked on successful and high-profile ministries. Many are of a Pentecostal disposition and have come to constitute what Peterson has dubbed the "Electronic Sisters."[66] They are women of a vast variety of backgrounds and ministerial styles. Collectively they constitute a colorful kaleidoscope of charismatic personalities.

Finally, there are further rationalizing impulses to be observed in Pentecostalism, and these are associated with its globalization process. A number of such developments would seem to be in contradiction to the diversity propagated by Pentecostalism in the late/postmodern world. One innovation is that identified as "McDonaldization"—a term usually attributed to the work of George Ritzer,[67] which suggests that economic products, along with accompanying cultural attributes, are suitably packaged and disseminated across the world. Despite its esoteric practices, the spread of the Toronto blessing has been viewed in this way. Certainly, it displayed changing cultural attitudes toward bodily disinhibitions that have impinged on the Charismatic movement, altering communication patterns and new gender perceptions of God.[68] Yet it has also been described as the "McDonaldization of mysticism" because of its unique but standard esoteric apparitions and means of dissemination.[69] Such McDonaldization tendencies have more recently been identified in evangelizing programs typified by the global popularity of the Alpha courses, with their standardization of Charismatic doctrines and praxis.[70]

CULTURAL INNOVATION

I began this chapter with the observation that today the sociological study of religion is enjoying something of a new lease on life. The rise of global Pentecostalism has contributed to this resurgence. In part this is because it has proved culturally accommodating, even endorsing. Yet in line with other new forms of religiosity, perhaps most obviously the New Age movement, Pentecostalism, at least in its "neo" forms, has proved culturally innovating. This innovation is bound up with the antirationalizing impulses of late/postmodernity that are in marked contrast to the rationalizing tendencies of Pentecostalism explored above. Such antirationalism allows religiosity to reenter the world, perhaps reversing the secularity of the West.

There are various considerations here. One is Pentecostalism's ability to advance what Harvey Cox calls a "primal spirituality."[71] In short, the movement seeks the very nature of spiritual experience behind the Christian faith specifically and the very essence of religiosity generally. This includes, first, "primal speech" via the ecstatic utterance of glossolalia—"a language of the heart." Second, there is what Cox refers to as "primal piety": the articulation of archetypal religious experiences of trance, vision, healing, dreams, praise, and supplication. Third, there is the "primal hope" that looks forward to a new age, God's millennial kingdom on earth. In the search for this primal spirituality Pentecostalism is innovative in that it breaks down conventional understandings of religiosity in much the same way that it seeks to escape traditional organizational forms.

While such religious experience may be perceived as primal and premodern, there is much in this experience that reflects postmodern spirituality. According to postmodernist writers, religion in the contemporary epoch expresses individualistic religious "experience," mirroring today's culture of the fleetingly dramatic, titillating, and exotic.[72]

Although Pentecostals may be in line with postmodern spirituality and mysticism,[73] this religious experience remains exclusive. For Pentecostals, "primal" spirituality amounts to a return to a distinct cultural worldview that can be described as "restorationist," a tendency already noted. For those subscribing to the movement, spiritual renewal means "revival," "awakening," and the "outpouring of the Holy Spirit"—terminology that frequently designates a return to the Pentecostal experience of the early church. This does not, however, deny spiritual innovation that sports its own postmodern playfulness and eclecticism.[74] Nonetheless, such spiritual experiences as prophecy are intimately linked with Pentecostal eschatology. D. J. Wilson writes, "For most Pentecostals the future determines the present, their view of eschatology governs their view of current events. Their interpretation of prophecy has had a very significant effect on their perception of world historical events and on their political and social response to those events. On a smaller scale their eschatological views have affected their own history by stimulating evangelistic and missionary endeavours."[75]

THE FUTURE OF PENTECOSTALISM

At times, as explored above, Pentecostalism in both its "classical" and "neo" forms seemed to be reactionary, if not fundamentalist in tone. Yet the movement has not sat entirely comfortably with such designations. In short, if non-Pentecostal forms of conservative Christianity constituted a reaction to the contemporary world and pulled in a direction that attempted to take the faith back to some pristine and imagined past, then this did not hold on all fronts. The response by Pentecostals and Charismatics to the prevailing socioeconomic, political, and cultural conditions has always been far more complex and ambiguous. However, the difficulty of stating that the broad Pentecostal/Charismatic movement has proved simultaneously pre- or antimodern and in other ways modernist and even postmodernist is not to say very much that is illuminating. The reality is that the fluid nature of the movement has allowed it to adopt all these stances according to time and place and in response to the challenges that it faces. This underscores its wide appeal to different social groups in a variety of cultural contexts.

This brings us, finally, to speculations regarding the future of the universal Pentecostal movement.[76] Much would seem to be congruent with postmodernity and points the way to future possibilities. While postmodern theorists have explored such developments as religion and identity constructs and a growing spiritual marketplace and globalization processes, they have also been concerned with the general contemporary cultural conditions that lead to the increasing popularity of existential religiosity. Pentecostalism has come to exemplify a great deal. This is confirmed by the Charismatic theologian Henry Lederle, who writes that Charismatic thinking insists that reality consists of the "unseen" as well as "the seen" and reflects the broad cultural state that is in transition or experiencing a paradigm shift.[77] Jacques Theron similarly sees this cognitive shift as indicative of the rise of postmodernism—allowing narrative claims that make sense within particular communities of discourse, which, among other things, allow demons and demonology, a popular theme among Pentecostals and Charismatics, to reenter the world.[78]

So, what of the future? For Martyn Percy there is no doubt that Pentecostalism will remain a major shareholder in the totality of the Christian experience on a global level. Yet its instability makes predictions regarding future prospects problematic. Percy uses the analogy of a city to describe the nature of the movement. Like a city, its culture is pluralistic and diverse: its expression is not monobehavioral. The movement is multifaceted, complex, capable even at being at odds with itself. Pentecostals frequently speak of being hit by "waves" of revival rains and being drenched and soaked in the Spirit. These metaphors cover a multitude of occurrences, but whereas they bring energy and revival to some streams, they bring schism, erosion, and decline to others. This means that the city of neo-Pentecostalism is located on the unsure foundations of a beach. The waves or fashions wash and destabilize the movement at the same time that it has expanded. Health and wealth movements, the Toronto blessing, house churches, "shepherding" movements, healing ministries, and flamboyant charismatic leaders have all played their part.

The canopy for Percy's argument is that fissure and specialization in postmodernity are inevitable. This ensures that the city of the neo-Pentecostals will not in the future be governed by central fundamentals or core experiences. The movement thus takes various expressions that may continue into the foreseeable future. Some Pentecostals and Charismatics may follow a communitarian path. Alternatively, other factions of the movement may become apocalyptic in tone, becoming obsessed with Last Days scenarios. Then there may be those that become more authoritarian, embracing doctrinal "coping stones" by which to manage the uncertainties of postmodernity. Other groupings may become more political, turning to moral or political activism, endorsing left-wing as well as right-wing agendas.

CONCLUSION: THE FUTURE OF THE SOCIOLOGICAL STUDY OF PENTECOSTALISM

As evident in the overview presented in this chapter, the Pentecostal movement, in both its classical and neo forms, has drawn more than a passing interest from sociologists of religion for well over half a century. We have observed that several approaches—ranging from those derived from classical sociology to late/postmodern theorizing—have been employed in attempting to understand its multifaceted nature. None provides a wholesale account of what Pentecostalism is all about: they merely provide insights into certain aspects. Moreover, the problem with these contrasting approaches is that they tended to take a still picture of a movement that has constantly been in a state of transition and metamorphosis. Pentecostalism appears to change its colors not only according to wider cultural transformations from modernity to postmodernity but also as a result of dynamics within the movement itself, not least of all periods of routinization and revivalism.

The contribution of sociology to the study of Pentecostalism is by no means limited to a subdiscipline. The sociology of religion has been increasingly willing to break down the boundaries with rival subfields, including gender, ethnic, and organizational studies. Furthermore, it has also increasingly traversed the boundaries with rival academic traditions, including religious studies, cultural history, social psychology, political science, and, perhaps above all, social anthropology. Such a development might itself reflect the "pick 'n mix" culture of postmodernity. Yet it also results from the earnest endeavor to make the academic inquiry truly multidimensional.

Cross-discipline approaches are not the only likely future of the sociological enterprise. Developments in methodologies are also likely to occur. It is clear that macro sociological surveys will persevere in their contribution. This is ensured by the need to throw light on the sociocultural, economic, and political circumstances that give rise to and shape Pentecostalism in particular geographic contexts. The macro approach is also guaranteed of its survival by the need to conduct comparative analysis given truly global nature of Pentecostalism in all its diverse forms.

At the same time, the sociology of religion has discernibly moved toward more micro oriented approaches. These approaches tend to be the terrain of certain schools within sociology focusing on ethnographic accounts of Pentecostalism that have sought to negate or supplement crude reductionist sociological appraisals. Often phenomenological by nature, micro approaches attempt to come to grips with the "essence" of what Pentecostalism is really all about for the social actor.

In terms of methodologies, this simple distinction between macro and micro approaches tends to obscure the fact that the sociological study of religion has increasingly involved integrating the two. This is reflected in the analysis of Pentecostalism, so that the sociological inquiry now seems to be finely tuned in terms of broad approaches and methodologies. This, along with an increasing willingness to be interdisciplinary, will further safeguard the credibility of the sociology of religion. Certainly, developing approaches and methodologies will add to the sophistication of the sociological inquiry into Pentecostalism and overcome some of the limitations of earlier surveys. It goes almost without saying that this is clearly to be welcomed as the discipline continues to grapple with the diverse expressions and complexities of one of the most vibrant forms of religiosity in our time.

NOTES

1. David Martin, "Towards Eliminating the Concept of Secularisation," in *Penguin Survey of the Social Sciences,* ed. Julius Gould (Harmondsworth: Penguin, 1965), 169–82.

2. Robert Mapes Anderson, *Vision of the Inherited: The Making of American Pentecostalism* (Oxford: OUP, 1980).

3. Harvey Cox, *Fire from Heaven* (Reading, MA: Addison Wesley, 1996), 5.

4. Anderson, *Vision of the Inherited;* Listen Pope, *Millhands and Preachers* (New Haven: Yale University Press, 1942).

5. Peter Williams, *America's Religions: Traditions and Culture* (New York: Macmillan, 1990), 261–62.

6. Anton Boisen, "Religion and Hard Times: A Study of the Holy Rollers," *Social Action* 5 (March 1939): 8–35; John Holt, "Holiness Religion: Cultural Shock and Social Reorganization," *American Sociological Review* 5 (1940): 740–47.

7. Kilian McDonnell, "Holy Spirit and Pentecostalism," *Commonweal,* November 6, 1968, 198–204.

8. Vinson Synan, *The Holiness-Pentecostal Movement in the United States* (Grand Rapids: Eerdmans, 1971).

9. Malcolm Calley, *God's People: West Indian Sects in England* (London: OUP, 1965).

10. H. Richard Niebuhr, *The Social Sources of Denominationalism* (New York: World Publishing, 1929).

11. Max Weber, *The Protestant Work Ethic and the Spirit of Capitalism* (New York: Scriber, [1904] 1958).

12. Nathan Gerrard, "The Holiness Movement in Southern Appalachia," in *The Charismatic Movement,* ed. Malcolm Hamilton (Grand Rapids: Eerdmans, 1975), 159–60.

13. Clifford Hill, "Pentecostal Growth—Result of Racialism?" *Race Today* 3:3 (1971): 187–90.

14. Albert Miller, "Pentecostalism as a Social Movement: Beyond the Theory of Deprivation," *JPT* 9 (1996): 114.

15. Grant Wacker, Review of *Vision of the Inherited: The Making of American Pentecostalism* by Robert Mapes Anderson, *Pneuma* 4 (fall 1982): 53–62.

16. Cecil Bradfield, *Neo-Pentecostalism: A Sociological Assessment* (Lanham, MD: University Press of America, 1979).

17. Charles Glock, "On the Role of Deprivation in the Origin and Evolution of Religious Groups," in *Religion in Sociological Perspective,* ed. Charles Glock (Belmont: Wadsworth, 1973), 24–36.

18. Bradfield, *Neo-Pentecostalism,* 16–17.

19. See, e.g., John Loftland and Rodney Stark, "Becoming a World-Saver: A Theory of Religious Conversion," *American Sociological Review* 30 (1965): 862–74.

20. Luther Gerlach and Virginia Hine, "Five Factors Crucial to the Growth and Spread of a Modern Religious Movement," *JSSR* 7 (spring 1968): 23–40.

21. Stephen Hunt, Malcolm Hamilton, and Tony Walter, eds., *Introduction to Charismatic Christianity: Sociological Perspectives* (Basingstoke: Macmillan, 1997), 1–16.

22. Stephen Hunt, "Deprivation and Western Pentecostalism Revisited: The Case of 'Classical' Pentecostalism," *PentecoStudies* 1 (2002); Stephen Hunt, "Deprivation and Western Pentecostalism Revisited: The Case of Neo-Pentecostalism," *PentecoStudies* 1 (2002), available at www.glopent.net/pentecostudies/2002.

23. Anderson, *Vision of the Inherited,* 229.

24. Steve Bruce, *Religion in the Modern World: From Cathedrals to Cults* (Oxford: OUP, 1996).

25. Andrew Walker, *Restoring the Kingdom,* 4th ed. (London: Eagle, 1998),6.

26. Charles Harper, "Spirit-Filled Catholics: Some Biographical Comparisons," *Social Compass* 31 (1974): 311–24.

27. Roy Wallis, *The Elementary Forms of the New Religious Life* (London: Routledge, 1984).

28. Wallis, *Elementary Forms,* 36–37, 69.

29. Dick Anthony and Thomas Robbins, *Civil Religion and Recent American Religious Ferment: In Gods We Trust* (New Brunswick, NJ: Transaction, 1982).

30. Robert Bellah, "The New Religious Consciousness and the Crisis in Modernity," in *The Consciousness Reformation,* ed. Charles Glock and Robert Bellah (Berkeley: UCP, 1976), 335–43.

31. David Gordon, "The Jesus People: An Identity Synthesis," *Urban Life and Culture* 3:2 (1974): 159–78; John Marx and David Ellison, "Sensitivity Training and Communes: Contemporary Quests for Community," *Pacific Quarterly Review* 18:4 (1974): 442–62.

32. Bellah, "New Religious Consciousness and the Crisis in Modernity."

33. Steven Tipton, *Getting Saved from the Sixties* (Berkeley: UCP, 1982), 30.

34. Tipton, *Getting Saved from the Sixties,* 46.

35. Mary Jo Neitz, *Charisma and Community: A Study of Religious Commitment within the Charismatic Movement* (New Brunswick, NJ: Transaction Books, 1988), 67–68.

36. Daniel Bell, *The Cultural Contradiction of Capitalism* (Oxford: Heinemann, 1976).

37. McDonnell, "Holy Spirit and Pentecostalism."

38. Meredith McGuire, "Words of Power: Personal Empowerment and Healing," *Culture, Medicine and Psychiatry* 17 (1983): 221–40.

39. Peggy Shiver, *The Bible Vote* (New York: Pilgrim Press, 1981).

40. Allan Hertzke, *Echoes of Discontent: Jesse Jackson, Pat Robertson, and the Resurgence of Popularism* (Washington, DC: CQ Press, 1993).

41. Jeremy Rifkin, with Ted Howard, *The Emerging Order—God in the Scarcity* (New York: Putnam, 1979), 231.

42. Margaret Poloma, "Pentecostals and Politics in North and Central America," in *Prophetic Religion and Politics: Religion and the Political Order,* ed. Jeffrey Hadden and Anson Shupe (New York: Paragon House, 1986), 374.

43. Ted Jelen, "The Political Consequences of Religious Group Attitudes," *Journal of Politics* 55:1 (1993): 178–90.

44. Margaret Poloma, *The Assemblies of God at the Crossroads: Charisma and Institutional Dilemmas* (Knoxville: University of Tennessee Press, 1989).

45. Andrew Walker, *Restoring the Kingdom,* 2nd ed. (London: DLT, 1988), 333.

46. Stephen Hunt, "The 'Toronto Blessing': A Rumour of Angels?" *Journal of Contemporary Religion* 10:3 (1995): 257–71.

47. Philip Richter, "Charismatic Mysticism: A Sociological Analysis of the Toronto Blessing," in *The Nature of Religious Language,* ed. S. Porter (Sheffield: SAP, 1997), 97–119.

48. Letha Scanzoni and Susan Setta. "Women in Evangelical, Holiness, and Pentecostal Traditions," *Women and Religion in America* 8 (1986): 223–65.

49. Edith Blumhofer, "Women in American Pentecostalism," *Pneuma* 17:1 (1995): 19–32.

50. Poloma, *Assemblies of God at the Crossroads.*

51. David Martin, *Pentecostalism: The World Their Parish* (Oxford: Blackwell, 2002).

52. Nils Bloch-Hoell, *The Pentecostal Movemen* (Oslo: Universitetsforlaget, 1964).

53. Stephen Hunt, "The British Black Pentecostal 'Revival': Identity and Belief in the 'New' Nigerian Churches," *Ethnic and Racial Studies* 24:1 (2001): 104–24; Stephen Hunt, "'Neither Here nor There': The Construction of Identities and Boundary Maintenance of West African Pentecostals," *Sociology* 36:1 (2002): 147–69.

54. Sabino Acquaviva, *The Decline of the Sacred in Industrial Society* (Oxford: Blackwell, 1995).

55. Cox, *Fire from Heaven;* David Martin, *Tongues of Fire: The Explosion of Protestantism in Latin America* (Oxford: Basil Blackwell, 1990).

56. Martin, *Tongues of Fire,* 13.

57. Steve Brouwer et al., *Exporting the American Gospel* (New York: Routledge, 1996).

58. Roswith Gerloff, "Pentecostals in the African Diaspora," in *Pentecostals after a Century: Global Perspectives on a Movement in Transition,* ed. Allan Anderson and Walter Hollenweger (Sheffield: SAP, 1999), 115–20.

59. Hunt, "Deprivation and Western Pentecostalism Revisited."

60. Robin Perrin and Armand Mauss, "Strictly Speaking . . . : Kelley's Quandary and the Vineyard Christian Fellowship," *JSSR* 32:2 (1993): 125–35.

61. Dean Kelley, "Why Conservative Churches are Still Growing," *JSSR* 17:2 (1978): 165–72.

62. Donald Miller, *Reinventing American Protestantism: Christianity in the New Millennium* (Berkeley: UCP, 1997).

63. Scott Thumma, "The Kingdom, the Power, and the Glory: The Megachurch in Modern American Society" (Ph.D diss., Emory University, 1996).

64. Miller, *Reinventing American Protestantism,* 2.

65. J.N. Horn, *From Rags to Riches* (Pretoria: Unisa Press, 1989).

66. Richard Peterson, "The Electronic Sisters," in *The God Pumpers: Religion in the Electronic Age,* ed. Marshall Fishwick and Ray Browne (Bowling Green: Bowling Green State University Popular Press, 1987), 116–40.

67. George Ritzer. *The McDonaldization of Society* (Newbury Park, CA: Pine Forge, 1996).

68. Richter, "Charismatic Mysticism."

69. Martyn Percy, *The Toronto Blessing* (Oxford: Latimer Press, 1996), 8.

70. Stephen Hunt, *The Alpha Enterprise: Evangelism in the Post-Christian Era* (London: Ashgate, 2004).

71. Cox, *Fire from Heaven.*

72. Wade Roof and William McKinney, *American Mainline Religion: Its Changing Shape and Future* (New Brunswick, NJ: Rutgers University Press, 1987).

73. Margaret Poloma, *Main Street Mystics: The Toronto Blessing and Reviving Pentecostalism* (New York: AltaMira Press, 2003).

74. André Droogers, "The Normalization of Religious Experience: Healing, Prophecy, Dreams and Visions" in *Playful Religion: Challenges for the Study of Religion,* ed. André Droogers et al. (Delft: Eburon, 2006), 33–49.

75. D. J. Wilson, "Pentecostal Perspectives on Eschatology," in *DPCM,* 264.

76. Martyn Percy, "The City on a Beach: Future Prospects for Charismatic Movements at the End of the Twentieth Century," in Hunt et al., *Introduction to Charismatic Christianity,* 205–28.

77. Henri Lederle, "Life in the Sprit and Worldview: Some Preliminary Thoughts on Understanding Reality, Faith and Providence from a Comparative Perspective," in *Spiritual Renewal: Essays in Honour of J. Rodman Williams,* ed. Mark Wilson (Sheffield: SAP, 1994), 24–25.

78. Jacques Theron, "A Critical Overview of the Church's Ministry of Deliverance from Evil Spirits," *Pneuma* 18:1 (spring 1996): 84.

10

Historical Approaches

Cornelis van der Laan

In 1981, at the commemoration of the seventy-fifth anniversary of the Pentecostal Assembly of Amsterdam, an American missionary spoke about how the Pentecostal message had started in the United States and from there had come to Europe. The next speaker was Emmanuel Schuurman, the oldest living Dutch Pentecostal pioneer. The aged warrior corrected his American colleague by stating that Pentecost had not come from the United States but from heaven.[1] The sympathy of the audience clearly was with the latter, but for a historical reflection on European Pentecostalism neither of the two explanations suffices. But they illustrate how one's perspective influences one's view on the origins of Pentecostalism. This is one aspect of the methodology of historical research on Pentecostalism.

In this chapter I compare methodological developments in general historical research with some interpretive approaches to Pentecostal history. Because the latter is seen as a subcategory of church history, I include a theological perspective. Next, I devote attention to finding and using sources and offer some examples of surprises and discoveries in archival research. In any writing of a Pentecostal history, the issues of the origin and definition of Pentecostalism are most important. The issue of origins is addressed in the discussion of interpretive approaches, and the even more difficult matter of definition is addressed together with statistics.

GENERAL HISTORIOGRAPHY

Writing history may be described as accurate research of relevant events and facts in order to arrive at coherent conclusions and interpretations concerning the past that will be of use for the present. Although pure objectivity is unattainable, the researcher must attempt to be objective by maintaining a critical distance from his material. Even the professional historian has convictions and emotions that influence his or her interpretations. Church historians, for instance, often write from an ecclesiastical perspective. Luther might be a hero for one but a heretic for another, depending on the background from which the historian comes. The researcher must be aware of his or her own perspective, bias, and methodology, always keeping track of the difference between facts and interpretation. To avoid tunnel vision the historian needs to trace as many sources, internal and external, as possible.

Everything that happens is an event, but not all events hold equal value for the future. What can be traced from the past forms the data or sources with which the historian works. The historian assembles, selects, orders, and conducts a critical evaluation of the data before drawing conclusions. Looking for the connections between the facts, historians select from among the facts those that are important for their research. The importance depends on the research question that is being asked. Because research questions change over time, one could say that "every present has the past for which it asks."[2] This means that in a way the past is dynamic. Or perhaps better stated, the way we perceive the past is dynamic.

Several approaches to history can be distinguished. Up to the nineteenth century, historians were typically focused on political and military events. This old focus on a small (often-male) elite of educated and powerful is now often described as a history that is written "from above." During the twentieth century concern shifted toward economic and social life. Decolonization and the rise of feminism had a further impact on historical writings. A new kind of history, written "from below," took the perspective of the poor and powerless.[3] Ordinary people's views and oral forms of history were taken more seriously. Approaches such as social history and cultural history follow this line. Asking new types of questions led to looking for new kinds of sources, such as oral histories, images, and rituals, or new ways to interpret the known sources. More recent is the employment of interdisciplinary approaches or the interest in global history, which compares developments in different countries or continents. Gradually we have come to understand that a world history is not the same as a European or a Western history. The extension of the geographic field suggests the relativity of the old Western perspective.

Another shift in interest can be detected in the purpose of history. In the past the purpose of history was educational or nationalistic.[4] It often served to demonstrate the supremacy of a particular class, nation, or church. Today the purpose is rather to get a better understanding of the present by studying its historical development.

DEFINITION AND NUMBERS

For a researcher it is necessary to have a working definition of the object of study. To study Pentecostalism one needs to be aware not only of the great diversity but also of the unifying characteristics, including the characteristics that are different from those common to Christianity at large. A broad definition of Pentecostalism that includes all of Christianity makes no sense.

How can we define such a diverse phenomenon as Pentecostalism? Various attempts have been made, but the question still remains a matter of much debate. The Norwegian theologian Nils Bloch-Hoell identified as the movement's most outstanding characteristic "the doctrine of Spirit baptism as an experience different from conversion, manifested by the speaking with tongues."[5] Herewith Bloch-Hoell follows the self-identification of earlier Pentecostal writers such as Stanley H. Frodsham (1926), Donald Gee (1941), and Carl Brumback (1946). This theological definition has two identification markers of Spirit baptism: it is different from conversion, and it is manifested by tongues. By implication this refers to the doctrines of subsequence (meaning subsequent to conversion) and evidential tongues, two prominent issues in Pentecostal self-definitions.

The first of these issues is generally accepted among Pentecostals, but the second is more controversial, certainly outside North America. Walter J. Hollenweger therefore qualified the second marker by saying that it is "usually, but not always, associated with speaking in tongues."[6] The marker of "evidential tongues" is left out since it has been questioned among Pentecostals from the beginning, and it is neither taught nor generally experienced by a number of Pentecostal denominations.

In the first half of the twentieth century Pentecostal research dealt with what we now call "classical" Pentecostalism. For the classical Pentecostals, a subcategory of the "first wave," the above definition was useful, and it remains so when Hollenweger's definition is taken into consideration. The second half of the century saw the rise of the Charismatic Renewal, or "second wave," to which a neo-Charismatic, or "third wave," category was later added. While the "second wave," when limited to the Charismatic Renewal movements within the mainline churches, is still an identifiable category, according to the editors of the *New International Dictionary of Pentecostal and Charismatic Movements,* the "third wave" is a "catch-all category" that is nearly impossible to define: "[It] comprises 18,810 independent, indigenous, postdenominational denominations and groups that cannot be classified either as pentecostal or charismatic, but share a common emphasis on the Holy Spirit, spiritual gifts, Pentecostal-like experiences (not Pentecostal terminology), signs and wonders, and power encounters. In virtually every other way, however, they are as diverse as the world's cultures they represent."[7]

When this definition is compared with that found in the 1988 *Dictionary,* it is clear that the "third wave" has been broadened and relabeled "Neocharismatic" in order to include "vast numbers of independent and indigenous churches and groups that cannot be classified as either pentecostal or charismatic" but which share Pentecostal-like experiences.[8] According to the statistics of D. B. Barrett and

T. M. Johnson in the 2002 *NIDPCM*, neo-Charismatics outnumber all Pentecostals and Charismatics. The largest numbers are found in (1) the prophetic African independent churches, (2) in Asia, especially the house church movement in China, and (3) in Latin American countries, especially in Brazil. By moving the nonwhite indigenous Pentecostals from the first wave to the third wave, the 2002 edition made the first wave nearly synonymous with classical Pentecostalism but limited to the Western-related denominations.

The confusion within these categories is apparent in the 2002 *NIDPCM*. The editor includes the Church of God in Christ in his description of classical Pentecostals, where it must be classified, but Barrett and Johnson move this denomination to the third wave in their statistics. The same confusion applies to the numbers. The editor notes that the number of classical Pentecostals has tripled between 1970 and 1990, but this growth is difficult to find in the statistics. A comparison of the figures (in millions) in the 1988 and 2002 editions gives us the following picture:

Statistics	1st Wave	2nd Wave	3rd Wave	Total
1988 (Barrett)	176	123	28	327
2002 (Barrett/Johnson)	66	176	295	537

The majority of those who were listed as first wave Pentecostals in 1988 have been relabeled "third wavers" in 2002. These categories are arbitrary. The third category, unclearly labeled with the container term "Neocharismatic," includes large numbers that should rather be labeled classical Pentecostals. In the wider literature the three "wave" categories are used in such a variety of ways that it is best to abandon them all together.

The broadening of the categories as shown in the above statistics, of course, suggests a broadening of the definition. The earlier definition suited classical Pentecostalism but not the Charismatic Renewal and much less the neo-Charismatics. Therefore, more inclusive definitions have been suggested. In 2002 Allan Anderson proposed that the Pentecostal movement includes "those movements with an emphasis on the experience of the power of the Holy Spirit with accompanying manifestations of the imminent presence of God."[9] In his *Introduction to Pentecostalism* (2004), he has chosen to follow the lead of Robert Anderson, emphasizing experience and practice rather than the doctrine informing an appropriate definition, and suggests that it is "a movement concerned primarily with the *experience* of the working of the Holy Spirit and the *practice* of spiritual gifts."[10] Building on this broad definition, Anderson in this volume identifies four overlapping types. Although the debate will no doubt go on, for the present time this taxonomy seems to be a promising way to address the whole range of Pentecostalism.

PENTECOSTAL ORIGINS

Until recently, it has been common to point to the United States at the turn of the twentieth century as the place of origin for Pentecostalism, with the two main players being Charles Parham and William Seymour. Although this view is no longer held as a satisfactory explanation for the global rise of Pentecostalism, the events at Topeka and Los Angeles have functioned as icons in telling the miraculous story of this movement.

According to Hollenweger, the questions of where and when the Pentecostal movement started are matters of definition. To him, such a historical judgment must also be a theological judgment. Hollenweger distinguishes between the *realgeschichtliche* approach, which he favors, and the *ideengeschichtliche* approach. The first approach focuses on history as an interaction of religious, cultural, and social traditions. It sees Pentecostalism as the encounter between black oral spirituality in the United States and Catholic spirituality as it was handed down in the American Holiness tradition. It promotes a holistic understanding of Pentecost. Baptism in the Holy Spirit breaks down racial and other social barriers in the body of Christ. The Azusa Street revival is viewed as the cradle of Pentecostalism. The second approach focuses on the history of theological ideas. In this case, it can be seen in the idea of the baptism with the Holy Spirit being evidenced by the speaking in tongues. Therefore, it points to Parham's Bible College in Topeka, Kansas, where this doctrine was formulated for the first time.[11]

Hollenweger's presentation begs a theological question as to how to define the essence of Pentecostalism. On this matter many might prefer the Azusa event, but the question must be asked whether this decision does justice to the historical quest for the origin of Pentecostalism. The blending of history and theology is a problematic issue. Hollenweger is fully aware of his theological approach. In the introduction to his *Pentecostalism: Origins and Developments Worldwide* (1997) he writes of his own work, "Compared to the earlier volume, *The Pentecostals,* this is a thoroughly theological book, but it tells theology in the form of histories. This seems to me to be a form of scholarly treatment which is more appropriate to the contextual spiritualities of Pentecostalism, than propositional, so-called universal statements and discussions, because it places Pentecostal convictions and practices in their different cultural contexts."[12] Hollenweger is probably correct in assuming that this theological approach is more appropriate to describe the essence of the Pentecostal story, but a historical question as to the origin of Pentecostalism should receive a historical answer.

Historically, Parham can receive credit for formulating the doctrine of Spirit baptism evidenced by tongues that has been so characteristic of classical Pentecostalism. At the same time, Seymour deserves credit for interpreting, reinterpreting, and applying this teaching in an interracial local church setting in Los Angeles, from which the Azusa Street version would receive national and worldwide attention and thereby greatly influence the global rise of Pentecostalism. Even if we were to limit the options to Parham and/or Seymour, there does not seem to be a clear-cut answer to the question of who is at the root of the Pentecostal movement. Both men played essential roles in the formation of Pentecostalism, but of the Azusa Street event it may be said that its effect went far beyond the national borders and, as a result, far beyond the direct influence of Parham.

Today we have become more aware of the great varieties within Pentecostalism. As a result, some prefer to speak of Pentecostalisms. Similarly we have become aware of the diversity that must be recognized in its beginnings. It is more appropriate to see the Azusa Street revival as part of a wider series of revivals that promoted the Pentecostal experience throughout the world.[13] Interestingly this interpretation of Pentecostal origins more closely resembles the early Pentecostal claim of spontaneous, simultaneous beginnings without any particular founder (see below), although it does not necessitate the theological claim made by Emmanuel Schuurman in 1981.

PENTECOSTAL INTERPRETIVE HISTORIES

In 1986 the historian Grant Wacker wrote an excellent evaluation of how history was written among early Pentecostals. He established that "at the most general level, pentecostals, like most Christians, assumed that history was linear, moving by divine guidance from a starting point to an ending point. That meant that ultimately history was providential, progressing inexorably from Creation to the Final Judgement, whether humans co-operated or not. But unlike many Christians, or at least many modern Christians, pentecostals also believed that God's governance of history was partly dependent on human responses."[14]

The movement's origins were quickly attributed to supernatural interventions. The revival came "Suddenly . . . from Heaven," as Carl Brumback would title his book on the history of the Assemblies of God in 1961. This "sacred meteor theme" (Wacker) also presented itself in the assertion that the Pentecostal outpouring more or less simultaneously fell in all parts of the world without the influence of any one person or group on another.[15] Although early histories show a strong disagreement as to the theological, geographic, and social origins of the movement, there is a remarkable agreement on its significance. The revival was given cosmo-centric relevance. It was the "Latter Rain," the final episode of history before the Lord's Return. Wacker observed, "Pentecostals were convinced beyond question that they—and they alone—were riding the crest of history."[16]

After discussing the various early histories, Wacker concluded that the "golden oldies" are unreliable as conventional historical works but are very useful as "ritualised" works. By this he meant that they present a version of the past that suited the contemporary theological and institutional needs of the movement. The data were filtered and the interpretations were "simplified and dramatised in order to make them serve the larger purpose of the movement."[17] These remarks refer to the histories written by Pentecostals during the movement's first decades. The Pentecostal authors themselves had experienced an encounter with the divine and interpreted the events from their perspective. In their mind there was no doubt that this movement was initiated by God. It would be dishonoring God for them not to testify about the divine interventions.

In his article on the methodology of pursuing Pentecostal history, William Kay addressed the role of providence in the formation of the movement.[18] Kay warned against secular historical models that may harm the interpretation of Pntecostal experiences. He believed it is impossible to write Pentecostal history without some reference to providence. He also held that Pentecostal history should have some resemblance to the historical writings of the Bible. The Pentecostal writer, like the biblical writers, is convinced of God's continuous action in history. Kay's plea demonstrates the struggle of Pentecostal historians to remain objective as scholars while at the same time remaining true to their personal convictions. Nevertheless, Pentecostal historians must adapt to academic standards if they want to communicate on that level. All writers must have their audiences in mind. Writing a popular history for a Pentecostal periodical is quite different from writing a research article for a scholarly journal. These are different worlds with different rules for communication. In scholarly writings the researcher must maintain a critical distance from his subject and therefore should be very reluctant to attribute activities directly to God. This is not so much a matter of objectivity versus subjectivity but rather the use of different categories. Secular historiography simply does not have the appropriate tools to include God.

The early Pentecostal writers were not trained historians. They were followed by a generation of academically trained historians, many of them Pentecostals (e.g., William Menzies and Vinson Synan), who introduced a new type of Pentecostal historiography.

In 1997 the historian Augustus Cerillo distinguished four interpretive approaches to the history of American Pentecostal origins: the providential, the historical roots, the multicultural, and the functional.[19] He noticed that historians often combined any number of these four approaches or even employed different approaches in separate publications. The providential approach has already been discussed. The historical roots approach stresses Pentecostal continuity with nineteenth-century religious and social developments, in particular, the holiness and evangelical movements. As an example of this approach, Cerillo refers to Donald Dayton's work on the theological roots of Pentecostalism. Dayton concluded that the rise of Pentecostalism "may be seen as a natural development of forces that had been set in motion much earlier."[20] The Pentecostal historians Menzies and

Synan combine the historical roots approach with the providential approach.[21] The third, multicultural approach stresses the role of ethnic and racial minorities, especially African Americans and Hispanics, in the American telling of the story, as in the pattern of Hollenweger advocated by Lovett, Nelson, and MacRobert, among others.[22] Since the emphasis is so heavily weighted in favor of a black origin, it might be better labeled the "black origin" approach. Finally, the functional approach seeks to connect Pentecostalism to its cultural setting. It has been used to understand Pentecostal thought and practice in order to learn why it attracts so many adherents. Cerillo divides this one group into two groups. One group focuses on the socially dysfunctional aspects, drawing on theories of social disorganization, economic and social deprivation, and psychological maladjustment. Robert Anderson's *Vision of the Disinherited* (1979) may serve as an example for this first group. The other group points to the positive functions of Pentecostal spirituality, such as its sensitivity to the largely poor and powerless adherents. Harvey Cox's *Fire from Heaven* (1995) is exemplary of this model.

Cerillo regards the four approaches as complementary. Each has its weaknesses and each its strengths. The providential interpretation cannot be verified by generally accepted research methods and therefore will not be taken seriously by secular historians. The historical roots approach fits well with regular religious historiography, but the emphasis on continuity can blur what is in fact new or at least different.[23] The multicultural (or black origin) approach has opened new ways to perceive the origins or essence of Pentecostalism, but it is in danger of being too subjective. The functional approach has given us more insight into the social and economic status of Pentecostal recruits and of social and economic transitions in society. However, it tends to disregard the continuity with nineteenth-century religious and social developments, as well as the specific character of Pentecostalism. As a result, Cerillo called for a more comprehensive and historically satisfying synthesis of the Pentecostal story. Although this goal might not yet have been fully attained, he saw the works of Grant Wacker and Edith Blumhofer as moving in this direction.[24] They connect the social location, mind-set, and subculture of the Pentecostals with broader cultural and social currents in North America. The recent study of the Azusa Street revival by Cecil M. Robeck Jr. is exemplary of how thorough research may unearth a large number of new sources that may be skillfully connected to broader socioreligous developments, thereby providing excellent insight into Pentecostal beginnings.[25]

Compared to North American historical studies, Europe, Africa, Asia, and, to a lesser extent, Latin America are still behind in Pentecostal research, although the many sociological, anthropological, and other works such as case studies and ethnic studies that have been completed on Latin American Pentecostals provide significant potential interpretive help to historians working on the region. For many areas much more groundbreaking work has to be done. One advantage of being somewhat behind in this process, however, is that one learns from earlier mistakes and misconceptions.

MISCONCEPTIONS

In reflecting on the misconceptions in the writing of Pentecostal history, Allan Anderson has advocated for a global perspective *and* a history written from below.[26] Anderson's plea follows the shift we have seen in general historiography. Both in his *Introduction to Pentecostalism* (2004) and in his *Spreading Fires* (2007), he has employed a global perspective. He has stressed the global nature of the movement right from the start, speaking of a metaculture brought into existence through periodicals and missionary networks in its early stage.

Anderson has also attempted to correct earlier distortions in the writing of Pentecostal history. Pentecostal histories written in English, for instance, have often reflected a Western bias, and the "golden oldies" have frequently included a "white racial bias" and a "persistent gender bias." In all of them the vital role of indigenous workers, especially in Latin America, Africa, and Asia, was ignored or minimized, bringing Anderson to lament, "Where have all the soldiers gone?"

If indigenous workers are mentioned at all, it is usually as anonymous "native workers," "or at best, they are mentioned by a single name, often misspelled."[27] Nevertheless, the rapid growth of Pentecostalism in Latin America, Africa, and Asia was accomplished more effectively by the indigenous evangelists and pastors than by the Western missionaries. As long as our histories depend on the published letters, reports, and periodicals of Western agencies and their missionaries, our understanding will be seriously distorted. These documents were written for Western consumption in order to raise support for the mission work. Therefore, Anderson has called for a "reading between the lines" when studying these sources. Such an appeal, although understandable, also calls for caution. If there is no other evidence to support our understanding derived from a reading between the lines, we must be careful about drawing conclusions from these spaces; otherwise we might argue in a circle. This underscores the importance of digging further in the quest for more primary sources such as correspondence of missionaries not written for publication and minutes of missionary board meetings, since these sources might tend to balance the picture derived from documents published for public consumption. Such an undertaking calls for more local and regional studies by researchers prepared to go the extra mile in their search for new sources.

SOURCES

Primary sources are firsthand or eyewitness accounts, testimonies, sermons, diaries, letters, notes, minutes, and official records. But they may also include publications from the period at hand, for example, books, articles, periodicals, songbooks, creeds, official records, newspapers, and even parts of unpublished work such as research papers or theses. Examples include the Minutes and Letters of the Pentecostal Missionary Union (PMU), kept in the Donald Gee Centre, and Thomas Barratt's diaries, kept in Oslo. Primary sources provide observations that were made by those who lived at the time of the events, whether insiders or outsiders. When the accounts are written down at a later stage, in retrospect, there is more interpretation involved. For example, the famous prophecy from Smith Wigglesworth on David du Plessis has several versions. Over time it was reinterpreted and expanded by du Plessis himself in relation to the developments that took place in his life.[28] Because of this reworking some might classify the latter under secondary sources.

Secondary sources are secondhand accounts such as books, articles, research papers, or theses that have described or studied these events in some way. These accounts are made at a later stage by those who had no part in the events described. They usually involve interpretation. They may be the work of either outsiders or insiders. Questions that are important in handling the sources critically include the following: Is the source authentic? Who is the author? Is he reliable? Which sources are used by the author? How were the sources used? With both secondary and primary sources, it is important to determine the perspective from which the person has written and to detect any potential or possible bias.

CASE STUDY

In the case of the PMU we are fortunate to have an excellent archive that contains all the minutes and letters to and from the missionaries who worked with that organization. As a case in point, Dutch Pentecostal missionaries founded the mission outpost of the PMU in Lijiang, China. The transition of leadership from the Dutch missionary Peter Klaver to the British missionary James Andrews in 1924 caused quite a stir and even led to a split. This disturbance did not appear at all in published sources. It could only be retrieved from these archival documents.

When Klaver was due for a furlough, the PMU thought it was time to put a British superintendent in charge of the mission at Lijiang and appointed James Andrews to the post. Klaver considered Andrews totally incapable of doing the job and urged the council to put his fellow Dutch missionary, Elize Scharten, in charge during his absence.[29] Elize Scharten also appealed to the council not to send Andrews to Lijiang. The PMU council forwarded extracts of Klaver's letter to Jessie Biggs, who was on furlough in England and who was also engaged to Andrews at the time, for comment. Not surprisingly, she strongly defended her future husband. As a result, the council saw no reason to alter its decision to send Andrews to Lijiang. The situation grew worse for Klaver when it became apparent that after his furlough he would not be allowed to return to Lijiang. A letter written by the Chinese church at Lijiang in favor of Klaver and a letter from another PMU missionary, Florence Ives, defending Klaver could not make the council change its decision.[30] Klaver left Lijiang in January 1924 but still planned to return. In July he resigned from the PMU after a conversation with Cecil Polhill. The Dutch Pentecostal Mission Council decided to send Klaver back to Lijiang "to continue the work given them by God Himself."[31] Since the Dutch leader G. R. Polman insisted in several letters on knowing the motives behind the decision to replace Klaver, secretary T. H. Mundell finally, in March 1925, provided the following information:

> The Council was much exercised about the Dutch Workers at Lijiang during the recent War with Germany when Mr. Polhill had special communications from our Government Officials in connection with the pro-German tendencies and utterances of our Dutch Missionaries at Lijiang and the Council then resolved that so soon as we could we would endeavour to have an English Superintendent over the work at Lijiang so that whilst allowing the Dutch Workers to remain, the Head of the work would be an Englishman. It was really in pursuance of that decision we ultimately decided that so soon as Mr. and Mrs. Klaver left on furlough we should replace them with Mr. and Mrs. Andrews. I am telling you candidly the reason so that we are not saying anything whatever against Mr. Klaver personally.[32]

This statement, however, can be interpreted as standing in contradiction to what Mundell wrote to Klaver in November 1923: "This decision my dear Brother, has been come to not because you are Dutch as we cannot recognise Nationalities in The Lord's work, Who has made one of all nations, but because we believe it will be entirely for The Glory of God and in His Will."[33]

From the Dutch point of view there was much to be said against the decision of the PMU to replace Klaver with Andrews. Yet with regard to the local witness, sending Klaver back seems also to have been the wrong response.[34]

Internal conflicts and characterizations like these are typically not mentioned in Pentecostal publications. All the above information was gathered from archival sources, sources that are not always available. It demonstrates the need to retrieve the early histories, to collect materials before they get lost, and to record oral traditions and memories before they die out. In view of its importance for pentecostal history, I want to elaborate on the issue of tracing and dealing with sources, in particular, the use of archival material.

ARCHIVAL RESEARCH

Archives, as well as libraries and museums, keep a wealth of material that relates to the past.[35] In the Netherlands, for instance, a researcher has access to all national, provincial, and city archives and to a large number of institutional, church, and private archives. How to gain access to these materials will vary from country to country, but the following discussion with reference to the Netherlands serves as an example.

Just before 1800, civil registration of births, marriages, and deaths became compulsory. Since 1829 there has been a national census every ten years up to 1971. Since 1850 every city has kept records of its citizens and their addresses. Every change of address is registered. Up to 1938 families were registered on one card; since then, each individual has had a separate card. These cards are forwarded when the person moves to another city. After the death of the individual, these cards end up in the Central Office of Genealogy in the Hague. Annual city directories are also important for names and addresses but may also include professions. City archives keep photographs and construction plans of most buildings.

Since 1838 the Cadastre has kept track of the exact measurements, rights, limitations, ownership, and mortgage of all real estate.[36] When selling or buying real estate, an official deed of sale or purchase, witnessed by a public notary, is compulsory. The same applies to mortgages. Since 1818 the tax collector has required a memorandum of succession when someone has died. It sums up all possessions and debts of the deceased, and the relatives are given access to this information. All testaments or wills transacted since 1890 can be traced through the Central Index. Income tax became compulsory in 1914; this information is not easy to consult, but it is available. All these documents end up in archives.

The chamber of commerce has information on all foundations and associations.[37] Church archives usually keep minutes of board meetings and letters addressed to and from the board. In some cases, when new pastors move into a church, they dispose of earlier records because they do not understand their value. A church historian would do well to point local pastors to a place where these materials can be preserved for future research purposes. All the above information can be traced. We need to be aware of what is present in libraries and how to find it.

Robeck found himself frustrated by the lack of imagination and the perpetuation of errors in most of the earlier attempts to tell the story of the Azusa Street Mission. He discovered a plethora of public and private documents, previously unknown, that made a significant contribution to our understanding of what took place. Among these resources he mentions city directories, a host of local newspapers, birth and death certificates, obituaries, cemeteries, repositories of photographs, city maps, census material, articles of incorporation, purchase and mortgage transactions, and court proceedings. All these contained hidden treasures waiting to be disclosed.[38]

Presence

When you start to research the early history of Pentecostalism, you will often find it difficult to locate primary sources of the early period. The early Pentecostals were not interested in saving materials for the next generation. They thought that the Lord was coming back within their lifetimes, so why worry about these earthly matters? The Dutch Pentecostal pioneer Polman must have had a vast number of letters from all over the world. None of these has been preserved, nor have the films he made. His extensive library was auctioned off after his death to help pay the bills. His children kept only some of his photographs, family poems, the guest book of the Mission Home, and some volumes of his periodicals. Most of the documents that eventually were found came from Reformed clergymen, who had the presence of mind to collect and save historical sources.

Three collections of letters from the early period were traced. Two belonged to Reformed ministers who had been in close contact with Polman: G. A. Wumkes (1869–1954) and J. H. Gunning J.Hz. (1858–1940). The third belonged to Martha Visser (1896–1985), who was a former coworker of Polman's but had returned to the Reformed Church. All three were interested in church history, in particular, in the stories of the dissenters; all three published their findings. They took a critical and at the same time sympathetic stance toward Pentecostals. Most important, they kept the sources they collected! This researcher was privileged to interview Martha Visser one year before she died. After her death the family donated the relevant material to the Pentecostal archive. The two Reformed ministers left their books, pamphlets, correspondence, and notes to libraries and archives, where they lay waiting for decades to be discovered by researchers. In this way, fifty-six pieces of correspondence from Polman, three from Mrs. Polman, and nine addressed to Polman were traced, providing valuable information not found in other sources. Next to the correspondence, rare brochures and pamphlets from early Pentecostals or anti-Pentecostals were found. Also interesting were Wumkes's research notes, some of which were never used in publications.

Accessibility

Even when sources are present in publications, public libraries, and archives, they are not always easily found. In particular, the small brochures, correspondence, pamphlets, and other ephemera and missing issues of periodicals are difficult to trace. If they are kept at all, they are usually filed under separate collections not directly recorded in library catalogs. Thus Gunning's whole collection went to the University of Utrecht. Once the items had been cataloged and processed into the library system, the books were easy to find. For the correspondence, however, it was necessary to consult the special collection of handwritten documents, which demands a specific search. Wumkes's collection was split up. The books went to the Friesian provincial library, while the other documents went to the Friesian Literature Museum. In his case the Friesian language provided an additional obstacle. Wumkes was a well-known historian and advocate of the Friesian cause

(Friesland is a province in the Netherlands with a distinct language and culture). Because his memoirs, *Nei Sawntich Jier* (1949), were written in Friesian, his later reflection on his contact with the Pentecostals remained unknown to the general public.[39] Since universities, libraries, and some archives are increasingly digitalizing their holdings, including handwritten materials, the correspondence between Gunning and Polman is now available on-line (http://picarta.pica.nl). The same is true for others.

To cite another example, the Hollenweger collection is also split up. The books and periodicals are integrated into the library of the VU University, Amsterdam, and are therefore easily located, even on the Internet (www.ubvu.vu.nl). The archival material went to the Historical Documentation Center of the same university (www.hdc.vu.nl). The latter is cataloged in general terms and can be consulted in the reading room. Meanwhile a number of other Pentecostal research and documentation centers have been established.[40]

As electronic databases emerge it is becoming easier to trace obscure collections of handwritten documents, pamphlets, correspondence, and the like. For this reason it seems of paramount importance that libraries and archives develop these databases and make them available to researchers, preferably through the Internet.

A number of Pentecostal periodicals have been scanned and are now available on CD-ROM. Some are available through the Revival Library Web site, and a growing number of them are available through the Flower Pentecostal Heritage Center.[41] Dutch, German, and Swedish periodicals are currently being scanned. The benefits of these digital resources are evident. Not only do researchers and historians have easier access to the documents, but also in many cases the digital search machine at their disposal is a time saver.

In order to understand the importance of Azusa Street in the early Pentecostal papers, one can now check digitally how often the names (in various spellings) Azusa, Seymour, Los Angeles, Topeka, Parham and Ozman occur. This reveals that in the early British Pentecostal periodicals, as in the Dutch periodicals, the Topeka event and Parham were completely absent, whereas Azusa Street played a very important role as the place where the fire first fell and from where it spread throughout the world.[42]

Discoveries

Archival research may reveal delicate details unknown even to close relatives. In the case of Polman, it was revealed that he was born an illegitimate child, a fact he had kept from his children all his life. When Wumkes wrote a short biography of Polman, Polman explicitly requested that he not mention the names of his parents for personal reasons. As an infant of fifteen days old Polman was marked "onecht" (illegitimate, or more literally, "not genuine") in the baptismal record of the Netherlands Reformed Church. This mark was not washed away with the sacred water but left its imprint in the life of Polman.

In order to research the financial situation of the Pentecostal Assembly in Amsterdam, all deeds of purchase, sale, and mortgage in governmental archives and in the archives of the Cadastre were traced. With the help of Polman's children, access was given to the memorandum of succession and also to the last will. Information from Cecil Polhill's private bookkeeping record, kept by the Bedford County Record's Office, showed the large sums of money that he loaned to Gerrit Polman for the building.[43] With all this information and some references in the periodicals, it was possible to reconstruct the financial state of affairs with regard to the real estate. It could be established that the Pentecostals never bothered to clear the mortgage. Large sums of money were donated to the foreign mission field, but as to the building only the interest of the mortgage was paid. In light of the speedy return of the Lord, it was considered more important to bring the gospel to the uttermost parts of the earth than to pay for a building. The debt owing on the property was about equal to its value.

In June 1912 the Pentecostal Assembly opened the newly built Immanuel Hall in Amsterdam. Because the building was specially designed to suit the requirements of a Pentecostal meeting place, its floor plan deserved a closer look. As far as we know, the only other Pentecostal hall in Europe that was built before the one in Amsterdam was opened in Bournemouth, England, in November 1908. Although the Amsterdam hall was built solely for Pentecostal purposes, it did not have a baptistry until 1925, which was one of the surprising discoveries made during the archival research. None of the eyewitnesses had ever informed me of this fact, nor was it mentioned in any of the Pentecostal sources. Only the construction blueprints, kept in the archives of the city department responsible for issuing building licenses, revealed this secret. This fact has important theological significance. It substantiates the view that the Dutch Pentecostals initially saw themselves as a short-term revival movement, intended to bless the existing churches but not intending to build a separate Pentecostal denomination.

CONCLUSION

Bearing in mind the question I started with (America or Heaven?), we would conclude that the events of the Azusa Street revival in Los Angeles (1906) certainly influenced the start of Pentecostalism in Europe, while at the same time the element of the supernatural must not be overlooked. Yet religious revivals are not merely the product of export, whether from America or from Heaven. Revivalist movements always arise in a historical context and as a rule are reactions against the status quo in church or society. This calls for a thorough study of the historical context, including its religious, social, and cultural life. Attention should be given to what is continuous and what is new. Due credit must be given to the indigenous pioneers. Writing from a global perspective provides a helicopter view. It enables us to make comparative studies, but it should not cause us to neglect valuable local and national research. As a national history is founded in the local and regional history, so the global perspective must be founded on thorough national and continental studies. Much work is still to be done making use of all the resources and disciplines available. Anthropologists, sociologists, and other social scientists have contributed considerably to our understanding of modern Pentecostalism. While this chapter has focused on historical research, it is obvious that research skills and methodology from the social sciences can supplement those of the historian and vice versa.[44] Pentecostal historians are now addressing social and cultural issues, which require a more structural explanation as well as dialogue with other disciplines. GloPent has become an important player in this field by pulling together institutions and researchers from various disciplines. Some areas where GloPent could be of help for further archival research include the stimulation, collecting, and preservation of archival material, especially throughout the developing world; the initiation of an international database and the interchange of available archival material; and the creation of a global network of Pentecostal archivists.

If "every present has the past for which it asks," then there is a dynamic relationship between the past and the present. To a great extent, our present questions determine what we will find. To be "present-driven" is not a problem as long as we realize that we see only in part and thus must remain open to complementary approaches. Cooperating in the venture of recapturing the Pentecostal past is the way to acquire a better understanding of the present.

NOTES

1. Cornelis van der Laan, *Sectarian against His Will: Gerrit Roelof Polman and the Birth of Pentecostalism in the Netherlands* (Metuchen, NJ: Scarecrow Press, 1991), 1.

2. Bernard Slicher van Bath, *Geschiedenis: Theorie en praktijk* (Utrecht: Het Spectrum, 1978),17, cited from R. F. Beerling, *Heden en verleden: Denken over geschiedenis* (1962), 18.

3. Peter Burke, ed., *New Perspectives on Historical Writing* (Pennsylvania: Pennsylvania State University Press, 2001); John Tosh, *The Pursuit of History: Aims, Methods and New Directions in the Study of Modern History* (Harlow: Longman, 2000).

4. Slicher van Bath, *Geschiedenis,* 18.

5. Nils Bloch-Hoell, *The Pentecostal Movement* (Oslo: Universitetsforlaget, 1966), 2. Originally published in Norwegian in 1956.

6. W. J. Hollenweger, *Enthusiastisches Christentum: Die Pfingstbewegung in Geschichte und Gegenwart* (Zurich: Zwingli Verlag, 1969), xxi.

7. *NIDPCM,* xx.

8. *NIDPCM,* xx.

9. Allan Anderson, "Diversity in the Definition of 'Pentecostal/Charismatic' and the Ecumenical Implications," paper presented at the 31st Annual Meeting of the Society for Pentecostal Studies, Lakeland, Florida, 2002.

10. Allan Anderson, *An Introduction to Pentecostalism* (Cambridge: CUP, 2004), 14; original emphasis.

11. W. J. Hollenweger, "Priorities in Pentecostal Research: Historiography, Missiology, Hermeneutics and Pneumatology," in *Experiences of the Spirit: Conference on Pentecostal and Charismatic Research in Europe at Utrecht University 1989,* ed. J. A. B. Jongeneel et al. (Frankfurt: Peter Lang, 1991), 8–10.

12. Walter J. Hollenweger, *Pentecostalism: Origin and Development Worldwide* (Peabody: Hendrickson, 1997), 2.

13. See Allan Anderson, *Spreading Fires: The Missionary Nature of Early Pentecostalism* (London: SCM, 2007), 290–91.

14. Grant Wacker, "Are the Golden Oldies Still Worth Playing? Reflections on History Writing among Early Pentecostals," *Pneuma* 8:2 (1986): 83.

15. Wacker, "Golden Oldies," 86.

16. Wacker, "Golden Oldies," 93.

17. Wacker, "Golden Oldies," 95.

18. William K. Kay, "Three Generations On: The Methodology of Pentecostal History," *EPTA Bulletin* 11 (1992): 58–69.

19. Augustus Cerillo Jr., "Interpretive Approaches to the History of American Pentecostal Origins," *Pneuma* 19:1 (1997): 29–52. See also Augustus Cerillo Jr., "The Beginning of American Pentecostalism: A Historiographical Overview," in *Pentecostal Currents in American Protestantism,* ed. Edith L. Blumhofer, Russel P. Splittler, and Grant A. Wacker (Chicago: University of Illinois Press, 1999), 229–59.

20. Cerillo, "Interpretive Approaches," 38.

21. William Menzies, *Anointed to Serve: The Story of the Assemblies of God* (Springfield: GPH, 1971); Vinson Synan, *The Holiness-Pentecostal Movements in the United States* (Grand Rapids: Eerdmans, 1971).

22. Leonard Lovett, "Black Holiness-Pentecostalism: Implications for Ethics and Transformation" (Ph.D. diss., Emory University, 1978); Douglas Nelson, "For Such a Time as This: The Story of Bishop William J. Seymour and the Azusa Street Revival" (Ph.D. diss., University of Birmingham, 1981); Iaian MacRobert, *The Black Roots and White Racism of Early Pentecostalism in the USA* (New York: St. Martin's Press, 1988).

23. Cerillo, "Interpretive Approaches," 51.

24. Edith Blumhofer, *Restoring the Faith: The Assemblies of God, Pentecostalism, and American Culture* (Urbana: University of Illinois Press, 1993); Edith Blumhofer, *Aimee Semple McPherson: Everybody's Sister* (Grand Rapids: Eerdmans, 1993); Grant Wacker, *Heaven Below: Early Pentecostals and American Culture* (Cambridge, MA: HUP, 2001).

25. Cecil M. Robeck, *The Azusa Street Mission & Revival* (Nashville: Thomas Nelson, 2006).

26. Allan Anderson, "Where Have All the Soldiers Gone? Revising Pentecostal History in Global Perspective," paper presented at the International Conference on Asian Pentecostalism, 17–20 September 2001, University of Birmingham.

27. Anderson, "Where Have All the Soldiers Gone?" 4.

28. See Martin Robinson, "To the Ends of the Earth: The Pilgrimage of an Ecumenical Pentecostal, David du Plessis, 1905–1987" (Ph.D. diss., University of Birmingham, 1987); Brinton Rutherford, "From Prosecutor to Defender: An Intellectual History of David J. DuPlessis, Drawn from the Stories of His Testimony" (thesis, Fuller Theological Seminary, 2000).

29. P. Klaver to PMU Council, Lijiang, 20 August 1923. PMU sources are in the Donald Gee Centre at Mattersey.

30. Letter from Lijiang Pentecostal Church written in Chinese with an English translation by Klaver was enclosed in Klaver's letter to the PMU Council, Amsterdam, 24 May 1924. Florence A. Ives to PMU Council, Yunnan-fu, 25 September 1924.

31. Dutch Pentecostal Council to PMU Council, Amsterdam, 11 February 1925.

32. T. H. Mundell to G. R. Polman, London, 25 March 1925.

33. T. H. Mundell to P. Klaver, London, 16 November 1923.

34. Cornelis van der Laan, "Beyond the Clouds: Elize Scharten (1876–1965). Pentecostal Missionary to China," in *Pentecostalism in Context,* ed. Wonsuk M. and Robert P. Menzies (Sheffield: SAP, 1997), 337–60.

35. J. A. M. Y. Bos-Rops, M. Bruggeman, and F. C. J. Ketelaar, *Archiefwijzer: Handleiding voor het gebruik van archieven in Nederland* (Muidenberg: Dick Coutinho, 1987).

36. The Netherlands' Cadastre and Public Registers Agency is responsible for managing and supplying information about the legal situation of registered property. In the Public Registers, the Cadastre archives the various notarial deeds relating to real rights and mortgages. It also manages the topographic map, which includes a large collection of aerial photos.

37. The Netherlands Chamber of Commerce manages the trade register. The trade register contains a comprehensive list of all foundations and associations. It includes names of founders or owners and keeps a copy of the constitution. All BVs (private limited companies), NVs (public limited companies), cooperatives, and bonding companies are required to publish financial annual reports. These reports must also be filed with the chamber of commerce, where it is made available for public inspection. More than 1.4 million businesses, associations, and foundations throughout the Netherlands are entered in the trade register.

38. Cecil M. Robeck Jr., "The Use of Public Material for Instruction on Pentecostal Origins," paper presented at the Conference on Resources for Advancing Pentecostal Studies, Springfield, MO., April 17, 2004; Cecil M. Robeck Jr., "Finding Buried Treasures: Telling the Pentecostal Story Using Public and Private Sources," Azusa Street Centennial Celebration, Archivists' Track, Los Angeles, April 26, 2006.

39. G. A. Wumkes, *Nei Sawntich Jier* (Boalsert: A. J. Osinga, 1949).

40. Flower Pentecostal Heritage Center (Assemblies of God, Springfield, MO), Dixon Pentecostal Research Center (Church or God, Cleveland, TN), David du Plessis Center for Christian Spirituality (Fuller Theological Seminary, Pasadena, CA), Holy Spirit Research Center (Oral Robert University, Tulsa, OK), Donald Gee Centre (Mattersey, U.K.), Centre for Pentecostal and Charismatic Studies (University of Wales, Bangor), Centre for Pentecostal and Charismatic Studies (University of Birmingham), Hollenweger Center for the Interdisciplinary Study of Pentecostal and Charismatic Movements (VU University, Amsterdam), Interdisziplinäre Arbeitskreis Pfingstbewegung (University of Heidelberg), Swedish Pentecostal Research and Information Center (Stockholm). The most recent addition is GloPent, the European Research Network on Global Pentecostalism, a cooperative venture of the centers in Birmingham, Amsterdam, and Heidelberg.

41. E.g., *Confidence, Flames of Fire, Elim Evangel, Redemption Tidings, Apostolic Faith, Pentecostal Evangel.*

42. See my "What Good Can Come from Los Angeles? Changing Perceptions of the North American Origins in Early West-European Pentecostal Periodicals," in *The Azusa Street Revival and Its Legacy,* ed. Harold D. Hunter and Cecil M. Robeck Jr. (Cleveland: Pathway Press, 2006), 141–59.

43. Polhill's bookkeeping was traced by Desmond Cartwright. It also revealed that Polhill paid off the balance that was still owing on Azusa Street in February 1908. The following day Polhill received his Spirit baptism.

44. See Peter Lambert and Phillipp Schofield, eds., *Making History: An introduction to the History and Practices of a Discipline* (London: Routledge, 2004), 121–24.

PART THREE

Theology

11

Pneumatologies in Systematic Theology

Veli-Matti Kärkkäinen

FIRST WORDS ON METHODOLOGY AND APPROACH

The aim of this chapter is to look at the state of Pentecostal theology. Surveying the literature available, I was reminded of the important piece written by the leading Pentecostal systematician Frank Macchia in the revised edition of the *New International Dictionary of Pentecostal and Charismatic Movements,* titled "Theology, Pentecostal."[1] That article gives a succinct, balanced, and informative description of the main systematic contributions to developing Pentecostal theology. It discusses both the question of methodology and the main loci of Pentecostal theologies. Consequently, I came to the conclusion that attempting something similar but in a more modest way, focusing on the most obvious point of entry for Pentecostals to systematic theology, namely, the Spirit, might offer an alternative way to take stock and give a critical assessment of the state of affairs. Thus my aim here is to look at the state of Pentecostal theological scholarship by locating emerging Pentecostal theologizing of the Spirit within the larger matrix of rapidly developing constructive systematic theology done by Pentecostals, especially the younger generation of academically trained persons.

Challenges to this kind of task abound, however, and they should be highlighted up front. While there might be many more challenges, I was—and continue—tackling the following ones. First, who is to define what *Pentecostal* theology in general and pneumatology in particular are? In other words, who are the Pentecostals at the global and international levels we ought take as the shapers of the identity? Second—related to the identity question—is the overwhelming diversity of Pentecostalism at the global level. Third, is it really the case that the

Spirit is the "first theology" for Pentecostals? Or should it even be? And finally, where do we find the proper (re)sources for this kind of task?

Let me take one challenge at a time, beginning with the last. Until recently, Pentecostalism has not produced much theological literature; its contribution to Christian faith has been in the form of occasional pastoral and missional writings, testimonies, dreams, prophecies, and the like, which do not easily translate into an analytic, discursive theology.[2] The basic dilemma here is therefore obvious: should the scholar depend primarily on written, discursive writings or on grassroots testimonies from the believers in the pews and on the streets? If the former, then power is relegated—as in most traditional churches—to the priestly and academic elite. If the latter, then the question of *method* in theology becomes acute; in other words, how to collect and process testimonials, visions, prophecies, and similar material and make them "useful" for an academic setting. To make the issue even more complicated: it is not only a matter of the divide between Pentecostal academicians and laypeople in the congregations. There is a middle layer, namely, Pentecostal practitioners, pastors, elders, deacons, and other leaders, who are producing Pentecostal theology and pneumatology using other forms than academic treatises (though much of that can be found in occasional writings). For this presentation, I have relied predominantly on Pentecostal academic theologians' contributions; for scholarly writings, without extensive field study with interviews and observations, there is hardly an alternative.

With regard to the question of Pentecostal identity[3]—against the assumptions of uninformed outsider observers—pneumatology does not necessarily represent the center of Pentecostal spirituality. An emerging scholarly consensus holds that at the heart of Pentecostal spirituality lies the "Full Gospel," the idea of Jesus Christ in his fivefold role as Savior, Sanctifier, Baptizer with the Spirit, Healer, and Soon-Coming King. Since this is an issue so well documented and argued, for the purposes of this chapter I do not need to delve into details.[4] Consequently—and this is of utmost significance to my purposes here—the key to discerning and defining Pentecostal identity lies in Christ-centered Charismatic spirituality with a passionate desire to "meet" with Jesus Christ as he is being perceived as the Bearer of the Full Gospel. Spirituality, rather than theology/creeds or sociology of religion, is the key to understanding Pentecostalism.[5]

A critical facet to the question of identity is the overwhelming diversity of Pentecostalism—to the point that one should probably speak of Pentecostalisms (plural). The diversity arises in two dimensions: the cultural and the theologico-ecumenical. Pentecostalism, unlike any other contemporary religious movement, Christian or non-Christian, is spread across most cultures, linguistic barriers, and social locations.[6] Related to this is the theological and ecumenical diversity, which simply means that there are several more or less distinct Pentecostalisms—not only with the emerging three-tiered scholarly typology "Classical Pentecostalism,"

"Charismatic Movements," and "Neo-Charismatics,"[7] but also within Pentecostal movements themselves. I will say more about that in the following since it has everything to do with the presentation of Pentecostal pneumatologies. So, here we are: Who are the theological spokespersons for global Pentecostalisms and Charismatic movements and their understanding of the work of the Spirit in the world? Further, it is to be noted that "in Third World Pentecostalism, experience and practice are usually far more important than dogma. Pentecostalism today is in any case both fundamentally and dominantly a *Third World* phenomenon. In spite of its significant growth in North America, less than a quarter of its members in the world today are white, and this proportion continues to decrease."[8]

In addition to these challenges, others can be named. Unlike established Christian traditions such as Roman Catholicism, Pentecostalism cannot build on tradition for the simple reason that it came into existence only a century ago. Furthermore—and related to the question of identity—because Pentecostalism was birthed out of dynamic experience rather than a theological discovery, it has liberally incorporated elements from a number of theological traditions and sources such as Methodist-Holiness movements, the Protestant Reformation, mystical-Charismatic movements in the Roman Catholic and Eastern Orthodox Churches, as well as black or African American spirituality. Its theology is still in the making and represents a dynamic syncretistic exercise.

Following this overly long methodological introduction in which I have just presented the most obvious difficulties facing anyone attempting to assess the state of Pentecostal theology, let me present briefly the course of the discussion. First, I paint in a few strokes a picture of Pentecostal theologies and theological methods as a background and context to their pneumatologies. Second, I discuss the main features of Pentecostal spirituality as the bedrock for doing theology in general and pneumatology in particular. Third, I focus my efforts on discerning key features and distinctive contributions of Pentecostal theologians on the Spirit. Fourth, I attempt a comparison between Pentecostal theologies of the Spirit and those of mainline theologies as well as Charismatic counterparts. I conclude the chapter by recommending some tasks and suggestions for further research and reflections.

PENTECOSTAL THEOLOGY IN THE MAKING

Similar to their mainline counterparts, Pentecostals are yet to come to an agreement about what might be the most appropriate approach to theology. The tasks for such a reflection include the issue I mentioned above, namely, assessing the value and role of Charismatic spirituality, testimonies, visions, and similar things that are usually not incorporated into academic discursive theology. Macchia makes the helpful terminological note that rather than label all nonacademic theology "oral"—which certainly is not the case in the global North since much of Pentecostal thinking can be found written in journals, pamphlets, booklets, and similar occasional writings—it would be more appropriate to name it "nonaca-demic." This nonacademic theology can also be a great asset to the future of Pentecostal theological development. He writes:

> Important to note . . . is that the so-called nonacademic theology of pentecostals has not necessarily precluded disciplined exegetical work and theological reflection within the various theological *loci*. Such disciplined exegesis and systematic theo-logical reflection are significant, since nonacademic theology is not generally con-sciously critical, contextual, or methodical in its approach. Many pentecostals agree that the more rational exegetical and theological approaches to the gospel should still have a place in the development of various pentecostal theologies. Such rational approaches to theology, however, do not negate the significance of the nonacademic theologizing among pentecostals and similar free-church movements; nonacademic narrative and dramatic theologizing can offer a significant voice in the current theological climate. The older modernist problem of history . . . is now being expanded and intensified to include the challenges inherent in the complexities of social context and cultural pluralism. . . . In such an era of diversification and plural-ism, many are now becoming interested in a way of theologizing that is responsive to the unique experiences of various communities of faith, especially those that have been culturally marginalized without much access to academic citadels of learning, scientific methods, or literary analysis.[9]

If we look at the state of Pentecostal systematic theology today through the lens of the promise of the nonacademic theology described above, I suspect that the picture is somewhat confused. On the one hand, Pentecostal teachers—in keeping with the restorationist, "Back to the Bible" mentality of the movement—have always appreciated the importance of biblical materials for doing theology. In that sense, they have resisted the typical scholastic and later modernist paradigms of conceptual, philosophical, and analytic theological approaches. Indeed, a quick look at key theological works by Pentecostals reveals that what they have called "systematic" theologies are less that and mainly systematized outlines of biblical teachings. E. S. Williams's multivolume *Systematic Theology* (1953) is a prime example of that genre;[10] despite its title, the nature of the work is biblical theology grouped under main doctrinal loci rather than a systematic theological argumen-tation using also historical and philosophical insights. P. C. Nelson's widely used *Bible Doctrines* (1948) is appropriately titled in light of its contents.[11]

On the other hand, following in the footsteps of their evangelical colleagues and theological mentors, in the discussion of main theological topics, Pentecostals have rarely betrayed the influence of their own distinctive spirituality but have basically followed the agenda offered by others. A representative example here is the widely used *Foundations of Pentecostal Theology* (1983) written by two leading Foursquare Church theologians.[12] The discussion on God, revelation, Christology, soteriology, and eschatology follow the typical model of evangelical predecessors. The distinctively Pentecostal contributions are discussions of divine healing and Spirit baptism; apart from those chapters the reader could hardly tell that this is a distinctively Pentecostal discourse.

Newer-generation Pentecostal theologians have understandably raised the question of which approach, which method, would be most consonant with Pentecostal spirituality. The Chinese (from Singapore) Simon Chan and the American Steven J. Land have both argued vocally for the primacy of "spiritual" theology as the mode of doing theology for Pentecostals.[13] This would mean paying closer attention to the distinctively Pentecostal spirituality as the matrix out of which doctrinal discussions emerge, as well as giving proper account of prayer and other spiritual activities. Land's work also highlights the importance of the Wesleyan-Holiness tradition to emerging Pentecostalism with its focus on sanctification and Spirit baptism (the term adopted by Pentecostals and redefined by them in terms of empowerment) as well as of eschatology. The priority of eschatology for constructing Pentecostal theology is accentuated in William Faupel's historically oriented work, *The Everlasting Gospel* (1996).[14]

Macchia's essay in the *NICPCM* takes the fivefold Full Gospel template as a basic structuring guide to Pentecostal theology. At the same time, it makes an important addition by linking the discussion of Christology with that of Trinity. This is a badly needed corrective to a potential Trinitarian anemia in Pentecostalism.[15] Macchia rightly notes that in Pentecostal theology "excluded (or reduced to subordinate status) is the fatherhood of God, election, creation, Trinity, Scripture, and church." This is a critical observation, since "without a fundamental place for these doctrines, even Christology and pneumatology will suffer a lack of development."[16]

Though a full-scale academic systematic theology written by a contemporary Pentecostal theologian is yet to appear, Amos Yong's recent work, *The Spirit Poured Out on All Flesh: Pentecostalism and the Possibility of Global Theology,*[17] comes closest to being one. Yong discusses topics such as soteriology, ecclesiology, ecumenism, pneumatology, theology of religions, and creation from an authentically Pentecostal perspective and in mutual dialogue with Protestant and Roman Catholic theologies.

How does the state of Pentecostal pneumatology appear against the background of Pentecostal theology?

DISCERNING PENTECOSTAL SPIRITUALITY AS THE BEDROCK OF PENTECOSTAL PNEUMATOLOGIES

I am convinced that a proper way to assess and describe the state of Pentecostal pneumatology is to take a close look at Pentecostal spirituality and its implications for theologizing. What is significant about the Pentecostal experience of the Spirit was succinctly captured in the beginning of the Roman Catholic–Pentecostal dialogue in a Pentecostal position paper: "It may hardly be gainsaid, that the Pentecostal revivals of the present century have taken the *koinonia* of/with the Holy Spirit out of the cloistered mystical tradition of the Church, and made it the common experience of the whole people of God."[18] Pentecostal *koinonia* at its best represents a principle of democratization and reconciliation: not only is there access to God and "holy things" for all men and women, but there is also access to ministry and leadership. It is not about education, status, or wealth but about the empowerment of the Holy Spirit.

Consequently, it seems to me the most foundational feature and far-reaching contribution of Pentecostal views of the Spirit is what Pentecostals call "empowerment" and the Harvard theologian Harvey Cox names "primal spirituality." By this term Cox is referring to the largely unprocessed central core of humanity where an unending struggle for a sense of destiny and significance rages. For Cox, Pentecostalism represents a spiritual restoration of significance and purpose to lift the people from despair and hopelessness.[19] He considers this emphasis on "primal spirituality" evident in the contemporary (postmodern) world—as well as among Pentecostals in the Global South—as the key to its success. Pentecostalism "has succeeded because it has spoken to the spiritual emptiness of our time by reaching beyond the levels of creed and ceremony into the core of human religiousness, into what might be called 'primal spirituality,' that largely unprocessed nucleus of the psyche in which the unending struggle for a sense of purpose and significance goes on.... My own conviction is that Pentecostals have touched so many people because they have indeed restored something."[20]

Whereas for most other Christians the presence of the Spirit is just that, *presence,* for Pentecostals the presence of the Spirit in their midst implies *empowerment.*[21] While this empowerment often manifests itself in spiritual gifts such as speaking in tongues, prophesy, or healings, it is still felt and sought for by Pentecostals even when those manifestations are absent. The main function of the Pentecostal worship service, then, is to provide a setting for an encounter with Jesus, the embodiment of the Full Gospel, to receive the (em)power(ment) of the Spirit.[22] As important as sermon, hymns, and liturgy are, they all take second place to the meeting with the Lord.

Pentecostalism has thus offered a grassroots challenge to established churches and theologies, especially those endorsing the so-called cessationist principle, which holds that miracles or extraordinary charismata ceased at or near the end of the apostolic age. Often ridiculed for emotionalism, Pentecostals introduced a dynamic, enthusiastic type of spirituality and worship life to the contemporary church, emphasizing the possibility of experiencing God mystically. While it was the experience rather than doctrine that came first,[23] a novel and disputed doctrinal understanding of Spirit baptism emerged in the early years of the movement.

Though never uniformly formulated or followed by the worldwide movement, it is only fair to say that for the large majority of Pentecostals, this view came to be known as the "initial physical evidence." This simply means Pentecostals expect an external sign or marker of the reception of Spirit baptism, namely, speaking in tongues (glossolalia). Pentecostals claim this doctrine comes from the Book of Acts, their favorite book, and from contemporary experience. Theologically the initial evidence doctrine functions "sacramentally": it is an external confirmation of the inner grace received from God's Spirit. Pentecostals do not, of course, call it "sacramental," nor do they necessarily affirm the connection.[24]

Other gifts of the Spirit such as prophesying, prayer for healing, and works of miracles are enthusiastically embraced and sought for by Pentecostals. Belief in the capacity of the Spirit to bring about healing, whether physical or emotional/mental, is one of the hallmarks of Pentecostalism. In this Pentecostals echo the postmodern insistence on a holistic understanding of the body-mind relationship.[25]

A related belief is the capacity to fight "spiritual warfare" and exorcise demonic spirits, if necessary. This is a significant part of pentecostal spirituality, especially in the Global South.[26] In the words of the Ghanaian theologian Ogbu Kalu:

> Going through life is like spiritual warfare, and religious ardor may appear very materialistic as people strive to preserve their material sustenance in the midst of the machinations of pervasive evil forces. Behind it is a strong sense of the moral and spiritual moorings of life. It is an organic worldview in which the three dimensions of space are bound together; the visible and the invisible worlds interweave. Nothing happens in the visible world which has not been predetermined in the invisible realm. The challenge for Christianity is how to witness to the gospel in a highly spiritualized environment where the recognition of the powers has not been banished in a Cartesian flight to objectivity and enlightenment. . . . The argument here is that Pentecostalism in Africa derived its coloring from the texture of the African soil and from the interior of its idiom, nurture, and growth; her fruits serve the challenges and problems of African ecosystem more adequately than did the earlier missionary fruits.[27]

Two additional interrelated features need to be considered to aptly characterize the distinctiveness of any Pentecostal view of the Spirit: eschatology and missionary enthusiasm; these also bear directly on Pentecostals' view of the Spirit's role among religions. From the beginning, Pentecostals were convinced that the twentieth-century outpouring of the Spirit marked the beginning of the return of Jesus Christ to establish the kingdom. In the meantime, based on biblical promises such as Acts 1:8, Christians were supposed to be empowered by the Spirit to bring the gospel to all nations.[28] As a result of this "eschatological urgency," a massive missionary and evangelistic enterprise emerged, a main factor in the continuing rapid growth of the movement. While at times Pentecostals find suspect "liberal" churches' emphasis on the "social gospel" at the expense of the proclamation, they never withdrew from significant efforts to address physical needs even when at times those efforts were considered door openers for evangelization.[29]

PENTECOSTAL THEOLOGIES OF THE SPIRIT:
THE STATE OF THE QUESTION

Yong succinctly summarizes the nature of Pentecostal pneumatology and its relation to other traditional doctrines of the Spirit:

> In Pentecostalism, as in most conservative, traditionalist, and evangelical Christian traditions, the orthodox doctrine of the Holy Spirit as divine person continues to prevail. Yet pentecostals go beyond many of their orthodox Christian kindred to say that the Holy Spirit continues to act in the world and interact personally with human beings and communities. In this tradition, then, there is the ongoing expectation of the Holy Spirit's answer to intercessory prayer, of the Spirit's continual and personal intervention in the affairs of the world and in the lives of believers even when not specifically prayed for, and of the Spirit's manifestation in the charismatic or spiritual gifts (as enumerated by St. Paul in 1 Corinthians 12:4–7). Of course, amidst all that occurs in Pentecostal circles are some rather fantastic accounts . . . and discerning between the valid and the spurious is not always easy. Pentecostals face the tension of (on the one hand) accepting a rather traditional supernaturalistic worldview along with at least some of the more embarrassing claims that come with it resulting in their being excluded from scholarly or academic conversation, or (on the other hand) attempting to reinterpret Pentecostal testimonies within a more naturalistic framework so as to be able to proceed acceptably with rigorous scientific inquiry into Pentecostal spirituality and experience.[30]

This statement highlights the dynamic nature of emerging Pentecostal theologizing on the Spirit. On the one hand, Pentecostal theological works follow the traditional doctrine of the Holy Spirit and the Trinity and usually employ categories and terms borrowed from others. It is significant to note in this respect that no academic Pentecostal pneumatology yet exists. One would assume that a Spirit movement a century old would have had enough time to produce one. Nevertheless, Pentecostals are going beyond the established contours of traditional theologies and instinctively and nonthematically pushing the boundaries of pneumatology based on their distinctive spirituality, as described above.

As with theology in general, the few theological studies on some aspects of pneumatology written by Pentecostals represent the genre of biblical theology. Indeed, the only available Pentecostal pneumatologies have been written by biblical scholars, mainly New Testament ones. With their love of Luke-Acts as the paradigm of Pentecostal spirituality and empowerment, it is no surprise that scholarship has paid special attention to that part of the New Testament. One of the leading ideas of the Canadian R. Stronstad's *A Charismatic Theology of St. Luke* is the transfer of the charismatic Spirit from Jesus to the disciples.[31] The transference of the Spirit at Pentecost means transference of Jesus' own mission to the church. In keeping with the missionary orientation of the Lukan narrative, Pentecostal biblical scholars have highlighted the important connection between mission and Spirit. Likewise, Robert Menzies has written on distinctive features of Lukan pneumatology with a view to mission. In his *Empowered for Witness* he argues that the church, by virtue of its reception of the pentecostal gift, is a prophetic community of empowerment for missionary service.[32] The main dialogue partners for Menzies and some other Pentecostal theologians have been the mainline New Testament scholars James D. G. Dunn and Max W. Turner.[33] The Australian J. M. Penney, in his recent *Missionary Emphasis of Lukan Pneumatology,*[34] contends that the reason Luke-Acts has been so dear to Pentecostals is that Pentecostalism—from inception a missionary movement—saw in the Spirit baptism of Acts 2 a normative paradigm for the empowerment of every Christian to preach the gospel. He writes, "Acts is more than history for the Pentecostal: it is a missionary manual, an open-ended account of the missionary work of the Holy Spirit in the church, concluding, not with ch. 28, but with the ongoing Spirit-empowered and Spirit-directed gospel preaching of today."[35]

Another Australian theologian, Andrew Lord, has developed a Pentecostal pneumatology that also incorporates the eschatological perspective into its matrix, "Mission Eschatology: A Framework for Mission in the Spirit."[36] Lord argues for a holistic pneumatology that enables Pentecostals "to have a holistic, hope-filled approach to mission."[37] He quotes with approval Oscar Cullmann, who stated that the "missionary work of the Church is the eschatological foretaste of the kingdom."[38] Out of this framework, Lord outlines seven leading characteristics of an eschatologically driven Pentecostal pneumatology: acknowledging the Lordship of Jesus, healing, justice, unity in diversity, creation set free, praise and worship, love and fellowship.[39] It is significant theologically that this paradigm attempts to view the Spirit's work holistically, from proclamation to fellowship to healing to social justice. Lord calls this holistic approach "realistic."[40] This holistic approach corresponds to what Lord calls two kinds of working of the Spirit in mission: "growing" (of the good things that are already happening in this world) and "inbreaking" (to challenge the way things are and to usher in the new).[41] Pentecostals, of course, with their emphasis on the supernatural, have opted for the latter orientation, and rightly so. The only concern is to have a proper balance.

Some contemporary theological contributions point to the widening scope of Pentecostal theologies of the Spirit. Two examples well illustrate this orientation. The American Paul W. Lewis has attempted to construct what he calls "a pneumatological approach to virtue ethics"; that project highlights the role of the Spirit with regard to ethical concerns.[42] The Korean Wonsuk Ma has worked with a project that aims at a distinctively Asian Pentecostal theological framework that intentionally attempts to find a balance between divine revelation and human agency.[43]

Though the topic is old for Pentecostals, the way of discussion is new in F. Macchia's recent work, *Baptized in the Spirit: A Global Pentecostal Theology*.[44] Taking up the most distinctive doctrine in Pentecostal theology, Spirit baptism, Macchia launches an ambitious project. His ultimate goal is to begin to develop not only a full-scale theology of Spirit baptism but also a theological lens through which a Pentecostal theology in general and ecclesiology in particular could be constructed. For Macchia, Spirit baptism is a thoroughly and genuinely communal event. Macchia further believes that his project can be best done in critical and mutually informing ecumenical dialogue with both Protestant and Roman Catholic theologians. In this respect, Macchia's approach resembles that of Yong. Previously, Macchia and some other Pentecostal theologians had suggested that Spirit baptism may also be conceived as a "semi-sacramental" event in which Pentecostals are being affirmed of the presence of the grace of God somewhat similarly to the way traditional church people look upon sacraments.[45]

Once again, the all-important questions, Whose Pneumatology? Which Spirit?[46] on which I touched in the introduction should be revisited. Neither Pentecostals themselves nor outsider theological observers have yet reached an agreement on *the* Pentecostal view of the Spirit and the Spirit's role in the world. Let me take a few obvious examples. African Pentecostalism gleans from the African spirit world,[47] similarly to the way Latin American Pentecostalism conceptually encounters folk Catholicism and spiritism;[48] some Korean pentecostals have made use of shamanistic traditions in the culture,[49] and so on.[50] Not all Pentecostal theologians, however, are willing to admit that these nonwhite, non-Western Pentecostalisms, with their contextualized and "syncretistic" pneumatologies, represent genuine Pentecostalism. The dispute continues and is not likely to find a resolution. The American Assemblies of God historian-theologian Gary McGee speaks of those whose "classification garners together a bewildering array of indigenous churches reflecting varying degrees of syncretism along with classical pentecostal and charismatic constituencies" and who are "loading the terms . . . with this much diversity."[51] He implies that such groups as Zionists in southern Africa, Kimbanguists in central Africa, and Spiritual Baptists in Trinidad should not be termed Pentecostal at all.

At the moment, when attempting to offer a theological reading of Pentecostal theologies in general and pneumatologies in particular, the best thing to do is to acknowledge and live with the lack of consensus. Diversity is the hallmark of this Spirit movement.

ATTEMPTING A COMPARISON

So, how does classical Pentecostal pneumatology fare in comparison with mainline Christian doctrines of the Spirit on the one hand and with Charismatic and neo-Charismatic views on the other? Discerning both similarities and continuities helps us more accurately discern the unique features of Pentecostal theology in general and pneumatology in particular, as well as point to further challenges and potential.

With regard to the state of current theological reflection among mainline Protestant and Roman Catholic theologies, a general observation can be made: Whereas in the past the doctrine of the Spirit was mainly and often exclusively connected with topics such as the doctrines of salvation and inspiration and some issues of ecclesiology, as well as individual piety,[52] contemporary pneumatologies include a strong and intentional drive toward expanding pneumatological categories to embrace the whole curriculum of theological topics from creation to anthropology to Christology and eschatology.[53] There is an attempt to give the Spirit a more integral and central role in theology. Political, social, environmental, liberationist, and other "public" issues are being invoked by the theologians of the Spirit in the beginning of the third millennium.[54]

Alongside the expansion of topics linked with pneumatology, especially under the influence of postmodernism and the growing impact of testimonies from the Global South, contemporary theologies embrace the importance of experience in a new, fresh way. The Old Testament idea of the Spirit of God as the Spirit of life has gained a new significance;[55] one of the exciting results is a new dialogue between the Spirit and science.[56] Furthermore, contemporary pneumatology both acknowledges and desires to relate itself to particular contexts, thus, for example, allowing women to express their experience of the Spirit in a unique way.[57] Contemporary pneumatology gives voices to the poor and oppressed and to testimonies from Africa, Asia, and Latin America in a way never before in the history of reflection on the Spirit.[58] Last but not least, contemporary theology includes an enthusiasm for relating the Spirit of God to other religions; indeed, we can talk about the "turn to the Spirit" in the Christian theology of religions (as it is technically known).[59]

When we put these developments among mainline pneumatologies side by side with emerging Pentecostal theologizing, some important parallels can be discerned. Pentecostalism's belief in the ongoing, dynamic work of the Spirit in the world is in keeping with the contemporary postmodern dynamic worldview, with its "turn to experience."

Alongside this emphasis on experience and primal spirituality, Pentecostalisms share with contemporary trends in pneumatology (as well as in many postmodern expressions) the new appreciation of the affectivity of religious experience and knowledge—a feature the philosopher J. K. A. Smith also finds in common between Pentecostalism and radical Orthodoxy.[60] For any observer of Pentecostal worship services, the presence of an affective element is visible in terms of music, dance, drama, movements, tears and laughter, and so on. Smith even argues that the adoption by Pentecostals of these kinds of features also speaks to what he calls "affective epistemology," which does not privilege only, and at times not even primarily, discursive, analytic argumentation but gives a fair place to intuition, emotions, and other nonrational aspects of the human being.[61]

Smith further contends that because of an emphasis on the role of experience and its roots in affective epistemology, Pentecostal theology—unlike evangelical theology—resists the kinds of dualisms also critiqued by postmodernists and radical Orthodoxy advocates.[62] Closely related to this is Pentecostalism's embrace of a holistic view of the work of the Spirit, including healing and deliverance from evil powers, which echoes the holistic approach of current trends.[63]

What distinguishes Pentecostals' understanding of the work of the Spirit from their mainline counterparts' is the reluctance to consider the role of the Spirit in relation to science (with the exception of the recently launched Pentecostalism and Science project under the leadership of Amos Yong and James K. A. Smith), politics, the environment, issues of equality, and similar public matters. Whether this neglect by Pentecostals reflects the mind-set of religious and theological conservatism or the alleged nonbiblical basis of the above-mentioned enterprises, or just lack of interest for other reasons, is yet to be determined. There seems to be little if anything in the structure and orientation of Pentecostal spirituality that seems to oppose tackling scientific, political, and public issues. As I note in the following, the theology of religions question has not been on the radar screen of Pentecostals either when thinking of the Spirit's role in the world.

Finally, an area of interest that is common to both mainline theologies and Pentecostals—even though their approaches and opinions may not often converge—has to do with the question of the theology of religions. In keeping with the overall wide interest in the question of how Christian faith in general and the Spirit's work in particular relates to other religions, Pentecostals have engaged in dialogue on the topic with other churches, and some Pentecostal theologies are emerging. In general, Pentecostals have been very cautious about speaking of any kind of salvific role of the Spirit among religions outside the work of the Spirit in preparing people for hearing the gospel.[64] Since the 1970s Pentecostals have had several significant ecumenical encounters and dialogues with Roman Catholics,[65] the Reformed, and the World Council of Churches (WCC) that have challenged them to formulate in a more precise way their understanding of this vital topic.[66] The rationale for Pentecostals' exclusivist attitude is found in the fallen state of humankind and in a literal reading of the New Testament, which for Pentecostals does not give much hope for non-Christians.[67] Furthermore, Pentecostals, like many of the early Christians, tend to point out the demonic elements in other religions rather than common denominators.[68]

As in the theology of religions in general, new developments are under way among some younger-generation Pentecostal theologians who are reconsidering the role of God's Spirit among the spirits in religions. Several reasons have been listed as to why Pentecostals and Charismatics should engage the urgent task of a theology of religions: their international roots and global presence, the need to tackle present missiological issues such as syncretism, the denunciation of local traditions as a sign of a dualistic approach to questions regarding the gospel and culture, and the balance between gospel proclamation and work for social justice, to name a few of the most obvious.[69] A leading champion of a more inclusive and comprehensive attitude toward other religions—based on a robust Pentecostal *pneumatological* theology of religions—is the Chinese Malaysian Amos Yong. His latest monograph on this topic is *The Spirit Poured Out on All Flesh: Pentecostalism and the Possibility of Global Theology*. In chapter 6, "The Holy Spirit and Spirits," he issues a call to all Pentecostals to work toward a public theology by engaging Pentecostal pneumatology with interfaith dialogue. His thesis is that "a pneumatologically driven theology is more conducive to engaging [interfaith issues] . . . in our time than previous approaches. . . . [R]eligions are neither accidents of history nor encroachments on divine providence but are, in various ways, instruments of the Holy Spirit working out the divine purposes in the world[,] and . . . the unevangelized, if saved at all, are saved through the work of Christ by the Spirit (even if mediated through the religious beliefs and practices available to them)."[70]

My own work in the field of interfaith studies has focused on developing a Trinitarian understanding of the role of the Spirit in the world. Unlike Yong and other Pentecostal colleagues,[71] my dialogue partners have been Protestant and Catholic colleagues outside Pentecostalism.[72]

When compared to non-Western Pentecostal and Charismatic/neo-Charismatic Christians' views of the Spirit, something similar comes to the fore: while sharing a lot in common—from an underlying Charismatic spirituality to an expectation of the miraculous as part of the Christian's everyday life—it is also clear that classical Pentecostal pneumatologies in general shy away from political, social justice, environmental, and similar pursuits, even though there are some individual Pentecostal theologians who have developed those themes.[73] Non-Western Pentecostal and Charismatic movements are much less likely to define themselves in terms of the doctrine of initial evidence and to more liberally incorporate insights from various local sources, unless they are tutored by "missionary parents" from the West.[74] The South African Charismatic Reformed theologian Henry I. Lederle strikes a note that challenges Pentecostals who have been slower to reflect on the wider ministry of the Spirit in the world:

For too long the Spirit and his work has been conceived of in too limited a sense. There was a capitulation at the beginning of the modern era in which faith became restricted to the private devotional life and the latter was then described as "spiritual." The Spirit should not be limited to spiritual experiences and charisms—even though it needs to be recognized that this element still awaits acknowledgment in much of Christianity. We need, however, to set our sights much higher. Not only the reality discovered by Pentecostalism needs to be reclaimed but also the cosmic dimensions of the Spirit's work. The Spirit is at work in the world and should not be degraded to an ornament of piety.[75]

An illustration of the difference of ethos between classical Pentecostalism's and Charismatic movements' approaches to the Spirit's role in the world comes from a consultation on Charismatic theology sponsored by the WCC at Geneva in 1980.[76] The theological task force identified three arenas of the work of the Spirit in the world:[77] (1) an ecclesiological approach: the Spirit works for the unity and united witness of all churches; (2) a cosmological approach: the Spirit renews creation and bestows fullness of life; this encompasses physical healing and healing of social relationships as well; (3) a sacramental approach: the Spirit is mediated through personal conversion, baptism, confirmation, and ordination as sacramental theologies renew their focus on the Spirit.

IN LIEU OF CONCLUSIONS: TASKS FOR FURTHER STUDY AND REFLECTION

Let me conclude this chapter with some final reflections on the state of Pentecostal theology in general and pneumatologies in particular and suggest some tasks for further research and reflection.[78] Though Pentecostal scholarship has paid due attention to the empowerment dimension of the Holy Spirit, especially with regard to mission and ministry, more work should be done with regard to other aspects of the Spirit's work in the life of the church and individuals. This is what the Dutch missiologist and observer of Pentecostalism, Jan A. B. Jongeneel, means when he speaks of the need for Pentecostals (and Charismatics) to reflect on the fruit of the Spirit in Christian life and mission.[79] There needs to be a balance between the "mighty works" of the Holy Spirit, under which Jongeneel also includes God's mighty works in creation,[80] and a less spectacular, growth-oriented fruit of the Spirit. Pentecostal and Charismatic ministry offers too many sorrowful examples of the lack of the fruit of the Spirit. Charisma obviously cannot replace character.

A related concern is the apparent desire to limit the scope of the Spirit among Pentecostals. Jürgen Moltmann asks, where are the "charismata of the 'charismatics' in the everyday world, in the peace movement, in the movements of liberation, in the ecology movement"? He continues: "If charismata are not given to us so that we can flee from this world into a world of religious dreams, but if they are intended to witness to the liberating lordship of Christ in this world's conflicts, then the charismatic movement must not become a nonpolitical religion, let alone a de-politicized one."[81] While one may be a bit critical of Moltmann's tendency to label almost everything "charismatic," his call for a widening and more inclusive view of the charismatic is definitely needed for Pentecostals.

Classical Pentecostalism's location in the theologically (and in the American scene, often politically and socially) conservative camp has significantly shaped its view of the Spirit and the Spirit's work in the world. The pneumatology of the Pentecostal denominations, with their predominantly white American and European origins, is characterized by openness to the continuing, dynamic, and miraculous work of the Spirit in the church and in the lives of individual believers. Their pneumatology of religions, for example, is characterized by serious reservations about any kind of salvific role of the Spirit apart from the preaching of the gospel.[82] Their Charismatic counterparts derive their pneumatologies in general and pneumatologies of religions in particular from the theologies of their respective churches—whether contemporary Roman Catholic or mainline Protestant churches' inclusivism—and are at times critical of classical Pentecostalism's exclusivism. Charismatic pneumatologies reflect the orientations of other mainline theologies in their desire to move beyond the domain of individual believers and churches to consider the Spirit's role more inclusively and holistically. It seems to me the dividing line here has little to do with pneumatology per se and everything to do with underlying theological and biblical orientations, whether conservative/ fundamentalist or mainline. It is significant that pluralistic pneumatologies, quite widely embraced by many in mainline academia, are pretty much unknown in the whole Pentecostal/Charismatic constituency, even when using the most inclusive definition.

An interesting research task would be then to study further the locatedness of pneumatology in given theological and ecclesiastical contexts. This kind of study would give us an opportunity to test the hypothesis that Pentecostal-type pneumatology—perhaps better than any other spirituality—can fit in more than one type of theological outlook. Support for that suggestion can be found in the more general observation that it is Pentecostalism's ingenuity to be able to find a dwelling place in so many different Christian families. How else can you explain the presence of Pentecostalisms among the most fundamentalistic American southerners, liberationist Latin American Catholics, mainline British Anglicans, and so on? Or where else can you find worship patterns from structured high church liturgies to the most spontaneous independent churches' enthusiasm?

An interesting topic of research would be something like this: What, if any, is the underlying spiritual common denominator that despite radical ecclesiastical, cultural, theological, and sociopolitical differences, still makes it reasonable to speak of Pentecostalism as a generic term? Does it have to do with their understanding of the Spirit?[83]

This brings me to another urgent task for Pentecostal theologians and pneumatologists: What are the connections if any between the Pentecostal "primal spirituality" and spiritualities of religions, say, in Africa and Asia? It seems to me that Pentecostal pneumatology—even when its potential to pursue that question seems to be trapped in a particular fundamentalistic/conservative milieu—has striking similarities with living religions such as Hinduism and Buddhism in their resistance to modernity's reductionistic, overrationalistic, and at times dualistic worldview. The movement toward a post-/late-modern dynamic worldview, with its willingness to reassess the canons of modernity, has certainly opened up mainline Christian pneumatologies to a more holistic, dynamic reflection on the Spirit. Pentecostalism has that kind of undergirding primal spirituality as a wonderful asset. It is yet to be seen if suggestions such as those by Yong will elicit a wideranging resurgence of Pentecostal reflection or if that task will be left only for Charismatic and neo-Charismatic movements. The Charismatic theologian Clark Pinnock makes a challenging remark to his Pentecostal counterparts: "One might expect the Pentecostals to develop a Spirit-oriented theology of mission and world religions, because of their openness to religious experience, their sensitivity to the oppressed of the Third World where they have experienced much of their growth, and their awareness of the ways of the Spirit as well as dogma."[84]

This has not, however, been the case for the most part. While Pentecostals have excelled in missionary activities with impressive results by any standards, their thinking about the ministry of the Spirit in the world lags behind.[85]

The location of Pentecostalism in the camp of conservative Christians, especially in the United States and many parts of Europe and as a result of aggressive missionary work also in many former mission lands, explains to a large extent the reservation about considering the Spirit's role in relation to politics and other public domains as well as in religions. The alliance with fundamentalism, however, is a complicated and in a way self-contradictory development. Among all Christians it is the fundamentalists who have most vocally opposed the Pentecostal claim for the continuing miraculous work of the Spirit. Similarly, the rather fundamentalistic understanding of revelation and inspiration they inherited may be at odds with a Pentecostal worldview.[86]

Another exciting study task would be to examine the issue of contextualization from a *theological* perspective and from the perspective of the theology of Spirit. As is well known, Pentecostals have been entrepreneurial in their approach to church structures, methods of mission and evangelism, styles of worship, and training of leaders, to take just a few examples. Pentecostals have also been enthusiastic about applying whatever methods seem to work in their approach to other cultures and religions in mission work. And this is despite their sometimes quite conservative theological outlook. I wonder if any of this entrepreneurial, explorative, and risk-taking mentality could be channeled into Pentecostal reflection on pneumatology. Pentecostals have never eschewed controversies or avoided conflicts with views (such as cessationism) they deem wrong and limiting to the free flow of the Spirit. What would a Pentecostal pneumatology look like when done with the radical boldness with which some other Pentecostal views were advanced in the beginning decades of the movement?

One more challenging and probably somewhat controversial task lies ahead of us as we think of the future of Pentecostal reflections on the Spirit. What would be some of the ways to enhance dialogue within the wider Pentecostal family on the one hand and in relation to mainline theologies on the other? I am reminded of the very unexpected and ironic attitude of Pentecostals toward the emergence in the mainline churches of the Charismatic movements in the early 1960s. While an outsider would assume the spread of Pentecostal-type spirituality among established churches would have been seen as a sign and gift from God by classical Pentecostals, it brought to the surface the kinds of questions I have raised in discussing the task of identifying Pentecostal views. Pentecostalisms, no less than other Christian movements, are not free from the temptation to domesticate the Spirit. What will be the shape of a Pentecostal pneumatology of religions when Asian, African, and Latin American Pentecostal theologians—who already now represent the majority of the Pentecostal constituency—are enlisted side by side with their American and European colleagues in a common search?

According to the ancient biblical witness, *spiritus ubi vult spirat* ("The wind blows wherever it pleases"; John 3:8 NIV). To quote the programmatic monograph title on the pneumatological theology of religions, could Pentecostals of all stripes, along with their mainline counterparts, join hands and minds in "discerning the Spirit(s)"?[87]

NOTES

1. Frank Macchia, "Theology, Pentecostal," in *NIDPCM*, 1120–41.

2. This is of course not to say that Pentecostals have not produced theology. They have, but in forms that until recently have not been either appreciated or well known by the professional theological guild. Pentecostalism's way of doing theology—paralleling the way much of non-Western Christianity is still doing it—has been oral rather than discursive. See Macchia, "Theology, Pentecostal," 1120–21.

3. See further my "Free Churches, Ecumenism, and Pentecostalism," in *Toward a Pneumatological Theology*, ed. Amos Yong (Lanham, MD: University Press of America, 2002), chap. 4. See also Russell P. Spittler, "Spirituality, Pentecostal and Charismatic," in *NIDPCM*, 1096–1102.

4. The classic study is Donald W. Dayton, *Theological Roots of Pentecostalism* (Grand Rapids: Zondervan, 1987). See also my "'Encountering Christ in the Full Gospel Way': An Incarnational Pentecostal Spirituality," *JEPTA* 37:1 (2007): 9–23.

5. No one else has argued so forcefully and convincingly for the primacy of spirituality as the way to define Pentecostalisms as Walter J. Hollenweger, whose many writings on the topic should be con-

sulted for details. According to him, the features that helped define Pentecostalism in the beginning of the movement are still critical for understanding its specific features and identity, such as orality of liturgy; narrativity of theology and witness; maximum participation at the level of reflection, prayer, and decision making in a community characterized by inclusion and reconciliation; inclusion of dreams and visions into personal and public forms of worship; and a holistic understanding of the body-mind relationship reflected in the ministry of healing by prayer.

6. For documentation, see the annual statistics lists in the January 2009 issue of *IBMR*.

7. This typology is followed, e.g., in *NIDPCM*.

8. Allan H. Anderson, "The Pentecostal Gospel and Third World Cultures," http://artsweb.bham.ac.uk/aanderson/ (accessed 21.8.2006), n.p.; original emphasis. I have recently edited a book titled *Spirit in the World: Emerging Pentecostal Theologies in Global Contexts* (Grand Rapids: Eerdmans, 2009) that attempts to give voice to and facilitate dialogue between diverse Pentecostal theologies from various contexts, primarily from the Global South.

9. Macchia, "Theology, Pentecostal," 1120–21.

10. Ernest Swing Williams, *Systematic Theology,* 3 vols. (Springfield, IL: GPH, 1953).

11. P. C. Nelson, *Bible Doctrines* (Springfield, IL: GPH, 1948).

12. Guy P. Duffield and Nathaniel M. Van Cleave, *Foundations of Pentecostal Theology* (Los Angeles: L.I.F.E. Bible College, 1983).

13. Simon Chan, *Pentecostal Theology and the Christian Spiritual Tradition* (Sheffield: SAP, 2001); Steven J. Land, *Pentecostal Spirituality* (New York: Continuum, 1993).

14. William P. Faupel, *The Everlasting Gospel: The Significance of Eschatology in the Development of Pentecostal Thought* (Sheffield: SAP, 1996).

15. An important work here is by the Anglican Charismatic Thomas A. Smail, *The Forgotten Father* (Portland: Wipf and Stock, 2001), which argues for the lack of attention to the Trinity and especially the first person of the Trinity among Pentecostals and Charismatics.

16. Macchia, "Theology, Pentecostal," 1124.

17. Amos Yong, *The Spirit Poured out on All Flesh: Pentecostalism and the Possibility of Global Theology* (Grand Rapids: Baker Academic, 2005).

18. Howard M. Ervin, "Koinonia, Church and Sacraments: A Pentecostal Response," Pentecostal Position Paper read at the International Roman Catholic–Pentecostal Dialogue in Venice, 1–8 August 1987, 8–9.

19. Harvey Cox, *Fire from Heaven* (Reading: Addison Wesley, 1995), 81ff. See also my "'The Re-Turn of Religion in the New Millennium': Pentecostalisms and Postmodernities," *Swedish Missiological Themes* 95:4 (2007): 469–96.

20. Cox, *Fire from Heaven,* 81.

21. In this distinction I am indebted to the Benedictine Catholic expert on Pentecostal-Charismatic movements, Fr. Kilian McDonnell, O.S.B.

22. See Daniel Albrecht, *Rites in the Spirit: A Ritual Approach to Pentecostal/Charismatic Spirituality* (Sheffield: SAP, 1999).

23. Jean-Daniel Plüss, "Azusa and Other Myths: The Long and Winding Road from Experience to Stated Beliefs and Back," *Pneuma* 15 (fall 1993): 191: "In the beginning there was an experience and a testimony; then came an explanation in the form of a theological construct."

24. Heribert Mühlen, "Charismatic and Sacramental Understanding of the Church: Dogmatic Aspects of Charismatic Renewal," *One in Christ* 12 (1976): 344–45; Frank Macchia, "Tongues as a Sign: Towards a Sacramental Understanding of Pentecostal Experience," *Pneuma* 15:1 (1993): 63.

25. See further, Hollenweger, *Pentecostalism,* chap. 18.

26. See Opoku Onyinah, "Deliverance as a Way of Confronting Witchcraft in Contemporary Africa: Ghana as a Case Study," in Kärkkäinen, *The Spirit in the World,* chap. 10.

27. Ogbu U. Kalu, "Preserving a Worldview: Pentecostalism in the African Maps of the Universe," *Pneuma* 24:2 (2003): 122.

28. For a helpful discussion, see Wonsuk Ma, " 'When the Poor Are Fired Up': The Role of Pneumatology in Pentecostal/Charismatic Mission," in Kärkkäinen, *The Spirit in the World,* chap. 3.

29. An important article here is Douglas Peterson, "A Moral Imagination: Pentecostals and Social Concern in Latin America," in Kärkkäinen, *The Spirit in the World,* chap. 4. See also my "Are Pentecostals Oblivious to Social Justice? Theological and Ecumenical Perspectives," *Missionalia* 29 (2001): 387–404.

30. Amos Yong, " 'The Spirit Hovers over the World': Toward a Typology of 'Spirit' in the Religion and Science Dialogue," *The Digest: Transdisciplinary Approaches to Foundational Questions* 4:12 (2004): n.p., www.metanexus.net/digest/2004_10_27.htm; accessed 21 August 2006.

31. R. Stronstad, *A Charismatic Theology of St. Luke* (Peabody: Hendrickson, 1984).

32. Robert Menzies, *Empowered for Witness* (Sheffield: SAP, 1994); see also his earlier work, *The Development of Early Christian Pneumatology with Special Reference to Luke-Acts* (Sheffield: SAP, 1991).

33. James D. G. Dunn, *Baptism in the Holy Spirit: A Re-Examination of the New Testament Teaching on the Gift of the Spirit in Relation to Pentecostalism Today* (Louisville: Westminster John Knox, [1975] 1977; Max Turner, *Power from on High: The Spirit in Israel's Restoration and Witness in Luke-Acts* (Sheffield: SAP, 1996).

34. J. M. Penney, *The Missionary Emphasis of Lukan Pneumatology* (Sheffield: SAP, 1997).

35. Penney, *The Missionary Emphasis,* 12.

36. Andrew M. Lord, "Mission Eschatology: A Framework for Mission in the Spirit, " *JPT* 11 (1997): 111–24.

37. Lord, "Mission Eschatology," 111.

38. Oscar Cullmann, "Mission in God's Eschatology," in *Classic Texts in Mission and World Christianity* (New York: Orbis Books, 1995), 307, quoted in Lord, "Mission Eschatology," 112.

39. Lord, "Mission Eschatology," 114; see also pp. 116 ff.

40. This term was coined by Michael Welker in his *God the Spirit* (Minneapolis: Augsburg, 1994). The program of Jürgen Moltmann's *Spirit of Life: A Universal Affirmation* (trans. Margaret Kohl [Minneapolis: Fortress, 1992]) runs, of course, in the same direction, although the terminology differs a bit.

41. Lord, "Mission Eschatology," 114–15.

42. Paul W. Lewis, "A Pneumatological Approach to Virtue Ethics," *AJPS* 1:1 (1998): 42–61.

43. Wonsuk Ma, "Toward an Asian Pentecostal Theology," *AJPS* 1:1 (1998): 15–41.

44. Frank Macchia, *Baptized in the Spirit: A Global Pentecostal Theology* (Grand Rapids: Zondervan, 2006).

45. Macchia, "Tongues as a Sign," 63.

46. I am of course playing here with one of the titles of A. McIntyre's well-known books.

47. For important insights, see Ogbu Kalu, "*Sankofa* Pentecostalism and African Cultural Heritage," in Kärkkäinen. *The Spirit in the World,* chap. 8. Also helpful are, e.g., Allan H. Anderson, *Moya: The Holy Spirit in an African Context* (Pretoria: Unisa, 1991); Allan H. Anderson, "Pentecostal Pneumatology and African Power Concepts: Continuity or Change?" *Missionalia* 19 (1991): 65–74.

48. See, e.g., Walter J. Hollenweger, *Pentecostalism: Origin and Development Worldwide* (Peabody: Hendrickson, 1997), chap. 7 (on Mexico) and chap. 10 (on Chile).

49. See Koo Dong Yun, "Pentecostalism from Below: *Minjung* Liberation and Asian Pentecostal Theology," in Kärkkäinen, *The Spirit in the World,* chap. 6; and Yoo Boo-Woong, *Korean Pentecostalism: Its History and Theology* (Frankfurt: Peter Lang, 1988).

50. See further, Allan H. Anderson and Walter J. Hollenweger, eds., *Pentecostals after a Century: Global Perspectives on a Movement in Transition* (Sheffield: SAP, 1999). The Indian Pentecostalist offers an intriguing analysis of the struggle of trying to define Pentecostalisms in his own homeland: Paulson

Pulikottil, "One God, One Spirit, Two Memories: A Postcolonial Reading of the Encounter between Western Pentecostalism and Native Pentecostalism in Kerala," in Kärkkäinen, *The Spirit in the World,* chap. 5.

51. Gary McGee, "Pentecostal Missiology: Moving beyond Triumphalism to Face the Issues," *Pneuma* 16:2 (1994): 276–77. An opposing view is represented by the South African expert on Pentecostalism, Allan H. Anderson, *Bazalwane: African Pentecostals in South Africa* (Pretoria: Unisa, 1992), 2–6.

52. With regard to the doctrine of salvation, the Spirit represented the "subjective" side, whereas Christology was the objective basis. With regard to Scripture, the Spirit played a crucial role in both inspiration and illumination of the Word of God. In various Christian traditions, from mysticism to pietism to classical liberalism and beyond, the Spirit's work was seen mainly in relation to animating and refreshing one's inner spiritual life. It is this reductionism that has elicited a number of new proposals, and as a result, the theological landscape is now changing rapidly.

53. Influential recent contributions include Moltmann, *Spirit of Life;* Welker, *God the Spirit;* W. Pannenberg, *Systematic Theology,* trans. Geoffrey W. Bromiley, 3 vols. (Grand Rapids: Eerdmans, 1991–98).

54. For political pneumatologies, see Geiko Müller-Fahrenholz, *God's Spirit: Transforming a World in Crisis,* trans. John Cumming (New York: Continuum, 1995); for "green" and ecofeminist pneumatologies, see Elizabeth A. Johnson, *Women, Earth and Creator Spirit* (New York: Paulist, 1993); for liberationist pneumatologies, see José Gomblin, *The Holy Spirit and Liberation,* trans. Paul Burns (Maryknoll: Orbis, 1989); for a "pneumatology of work," see Miroslav Volf, *Work in the Spirit: Toward a Theology of Work* (New York: OUP, 1991).

55. The main thesis of Moltmann's *Spirit of Life* is that the best way to discern the presence of the Spirit in the world is to look for work in support of life, growth, and development. The original subtitle in German, *Eine ganzheitliche Pneumatologie* ("holistic," "all-encompassing," or "comprehensive" pneumatology), expresses the main theme of the book better than the English subtitle, *A Universal Affirmation.*

56. For some insights into the dialogue between the Spirit and science, see Pannenberg, *Systematic Theology,* vol. 2, esp. §2; W. Pannenberg, "The Doctrine of the Spirit and the Task of a Theology of Nature," in Pannenberg, *Toward a Theology of Nature: Essays on Science and Faith,* trans. Ted Peters (Louisville: Westminster John Knox, 1993), chap. 5. Process theology, with its dynamic worldview, has been fertile soil for the dialogue, as illustrated by the work of Joseph Bracken, S.J., *Society and Spirit: A Trinitarian Cosmology* (Selinsgrove: Susquehanna University Press, 1991).

57. For feminist pneumatologies, see Elizabeth Johnson, *She Who Is: The Mystery of God in Feminist Theological Discourse* (New York: Crossroad, 1992); Rebecca Button Prichard, *Sensing the Spirit: The Holy Spirit in Feminist Perspective* (St. Louis: Chalice, 1999); and Nancy M. Victorin-Vangerud, *The Raging Hearth: Spirit in the Household of God* (St. Louis: Chalice, 2000).

58. For contributions to pneumatology from Asia, Africa, and Latin America, see Kärkkäinen, *Pneumatology,* chap. 6.

59. For a concise introduction, see Amos Yong, "The Turn to Pneumatology in Christian Theology of Religions: Conduit or Detour," *JES* 35 (1998): 437–54.

60. James K. A. Smith, "What Hath Cambridge to Do with Azusa Street? Radical Orthodoxy and Pentecostal Theology in Conversation," *Pneuma* 25:1 (spring 2003): 111.

61. Smith, "What Hath Cambridge to Do with Azusa Street?"

62. Smith, "What Hath Cambridge to Do with Azusa Street?"

63. It is ironic that some of the trailblazers of the new holistic understanding of the Spirit of God, such as W. Pannenberg, totally miss the topic of healing and exorcisms in their pneumatology (and consequently, anthropology and ecclesiology). See my "The Working of the Spirit of God in Creation

and in the People of God: The Pneumatology of Wolfhart Pannenberg," *Pneuma* 26:1 (2004): 17–35. In contrast to Pannenberg, Moltmann (*Spirit of Life,* chap. 9) discusses these topics in his pneumatology.

64. See, e.g., "Word and Spirit, Church and World," in *Final Report of the International Pentecostal-Reformed Dialogue* (Geneva: WARC, 2000), 12: "On the whole, Pentecostals do not acknowledge the presence of salvific elements in non-Christian religions because they view this as contrary to the teaching of the Bible. The church is called to discern the spirits through the charism of the Holy Spirit informed by the Word of God (1 Corinthians 12:10, 14:29; cf. 1 Thessalonians 5:19–21; 1 John 4:2–3). Pentecostals, like many of the early Christians, are sensitive to the elements in other religions that oppose biblical teaching. They are, therefore, encouraged to receive the guidance of the Holy Spirit."

65. For the most long-standing and theologically most significant dialogue, see further my *Spiritus ubi vult spirat: Pneumatology in Roman Catholic-Pentecostal Dialogue (1972–1989)* (Helsinki: Luther Agricola-Society, 1998); and *Ad ultimum terrae: Evangelization, Proselytism, and Common Witness in the Roman Catholic-Pentecostal Dialogue, 1990–1997* (Frankfurt: Peter Lang, 1999). For a scrutiny of specific missiological aspects, see V.-M. Kärkkäinen, "'An Exercise on the Frontiers of Ecumenism': Almost Thirty Years of the Roman Catholic-Pentecostal Dialogue," *Exchange* 29:2 (2000): 156–71; V.-M. Kärkkäinen, "Evangelization, Proselytism and Common Witness: Roman Catholic-Pentecostal Dialogue on Mission (1991–1997)," *IBMR* 25:1 (2001): 16–23.

66. Despite the long-standing ecumenical dialogues, probably the majority of Pentecostals to this day are at best ignorant of and at worst hostile to ecumenism for its alleged liberal theological agenda, compromising doctrinal purity, and similar reasons—again, gleaning from the typical fundamentalistic/conservative reasoning.

67. *Final Report 1978–1982,* #14. *Final Report 1991–1997,* #20. *Final Report* refers to the documents of the International Roman Catholic–Pentecostal Dialogue, unless otherwise indicated. "Perspectives on *Koinonia:* The Report from the Third Quinquennium of *The Dialogue* between the Pontifical Council for Promoting Christian Unity of the Roman Catholic Church and Some Classical Pentecostal Churches and Leaders, 1985–1989," *Information Service* 75 (1990): 179–91; *Pneuma* 12:2 (1990): 117–42.

68. *Final Report 1991–1997,* #21.

69. Amos Yong, *Discerning the Spirit(s): A Pentecostal-Charismatic Contribution to Christian Theology of Religions* (Sheffield: SAP, 2000), 206–15.

70. Yong, *Spirit Poured Out,* 235–36. See also Yong's *Beyond the Impasse: Toward a Pneumatological Theology of Religions* (Grand Rapids: Baker Academic, 2003); Yong *Discerning the Spirit(s);* Yong, "'Not Knowing Where the Spirit Blows . . . ': On Envisioning a Pentecostal-Charismatic Theology of Religions," *JPT* 14 (1999): 81–112.

71. See, e.g., Tony Richie, "'Azusa Era Optimism': Bishop J.H. King's Pentecostal Theology of Religions as a Possible Paradigm for Today," *JPT* 14:2 (2006): 247–60; and my response to Richie in the same issue.

72. Veli-Matti Kärkkäinen, *Trinity and Religious Pluralism: The Doctrine of the Trinity in Christian Theology of Religions* (Aldershot: Ashgate, 2004); "'How to Speak of the Spirit among Religions': Trinitarian 'Rules' for a Pneumatological Theology of Religions," *IBMR* 30:3 (2006): 121–27; "Trinity and Religions: On the Way to a Trinitarian Theology of Religions for Evangelicals," *Missiology* 33:2 (2005): 159–74; "Trinitarian Rules for a Pneumatological Theology of Religions," in *The Work of the Spirit: Pneumatology and Pentecostalism,* ed. Michael Welker (Grand Rapids: Eerdmans, 2007).

73. The Hispanic Eldin Villafañe has been one of the pioneers; see, e.g., his latest book, *Beyond Cheap Grace: A Call to Radical Discipleship, Incarnation, and Justice* (Grand Rapids: Eerdmans, 2006).

74. Robert Mapes Anderson, *Vision of the Disinherited* (Peabody: Hendrickson, 1979), 4.

75. H.I. Lederle, *Treasures Old and New: Interpretations of Spirit-Baptism in the Charismatic Renewal Movement* (Peabody: Hendrickson, 1988), 338

76. The conference proceedings can be found in Arnold Bittlinger, ed., *The Church Is Charismatic* (Geneva: World Council of Churches, 1981).

77. "Towards a Church Renewed and United in the Spirit," in Bittlinger, *The Church Is Charismatic,* 21–28.

78. In this final section I am dependent on my essay "Pentecostal Pneumatology of Religions: The Contribution of Pentecostalism to Our Understanding of the Work of God's Spirit in the World," in Kärkkäinen, *The Spirit in the World,* 155–80.

79. Jan A. B. Jongeneel, "Ecumenical, Evangelical and Pentecostal/Charismatic Views on Mission as a Movement of the Holy Spirit," in *Pentecost, Mission and Ecumenism: Essays on Intercultural Theology,* ed. J. A. B. Jongeneel et al. (Frankfurt: Peter Lang, 1992), 235–37.

80. Jongeneel, "Ecumenical, Evangelical and Pentecostal/Charismatic Views on Mission as a Movement of the Holy Spirit," 239 ff.

81. Moltmann, *Spirit of Life,* 186.

82. See my "Toward a Pneumatological Theology of Religion: Pentecostal-Charismatic Contributions," *IMR* 41:361 (April 2002): 187–98.

83. Albrecht (*Rites in the Spirit,* 28) speaks of an "underlying or core spirituality" among various types of Pentecostalisms. In addition to speaking of primal spirituality, Harvey Cox also speaks of "primal piety" (*Fire from Heaven,* 99 ff.) and "primal hope" (111–22) in relation to a distinctive Pentecostal spirituality.

84. Clark Pinnock, *Flame of Love: A Theology of the Holy Spirit* (Downers Grove, IL: IVP, 1996), 274.

85. For discussion of Pentecostal missiology and the Spirit's role therein, see Hollenweger, *Pentecostalism,* 288–306; V.-M. Kärkkäinen, "'Truth on Fire': Pentecostal Theology of Mission and the Challenges of a New Millennium," *AJPS* 3:1 (2000): 33–60; "Mission, Spirit, and Eschatology: An Outline of a Pentecostal-Charismatic Theology of Mission," *Mission Studies* 16–1:31 (1999): 73–94; V.-M. Kärkkäinen, "Pentecostal Missiology in Ecumenical Perspective: Contributions, Challenges, Controversies," *IMR* 88:350 (1999): 207–25; and V.-M. Kärkkäinen, "Missiology, Pentecostal and Charismatic," in *NIDPCM,* 877–85.

86. For an important discussion, see Gerald T. Sheppard, "Pentecostalism and the Hermeneutics of Dispensationalism: The Anatomy of an Uneasy Relationship," *Pneuma* 6:2 (1984): 5–34.

87. Yong, *Discerning the Spirit(s).*

12

Missiology and the Interreligious Encounter

Amos Yong and Tony Richie

Pentecostals have always been heavily involved in missions and hold missionaries in high esteem as extraordinary heroes of the faith.[1] But they have traditionally not given as much thought to the topic of theology of religions, or interreligious dialogue and encounter, as to other theological loci.[2] Why this is the case may be related in part to the fact that academic Pentecostalism is but a recent arrival to the theological scene, with its first generation of professionally trained theologians—as opposed to historians or biblical scholars—emerging only since the early 1990s.[3] Yet Pentecostal scholars can no longer avoid giving serious attention to these topics for various reasons, whether because the Pentecostal commitment to carrying out the Great Commission leads many of its missionaries and ministers into environments and situations in which they are interacting with people of other faiths, because the question of how Christianity is to respond to other religions has become a more intensely debated social, political, and ideological question in an increasingly globalized world after 11 September 2001, or simply because they are led to engage in the wider academic conversation. There is now no denying the need to think through the theological question of the religions from a distinctively Pentecostal perspective.

Of course, missiology, theology of religions, and interreligious dialogue are characterized by closely interlocking concerns. A fundamental focal point shared by all three is that of intentional Christian encounter with religious others. This chapter first surveys Pentecostal theologies of mission and theologies of religions, respectively, before finally attempting to articulate a Pentecostal theology of the interreligious encounter.

245

PENTECOSTAL THEOLOGIES OF MISSION

Pentecostals are well and widely known for missionary practice; however, in many ways our reflection and articulation have been left behind. Recently, however, that has begun to change.[4] In this section we discuss first earlier and then later theologies of mission among classical Pentecostals, before turning to explore more recent developments in the wider domain of Pentecostal-Charismatic missiology. In a transitional section, we note the growing importance of theology of religions and the interreligious encounter for Pentecostal missiology.

Classical Pentecostal Missiology

Credited with developing the distinctive doctrine of tongues as initial evidence,[5] Charles Fox Parham has been recognized as the father or founder of the modern Pentecostal movement. Yet his greatest legacy to modern Pentecostalism may well be his missionary vision. Goff notes that Parham "instilled within the movement a fervent missionary emphasis."[6] Though his belief in xenolalia (i.e., tongues as known languages used in an unprecedented wave of end-time missionary activity and revival) failed on the mission field and was discarded by the embryonic movement, his emphasis on the gift of the Holy Spirit's power for evangelistic witness continues to be of central significance in Pentecostalism. These motifs came together in one of the central scriptural texts for Pentecostals: "But you will receive power when the Holy Spirit has come upon you; and you will be my witnesses in Jerusalem, in all Judea and Samaria, and to the ends of the earth" (Acts 1:8, NRSV). When linked with Peter's explanation of the events of the Day of Pentecost (drawn from the prophet Joel), that this outpouring of the Spirit was God's special work in the last days (Acts 2:17), Parham's eschatological emphasis and sense of urgency provided Pentecostalism with immense missionary momentum.

Yet it needs noting that Parham's (onetime) disciple William J. Seymour and the Azusa Street Mission's actual and sacrificial missionary practices also deserve considerable credit for much of the effective missionary thrust of early Pentecostalism.[7] If today's Pentecostal denominations like to highlight their "evangelism distinctive" and talk about evangelism as part of "a unified experience of the Holy Spirit," it is largely due to the early influence of Parham and Seymour.[8] Parham guaranteed that Spirit baptism and evangelism or missions would be permanently connected for most Pentecostals, while Seymour's Azusa Street Mission was what actually launched a large number of the first Pentecostal missionaries around the world.

But neither Parham nor Seymour, nor anyone else early in the movement for that matter, systematized Pentecostal missiology. Melvin L. Hodges, an experienced missionary and prolific author, was the first to begin articulating a distinctive Pentecostal missiology in the mid-twentieth century. Though in some ways he basically followed previously trodden Evangelical paths, his practical missionary expertise building indigenous churches and his overt Pentecostal pneumatology greatly shaped his approach and contributed to its overall effectiveness.[9] Following the lead of Parham and other early Pentecostal missionaries, Hodges took his missiological cues from the Book of Acts. From this he discerned not only that the church is God's missionary agency to the ends of the earth but also that the Spirit empowers the church for her ministry and mission in various contexts. At the level of the individual, all persons, including nominal Christians, are to be brought into an experiential knowledge of the gospel and "into the fellowship of the life in the Holy Spirit."[10] At the corporate level, the Christian mission is to establish self-propagating, self-governing, and self-supporting local congregations and ministries. These would be the dominant features of what Hodges calls "the indigenous church": established, overseen, organized, and developed by local (i.e., "native") leadership in their own language and according to their own cultural customs, with missionaries (in Hodges's mind, from the West, although in our new context, perhaps not exclusively so) serving only in the role of consultants.[11]

Clearly the earliest Pentecostal missionaries were motivated first and foremost by the practical exigencies of fulfilling the Great Commission. What was distinctive about Pentecostal missiology during this early period, however, even if not as explicitly articulated as later generations might have hoped, was its being informed by the early Christian and apostolic paradigm. Hence the mission for the church, for classical Pentecostals, was linked essentially to the outpouring of the Spirit on the Day of Pentecost. Even Hodges's indigenous principle is, in effect, a practical missionary vision shaped in part by the many tongues manifest and validated by the apostolic experience.[12]

Contemporary Pentecostal Missiologies

From Paul Pomerville, an Assemblies of God missionary, we have one of the first insider analyses of Pentecostal missions from a more formal missiological perspective.[13] Pomerville follows the church growth movement but denies the evangelical argument that the primary motivation for missions is obedience to the Great Commission of Matthew 28:19–20. Rather, he insists that the Holy Spirit of Pentecost is a missionary Spirit and that that makes the Spirit-filled church a missionary church. Furthermore, what is true collectively is also true individually. Every Spirit-filled believer is an evangelist or a witness of Christ. Pomerville hence emphasizes the centrality of Spirit baptism and its accompanying impetus for Pentecostal missions. Yet he resists defining and describing Pentecostal missions one-dimensionally. Accordingly, he lists five prescriptions for Pentecostal missions: a thoroughgoing Trinitarian theology of mission based on Acts; a reemphasis of Great Commission missions based on the power of the Spirit, with accompanying charismatic confirmations; a holistic view of missions with a priority on evangelism; evangelism directed toward church planting, viewing the local church as the Holy Spirit's instrument and the Pentecostal experience as its primary dynamic; and, especially in the non-Western world, respect for independent movements.[14] Pomerville's work can thus be seen as a contemporary retrieval but also reappropriation of classical Pentecostal theologies of mission.

Similarly, Grant McClung, a Church of God (Cleveland) missionary and educator, is convinced of the centrality of experiencing the power of the Holy Spirit for Pentecostal missions.[15] He observes that signs and wonders, especially divine healing, can serve as powerful openings for evangelistic opportunities.[16] Indeed, miracles often serve to draw unbelievers to Christ. Such experiences can also function as great levelers, catapulting women, the poor and illiterate, and other marginalized people into positions of prominent ministry and thus multiplying the missionary task force. With Hodges, then, McClung understands Pentecostal missions in terms of indigenization. McClung also contends, in the tradition of Parham and the early Azusa Street experience, that there is a need for a continuing sense of eschatological urgency and for a strong commitment of vocational calling for missionary effectiveness.[17] Overall he emphasizes Pentecostal missions as a process of explosion, motivation, and consolidation; an eschatological urgency, sense of destiny, and high regard for the supernatural working of the Holy Spirit as the heart of these missions; a combination of "a spontaneous strategy of the Spirit" with pragmatic calculation; parallels with the church growth movement; and a visionary commitment to the future, acknowledging concerns and preparing for challenges. McClung's contributions to a contemporary restatement of classical Pentecostal missiology cannot be overlooked.

Gary McGee is a historian and missiologist who teaches at the Assemblies of God Theological Seminary. Drawing on historical perspectives for missiological application, he notes that opposition to signs and wonders of the Spirit *and* expectation of their occurrence have been, paradoxically, common throughout the church's existence in the extension of its witness.[18] Pentecostalism's extensive use of this radical strategy of divine power certainly has been important for its success. Yet McGee is also quick to contend that Pentecostal missions need to increase their understanding and practice of social ministry and activism if they are to meet the needs of oppressed and underprivileged peoples today. However, a biblical hermeneutic including powerful spiritual experience remains a key to missionary effectiveness in the non-Western world. Supernatural experiences or occurrences are a major element of missions, especially of Pentecostal missions. Clearly, missiologists like McGee, Pomerville, and McClung are working to provide the discipline of missiology with distinctive Pentecostal perspectives but also to update classical Pentecostal missiology in dialogue with the wider missiological conversation.

Recent Developments in Pentecostal-Charismatic Missiology

In many ways Walter J. Hollenweger is largely responsible for making the wider scholarly world more aware of Pentecostalism.[19] A Swiss scholar of Pentecostalism and an intercultural theologian, he has been the preeminent analyst of the world Pentecostal movement from his post at the University of Birmingham.[20] Hollenweger insists Pentecostals themselves need new appraisals of Pentecostalism's relations with pre-Christian cultures and religions, especially in the so-called third world. He suggests these have been "taken and transformed" by Pentecostalism but laments that Pentecostals have not consistently acted on Seymour's ecumenism. As the real founder of the movement (according to Hollenweger), Seymour's roots in the black spirituality of his past provide important insights into the original and authentic nature of a Pentecostal identity that is rich with ecumenical and interreligious possibilities.[21] Hollenweger suggests that Pentecostals must come to grips with the bewildering pluralism within the global movement and that this can be done by attending to the pluralism at the origins of modern Pentecostalism itself. Further, he argues that first-century Christians weren't "theologically homogeneous" either, and that idea could be helpful for Pentecostals today. This is especially relevant as all Christianity and churches—including Pentecostal churches, are syncretistic, taking "on board many customs and ideas from our pagan past."[22] Thus rather than the traditional "aggressive evangelism," Hollenweger proposes "dialogical evangelism" as a biblical model for mission in which Pentecostals and Charismatics can learn from those they are evangelizing even as Peter learned from his encounter with Cornelius (Acts 10).[23] In the end, his goal is to help Pentecostals and Charismatics guard against losing their original ecumenical vision and perhaps even encourage its restoration.[24]

Alan Anderson, the successor to Hollenweger at Birmingham, agrees with Hollenweger that Pentecostals "must rediscover their roots," lest they "betray the origins of the movement."[25] He especially stresses the need for Pentecostal social involvement and suggests that the essence of the Pentecostal gospel is pragmatic and meets practical needs. Yet Pentecostal spirituality includes both strong liberationist overtones and a high priority on evangelism. Anderson also says some Pentecostals and Charismatics have so adapted to their cultural and religious context that many Western Pentecostals would probably doubt the Christian identity of such communities. He himself, however, tends to view authentic Pentecostalism as much more diverse than may be common for classical Pentecostals. For example, he observes that Pentecostal interaction with (not capitulation to) Korean shamanism can be a positive development. There is an "inherent flexibility" in Pentecostalism, he argues, that "makes it more easily able to adjust to any context," and this is its missiological advantage.[26] Hence Anderson sees the major features of Pentecostal missiological theology to include the interrelatedness of the missionary Spirit and church growth; the importance and prevalence of signs and wonders; connections between Spirit baptism and global mission, including social activism; the significant experiential impact of Pentecostal liturgy and indigenous churches; and the adaptability of Pentecostal forms of evangelism.[27] Like Hollenweger before him, Anderson also is especially insistent on the worldwide scope and variety of Pentecostalism and Pentecostal missions.[28]

Andrew Lord, an Anglican Charismatic missiologist influenced by this "Birmingham school," grounds Pentecostal missions more directly in pneumatology. For example, in comparing the pneumatology of Pentecostal scholars and Jürgen Moltmann, he examines two key differences in understanding and their implications for missions.[29] First, Pentecostals tend to focus on the "particular" and the "transcendent," whereas Moltmann emphasizes the "universal" and the "immanent." Second, and related to this, Pentecostals have adopted a more evangelical posture on mission in contrast to Moltmann's more ecumenical approach. Together, these differences are significant for the theology and practice of mission. Although both Moltmann and Pentecostals share a desire for mission to be holistic and experiential, they differ over the means and characteristics of mission. Pentecostal missions and evangelism have focused on salvation of the individual soul, in contrast to ecumenical missions, which are focused on social presence and transformation. Lord suggests a way beyond these differences by presenting a pneumatological framework for grounding mission in movement of the Holy Spirit. The Spirit is universally present and active, as well as involved in the particularities of human embodiment and the personal transformation of human hearts in anticipation of eschatological salvation. Hence a pneumatological theology of mission is holistic, experiential, contextual, community forming, and spirituality sensitive. In this way, Pentecostals and Charismatics are encouraged to develop a holistic missiological theology more cognizant of cultures and globalization.[30]

From Pentecostal Missiology to Theology of Religions and Interreligious Dialogue

We have shown in this brief survey of the field of Pentecostal missiology a growing recognition of the importance of theology of religions and of the interreligious dialogue. These connections have also been observed by the Finnish Pentecostal systematician, Veli-Matti Kärkkäinen.[31] He suggests that the next steps for Pentecostal missiology involve a threefold challenge: (1) to continue to highlight and articulate the theological basis of distinctive pentecostal mission; (2) to clarify the relationship between proclamation and social concern or service; and (3) to explore further how Pentecostals should understand and interact with followers of other religions. With regard to the first two points, Kärkkäinen has proposed that the church needs to be seen as the Trinitarian movement sent by the Spirit into the world even as the Spirit participates in the sending of the Father in behalf of the Son (in this way opening up to a distinctively Trinitarian and pneumatological theology of mission) and that Pentecostals need to realize that kingdom works remain to be done today and social activism can have eschatological significance (in this way, further strengthening the connections made by Anderson and Lord, for example, between mission as social witness).

Our focus, however, lies in Kärkkäinen's third point, concerning Pentecostal relations with other (world) religions and their adherents.[32] Pentecostals typically duck the issue. Often they default to standard (Evangelical) exclusivism. That is no longer satisfactory—if it ever was. Dialogue with other Christians, such as Roman Catholics, increasingly challenges Pentecostals to face up to the diversity within the Christian movement and to the plurality of Christian views regarding the religions. Furthermore, developing pneumatology within Pentecostalism's own ranks suggests room is being made for the Spirit in the world and, perhaps, in the world's religions. Significantly, a pneumatological theology of religions does not and must not downplay the importance of evangelization.

A few summary remarks can be made at this point with regard to Pentecostal missiology. First, that pneumatology is the area (or experience!) that makes Pentecostal missions most distinctive seems generally assumed, but how that may specifically apply is not agreed on. For example, do we view mission through pneumatology or pneumatology through mission or both through yet another lens such as eschatology? Interestingly, almost everyone agrees about the recipe itself, but many remain unclear about how to assess the resulting shifts in missionary practice. Second, there are tensions between the historic versus contemporary aspects of Pentecostalism. The former seems to some more exclusive, antiecumenical, and anti-interreligious, whereas the latter seems to others too open-ended and ideologically pluralistic. Again, one senses a growing movement in the latter direction, even while there is reluctance to abandon completely the legacy of the historical tradition. Third, there is the question of emphasizing the Evangelical identity of Pentecostalism that may incline us to embrace a North American version, with all of its cultural and geographic baggage, or of opting instead for an ecumenical vision of Pentecostal identity that opens us up to a global Charismatic movement based in the majority non-Western world with implications for relating to other religions. Again, one is tempted to argue that it doesn't have to be either/or, that it can be both/and. The trajectories of Pentecostal missiology explored above certainly seem to suggest developments in the ecumenical, global, and interreligious direction. Hence it appears that Pentecostal missiology is intertwined with and cannot avoid thinking about theology of religions.

PENTECOSTAL THEOLOGIES OF THE RELIGIONS

One of the oft-repeated errors regarding Pentecostalism (frequently even by Pentecostals) is an assumption that the movement is monolithic. It is not, and this diversity is reflected as well in the theology of religions.[33] In the following discussion, we present the classical Pentecostal exclusivist view regarding the religions, discuss the inclusivism that has reappeared more recently among Pentecostals and Charismatics, and then look at efforts to think theologically about the religions from a distinctively Pentecostal perspective. In a transitional section, we note that there is a general correlation between developments in Pentecostal theologies of mission (as presented above) and Pentecostal theologies of religions.

Classical Pentecostal "Exclusivism"

As used in the context of the discipline of the theology of religions, "exclusivism" reflects a closed attitude, positing that a conscious personal response to the preached gospel is not only normative but also necessary for salvation. It basically argues that there is no salvation outside the church or apart from the church's proclamation of the gospel. On the other end of the spectrum, "pluralism" essentially equates all religions while denying superiority to any. It focuses at the more general level of God or "ultimate reality" rather than on the particularity of Christ (or Buddha, or Mohammed, etc.). The moderating position, "inclusivism," is a Christocentric and pneumatic openness regarding the present state and eternal fate of the unevangelized or adherents of other religions. It affirms salvation ultimately of and by Christ, even if it allows for the possibility that the unevangelized or adherents of other faiths may experience salvation according to the mysterious grace and mercy of God. But a great deal of ambiguity and overlap admittedly exists among these broad categories.[34]

Usually Pentecostals are assumed to be exclusivists, and indeed there is a track record to that effect. At one level, Pentecostal exclusivism is connected to its understanding of the Great Commission. The call to go into the world and proclaim the gospel to everyone has led them to view religious others narrowly, primarily as objects of evangelism. Hence Pentecostals have asserted that the Spirit's saving work is limited to the church, and it is precisely as members of the church allow themselves to be used by the Spirit to witness to their non-Christian neighbors, even those of other religions, that salvation is also made available to the world.[35] Insofar as Pentecostals think that the evangelism mandate and inclusivist openness to the possibility of the salvation of the unevangelized (not to mention pluralism) are incompatible, their ardent evangelistic orientation requires, they assume, that they must be exclusivists.

Another way to understand Pentecostal exclusivism is to note Pentecostals' historical connections with fundamentalism and conservative Evangelicalism. The historic Pentecostal closed-mindedness may be a remnant of their landing on the fundamentalist side of the fundamentalist-liberal (or modernist) divide during the first quarter of the twentieth century, an excessive literalist approach to biblical hermeneutics, and an overall suspicion toward ecumenism in general.[36] Since the early Pentecostals were shunned on both the left and the right—by liberals, because of Pentecostalism's uncultured and unsophisticated spirituality; by fundamentalists, because of their charismatic enthusiasm and experientialism— Pentecostals have imbibed a sectarian mentality, almost as if for reasons of self-preservation. This rejection has produced a long history of ecumenical isolationism vis-à-vis the other churches, as well as a theological exclusivism vis-à-vis other religions. And since Pentecostals have not given serious thought to developing a formal theology of religions of their own until very recently, they have historically not felt the need to go beyond the exclusivism they shared with Evangelicals (and fundamentalists) regarding the religions.

Of course, there is also the gloomy possibility that Pentecostals are just exclusivists by nature, and without further evidence deciding is difficult. Fortunately, there is additional evidence for investigation.[37]

Pentecostal-Charismatic "Inclusivism"

Clark Pinnock, himself a Charismatic Baptist, has worked closely with Pentecostal scholars and thus built a relationship of mutual respect. He is clearly inclusivist in his theology of religions.[38] While continuing to affirm unequivocally the incarnation and revelation of God in the person of Jesus Christ, he refuses to restrict the Spirit's reach to those who have specifically heard the gospel. In fact, it has been precisely his commitment to biblical authority and a high Christology that has led Pinnock to develop his pneumatology. The result has been an openly and optimistically inclusivist stance wherein he seeks to avoid the twin errors of overemphasizing either universality or particularity to the exclusion of the other. For Pinnock, the Spirit (though not entirely or only) represents universality and the Son (though not entirely or only) represents particularity.[39] This is not an either/ or but a both/and proposition. Building on John Wesley's concept of prevenient grace (the grace that goes before), Pinnock posits the Spirit's presence in the religions bringing God's revelation into contact with some who will receive and then perhaps be saved. He does not see non-Christian religions as vehicles of salvation, yet he resists restricting God the Spirit to the church. One may discern this prevenient process in action through the presence of the Spirit's fruit. Pinnock, therefore, refers in hope to the unevangelized or adherents of other religions as "pre-Christian" rather than "non-Christian."[40]

No doubt some Pentecostals have been influenced by Pinnock. But is inclusivism simply a choice between historical Pentecostal and contemporary Charismatic stances? No, because even in historical, classical Pentecostalism "strands of openness" to religious others crop up sporadically in the midst of a history and environment of exclusivity.[41] Tony Richie has recently drawn attention to the fact that early and original elements of Pentecostalism had significant inclusivist strains.[42] Such a stance may be gleaned from the theology of none other than Charles Fox Parham. Parham advocated an eschatological inclusivism of uncompromising loyalty to Christ coupled with compassionate openness to devout adherents of other religions.[43] For Parham, commitment to the absolute uniqueness and necessity of Jesus Christ as Lord and Savior complements openness to a possibility of divine reality and redemption in extra-Christian religions that are consummated in the eschaton by Christ.

Contemporary Pentecostals can also respond to the challenges of religious pluralism through an appropriation of the optimistic and hopeful theology of Bishop J. H. King, an important and early Pentecostal pioneer leader and thinker.[44] Central and crucial for King was the universal significance of Christ, a refined doctrine of universal atonement, the reality and efficacy of general revelation, a qualified acceptance of religious experience over rigid doctrinal propositionalism, and, though somewhat less directly, a dynamic and progressive view of the process of salvation. King also accepted that "the religion of Christ"—the religion centered in the person of Christ himself rather than in institutional Christianity—predates and exists apart from ecclesial Christianity, that is, among other world religions, though Christianity may be in a special sense truly called "the only true religion." When put together to address the questions of religious pluralism, Bishop King's theology invites a more inclusive stance toward the religions than the rhetoric of classical Pentecostalism suggests.

In fact, we suggest, a generally and genuinely inclusive theology of religions flows quite naturally out of the Wesleyan-Arminian heritage of the Holiness-Pentecostal revival.[45] The time is ripe for Pentecostals to explore a "balanced pentecostal approach to Christian theology of religions."[46] Hollenweger's suggestion of "dialogical evangelism" provides an interactive mode of engaging religious others that is not contradictory to but compatible with Pentecostal history, identity, missiology, spirituality, and theology. Neither dialogical evangelism nor traditional Pntecostal evangelism usurps the other, but both are appraised as attractive options in their appropriate places. Such an inclusive Pentecostal theology of religions, especially of the kind articulated by Richie in dialogue with major streams of the early Pentecostal tradition, is a "back to the future" approach that simultaneously looks backward and forward and stresses both continuity and creativity.

Toward a Pentecostal Theology of Religions

One recognized Pentecostal theologian who has led the way on the issue of theology of religions is Veli-Matti Kärkkäinen.[47] If theology of religions "attempts to account theologically for the meaning and value of other religions,"[48] then a distinctively Christian theology of religions, Kärkkäinen suggests, must be Trinitarian. Very briefly, Kärkkäinen's Trinitarian theology of religions suggests that Trinitarian theology serves as a critique of a so-called normative pluralism (which usually collapses the differences between religions); that the Triune God of the Bible is unique; that a high Christology plays a critical role in the doctrine of the Trinity; that the church in the power of the Holy Spirit anticipates the Kingdom of God, always pointing beyond itself to the eschaton, or the coming of the Kingdom and unity of all people under one God; that the doctrine of the Trinity indicates the communal nature of God capable of relating in unity and difference; and that Trinitarian communion can include critical relationship with religious others in tolerance. Essentially, Kärkkäinen is suggesting that a full-orbed Trinitarian theology emphasizes the role of the Spirit not only in the Trinitarian life of God but also in the presence of relationship between God and the church and in the relationship between the church and the world.

Obviously pneumatologically robust, Kärkkäinen is nonetheless faithfully Christocentric and ecclesiological.[49] The Spirit who reaches out beyond the church into the Kingdom and into the world is always the Spirit of Christ who abides in unique relation with his church. No wedge is driven between the Spirit and Christ, or between the Spirit and the church. Thus other religions are not salvific, but discerning appreciation for the presence of the Triune God in their midst is possible. This opens the way wide for relational engagement and includes a responsibility for genuinely appreciative and cautiously critical interreligious dialogue and encounter. For Kärkkäinen, a truly Trinitarian theology of religions enables interreligious dialogue as a mutually respectful process of learning and sharing.

If Kärkkäinen has reflected theologically on the religions as a Pentecostal, it has been Amos Yong who has attempted to develop a distinctively Pentecostal theology of religions.[50] He advises fellow Pentecostals to develop a theology of religions because of their international roots and global presence; because of their need to attend to urgent missiological issues such as syncretism, the relations between gospel and culture, and the balance between proclamation and social justice; and because of the importance of this topic for further delineating Pentecostal identity. Yet the Pentecostal experience produces its own "pneumatological imagination"—a way of thinking and theologizing informed by the Pentecostal-Charismatic experience of and orientation toward the Holy Spirit—which suggests the possibility of the Spirit's presence and influence in the world in general and in the world's religions more particularly. Further, such a Pentecostal theology is also sensitive to the fact that there are many "spirits" in the world, much less in the world of the religions, which require Christian discernment. The criteria for discerning the Holy Spirit from other spirits, then, includes the fruits of the Spirit, ethical conduct, and the signs of the coming Kingdom. In such a Pentecostal theological framework, then, Yong also emphasizes that "the pneumatological imagination derived from the outpouring of the Spirit" enables a relatively impartial, sympathetic, yet critical engagement with the religions.[51]

For Kärkkäinen and Yong, then, it is important that a Pentecostal theology of religions should help Pentecostal Christians engage the religions through discernment rather than through any a priori views about the religions. This means that people of other faiths need to be heard first on their own terms, even while (Pentecostal) Christians would also be invited or even required to testify in their own tongues. The key here is to be able to comprehend other religions according to their self-understanding, without prejudging or defining them according to our own Christian (or Pentecostal) theological categories (e.g., in exclusivist, inclusivist, or pluralist terms). Such a Pentecostal approach thus sustains and motivates the interreligious encounter, and it does so as part of the Christian mission.

Assessing Pentecostal Theologies of Religions

We will momentarily expand on these insights toward a Pentecostal and pneumatological theology of religions. Before doing so, however, some assessment is in order. To begin, we should clearly state, as Kärkkäinen has already pointed out, that pluralism is not an option for Pentecostals.[52] At the same time, a narrow exclusivism, that is, a view that Christ and the Spirit are restricted entirely to the church or its members, sits uncomfortably with the theology of religions proposed by Pinnock, Richie, Kärkkäinen, and Yong. However, as a more open inclusivism could fit with any of them, it is noteworthy that those working most directly and pointedly in the area of Pentecostal theology of religions seem to be developing in generally inclusivist directions. As of yet, no major theological voice from within the movement itself is sounding an alarm (even while recognized Pentecostal theologians such as Frank Macchia are turning in what might be called inclusivist directions).[53] Though that may happen at some point, likely the burden of proof rests with those seeking to limit or restrict the Spirit rather than otherwise.

But it is interesting to ask why Pentecostal scholars and theologians who are publishing on the religions have not resorted to the established categories of exclusivism, inclusivism, and so on. Perhaps there are more exclusivists present than we are aware of, but if they are not explicitly using (or defending) the exclusivist model in their writings, they would be identifiable as exclusivistic only with difficulty.[54] Hence concluding that inclusivism has won or will win the day is premature.

Of course, inclusivism itself is not without its challenges. One of the major hurdles that inclusivists need to confront is that their theological paradigm remains wedded to the soteriological question about the salvation of the unevangelized or of those in other religions. Inclusivism, in other words, was developed more for Christian self-understanding than for answering the questions related to theology of religions. Hence inclusivism is inappropriate when applied in a dialogue with people of other faiths since that would entail Christians either granting salvation to people of other faiths who are not seeking such salvation (of union with God in Christ) or Christians labeling people of other faiths according to categories foreign to those religious traditions. In our contemporary pluralistic world, the challenge is to understand religious others on their own terms, even while remaining committed to our own religious vision, including that of bearing witness to Christ in the power of the Spirit.

In a real sense, the theologies of religions of Kärkkäinen and Yong are in search of ways to resolve this inclusivist dilemma. Both emphasize a robust Trinitarian pneumatology (even if Kärkkäinen stresses the Trinitarian a bit more and Yong the pneumatology) precisely in order to open up theological space to appreciate the particularities of the religions and their differences from Christian faith. While Kärkkäinen's emphasis is on how the real Trinitarian differences may correlate with real differences between the religions, Yong's "pneumatological imagination" is designed to both recognize and bridge the vast chasm separating Christian faith from other religions. In this sense, both recognize the shortcomings of the dominant categories of exclusivism, inclusivism, and pluralism and have explored the questions of if and how we might advance beyond this paradigm.[55] Yet their efforts, along with those of Pinnock and Richie, are also indications that a Pentecostal theology of religions is an exciting but complex undertaking. They suggest that Pentecostals are ready to take their place in the global community amid the interreligious encounter. Might Pentecostal approaches to mission and the theology of religions point the way forward for such a task?

PENTECOSTALISM, MISSIONS, AND THE CONTEMPORARY INTERRELIGIOUS ENCOUNTER

In this final part of our chapter we want to focus both on pneumatological-theological issues and on performative-practical proposals for a Pentecostal pneumatological theology of religions. We argue first that the many tongues of Pentecost could represent even the religious traditions of the world and second that this same multiplicity of tongues invites and empowers various kinds of practices for the interfaith encounter. Our goal is to make explicit the connections between a distinctive Pentecostal missiology (discussed in the first section) and a distinctive Pentecostal theology of religions (just introduced), with an eye to explicitly fleshing out how such a Pentecostal and pneumatological approach to the religions works itself out in the practice of missions.

Toward a Pentecostal and Pneumatological Theology of Religions

As we have seen, one of the main problems that plague traditional theologies of religions is how to honor and respect the particularities of other faiths, even while remaining committed to one's own (in our case, Pentecostal Christianity). This is parallel to the perennial philosophical challenge of the relationship between the one and the many. Historically, responses have either privileged the one, which risks rejecting the many, or emphasized the many, which lapses into anarchy or relativism.[56] Does a Pentecostal and pneumatological perspective shed light on this ancient debate?

The Day of Pentecost narrative in Acts 2 provides some perspective on this issue. Two observations can be made.[57] First, it should be noted that the one outpouring of the Spirit did not cancel out but rather enabled an eruption of a diversity of tongues. On the one hand, there is a cacophony of tongues; on the other, there is a harmony of testimonies, each witnessing in its own way to God's deeds of power. Correlatively, there is mass confusion but yet also an astonishment born of understanding.[58] In these ways, Pentecost signifies, perhaps, a unique resolution of the one and the many: the many (tongues) retain their particularities even as they participate in the one (Spirit's outpouring).[59] Whereas before there were just the many tongues, now the many tongues are brought together, not so that they might cancel or drown one another out, but so that precisely out of the plurality of utterances strangers might be brought together and the goodness of God might be declared.

This leads, second, to the observation that the many tongues of Pentecost did indeed signify the many cultures of the ancient Mediterranean world. Whereas the cultural and religious domains of human life are neither identical nor synonymous, we argue that they are also not completely distinct. Rather, languages are related to cultures, and both are related to religious traditions, even if each is a distinguishable aspect of human life. Given this interrelationship, however, might we suggest that the many tongues of Pentecost represent not only many cultures but also, at least potentially, many religious traditions? If so, then the outpouring of the Spirit points not only to the redemption of the many languages but also to the redemption of many cultures and perhaps of many religious traditions.

What we mean by redemption, however, should be qualified. First, the claim about the redemption of other faiths is an eschatological one: "In the last days it will be, God declares, that I will pour out my Spirit upon all flesh" (Acts 2:17a). If the eschatological gift of the Spirit means, in part, that the outpouring of the Spirit has occurred, is occurring, and will continue to occur, then the redemption of any thing, the religions included, may have past, present, and, most important, future aspects to it. In that sense, then, every person, including persons in other faiths, is a candidate for the future reception of the Spirit (if not already having been touched by the Spirit whose winds blow where they may), and such reception may depend in part on their interactions with us (as Christians). How we approach or respond to people of other faiths may determine if and when the gift of the Spirit will be given to them. And, given the fact that there are varying degrees of ignorance and knowledge about Christ, we would underscore God's redemptive work in the lives of individuals as a dynamic process depending not on our certification of their salvation but on the gracious gift of God in Christ and the Holy Spirit. So in anticipating the possibility of the redemption of the religions, then, we are saying neither that Luke means every person since the Day of Pentecost has received the Spirit nor that all people of other faiths are already saved.

Second, in speaking about the redemption of cultures and of religious traditions, we are by no means suggesting that all cultures or religious traditions as wholes are now conduits of the saving grace of God. Cultures and religions, like languages, are not monolithic, and aspects of each of them are antithetical to the purposes of God (hence their fallenness). At the same time, neither are languages, cultures, and religions static, so that whatever in them might be hostile to the purposes of God today might not be so tomorrow. The Day of Pentecost attests to God's gracious and incomprehensible freedom to redeem—take up and use—the diversity of languages for his purposes. Similarly, we suggest, God has the freedom to do this redemptive work with the various cultures and religions of the world.

But, further, we must also avoid any unqualified optimism, as critics of inclusivism have warned. Hence discussion of the redemption of the religions, even if understood in eschatological perspective, must provide guidelines for discerning engagement with them on this side of the eschaton. If our position is to avoid both a universalistic soteriology in which all people are finally saved (which we repudiate) and a blanket endorsement of the religions as already redeemed of God (which we reject), then what is the proper posture with which we should approach people of other faiths? For this task, we must be discerning not only of the many tongues (beliefs or doctrines) of other religious traditions but also of their many practices. Let us outline a Pentecostal and pneumatological approach to discerning the religions, then, that avoids the pitfalls identified above in the traditional approaches.

To begin, a Pentecostal and pneumatological theology of religions underwrites an a posteriori approach to interreligious engagement. Just as in a congregational context, "Let two or three prophets speak, and let the others weigh what is said" (1 Cor. 14:29), so also in the interfaith encounter: we must look and listen carefully before rendering judgment. The goal is to allow the tongues (testimonies) of other religious people to be heard first on their own "insider's" terms (just as we clamor to be heard on our terms). Any theology *of religions,* even a pneumatological one, must be deeply informed by the empirical reality of the religions rather than an a priori projection of the Christian imagination.

Second, a Pentecostal and pneumatological theology of religions engages in critical analysis (discernment) of the religious phenomenon or teaching under scrutiny. Here we might bring to bear a multitude of disciplinary perspectives, being cautious about not imposing a reductionist interpretation on what we are attempting to discern. Also here, we attempt to compare and contrast what we are looking at or listening to with our Christian convictions (beliefs and practices).[60] Such analysis is not always straightforward. At one level, we might be attempting to compare very disparate realities, and if so, any conclusions will have missed the point.[61] Part of the task involves application of what might be called a "hermeneutics of charity" that attempts to empathize with the other faith perspective as much as possible from their point of view. Always at work, however, will be the Christian (and Pentecostal) "hermeneutics of suspicion" (regarding the other faith) that is vigilant about the urgency of the gospel.

At some point in the discerning process, we might have to "come to a decision." So long as we remember that any such judgments are always provisional, subject to later confirmation (or not), we recognize that as historically situated beings, life requires that we discern the Holy Spirit's presence and activity to the best of our ability. Decision is followed by action. The hermeneutical circle requires, however, if we are to be honest, that we then reassess the process of discernment to see if we have missed the mark.

Many Tongues, Many Practices: Hospitality, Missions, and Interfaith Practices

We have suggested that a Pentecostal-pneumatological perspective sheds new light on the perennial question of the one and the many in ways that allow us to affirm the diversity of tongues, cultures, and religions without being uncritical in our affirmation. We proposed that holding together our conviction about Christian faith amid the many religions invites a posture of engagement and discernment. Now we expand on this by arguing that a pneumatological approach that begins with the many tongues of Pentecost opens up to the many practices of the empowering Spirit. More precisely, we argue that the Spirit of encounter is also the Spirit of hospitality and that a pneumatological theology of hospitality nourishes many practices through which Christians can and need to bear witness to the gospel in a pluralistic world. We present this line of thought first by looking at the life of Jesus and then that of the early church. As Pentecostal theologians, we turn to the two volumes of Luke and Acts.[62]

Jesus himself can be understood both as the paradigmatic host of God's hospitality and as the exemplary recipient of hospitality. From his conception in Mary's womb (by the Holy Spirit) to his birth in a manger through to his burial (in a tomb of Joseph of Arimathea), Jesus was dependent on the welcome and hospitality of others. As "the Son of Man has nowhere to lay his head" (Lk. 9:58), he relied on the goodwill of many, staying in their homes and receiving whatever they served. But it is in his role as guest that Jesus also announces and enacts the hospitality of God. Empowered by the Spirit, he heals the sick, casts out demons, and declares the arrival of the reign of God in the midst of the downtrodden, the oppressed, and the marginalized. While he is the "journeying prophet" who eats at the tables of others, he also proclaims and brings to pass the eschatological banquet of God for all who are willing to receive it. So sometimes Jesus breaks the rules of hospitality, upsets the social conventions of meal fellowship (e.g., Jesus does not wash before dinner), and even goes so far as to rebuke his hosts. Luke thus shows that it is Jesus who is the broker of God's authority, and it is on this basis that Jesus establishes the inclusive hospitality of the Kingdom to the marginalized of his day (women, children, and the "disabled").

This more inclusive vision of divine hospitality is most clearly seen in the parable of the Good Samaritan (10:25–37). It is the Samaritan, the religious "other" of the first-century Jewish world, who fulfills the law, loves his neighbor, and embodies divine hospitality. What are the implications of this parable for contemporary interreligious relationships? Might those who are "others" to us Christians not only be instruments through whom God's revelation comes afresh but also perhaps be able to fulfill the requirements for inheriting eternal life (10:25) precisely through the hospitality that they show to us, their neighbors?[63]

In Acts, the hospitality of God manifested in Jesus the anointed one (the Christ) is now extended through the early church by the power of the same Holy Spirit. As with Jesus, his followers are also anointed by the Spirit to be guests and hosts, in either case representing the hospitality of God. Saint Paul, for example, is also both a recipient and a conduit of God's hospitality. He was the beneficiary of divine hospitality through those who led him by the hand, Judas (on Straight Street), Ananias, other believers who helped him escape from conspiring enemies, and Barnabas. Then during his missionary journeys, he is a guest of Lydia, a new convert, and has his wounds treated by the Philippian jailer. Paul the traveling missionary is also a guest of Jason of Thessalonica, Prisca and Aquilla and Titius Justus at Corinth, Philip the Evangelist (and his daughters) at Caesarea, Mnason in Jerusalem, and unnamed disciples at Troas, Tyre, Ptolemais, and Sidon, and so on. Along the way, Paul is escorted by Bereans, protected by Roman centurions, and entertained by Felix the governor. During the storm threatening the voyage to Rome, Paul hosts the breaking of bread. After the shipwreck, Paul is guest of the Maltese islanders (*barbaroi,* according to the original Greek of Acts 28:2) in general and of Publius the chief official in particular, and then later of some brothers on Puteoli. Acts closes with Paul as host, welcoming all who were open to receiving the hospitality of God. Throughout, Paul is the paradigmatic guest and host representing the practices of the earliest Christians who took the gospel to the ends of the earth by the power of the Holy Spirit.

The Spirit's empowerment to bear witness to the gospel takes the form of many different practices in the lives of Jesus and the early Christians, each related to being guests and hosts in various times and places. We suggest that these many practices of the Spirit are related to the diversity of tongues spoken on the Day of Pentecost. Even as the many tongues of the Spirit announce the redemptive hospitality of God, so also the many works of the Spirit enact God's salvation through many hospitable practices. As believers interact with and receive the hospitality, kindness, and gifts of strangers of all sorts, even Samaritans, public or governmental officials, and "barbarians," a diversity of practices ensues. In short, many tongues require many hospitable practices because of the church's mission in a pluralistic world.

How do these many practices redeem the traditional theologies of exclusivism, inclusivism, and pluralism? We suggest that a Lukan, Pentecostal, and pneumatological theology of hospitality allows us to retrieve and reappropriate the wide range of practices implicit in these models without having to endorse the full scope of their theological assertions. From the pluralist perspective, for example, an emphasis on social justice is prevalent in Jesus' concerns for the poor and the marginalized and in the Spirit's producing a new community, the church, in which the traditional barriers of class, gender, and ethnicity no longer hold; but pluralism's all-roads-lead-to-God idea can be rejected. The inclusivist insistence on recognizing the possibility of divine revelation and activity among the unevangelized is likewise preserved, especially given the Pentecostal conviction regarding the miraculous gift of the Spirit that enables understanding amid the cacophony of many tongues; at the same time, inclusivism's crypto-imperialistic stance can be recognized and guarded against. And finally, the exclusivist commitment to the proclamation of the gospel is upheld since authentic hospitality is redemptive, and this includes declaration of the gospel in the proper time and place; but exclusivism's triumphalism and arrogance can be rejected. In short, the practices of the models are redeemed without their theological and attitudinal liabilities.

Hence a pneumatological theology of hospitality empowers a much wider range of interreligious practices more conducive to meeting the demands of our time. This is in part because Christians often find themselves as guest or as hosts, sometimes (as in the lives of Jesus and Paul) simultaneously. In these various circumstances, there are many sociocultural protocols that will inform Christian practices. Sometimes Christians will defer to their hosts, embodying epistemic humility, and in the process be enriched by their interactions with people of other faiths. In other cases, Christians are hosts, with the responsibility to care for their guests of other faiths and to do so at the many levels at which such care can be given (the physical, the material, the intellectual, the spiritual, etc.). In all cases, however, the conventions of hospitality will resist imperialistic approaches or better-than-thou attitudes, even as such conventions mediate honest dialogue and mutual interaction.

Perhaps most important, a Pentecostal-pneumatological approach to theology of religions opens up to the kinds of Christian practices through which Christians themselves are transformed and even saved. A parallel parable to the Good Samaritan is that of the Sheep and the Goats (Matt. 25:31–46), and in this case the salvation of the Sheep was mediated by their ministering to Jesus through their encounter with the poor, the naked, the hungry, and those in prison. Of course, many people of faith, both Christian and non-Christian, are poor, hungry, and marginalized. Will we who have experienced the redemptive hospitality of God in turn show hospitality to such people? And if so, the Spirit has surely empowered us to bear witness to the gospel in these encounters. But at the same time, such hospitable interactions become the means of the Spirit to lavish on us the ongoing salvific hospitality of God. In these cases, instead of "looking down" on those in other faiths because we have something they do not, we are ourselves in a position similar to that of the Jewish man by the wayside in the parable of the Good Samaritan: thankful to the God of Jesus Christ for revealing himself to us and saving us by the power of the Holy Spirit in and through the lives of our many neighbors in a pluralistic world.

CONCLUSION

We have suggested that Pentecostal missiology, theology of religions, and interreligious encounter and dialogue are or ought to be interrelated and interdependent. These important disciplines should not be developed or practiced in isolation. Further, we have suggested that fresh and vigorous Pentecostal-pneumatological insights, while building on long-standing classical commitments, yield exciting possibilities for their theological development and practical implementation. Continuity and creativity here may be integrated and applied profitably. While existing conceptual categories—such as exclusivism, pluralism, and inclusivism—are relatively helpful, the conversation needs to be able to move past those boundaries to explore potentially fertile regions beyond. The challenge of today is for Pentecostal scholars, missionaries, theologians, dialogue participants, and others to move forward into the future under the power of the anointing of the Holy Spirit.

NOTES

1. Possibly the closest that Pentecostals have come to hagiography has been in their praise of extraordinary missionaries, e.g., Peggy Humphrey, *J. H. Ingram: Missionary Dean* (Cleveland: Pathway, 1966).

2. Amos Yong discusses this in "The Inviting Spirit: Pentecostal Beliefs and Practices regarding the Religions Today," in *Defining Issues in Pentecostalism: Classical and Emergent,* ed. Steven Studebaker (Eugene: Wipf & Stock, 2008), 29–45.

3. Developments in Pentecostal scholarship are documented in Amos Yong, "Pentecostalism and the Theological Academy," *Theology Today* 64:2 (2007): 148–57.

4. See Murray W. Dempster, Byron D. Klaus, and Douglas Petersen, eds., *Called and Empower: Global Mission in Pentecostal Perspective* (Peabody: Hendrickson, 1991); and Veli-Matti Kärkkäinen, "Pentecostal Theology of Mission in the Making," *JBV* 25:2 (August 2004): 167–76.

5. James R. Goff Jr., "Initial Tongues in the Theology of Charles Fox Parham," in *Initial Evidence: Historical and Biblical Perspectives on the Pentecostal Doctrine of Spirit Baptism,* ed. Gary B. McGee (Peabody: Hendrickson, 1991), 57–71.

6. J. R. Goff, "Parham, Charles Fox," in *NIDPCM,* 955–57(955). For Goff's definitive treatment of Parham, see James R. Goff Jr., *Fields White unto Harvest: Charles F. Parham and the Missionary Origins of Pentecostalism* (Fayetteville: University of Arkansas Press, 1988).

7. See Cecil M. Robeck Jr., *The Azusa Street Mission & Revival* (Nashville: Nelson, 2006), 235–80.

8. E.g., Ray H. Hughes, *Church of God Distinctives* (Cleveland: Pathway, 1989), 49–62; and Stanley M. Horton, *What the Bible Says about the Holy Spirit* (Springfield: GPH, 1992), 149.

9. See G. B. McGee, "Hodges, Melvin Lyle," in *NIDPCM,* 723–24.

10. Melvin L. Hodges, *A Theology of the Church and Its Mission: A Pentecostal Perspective* (Springfield: GPH, 1977), 95.

11. See Melvin L. Hodges, *The Indigenous Church* (Springfield: GPH, 1953).

12. Amos Yong argues this point in his *The Spirit Poured out on All Flesh: Pentecostalism and the Possibility of Global Theology* (Grand Rapids: Baker Academic, 2005), 123–24 and chap. 4.

13. See Paul A. Pomerville, *Third Force in Missions: A Pentecostal Contribution to Contemporary Mission Theology* (Peabody: Hendrickson, 1985).

14. Paul A. Pomerville, "Pentecostals and Growth," in *Azusa Street and Beyond,* ed. Grant L. McClung Jr. (Gainesville: Bridge-Logos, 2006), 151–55.

15. See McClung, ed., *Azusa Street and Beyond,* esp. his introduction to each section; Grant L. McClung Jr., *Globalbeliever.com: Connecting to God's Work in Your World* (Cleveland: Pathway, 2004).

16. Along this line contemporary the Pentecostal New Testament scholar John Christopher Thomas argues for "an intricate and significant connection" between healing and mission. See his *The Spirit of the New Testament* (Leiderdorp: Deo, 2005), 21–47.

17. Other Pentecostal scholars have also noted the connection between pneumatology, eschatology, and mission for Pentecostalism; see, e.g., Byron D. Klaus, "The Holy Spirit and Mission in Eschatological Perspective: A Pentecostal Viewpoint," *Pneuma* 27:2 (2005): 322–42.

18. Gary McGee, "Pentecostal Missiology: Moving beyond Triumphalism to Face the Issues," *Pneuma* 16:2 (fall 1994): 275–81. See further Gary B. McGee, *This Gospel Shall Be Preached: A History and Theology of Assemblies of God Foreign Missions,* 2 vols. (Springfield: GPH, 1986, 1989); "Pentecostal and Charismatic Missions," in *Toward the Twenty-first Century in Christian Mission: Essays in Honor of Gerald H. Anderson,* ed. James M. Philips and Robert T. Coote (Grand Rapids: Eerdmans, 1993), 41–56; and "The Radical Strategy in Modern Missions: The Linkage of Paranormal Phenomena with Evangelism," in *The Holy Spirit and Mission Dynamics,* ed. C. D. McDonnell (Pasadena: William Carey Library, 1997), 69–95.

19. See his now-classic text, *The Pentecostals* (Peabody: Hendrickson, 1988; first published, London: SCM, 1972); cf. Walter J. Hollenweger, *Pentecostalism: Origins and Development Worldwide* (Peabody: Hendrickson, 1997).

20. Cf. D. D. Bundy, "Hollenweger, Walter Jacob," in *NIDPCM,* 729.

21. Walter J. Hollenweger, "Black Roots of Pentecostalism," in *Pentecostals after a Century: Global Perspectives on a Movement in Transition,* ed. Alan Anderson and Walter J. Hollenweger (Sheffield: SAP, 1999), 33–44.

22. Walter J. Hollenweger, "Critical Issues for Pentecostals," in Anderson and Hollenweger, *Pentecostals after a Century,* 176–91 (85–86).

23. See Tony Richie, "Revamping Pentecostal Evangelism: Appropriating Walter J. Hollenweger's Radical Proposal," *IMR* (July–October 2007): 343–54; cf. Richie, "A *Pentecostal* in Sheep's Clothing: An Unlikely Participant but Hopeful Partner in Interreligious Dialogue," *Current Dialogue* 48 (December 2006): 9–15.

24. Hollenweger, "Critical Issues for Pentecostals," 176–91. See Lynne Price's excellent study, *Theology Out of Place: A Theological Biography of Walter J. Hollenweger* (Sheffield: SAP, 2002), which shows that Hollenweger is deeply committed to the ecumenical and interreligious nature of Pentecostalism and that his missiology is significantly shaped by it.

25. Allan Anderson, "Global Pentecostalism in the New Millennium," in Anderson and Hollenweger, *Pentecostals after a Century,* 210.

26. Allan Anderson, "Introduction: World Pentecostalism at a Crossroads," in Anderson and Hollenweger, *Pentecostals after a Century,* 19–31.

27. See Alan Anderson, "Towards a Pentecostal Missiology," n.d., available at http://artsweb.bham .ac.uk/aanderson/Publications/towards_a_pentecostal_missiology.htm.

28. This is a main point of his recent books, *An Introduction to Pentecostalism: Global Charismatic Christianity* (Cambridge: CUP, 2004); and *Spreading Fires: The Missionary Nature of Early Pentecostalism* (London: SCM, 2007).

29. Andrew Lord, "The Pentecostal-Moltmann Dialogue: Implications for Mission," *JPT* 11:2 (2003): 271–87.

30. Andrew Lord, *Spirit-Shaped Mission: A Holistic Charismatic Missiology* (Carlisle: Paternoster, 2005).

31. Veli-Matti Kärkkäinen, "'Truth on Fire': Pentecostal Theology of Mission and the Challenges of a New Millennium," *AJPS* 3.1 (January 2000): 33–60.

32. See also Amos Yong, "'Not Knowing Where the Spirit Blows . . .': On Envisioning a Pentecostal-Charismatic Theology of Religions," *JPT* 14 (April 1999): 81–112.

33. Cf. Veli-Matti Kärkkäinen, *An Introduction to The Theology of Religions: Biblical, Historical, and Contemporary Perspectives* (Downers Grove, IL: IVP, 2003), 139–40.

34. For the classic presentation of the categories of exclusivism, inclusivism, and pluralism in theology of religions, see Alan Race, *Christians and Religious Pluralism: Patterns in the Theology of Religions* (Maryknoll, NY: Orbis, 1983).

35. Cf. Kärkkäinen, *An Introduction to The Theology of Religions,* 140–42.

36. Amos Yong, *Discerning the Spirit(s): A Pentecostal-Charismatic Contribution to Christian Theology of Religions* (Sheffield: Sheffield Academic, 2000), 185–87.

37. See, e.g., Tony Richie, "Precedents and Possibilities: Pentecostal Perspectives on World Religions," *Pneuma Review* (January 2006), available at http://pneumafoundation.org/article.jsp?article=/ article_0042.xml#note15.

38. Clark Pinnock, *A Wideness in God's Mercy: The Finality of Jesus Christ in a World of Religions* (Grand Rapids: Zondervan, 1992).

39. Clark H. Pinnock, *Flame of Love: A Theology of the Holy Spirit* (Downers Grove, IL: IVP, 1996), 185–214.

40. For further discussion of Pinnock's charismatic and inclusivist theology of religions, see Amos Yong, "Whither Theological Inclusivism? The Development and Critique of an Evangelical Theology of Religions," *Evangelical Quarterly* 71:4 (October 1999): 327–48.

41. See Yong, *Discerning the Spirit(s)*, 187–97.

42. Tony Richie, "The Unity of the Spirit," *JEPTA* 26 (2006): 21–35.

43. Tony Richie, "Eschatological Inclusivism: Exploring Early Pentecostal Theology of Religions in Charles Fox Parham," *JEPTA* 27:2 (2007): 138–52.

44. Tony Richie, "Azusa-Era Optimism: Bishop J. H. King's Pentecostal Theology of Religions as a Possible Paradigm for Today," *JPT* 14:2 (April 2006): 247–60.

45. See Tony Lee Richie, "John Wesley and Mohammed: A Contemporary Inquiry concerning Islam," *Asbury Theological Journal* 58:2 (fall 2003): 79–99; and Yong, *Spirit Poured Out*, chap. 6.

46. Tony Richie, "Neither Naïve nor Narrow: A Balanced Approach to Christian Theology of Religions," *CPCR* 15 (February 2006), available at www.pctii.org/cyberj/cyber15.html.

47. For an explication of how Kärkkäinen's Pentecostal identity informs his work as a theologian in general and as a theologian of religions in particular, see Yong, "Whither Evangelical Theology? The Work of Veli-Matti Kärkkäinen as a Case Study of Contemporary Trajectories," *Evangelical Review of Theology* 30:1 (2006): 60–85.

48. See especially Veli-Matti Kärkkäinen, *Trinity and Religious Pluralism: The Doctrine of the Trinity in Christian Theology of Religions* (Aldershot: Ashgate, 2004), 2; see also his *Toward a Pneumatological Theology: Pentecostal and Ecumenical Perspectives on Ecclesiology, Soteriology, and Theology of Mission*, ed. Amos Yong (Lanham, MD: University Press of America, 2002), chap. 14.

49. E.g., Veli-Matti Kärkkäinen, "Toward a Pneumatological Theology of Religions: A Pentecostal-Charismatic Inquiry," *IMR* 91: 361 (2002): 187–98; and "How to Speak of the Spirit among Religions: Trinitarian 'Rules' for a Pneumatological Theology of Religions," *IBMR* 30:3 (2006): 121–27.

50. See Yong, *Discerning the Spirit(s)*; and also his *Beyond the Impasse: Toward a Pneumatological Theology of Religions* (Grand Rapids: Baker Academic, 2003).

51. Yong, *Spirit Poured Out*, 254.

52. See Kärkkäinen, "A Response to Tony Richie's 'Azusa-Era Optimism: Bishop J. H. King's Pentecostal Theology of Religions as a Possible Paradigm for Today,'" *JPT* 5:2 (April 2007): 263–68.

53. While Macchia rejects the philosophy of religious pluralism, he skillfully argues that Christ's role as Spirit Baptizer indicates that the church is the locus of the Spirit's work and that the Spirit still works in the wider religious world because the Kingdom extends in gracious ways beyond ecclesial borders. Pluralist equalizations of all religions are thereby refuted without falling into the equal and opposite error of exclusivist incriminations. Accordingly, Macchia adds his voice to others assisting Pentecostals in advancing toward a mature, moderate theology of religions. See Frank D. Macchia, *Baptized in the Spirit: A Global Pentecostal Theology* (Grand Rapids: Zondervan, 2006), 178–90.

54. For example, it appears that the exclusivist position is defended in this essay—Robert L. Gallagher, "The Holy Spirit in the World: In Non-Christians, in Creation, and Other Religions," *AJPS* 9:1 (2006): 17–33—although the author does not put it in those terms.

55. As suggested in Amos Yong, "Can We Get 'Beyond the Paradigm' in Christian Theology of Religions? A Response to Terry Muck," *Interpretation* 61:1 (January 2007): 28–32. Note that Kärkkäinen himself organized his introductory textbook, *An Introduction to the Theology of Religions*, using a set of categories different from exclusivism, inclusivism, and pluralism. For further discussion of the unresolved difficulties for each of these approaches, see Amos Yong, "The Spirit, Christian Practices, and the Religions: Theology of Religions in Pentecostal and Pneumatological Perspective," *Asbury Journal* 62:2 (2007): 5–31 (14–19).

56. See F. C. Copleston, *Religion and the One: Philosophies East and West* (New York: Crossroad, 1982).

57. What follows is a condensed version of what Yong has argued at greater length elsewhere: "'As the Spirit Gives Utterance . . .': Pentecost, Intra-Christian Ecumenism, and the Wider *Oekumene*,"

IMR 92:366 (July 2003): 299–314; "The Spirit Bears Witness: Pneumatology, Truth, and the Religions," *Scottish Journal of Theology* 57:1 (2004): 14–38; and *Spirit Poured Out,* chap. 4.

58. On these points, we follow the brilliant reading of the Acts 2 narrative provided by Michael Welker, *God the Spirit,* trans. John F. Hoffmeyer (Minneapolis: Fortress, 1994), chap. 5.

59. See Jean Jacques-Suurmond, *Word and Spirit at Play: Towards a Charismatic Theology,* trans. John Bowden (Grand Rapids: Eerdmans, 1995), 201.

60. Yong describes the task of comparative theology in a religiously plural world in *Beyond the Impasse,* chap. 7.

61. The difficulties associated with obtaining adequate comparative categories across religious lines are discussed extensively throughout Robert Cummings Neville, ed., *The Comparative Religious Ideas Project,* 3 vols. (Albany: SUNY Press, 2001).

62. What follows condenses lengthier arguments in Amos Yong's "Guests, Hosts, and the Holy Ghost: Pneumatological Theology and Christian Practices in a World of Many Faiths," in *Lord and Giver of Life: A Constructive Pneumatology,* ed. David Jensen (Louisville: Westminster John Knox Press, 2008), pt. 1; and *Hospitality and the Other: Pentecost, Christian Practices, and the Neighbor* (Maryknoll, NY: Orbis, 2008), esp. chaps. 2 and 4.

63. Yong probes these questions at greater length in *Spirit Poured Out,* 241–44.

13

Practical Theology

Mark J. Cartledge

The discipline of practical theology is one that appears to be in constant redefinition in recent times, although there might at last be some consensus emerging. It was once regarded as the crown of theological study, placed toward the end of theological education for the ordained ministry. At this point in the process all the necessary "tips and hints" were added under the rubric *pastoralia.* In this context it was closely aligned with education for ministry and by extension church education in a broader sense. Thus would-be clergy learned how to preach, lead worship, conduct pastoral conversations with the insights of psychology, administer congregational education programs, and, of course, integrate spirituality into ministerial practice. But fundamentally with this model the minister applied theological knowledge from elsewhere (the Bible, systematic theology, church history and philosophy) to the issue of church leadership with the aid of *pastoralia* (hints and tips). This is often referred to as the formational or ministerial model. However, with the advent of liberation theology there came a turn to contemporary praxis as the starting point and in particular the use of Marxist social theory to diagnose the "problem" to be solved by liberating practices.[1] This meant that practitioners and academics used the hermeneutical tools of liberation theology to be suspicious about power relations and the need for those on the margins to be heard and empowered. It has also been allied with mission theology as liberation is conceived as part of the missionary imperative and contextual theology. This liberationist model of practical theology is now a dominant one in the academy. The third model arises from the use of the social sciences by theologians in the twentieth century, in particular, the use of both qualitative and quantitative empirical research methods within the discourse of theology. This model was developed toward the end of the 1980s as theologians started to consider the idea of theory development by using the actual beliefs and practices of religious individuals and groups rather than by simply reflecting on theological traditions historically. This model has been named *empirical theology* but must not be confused with later versions of the Chicago school, which allied itself with process theology and philosophy. North American readers, in particular, must be aware of the very real differences here, even if there are common roots in both traditions.[2]

The International Academy of Practical Theology (IAPT) was founded in 1993 and now has more than 140 members around the world. It is probably best placed to comment on the nature of the discipline as it is practiced by academics globally. It is this academy that first acknowledged, in 2005, the existence of these three strands of practical theology as represented by its members. Of course, they are not exclusive strands, and it is the case that scholars combine them according to their own commitments and interests. Nevertheless, there is an agreed-on common focus or direct object of inquiry, namely, contemporary religious praxis; that is, the value-laden practices of ecclesial and religious communities in global contexts. Of course, such a definition means that other areas or disciplines conceived in this manner can, in effect, become subdisciplines of practical theology, for example, mission, worship and liturgy, spirituality and education. Therefore, it is inevitable that there will be some form of overlap, even if in all cases the horizon of interest is principally the contemporary one. For some, practical theology is more like a field of study than a discipline.

For the purposes of this chapter, I focus on the theology and value-laden practices of Pentecostal and Charismatic Christians. For the *formational* strand, theology is conceived as prior to and therefore applied to subsequent practice: hence theology *for* practice. For the *liberationist* strand, theology is conceived as providing a challenge to values embedded in existing unjust practices in order to transform them: hence a critical theology *of* practice. For the *empirical* strand, theology arising from contemporary practice, as it is explored and tested by means of empirical research methods, is refined by critical reflection and a process of theory building in order to offer recommendations for a renewal of practice: hence theology *from and with* practice.

The use of the discipline of practical theology in the field of Pentecostal and Charismatic studies can be understood in terms of two main categories. First, there are studies by those who are Pentecostals and who reflect on their own praxis in a confessionally oriented manner. Second, there are studies of Pentecostal praxis by non-Pentecostal practical theologians, who reflect theologically on the praxis of others but in a nonconfessional manner.

In what follows, I attempt to chart the "state of the art" by means of these two categories (Pentecostal and non-Pentecostal), and I also comment on the relationship between formational/ministerial, liberationist, and empirical approaches to the subject and how in the very different writers these strands are represented. Material for this chapter is drawn from key monographs, the main journals associated with Pentecostal and Charismatic studies, and Society for Pentecostal Studies conference papers from 1998 to 2007. I have used studies that focus on contemporary praxis even if they start with biblical, historical, and systematic theological studies.

STUDIES BY PENTECOSTAL-CHARISMATIC SCHOLARS

The vast majority of publications by Pentecostals refer to their own ecclesial practices and are confessional in nature. The most recent literature focuses on formation and spirituality as the basis for discipleship, leadership, and ministry. These studies tend to be largely theoretical and suggest new frameworks or models, or perhaps offer insights for the application to practice.

Formation, Ministry, and Education

Formation, Leadership, and Spirituality.   On the subject of *spiritual formation and leadership* in the Pentecostal tradition one of the most significant texts to emerge in the past fifteen years is Cheryl Bridges Johns's *Pentecostal Formation,* in which she adapts the educational paradigm developed by the Brazilian Paulo Freire to Pentecostal spirituality.[3] Johns critiques Freire in light of her Pentecostal theological commitments and then offers an approach to catechesis for the Pentecostal tradition. Using the biblical notion of *yada* as personal knowledge of God, she critiques the concept of praxis on epistemological grounds. Following from this, she offers a Pntecostal approach to Bible study that includes starting with personal testimony, followed by a search of the Scriptures, yielding to the Spirit, and responding to the call in a fourfold movement.[4] This landmark study has been used widely within the field.

Jackie D. Johns considers church leadership and decision making based on educational theory, in particular, the idea of Christian transformational leadership (visionary and team building). He suggests, however, that a Pentecostal leadership model must flow out of a Pentecostal worldview and a "corresponding paradigm of the church." Building on the educational cycle of LeBar, he offers a "cycle of ministry development" that includes seven stages: (1) analyze: where are we? (2) set goals: where does God want us to be? (3) select a course: what course should we follow to get there? (4) plan for action: what must we do to make the trip? (5) work the plan: let's go! (6) evaluate: are we there yet? and (7) celebrate: remember the journey! This process has been made more "Pentecostal" by being translated into language that can be used by Pentecostals. Therefore the sevenfold cycle is also offered as a threefold cycle titled, "Sharing the Vision: A Covenant of Planning," and includes (1) revisioning (stages 1 and 2); (2) envisioning (stages 3 and 4); and (3) supervisioning (stages 5–7).[5]

In a similar manner, James P. Bowers advances an approach to Christian formation from an explicitly Wesleyan-Pentecostal perspective.[6] He suggests that Pentecostals have suffered from an identity crisis that has, in effect, meant that their approach to formation has been pragmatist and denominationally driven. His answer to this problem is to quarry the resources of the Wesleyan-Pentecostal tradition, suggesting that the fivefold gospel can offer formational experience of life in the Spirit to transform and energize individuals and communities. He further suggests that this discipleship process can be translated into appropriate objectives and educational practices, such as experiential knowledge, spiritual transformation, responsiveness and moral fullness, prophetic engagement, covenant relationships, discernment of truth, mission and ministry call, and a kingdom-centered eschatological vision. Having articulated these objectives, he then suggests that they can be applied to the curriculum, parenting, the church community, pastors and the eldership, small discipleship groups, church structures and decision-making processes, membership and church discipline, and the ministry of believers.

Moving to the subject of *spirituality* more directly, there are a number of useful studies. Jeanne Porter investigates the beliefs and practices of Pentecostals in order to demonstrate that they are situated within the larger stream of Christian spirituality, showing how recent Pentecostal scholarship can make an impact on the broader discourse of spirituality studies. She articulates three levels of academic study: (1) experiences of life in the Spirit through the analysis of corporate practices and the lives of leaders; (2) theorizing about life in the Spirit, which aims to explain the experiences internal to the tradition; and (3) discourse of life in the Spirit, which is the study of what scholars working at levels (1) and (2) have produced but with regard to wider Christian tradition and scholarship.[7] Similarly, Jay A. Herndon aims to introduce Pentecostals to the ministry of spiritual direction by considering its history, theology, and practice based on biblical foundations. It is a response to God's actions and forms faith in the person being directed that is holistic; and, being holistic, it can provide resources for pastoral ministry. To be a spiritual director requires spiritual experience, ability to listen, discernment, and ability to direct others.[8]

Church, Worship, and Ministry.   When discussing issues relating to the church's ministry Pentecostals tend to focus on the worshiping context and allied issues such as song, testimony, preaching, healing, counseling, spiritual warfare, revivalism, and physical manifestations of the Spirit's presence. R. Jerome Boone gives a helpful account of the key components of the Pentecostal worshiping community as the main context for spiritual formation and thus links spirituality to church ministry. He describes the components of worship services as including congregational singing, prayer, testimony, and the sermon.[9] His study provides a useful framework for analysis.

A number of studies have aimed to analyze Pentecostal and Charismatic *hymnody* in the United Kingdom. The first, by Jeremy Begbie, identifies five types of song: (1) praise, (2) love and commitment, (3) intercession, (4) ministry, and (5) awe and glory.[10] This typology is elaborated by Victoria Cooke through an analysis of the songs of Matt Redman, the British Vineyard movement, and Hillsongs, Australia, before suggesting a Charismatic theology of worship through song that includes attention to the glory of God, the Holy Spirit, healing power, confidence in God, and a response of praise.[11] In addition, Anne Dyer, independently of these studies, surveys 2,500 songs composed between 1970 and 2005 and analyzes them by means of three theological themes: (1) Jesus and his life, death, and exaltation; (2) triumphal ecclesiological ideas such as the church as priests and mediators exercising a prophetic and military ministry to the world; and (3) individualism, intimacy, and experience of God.[12]

The most significant study of American and British Pentecostal and Charismatic hymnody is by Pete Ward, using a combination of popular cultural analysis and theology. He traces the development of songs from the 1960s to the early 2000s and the spread of a culture of worship by means of these songs. He observes that the growth of the worship song market is a growth in the selling of information through song and ultimately suggests that songs in Charismatic Christianity focus on an experience of an encounter with God.[13] David Morgan has developed Ward's idea, namely, that worship is sold in the sense that Pentecostal worship songs have been brought not just in CDs but in terms of the exchange of information, theology, and values. He discusses three Hillsong texts and the information that has been bought by those using them.[14]

Also in the context of Pentecostal worship, Jean-Daniel Plüss offers an analysis of *testimony*. He discusses the problem of self-deception, the problem of language, and the role of the audience or community of the church.[15] He also considers the hermeneutics of testimony by drawing on the work of Paul Ricoeur, who identified three aspects of testimony: its quasi-empirical character, the struggle of opinion each testimony evokes, and the notion of false testimony.[16] He suggests that testimony's function is to relate to the "cloud of witnesses" and to stress the unity within the Body of Christ, causing members to worship God in song or by clapping and encouraging those listening to it in their faith. His main work in the area, a published Ph.D. dissertation, offers theological, philosophical, and sociological analyses of Pentecostal testimony in the context of worship and advances a liturgical thesis of oral narratives as a bridge between secular and religious discourse.[17]

John Gordy acknowledges that a weakness of Pentecostal scholarship is that it has failed to reflect critically on the practice of *preaching*. He aims to address this weakness by exploring the nature of Pentecostal preaching, its internal dynamics and parameters, and by proposing a framework for understanding it.[18] Another study, by Aldwin Ragoonath, compares Pentecostal preaching with Protestant and Roman Catholic preaching and suggests by means of such a comparison that it may be possible to define the contours of a distinctly Pentecostal approach. This is achieved by starting from an exegesis of Luke 4.16–20, from which he argues that Pentecostal homiletics (1) contains a commitment to the whole of the Scriptures; (2) operates from a Spirit worldview, (3) starts with the preacher reexperiencing the text and subsequently drawing out the symbolic meaning of it, (4) moves the congregation to experience the presence of God through the sermon, (5) seeks to preach to the needs of the congregation, (6) preaches in a variety of genres (topical, textual, need centered, counseling, expository), (7) is not dependent on any specific mode of communication (monologues and dialogues), and (8) uses blocks of thought, especially when preaching from narratives.[19]

Moving to other aspects of ministry, Jacques P. J. Theron conducts a practical theological reflection on the subject of *healing* by considering Pentecostal theory as part of the full gospel. He sees it as "provided for all in the atonement," noting the biblical texts used. He subsequently identifies practical theological issues by studying the "faith communicative actions which relate to the healing ministry of Pentecostals."[20] He observes how the theory has been modified in light of experience and raises issues for further consideration: the state of the grassroots healing ministries, pastoral care, manipulation and excessive claims, the unhealed, prolonged illness, the demonic,[21] the influence of the Western worldview, the implications of the Eucharist for healing, the use of the anointing with oil, the relationship between the gifts, the gifts of healing and the ministry of healing, the use of healing teams, the terminology in use, the healing of societies, and the influence of non-Pentecostals on Pentecostals in the healing ministry. In another paper he offers a reflection on the nature of spiritual warfare in the context of South Africa and asks whether Pentecostal churches deal adequately with the issue.[22] It must be said that although demonology is extremely significant for Pentecostals and Charismatic Christians, it is hardly represented in the academic literature in practical theology.

Healing and *suffering* are inevitably related, and Jeff McAffee offers a pastoral theological model of co-suffering that allows for spiritual healing and transformation of the individual who is suffering as well as the "co-suffering sojourner." He suggests a methodology in two phases: transformation (co-sufferers assume the right disposition, thinking, and skills) and bearing the burdens (co-sufferers assess and assist the sufferers).[23] Johan Mostert also offers pastoral insight by reporting on the Apostolic Faith Mission of South Africa and its response to the HIV/AIDS crisis. He argues that this church has been poor in its response to this huge problem and suggests that there are four reasons for this: (1) the traditional problem that Pentecostals have integrating a compassionate response within their theology because of the suspicion of a "social gospel"; (2) the influence of Western models of ecclesiology and definitions of revival; (3) the impact of Western evangelical thinking on the course of human destiny; and (4) the so-called prosperity gospel, which denies the realities of poverty and suffering.[24]

Richard Castleberry discusses the state of contemporary *youth ministry* and how the "cutting edge" ministries have moved away from an entertainment program to a more contemplative and spiritual focus. He suggests six tenets for a postmodern youth ministry: (1) it has a communal nature; (2) it stresses broad ethical principles rather than dogmatic rules; (3) it is concerned with a living faith rather than a theological faith; (4) it stresses integration of the social and spiritual life; (5) it emphasizes holiness by precept rather than program; and (6) it requires long-suffering patience. In summary, it should be incarnational, it should use sacred space and sacraments, and it should be integrative.[25]

Finally, the issue of *revivalism* is considered by Mark Stibbe, who offers a practical theology for analyzing and discerning revival in terms of a fivefold pattern: (1) exegesis of Scripture; (2) experiential narratives from churches (using historical sources) and individuals (from people known to him); (3) devotional material in the sense that ideas contained in the book have been generated out of worship; (4) communal ideas through using the contributions of many and the commissioning of his congregation; and (5) a practical orientation through the inclusion of study sections at the end of chapters suggesting ideas for response.[26]

Theological Education.   Like many other church traditions, Pentecostals have been influenced by the debates surrounding theological education. There are a number of features to this, including the relationship of the "secular" university to the "confessional" seminary, the imposition of Western intellectual patterns on non-Western cultures, the nature of training for church leaders in the contemporary context, and the power of the church to decide what it wants from its ministers. All these issues are reflected in the literature.

At the thirtieth annual meeting of the Society for Pentecostal Studies in 2001 the theme of discipleship and education was explored. A number of the papers were published the same year in the Society for Pentecostal Studies journal, *Pneuma*. First, Michael Palmer asks the question why texts and subjects that have no discernible application to contemporary church life should continue to be studied as part of a liberal arts education. He responds by arguing that this study is vitally important and should be regarded as essential for "appropriating the past and informing moral consciousness."[27] Second, Jeffrey S. Hittenberger advances a

Pentecostal philosophy of education by seeking to understand what Pentecostals say about the ways in which their experience and theology influence their educational thought and practice. These ideas are assessed by means of philosophies of education and Pentecostal educational praxis before a framework is proposed that allows Pentecostals to articulate their theory and practice in more suitable terms.[28] The framework advances four categories of thought: (1) worldview formation, which consider issues of ontology, epistemology, and values; (2) educational goals and how these are framed by different contexts; (3) educational issues and applications, such as the nature of the student, the role of the teacher, and what should be learned and taught; and (4) educational practice in terms of how ideas are translated into practice and how practice informs ideas. Third, Allan Anderson discusses non-Western Pentecostalism and the need to contextualize theological education, overcoming the dichotomy of training for ministry and academic theology.[29] In a later article Anderson argues that contextualization must also be rooted in the Western as well as the non-Western academy and that this is even more pressing in the context of global Pentecostalism. European and North American theological institutions should focus more on the "rest of the World" by means of social and cultural studies, history, and local theology. In particular, Pentecostal spirituality in Africa, Asia, and Latin America should be given attention as providing fundamental challenges to Western theology.[30]

Jon Ruthven is a Pentecostal scholar who has been struggling with the issue of the best context in which to train Pentecostal church leaders.[31] He offers a critique of traditional theological education and advocates an approach to education that is grounded in a biblical epistemology, goals for ministry, and teaching modalities. He argues that training should be by apprenticeship for those already involved in local church ministry and supported by academics through short intensive blocks of instruction and by withdrawing the grading system. Unemployed seminary professors can move to the university![32]

This North American debate is also mirrored in Europe. Volume 23 of the *Journal of the European Pentecostal Theological Association* contains a number of articles addressing the question of theological education. First, Keith Warrington asks whether Jesus would have sent his disciples to Bible college; by so doing, he critiques some of the contemporary educational practices by means of biblical insights from the ministry of Jesus, namely, interactively, contextually, and regularly.[33] Second, Neil Hudson charts the development of Pentecostal theological colleges, examining criticisms of these settings, for example, that they kill the sense of wonder, lose the sense of belonging to a constituency, focus on the irrelevant, assess the wrong skills, do not model Pentecostal spirituality, and price themselves out of the market. Echoing Ruthven, he anticipates that new church-based theological models will emerge that are flexible and engage more proactively in Pentecostal formation.[34] Third, Matthias Wenk offers a survey of Pentecostal theological education and suggests that the praxis/theory dichotomy, as well as the role of the Spirit, needs to be addressed. He proposes that a relational model accounting for the role of the Spirit and overcoming the praxis/theory dichotomy should be developed.[35]

Finally, other areas of debate consider questions of intercultural theology for ministry. For example, Ridley N. Usherwood argues that theological competence should include intercultural skills while acknowledging that any particular expression of the gospel is bound to be culturally conditioned. Part of the problem that the American church faces is due to the "segregated, monocultural, homogeneous and racist approach to ministry."[36] Racism must be confronted first before peace and justice can be experienced, and it is here that the Church of God (Cleveland, Tenn.) might be able to play a role in uniting white and black churches. This will be achieved by acknowledging the link to racism in the past and by doing theology from an intercultural perspective.

Liberation Theology, Ethics, and Public Issues

Pentecostals have also addressed issues of social and ethical concern. A few studies use the liberationist paradigm in relation to American, Latin American, and British contexts.

Liberation Theology.   Eldin Villafañe in his presidential address to the Society for Pentecostal Studies in 1996 challenged the society to consider liberation not in terms of liberal and Enlightenment ideals but in terms of the biblical promise that is linked to the gospel. He argues that this liberation is part of the Spirit's work for personal and social transformation. This means that the Spirit has a political agenda for God's creation and works this out through the church in the world. The "politics of the Spirit" must, therefore, be understood as part of the reign of God in-breaking into history. This means that Pentecostal action in the world is pneumatic political discipleship guided by biblical teaching and paradigms of divine action demonstrating God's preferential option for the poor.[37] This call builds on his established proposal for a Hispanic American Pentecostal social ethic, which aims to participate in the reign of God, confront structural sin and evil, and fulfill a prophetic and vocational role for those baptized in the Spirit.[38]

Tim Klingler explores the subject of liberation theology as a paradigm for Latin American Pentecostalism as it faces institutionalization, organization, and new ecclesiological models, as well as social and political dimensions. Working with the insights of Leonardo Boff, he suggests that the local church should be seen as a sacrament and sign of the kingdom, as a sacrament of the Holy Spirit, the Trinity, and the universal church. Klingler believes that Pentecostals would benefit from adopting such insights, in addition to seeing evangelism in a broader dimension that includes social and political involvement.[39] Similarly, Virginia T. Nolivos offers a theological argument for the Latin American family being able to function as a means of transformation when allied with Pentecostalism.[40]

In the United Kingdom Robert Beckford analyzes Pentecostalism in the context of the immigrant churches in order to propose a political theology for the black church. Building on black scholarship, he advances a liberation theological praxis and locates this methodologically in the context of an action-reflection model, suggesting three phases to the process: experience, analysis, and action. He thereby advocates a theology that is holistic, transformative, and grounded in hope for the black Christian community.[41]

Ethics.   There are a limited number of studies in this area, but they are worth noting, even if they are not easily classified together.

David Castelo proposes that a Pentecostal approach to theological ethics can emerge out of worshiping experience and employs the "tarrying" motif to signal this connection to pneumatology. He argues that the two frameworks of affections and virtues can be used in a complementary way to shape the Pentecostal moral life.[42] This contribution by Castelo can be usefully set alongside the work of Paul W. Lewis, who argues for a pneumatological approach to virtue ethics in relation to Pentecostalism.[43] Lewis suggests a framework and ideas for dialogue, which include the view that virtues have their origin and mediation in the Holy Spirit acting via the avenues of the community, the Bible, and the self, and by these routes the Spirit brings ethical understanding and moral development.

In a different vein, Neil Hudson and Keith Warrington offer a joint reflection on the question of cohabitation and the church. This study considers the reasons that people give for cohabitation, the reactions of the Christian community, and biblical reflections before outlining "marital principles" for application to churches.[44]

Taking his cue from Pentecostal pacifist history, Paul N. Alexander established the Pentecostal Charismatic Peace Fellowship in 2002 as a way to recapture a tradition of the past and renew it in the present.[45] This is a project that is undergirded by a theological rationale and offers a nonviolent ethic for the orientation of Pentecostals in the contemporary world.[46]

Finally, Ed E. Decker advocates training for those wishing to minister prophetically in the power of the Spirit by not only paying attention to the voice of God but also by being attentive to the persons ministered to as well as the ethics of human service. These include "to do no harm, to avoid exploitation, to treat people with dignity, to protect confidentiality, and to allow for informed consent."[47]

Public Issues.   It is certainly the case that Pentecostals have not yet embraced the discourse of public theology. This may be because the nature of that discourse is largely liberal in theological terms and is also constructed by some of the most powerful individuals in academia. However, if one looks more closely at the theology that is emerging from the Society for Pentecostal Studies, it is clear that public issues are beginning to be reflected on and recommendations are being made. In this way a public theology is beginning to emerge, even if it is still not regarded as a dimension of practical theology. For example, Paul Alexander outlines a historical and contemporary critique of nationalism and in so doing offers an analysis of Pentecostal politics. He argues that Christian identity should be one's primary identity and that nationality, ethnicity, and gender are secondary identity markers.[48]

Empirical Theology

Here I focus on the term *empirical theology* as used by European scholars, which was established in 1988 with the publication of the *Journal of Empirical Theology*, edited by Johannes A. van der Ven. The founding of the International Society for Empirical Research in Theology in 2002 further advanced the paradigm, so that now it is firmly established in the discipline. As a young research student working in the 1980s, I looked for methodological tools from within the discipline of theology to study prophecy in Pentecostal and Charismatic Christianity. I could not find anything suitable and was forced to improvise using sociology and theology. However, it was only in the mid-1990s that I discovered the *Journal of Empirical Theology* and began to publish some of my empirical work.[49] The methodological text of van der Ven was used critically and the empirical-theological cycle (including the definition of the problem, induction, deduction, testing, and evaluation) was adapted to study the New Church movement in the United Kingdom from the discipline of practical theology.[50] The focus of this study was the nature and function of glossolalia, and it is the only study to develop a specifically empirical-theological theory of it.[51]

However, it was my second book that allowed me to develop my thinking in relation to practical theology and empirical methods. *Practical Theology: Charismatic and Empirical Perspectives* is the first textbook attempting to situate the empirical-theological paradigm within a Pentecostal-Charismatic theological framework.[52] I used both qualitative and quantitative data in order to illustrate the kinds of research that are possible within such a paradigm, including discussions of worship and spirituality, glossolalia, prophetic activity, charismatic experience, and healing. Further methodological thinking has allowed me to consider the role of the affections as part of the direct object of practical theology,[53] as well as the Trinitarian theology of Pentecostal and Charismatic Christians.[54] The practical theological paradigm was used recently to integrate multidisciplinary accounts of glossolalia, and a case study provided a means to reflect on various perspectives before recommendations for renewed praxis were made.[55] Finally, practical theology is being used to "rescript" Pentecostal theology, so that the ordinary theology of believers is illuminated by the social sciences and rescripted by means of systematic theological categories.[56]

Other studies that can be said to fall within this genre, even if they do not use the denotation "empirical theology," use empirical research methods in theological discourse. Stephen E. Parker's book, *Led by the Spirit,* marks a significant step in the Pentecostal tradition's adoption of a practical theological paradigm, which refers to *"critical theological reflection arising out of and giving guidance to the practices of a local faith community."*[57] This study positions itself in the emerging field of practical theology and contrasts itself with the handy tips for ministers associated with *pastoralia.* Parker investigates the Pentecostal practices of being led by the Holy Spirit, including spontaneous thoughts and feelings, and the processes of discernment and evaluation. His aim is to make a genuine contribution to Pentecostal practice by "helping pentecostals understand themselves and their practices more critically and of formulating better guidelines for evaluating these practices."[58] It is a study that is authentically Pentecostal; that is, theological reflection is conducted from within the Pentecostal community and at the same time uses the methodology of mutual critical correlation to interrogate and evaluate ethnographic material by means of object relations psychology and the criteria derived from the theology of Paul Tillich. The outcome is a set of multifaceted guidelines capable of being used to evaluate claims to the Spirit's guidance.

William K. Kay, a classical Pentecostal himself, is an important researcher in the field of Pentecostalism in the United Kingdom (Assemblies of God, U.K.). He combines history, theology, and the social sciences in a creative manner. Working from both church history and social psychology, a good number of his projects tend to offer both a historical context and empirical research into beliefs and values of Pentecostal Christians. The accent has been on what might be called historically informed descriptive theology with social-psychological or theological explanations, for example, personality theory or the influence of charismata on church life. Two important books have developed from his research. The first is titled *Pentecostals in Britain,* which includes a historical sketch of the classical Pentecostal denominations emerging in the twentieth century.[59] It subsequently describes data from a survey of classical Pentecostal ministers relating to denominational problems, vocal spiritual gifts, healing and the Toronto blessing, non-Charismatic beliefs (e.g., about the Bible, creation, Jesus and the Trinity, eschatology, demons, and women), and ethical issues such as divorce and remarriage, homosexuality, and the Holiness codes. The relationship between background variables, material conditions of service, and spirituality is mapped, as are ministerial experience, roles, and satisfaction, the relationship between charismata and church growth, and personality and burnout. In his second book, *Apostolic Networks in Britain,* Kay offers a historical overview of the thought and practices of the New Church movement in Britain from the 1960s to the present day.[60] He also looks at the cell movement, the Toronto blessing, immigration, the media, conferences, and the Alpha course before outlining the theology and mission of the apostolic networks and offering sociological analyses. He uses a questionnaire survey to map out the various beliefs and values of the network and builds on earlier work to consider the relationship between charismata and church growth. He concludes that there are similar dynamics in classical Pentecostal denominations in Britain and the United States, with greater charismatic activity correlating to church growth, greater ministerial charismatic activity correlating to increased congregational charismatic activity, and ministerial evangelistic activity being crucially important for smaller churches.

Finally, James H. S. Steven's study of charismatic worship in the Church of England is also worth noting.[61] Steven aims to describe the nature of worship and "prayer ministry'" in five different churches, and he does this by adopting a *Verstehen* approach using participant observation and interviews. He subsequently advances a theological analysis of this material in terms of the Trinity, pneumatology, liturgy, and healing. This theological rescripting of charismatic worship is the book's most significant contribution. My only real concern regarding this study is the nature of Steven's fieldwork. The time spent in the field is extremely limited and is not the best model of this kind of fieldwork, because rich and varied data are gathered through prolonged engagement rather than more superficial visits.

STUDIES BY NON-PENTECOSTAL-CHARISMATIC SCHOLARS

There are two practical theologians who would not be classified as Pentecostal or Charismatic but have nevertheless made a contribution to the field of Pentecostal-Charismatic studies. Don S. Browning is probably the elder statesman of practical theology in the United States, and his book, *A Fundamental Practical Theology*, is widely regarded as a classic in the discipline. He argues that practical theology moves from "theory-laden practice to a retrieval of normative theory-laden practice to the creation of more critically held theory-laden practices."[62] He claims that the "practical" is not a "subspeciality" of theology but rather that Christian theology is fundamentally practical by nature. Conceived in this way, practical theology has four submovements: descriptive theology, historical theology, systematic theology, and strategic practical theology (including religious education, pastoral care, preaching, liturgy, and social ministries). To this approach he inserts the revised critical correlation model of David Tracy, whereby "practical theology is the mutually critical correlation of the interpreted theory and praxis of the Christian faith with the interpreted theory and praxis of the contemporary situation."[63]

To illustrate how the submovements work within this framework three congregations are studied, including a black Pentecostal church called the Apostolic

Church of God pastored by the well-known Arthur Brazier and having over five thousand members. Browning offers a careful reflection on its congregational care of families and couples as his research focuses on the church's family ethic and the feminist ethic of mutuality and equal regard. He interviewed a number of church members and adopted a dialogical approach, which acknowledged that this research could have a mutual influence on him and the church. In his analysis of pastoral care in the context of this church, he observes the cultural context of black Pentecostal worship, preaching, and prayer. He situates the pastoral care theologically by reviewing the literature in Protestant theology and the hermeneutics of care, then offers a descriptive theology of the church and enters into a critical conversation from the perspective of his white, male, liberal theological identity. Thus Browning demonstrates reflexivity in his engagement with this church's praxis in order to offer insights in return.

Martyn Percy is another scholar who at times claims the label "practical theologian" and moves between the disciplines of sociology and theology. He is noted for two key studies. The first is his published dissertation, a study of the concept of power in the theology of John Wimber, although he aims to situate this discussion by framing Pentecostalism and the Charismatic Renewal as branches of "fundamentalism."[64] It is largely a theoretical piece that analyzes all the material that Wimber produced in tapes and books. Percy uses organizational theory, in particular, Clegg's "circuits of power," as an analytical tool to critique the ideology of power in Wimber's discourse and seeks to uncover Wimber's theology of power. This is an important study and one that is often noted without being engaged with in a serious manner.[65] Percy's second study concerns the Toronto blessing and resulted in a short monograph and a series of articles. In these pieces the Toronto blessing is analyzed in terms of sociological theory, in particular, exchange theory, or in terms of eroticism and gender.[66] Again, these are interesting and provocative studies, even if they appear to be ultimately reductionist. Nevertheless, all his work repays careful attention.

CONCLUSION

It can be said that practical-theological studies by Pentecostals are mostly concerned with formational or ministerial questions and concerns. This finding should come as no real surprise. There are some liberationist studies, and certainly this discourse has established itself within global Pentecostal studies, especially in relation to Latin America. However, there are only a very few empirical studies by Pentecostal or Charismatic scholars working from within a practical theology paradigm. This can be widened when we include interdisciplinary and social science studies that also attempt to engage with theological discourse.

It has been suggested that practical theology works at three levels: the church, the seminary, and the university. But these boundaries are not tight, and there is inevitable overlap. It would seem that most practical-theological discourse is produced by Pentecostal-Charismatic scholars at the level of the seminary but interfacing with the church and its mission. It appears to be largely theoretical in the sense that its major contribution is the provision of models, frameworks, and insights for subsequent application to ministry through the use of, for example, educational and counseling models but used with biblical and theological texts. The empirical work from this sector tends to emerge from the university in the sense that it is usually published Ph.D. work. This means that while practical theologians are serving the needs of the church by offering resources to church leaders, they rarely seem to engage with rigorous empirical study and therefore fail to explore and map the actual theological praxis of Pentecostals themselves, that is, the theology embedded in their beliefs, values, and practices. They offer a largely applicationist model of practical theology, and in this regard it is very similar to standard evangelical seminary education. This finding may come as a surprise to those who advocate a distinctive "Pentecostal" approach to theology.

Non-Pentecostal practical theologians have offered interesting and important studies, as have Christian social scientists who have stepped outside the "scientific" box. But, in my view, for practical theology to develop and flourish in the context of Pentecostal-Charismatic studies, there needs to be greater critical engagement with the liberationist and empirical traditions. This will inevitably lead to greater attention to public issues and indeed the emerging discourse of "public theology."[67] There is also a need to engage with the wider international academy in practical theology, where the Pentecostal-Charismatic tradition has been marginalized by the hegemony of the Americans and Europeans, who tend to be theologically liberal, liberationist, and/or empirical in orientation. Breaking into that club might be difficult, but more Pentecostals need to do so in order to open up the horizon of possibility both for themselves and for others.

NOTES

1. The most influential text is by Gustaf Guterriez, *A Theology of Liberation* (London: SCM, 1974).

2. See Randolph C. Miller, ed., *Empirical Theology: A Handbook* (Birmingham: Religious Education Press, 1992); and Johannes A. van der Ven, *Practical Theology: An Empirical Approach* (Kampen: Kok Pharos, 1993).

3. Cheryl B. Johns, *Pentecostal Formation: A Pedagogy among the Oppressed* (Sheffield: SAP, 1993).

4. Jackie D. Johns and Cheryl B. Johns, "Yielding to the Spirit: A Pentecostal Approach to Group Bible Study," *JPT* 1 (1992): 109–34.

5. Jackie D. Johns, "Formational Leadership: A Pentecostal Model for Using the Decision-Making Processes of the Congregation to Nurture Faith," paper presented at the 29th Annual Meeting of the SPS, Northwestern College, Kirkland, WA, 2000.

6. James P. Bowers, "A Wesleyan-Pentecostal Approach to Christian Formation," *JPT* 6 (1995): 55–86.

7. Jeanne Porter, "The Practice and Principles of Life in the Spirit: An Examination of Pentecostal Spirituality," paper presented at the 33rd Annual Meeting of the SPS, Marquette, Milwaukee, WI, 2004.

8. Jay A. Herndon, "Introducing Pentecostals to the Ministry of Spiritual Direction," paper presented at the 32nd Annual Meeting of the SPS with the Annual Meeting of the Wesleyan Theological Society, Asbury Theological Seminary, Wilmore, KY, 2003.

9. R. Jerome Boone, "Community and Worship: The Key Components of Pentecostal Christian Formation," *JPT* 8 (1996): 142.

10. Jeremy Begbie, "The Spirituality of Renewal Music: A Preliminary Exploration," *Anvil: An Anglican Evangelical Journal for Theology and Mission* 8:3 (1991): 227–39.

11. Victoria Cooke, *Understanding Songs in Renewal* (Cambridge: Grove Books, 2001).

12. Anne E. Dyer, "Some Theological Trends Reflected in the Songs Used by the British Charismatic Churches of 1970s–early 2000s," *JEPTA* 26:1 (2006): 36–48.

13. Pete Ward, *Selling Worship: How What We Sing Has Changed the Church* (Milton Keynes: Paternoster, 2005).

14. David Morgan, "Contemporary Australian Pentecostal Worship in Trouble: An Analysis of Hillsong Worship," paper presented at the 36th Annual Meeting of the SPS, Cleveland, TN, 2007.

15. Jean-Daniel Plüss, "How Public Are Public Testimonies? A Short Reflection on a Liturgical Practice," *EPTA Bulletin* 6:1 (1987): 4–12.

16. Jean-Daniel Plüss, "Religious Experiences in Worship: A Pentecostal Perspective," *PentecoStudies* 2:1 (2003): 4–12 (8).

17. Jean-Daniel Plüss, *Therapeutic and Prophetic Narratives in Worship: A Hermeneutical Study of Testimonies and Visions—Their Potential Significance for Christian Worship and Secular Society* (Frankfurt: Peter Lang, 1988).

18. John Gordy, "Toward a Theology of Pentecostal Preaching," *JPT* 10:1 (2001): 81–97.

19. Aaldwin Ragoonath, "Pentecostal Preaching," paper presented at the 36th Annual Meeting of the SPS, Cleveland, TN, 2007.

20. Jacques P. J. Theron, "Towards a Practical Theological Theory for the Healing Ministry in the Pentecostal Churches," *JPT* 14 (1999): 50, 52.

21. Cf. P. L. King, "Searching for Genuine Gold: Discerning Spirit, Flesh and Demonic in Pentecostal Experiences," paper presented at the 36th Annual Meeting of the SPS, Cleveland, TN, 2007.

22. Jacques P. J. Theron, "Ministry of Deliverance from Evil Forces: Reflections and Pastoral Concerns," paper presented at the 35th Annual Meeting of the SPS, Fuller Seminary, Pasadena, CA, 2006.

23. Jeff McAffee, "The Theology of Co-Suffering as a Model of Spiritual Help and Companionship," paper presented at the 34th Annual Meeting of the SPS, Regent University, Virginia Beach, VA, 2005.

24. Johan Mostert, "An Evaluation of the Pentecostal Response to HIV/AIDS in South Africa," paper presented at the 35th Annual Meeting of the SPS, Fuller Seminary, Pasadena, CA, 2006.

25. Richard Castleberry, "No More Youth Groups! A Polemic for Richard R Dunn's *Pacing-then-Leading* Model of Relational Youth Ministry," paper presented at the 36th Annual Meeting of the SPS, Cleveland, TN, 2007.

26. Mark Stibbe, *Times of Refreshing: A Practical Theology of Renewal for Today* (London: Marshall Pickering, 1995).

27. Michael Palmer, "Orienting Our Lives: The Importance of a Liberal Education for Pentecostals in the Twenty-first Century," *Pneuma* 23:2 (2001): 197–216.

28. Jeffrey S. Hittenberger, "Toward a Pentecostal Philosophy of Education," *Pneuma* 23:2 (2001): 217–44.

29. Allan Anderson, "The 'Fury and Wonder'? Pentecostal-Charismatic Spirituality in Theological Education," *Pneuma* 23:2 (2001): 287–302.

30. Allan Anderson, "Pentecostal-Charismatic Spirituality and Theological Education in Europe from a Global Perspective," *PentecoStudies* 3:1 (2004): 1–15.

31. Jon M. Ruthven, "'Between Two Worlds: One Dead, the Other Powerless to be Born?': Pentecostal Theological Education vs. Training for Christian Service," *Spirit & Church* 3:2 (2001): 273–97.

32. Jon M. Ruthven, "Are Pentecostal Seminaries a Good Idea?" *Pneuma* 26:2 (2004): 339–45.

33. Keith Warrington, "Would Jesus Have Sent His Disciples to Bible College?" *JEPTA* 23 (2003): 30–44.

34. Neil Hudson, "It's Not What We Do; It's the Way That We Do It: Uncomfortable Thoughts for a Lecturer in a Residential Bible College at the Turn of the Century," *JEPTA* 23 (2003): 45–57.

35. Matthias Wenk, "Do We Need a Distinct European Pentecostal/Charismatic Approach to Theological Education?" *JEPTA* 23 (2003): 58–71.

36. Ridley N. Usherwood, "The Importance of Intercultural Competence in Theological Education: A Mandate for the Church," in *The Spirit and the Mind: Essays in Informed Pentecostalism*, ed. Terry L. Cross and Emerson B. Powery (Lanham, MD: University Press of America, 2000), 279.

37. Eldin Villafañe, "The Politics of the Spirit: Reflections on a Theology of Social Transformation for the Twenty-first Century," *Pneuma* 18:2 (1996): 161–70.

38. Eldin Villafañe, *The Liberating Spirit: Towards a Hispanic American Social Ethic* (Grand Rapids: Eerdmans, 1993).

39. Tim Kingler, "Liberation Theology: An Ecclesiological Charisma for Latin American Pentecostalism," paper presented at the 32nd Annual Meeting of the SPS, Asbury Theological Seminary, Wilmore, KY, 2003.

40. Virginia T. Nolivos, "A Pentecostal Paradigm for the Latin American Family: An Instrument of Transformation," *CPCR* 11 (2002), available at www.pctii.org/cyberj/table.html; accessed 15 May 2007.

41. Robert Beckford, *Dread and Pentecostal: A Political Theology for the Black Church in Britain* (London: SPCK, 2000).

42. David Castelo, "Tarrying on the Lord: Affections, Virtues, and Theological Ethics in Pentecostal Perspective," *JPT* 13:1 (2004): 31–56.

43. Paul W. Lewis, "A Pneumatological Approach to Virtue Ethics," *AJPS* 1:1 (1998): 42–61.

44. Neil Hudson and Keith Warrington, "Cohabitation and the Church," *EPTA Bulletin* 13 (1994): 63–73.

45. Paul N. Alexander, "Spirit Empowered Peacemaking: Toward a Pentecostal Peace Fellowship," *JEPTA* 22 (2002): 78–102.

46. Paul N. Alexander, "A Pentecostal Theology of Peacemaking," paper presented at the 31st Annual Meeting of the SPS, Southeastern College, Lakeland, FL, 2002.

47. Ed E. Decker Jr., "What Do You Do with What You Know? The Ethics of Holy Spirit Empowering in Counselling," paper presented at the 31st Annual Meeting of the SPS, Southeastern College, Lakeland, FL, 2002.

48. Paul N. Alexander, "Historical and Contemporary Pentecostal Critiques of Nationalism," paper presented at the 34th Annual Meeting of the SPS, Regent University, Virginia Beach, VA, 2005.

49. Mark J. Cartledge, "Charismatic Prophecy," *Journal of Empirical Theology* 8:1 (1995): 71–88.

50. Johannes A. van der Ven, *Practical Theology: An Empirical Approach* (Kampen: Kok Pharos, 1993); Mark J. Cartledge, "Empirical Theology: Towards an Evangelical-Charismatic Hermeneutic," *JPS* 9 (1996): 115–26; Mark J. Cartledge, "Practical Theology and Empirical Identity," *European Journal of Theology* 7:1 (1998): 37–44; Mark J. Cartledge, "Empirical Theology: Inter- or Intra- Disciplinary?" *JBV* 20:1 (1999): 98–104.

51. Mark J. Cartledge, *Charismatic Glossolalia: An Empirical Theological Study* (Aldershot: Ashgate, 2002).

52. Mark J. Cartledge, *Practical Theology: Charismatic and Empirical Perspectives*, Studies in Pentecostal and Charismatic Issues (Carlisle: Paternoster, 2003); see also the earlier essay, Mark J. Cartledge, "Practical Theology and Charismatic Spirituality: Dialectics in the Spirit," *JPT* 10:2 (2002): 107–24.

53. Mark J. Cartledge, "Affective Theological Praxis: Understanding the Direct Object of Practical Theology," *International Journal of Practical Theology* 8:1 (2004): 34–52.

54. Mark J. Cartledge, "Trinitarian Theology and Spirituality: An Empirical Study of Charismatic Christians," *Journal of Empirical Theology* 17:1 (2004): 76–84; Mark J. Cartledge, "Empirical-Theological Models of the Trinity: Exploring the Beliefs of Theology Students in the United Kingdom," *Journal of Empirical Theology* 19:2 (2006): 137–62, which includes Pentecostal students.

55. Mark J. Cartledge, "The Practice of Tongues Speech as a Case Study: A Practical-Theological Perspective," in *Speaking in Tongues: Multi-disciplinary Perspectives*, ed. Mark J. Cartledge (Milton Keynes: Paternoster, 2006), 206–34.

56. Mark J. Cartledge, "Pentecostal Experience: An Example of Practical-Theological Rescripting," *JEPTA* 28:1 (2008): 21–33.

57. Stephen E. Parker, *Led by the Spirit: Toward a Practical Theology of Pentecostal Discernment and Decision Making* (Sheffield: SAP, 1996), 12; original emphasis.

58. Parker, *Led by the Spirit*,17.

59. William K. Kay, *Pentecostals in Britain* (Carlisle: Paternoster, 2000).

60. William K. Kay, *Apostolic Networks in Britain: New Ways of Being Church* (Milton Keynes: Paternoster, 2007).

61. James H. S. Steven, *Worship in the Spirit: Charismatic Worship in the Church of England* (Carlisle: Paternoster, 2002).

62. Don S. Browning, *A Fundamental Practical Theology: Descriptive and Strategic Proposals*, 2nd ed. (Minneapolis: Fortress Press, 1996), 7.

63. Browning, *A Fundamental Practical Theology*, 47.

64. Martyn Percy, *Words, Wonders and Power: Understanding Contemporary Christian Fundamentalism and Revivalism* (London: SPCK, 1996).

65. A recent exception is Pete Ward, "Affective Alliance or Circuits of Power: The Production and Consumption of Contemporary Charismatic Worship in Britain," *International Journal of Practical Theology* 9 (2005): 25–39.

66. Martyn Percy, *Power and the Church: Ecclesiology in a Age of Transition* (London: Cassell, 1998) 59–80, 101–20, 141–62.

67. The *International Journal of Public Theology* was inaugurated in May 2007 (www.brill.nl/ijpt).

14

Ecumenism

Cecil M. Robeck Jr.

Ecumenism is a topic that many Pentecostals find difficult to discuss. This is in part because most Pentecostals know very little about the subject, often just enough to condemn it. When asked why they are opposed to ecumenism, their responses are often anecdotal. Sometimes these anecdotes include personal experiences they have had, but more often than not they are stories they have received, stories passed on from pastor to parishioner, from parent to child, or from friend to friend. Generally there has been little or no attempt to assess their validity or to ask what events might lay behind such stories.

Unsettled issues between the East and the West—Orthodox and Catholic—as well as unresolved issues left over from the Reformation—Catholic and Protestant—continue to separate not only large ecclesial traditions but also nations and families.[1] The fundamentalist-liberal debates that marked so much of Protestantism during the early twentieth century also separated Christians from one another. Denominations split as Fundamentalists and Evangelicals withdrew from older denominations or were encouraged to leave and form new ones. In the heat of all these divisions calls were made either to preserve the "truth" in ways that divided Christian communities or to preserve "community" in ways that relativized any notion of "truth."[2] Differences were highlighted at the expense of shared convictions, pejorative labels were introduced, sides were drawn, and stereotypes were invented. The rhetoric that led to such divisions was often deeply contemptuous as proponents of one position or the other sought to demonize their opponents.

Over the past seventy years the rise in the number of independent and emerging congregations and ministries involving Pentecostals and Charismatics has only exacerbated the problem of division. Calls for unity have been confused with compromise. Calls for agreement have been described as demanding mindless conformity. Calls for greater cooperation have been portrayed as devaluing the integrity of local congregations and, in some cases, of individual leaders. And calls for surrender to a common ideal have been spun in ways that make that surrender sound like the quenching of the Holy Spirit.[3] As a result, for too many Pentecostals ecumenism is simply unworthy of consideration, a pointless effort, the beginning of a slippery slope that will inevitably lead to unwarranted concessions. As a result, writing about ecumenism from a Pentecostal perspective is a difficult and at times an acrimonious task.

REASONS FOR ECUMENICAL HESITATION

Any attempt to describe an effective ecumenical methodology for use by Pentecostals requires a brief overview of the realities that Pentecostals who work in the field must face. There are several factors that explain the ecumenical neuralgia that has led many Pentecostals either to be hesitant about the value of ecumenism or to reject ecumenism altogether.

First, earlier Pentecostal leaders, pastors, and "theologians" typically had little if any firsthand ecumenical experience with those from traditions that were unlike their own—Catholics, the Orthodox, Anglicans, and even historic Protestants. This lack of direct encounter weighed on their ability to function as ecumenical peers. Part of this undoubtedly came as a result of rejection on both sides. It would take at least forty years before Pentecostal leaders would begin to look outside the Pentecostal world for interdenominational friends. Interdenominational cooperation, however, is not the same thing as ecumenism.

Although groups that foster interdenominational cooperation are good places to begin, they typically do not go very far in working on root differences that separate churches from one another, nor are they typically willing to explore areas in which they might grow together. Pentecostal pastors may participate in local ministerial fellowships, but in many places these fellowships limit their membership to other Pentecostal or evangelical ministers. Pentecostal leaders might even join in a relationship with the broader evangelical community to cooperate on something like evangelism or the plight of persecuted Christians, but they would assiduously avoid discussions of visible unity that might prove more contentious. On the whole, the kinds of interdenominational groups that Pentecostals joined were formed to counter other groups with broader ecclesial membership. As such, their "ecumenical" agenda is, at best, a limited one.[4]

Second, even now, Pentecostal leaders often do not have an education that is equivalent to that of their peers in the historic denominations. While a personal testimony and a Divine call are essential for any kind of successful Pentecostal ministry, they are not always adequate when one engages in ecumenical discussion.[5] Those without formal theological education often lack the tools of language, history, philosophy, theology, and culture that most ecumenists find useful. As a result, it is difficult for Pentecostal leaders to compete in ecumenical conversations.[6]

They may participate actively on an interdenominational level in a Billy Graham meeting, for instance, because they recognize its form and they identify with its purpose, but they wouldn't necessarily know how to follow along with or appreciate a Roman Catholic, Russian Orthodox, an Anglican, or even a Lutheran liturgy. They may have learned how to work within the proscriptions of an evangelical statement of faith, but they would not necessarily know how to contextualize, exegete, or explain the Trinitarian nuances found in the Nicene-Constantinopolitan Creed.[7] They may know how to share their personal testimony, but they might not know how to respond theologically to a theological critique by someone from a different theological tradition. Their temptation would be to retreat into their personal experience or to lash out in a manner that missed the nuances if not the core of what is under discussion. Their lack of education places them at a disadvantage in any substantive ecumenical discussion. As a result, they frequently find it easier not to participate in broader ecumenical discussions than to participate, knowing that their training is inadequate to understand everything under discussion. Such a lack of understanding has led some to condemn the entire ecumenical program.[8]

Third, since the 1940s Pentecostals have found their greatest level of acceptance among Evangelicals, and many evangelical denominations have strong sentiments against ecumenism. These sentiments reflect earlier battles within the historic denominations from which many of these Evangelicals fled or were driven, and anyone who now takes a position that embraces or speaks positively about some of these older denominations is viewed with suspicion, or worse, as having in some way compromised the evangelical agenda. As a result, the accommodation of Pentecostals to the larger evangelical culture, even though they do not share the same history and may have had no direct experience of their own that would lead them to take this position, has meant that evangelical "enemies" have sometimes become Pentecostal "enemies."[9]

Fourth, there are places in the world where Pentecostals have suffered at the hands of other Christian communities. The suffering endured by Pentecostals in Italy under the Mussolini regime with the alleged complicity of the Catholic Church, for instance, is one such example.[10] Pentecostals have also pointed to Latin America as another region where they have suffered at the hands of the Catholic Church.[11] Similar claims have been made more recently regarding Orthodox actions in former Soviet bloc countries.[12] While it is important to take these charges seriously, to investigate them, and to take appropriate action, often it has been difficult to do so because charges are made but evidence is not always presented. Pentecostal leaders have seldom trusted the ecumenical process that might have helped to bring some resolution or healing in specific situations. Instead, they have chosen to isolate themselves not only from the alleged offending party but also, as in the case of the Italian Assemblies of God, from much of the Christian community.[13]

Fifth, while regional histories, experiences, and cultures differ, pentecostal missionaries, especially from Britain and North America, who have been influenced by their evangelical friends have often introduced negative readings on ecumenism and ecumenical cooperation into the missionary cultures among whom they minister. As a result, they have introduced mistrust of other churches and limited the ability of national churches to be truly indigenous or faithful to their unique histories, experiences, and cultures.[14]

Sixth and finally, because many Pentecostals have taken eschatological readings from the Bible and interpreted them as warnings against a future world system of religion that is corrupt, they have also convinced themselves that any move toward greater *visible* unity within the church, holds negative institutional consequences. To them, this institutional potential looks like a dangerous compromise that could ultimately move beyond a shared but invisible spiritual unity toward a visible and disastrous, compromised anti-Christian system. Thus they have condemned ecumenism altogether.[15]

These issues need to be acknowledged in any ecumenical methodology developed by Pentecostals, but it also needs to be recognized that there is a growing body of Pentecostals who are interested in Christian unity and a significant number of Pentecostals who have been active in the ecumenical movement for half a century.[16] For this reason, I intend to suggest a methodology by which Pentecostals are able to engage in ecumenism with confidence.

DEFINING THE ECUMENICAL TASK

The terms *ecumenism (oikoumene)* and *ecumenical (oikoumenikos)* are derivatives of the Greek noun *oikos,* meaning "house." By extension, they speak to issues involving the household. Historically, they have held several different meanings, all of them valid. In the Patristic era, for instance, *oikumenikos* meant "the whole world."[17] As a result, there are those who think of ecumenism as having cosmic implications, that is, that it has to do with the household of all creation. Ecumenists who view the church as having an ecological mandate in addition to other components generally think of ecumenism in this way. They would, in turn, call the rest of the church to join them in working on a common ecumenical agenda that includes explicit care for all creation.[18]

A second meaning of *oikoumene* may be applied to the whole of humankind. Again in the Patristic period, *oikoumene* also carried the meaning "the whole world" or "everybody." Christians were, after all, human before they were ever Christian, thus they hold many things in common with all of humankind, whether or not they are Christian. As the Catholic Bishops noted during Vatican II, all Christians share the hopes, dreams, pains, and sorrows that are common to all human beings.[19] Ecumenists who accept this definition see themselves as having been placed in the midst of humanity for specific purposes. While working on issues that currently divide denominations from one another, they also focus their attention on issues that have an impact on the entire human race: peace and justice, poverty and human dignity, health and education, racism and violence.[20] Because they recognize the need for greater communication between all human beings, such ecumenists sometimes highlight the importance of interreligious dialogue.[21] This second understanding of *oikoumene* is also a valid one.

The third and most common meaning of *oikoumene,* however, is narrower yet. According to this interpretation, the term refers to a "council" of the church. Thus, although it was applied directly to early councils such as Nicaea or Chalcedon, today it describes the growing sets of relationships between new and existing Christian churches and denominations. This is a dominant understanding among ecumenists associated with the World Council of Churches (WCC).[22] The basis for membership in the WCC describes that council as "a fellowship of churches which confess the Lord Jesus Christ as God and Savior according to the Scripture and therefore seek to fulfill together their common calling to the glory of the one God, Father, Son and Holy Spirit."[23] Its primary reason for being has been to address the issues that stand between its member denominations in a spirit of repentance, forgiveness, and reconciliation so that together they might act in common on issues of mutual concern. What has not been clear is what that unity should look like.

MODELS OF UNITY

Whatever definition of the *oikoumene* one adopts, it is important to recognize that models of unity vary. Some models suggest structural, institutional mergers. Some imagine theological uniformity. Some encourage diversity better than others. Most Pentecostals maintain that when Jesus prayed that his followers might be one (John 17:21), he was not speaking of *visible unity.* It was *spiritual unity* that he had in mind. When the Holy Spirit came to indwell his followers, Jesus' prayer was answered.[24] Thus the call to work for visible unity has often been portrayed as enlisting human effort alone to accomplish something that God has already given. It is easy to see why ecumenism has placed so low on the list of Pentecostal priorities. But does this *spiritual* reading do justice to Jesus' prayer, or is a *literal* reading of John 17:21 more appropriate? If Jesus spoke only of an invisible, spiritual unity, how would it commend the world toward belief?

Most ecumenists do not question the reality of spiritual unity; they believe that Jesus called for a tangible form of unity so that the world might believe. Through the centuries they have suggested various models for consideration. In 1559, for instance, the Elizabethan Settlement included the Act of Uniformity. It required *conformity to a uniform set of standards* for all English clergy. During the twentieth century, many independent and free churches advocated what was called *federal unity,* by which they remained independent but developed covenantal agreements with one another. Others, especially within the Anglican world, contended for some form of *organic unity,* in which existing denominations would cease to exist, though in their coming together, they would form a new organism with varying practices. Others pushed it further, by arguing that whereas denominations might *be united,* they need *not* be *absorbed.*

Cardinal Willebrands, then president of the Secretariat for Promoting Christian Unity, suggested a model in 1970 that included the pope overseeing what he described as a *communion of communions.* All Christians would come under papal leadership with a common dogma, sacraments, and ministry but with differences in things like biblical interpretation, canon law, liturgy, and spirituality.[25] Within the WCC, the Nairobi Assembly in 1975 set forth a model of *conciliar fellowship.* The ambiguity of the term *conciliar,* however, led to vague conclusions on how such a model would function on the local level.

The Lutheran World Federation suggested *unity in reconciled diversity,* apparently in response to the Anglican suggestion of organic unity. The fear of too much central control and the possibility that the unique contributions of the various denominations or movements might be lost seem to have led to this response.[26]

In the end, none of these visions of unity has found universal support. Since the 1990s many ecumenists have moved away from the quest for models. What is clear in most contemporary conversations is that ecumenism must be seen as Christ's will, as God's gift to the church, and as our calling as members of that church. Primary responsibility for our unity rests with God, but all Christians are called to participate in that call. The second prevalent recognition is that whichever form of unity the church ultimately recognizes, it must reflect the full and genuine *koinonia* that God has already given to us. As a result, the search for visible unity will continue, and Pentecostals have an opportunity to contribute to this discussion.

RESOURCES FOR ECUMENICAL FORMATION

Traditionally, the study of ecumenism has been placed in one of two areas in the theological curriculum, mission studies or church history. There are good reasons for each of these decisions. One needs only to look to the modern missionary movement to recognize that it has given a great deal of impetus to the modern "ecumenical movement." Those who attended the 1910 Edinburgh Missionary Conference, for instance, were engaged in an ecumenical activity. That their work would result in the birth of the International Missionary Conference, which would eventually become a part of the WCC, is a clear indication of this seminal trajectory. Its call for a multinational and multidenominational commission to look at issues of doctrine and practice that separated Christians from one another in 1910, with the power to follow up on these unresolved issues, contributed substantially to the founding of the Faith and Order movement.[27] Those who attach ecumenism to the field of church history do so in order to study the many ways and reasons that denominations have broken, established, or reestabalished fellowship with one another over the centuries. But since good history also looks to the future, it may suggest ways to heal the divisions of the past.

Much has transpired on the ecumenical front since 1910. The formation of the WCC brought an unprecedented number of denominations to the same table. That a number of Orthodox and several Pentecostal denominations joined the WCC at its 1961 New Delhi Assembly broadened the table considerably. The Second Vatican Council (1962–65) opened up the Roman Catholic Church in ways that were thought to be impossible a decade before. Since 1910 a number of important agreements have been reached, convergence documents have been developed,[28] and bilateral as well as multilateral discussions have been opened on many fronts. A wide range of ecumenical resources are now available to help Pentecostals who are interested in developing their knowledge of the field. They include such items as a dictionary of ecumenical subjects,[29] a handbook on ecumenical councils,[30] various histories of the ecumenical movement[31] or the World Council's Commission on Faith and Order,[32] important documents adopted at the Second Vatican Council,[33] and the published reports of various bilateral and multilateral dialogues.[34]

It is important for anyone developing a Pentecostal methodology for ecumenical work to acknowledge that valuable ecumenical work involving Pentecostals has been under way for at least half a century. While some pentecostal groups have been active members of the WCC since 1961, others from the Netherlands[35] and Finland,[36] for example, have engaged in discussions within their own countries. While this includes work that has been done by many of the historic denominations, it is also the case that since at least 1972 ecumenical work on the international level has been undertaken by some Pentecostal leaders and groups. In 1972 David du Plessis and the Secretariat for Promoting Christian Unity established a formal bilateral dialogue between Pentecostals and the Catholic Church.[37] In 2010 it will commence its sixth round of discussions. In 1996 a bilateral dialogue between the World Alliance of Reformed Churches and Pentecostals began. It published its first report in 2001 and will complete its second round of discussions in 2010.[38]

The WCC established the Joint Consultative Group between the WCC member churches and Pentecostals in 1999. It made its first report at the Ninth Assembly of the WCC in Porto Alegre, Brazil in February 2007.[39] A second round of discussions was authorized by the Assembly at that time, and it began in October 2007. Encouraged by executives from the Lutheran World Federation, a conversation between the Institute for Ecumenical Research, in Strasbourg, France and Pentecostals was begun in 2004. It is scheduled to become an official dialogue following the 2010 Assembly of the Lutheran World Federation.[40]

Finally, Pentecostals have played a formative role in the establishment and success of the Global Christian Forum. Although this forum is not a dialogue sponsored by any specific denomination or set of denominations, it has provided a unique space for seasoned ecumenists and ecumenically interested parties from the entire range of Christian traditions to come together for the first time. Its future is currently open and promising for further Pentecostal participation.[41]

DEVELOPING AN ECUMENICAL METHODOLOGY FOR PENTECOSTALS

With all these factors in mind, one can identify at least eight elements that are essential to any ecumenical methodology employed by Pentecostals.

1. Self-Awareness. This ancient axiom is the place to begin. Good ecumenists are "called" as much as they are formed. Ecumenism is a vocation, not simply a career. While good training clarifies what is at stake, informs one on how to advance an argument, how to mediate a conflict, or how to draft a document, it is no substitute for the conviction that comes from a Divine call. When the way forward becomes difficult or the ecumenist is the victim of personal attacks, only a sense of Divine call will keep the ecumenist going. The ecumenical path can be a very lonely endeavor, especially for Pentecostals, whose tradition has little experience with the subject.

Good ecumenism is first of all relational. It is about giving and receiving, about listening and speaking. It is about growing together through confession, repentance, and acceptance. Good ecumenists do not pursue personal ideologies, press their own convictions, or succumb to pressures to conform. Their search is for the truth within community insofar as it can be determined. Consequently, there is no place for them to engage in unilateral actions as they seek the common good. One of the best ways to engage in ecumenism is to improve one's ecumenical sensitivity to "the other." This requires that we think of the other as though they were us. It requires that we pray specifically for their needs as though they were ours. It anticipates that our minds can be changed and that we are tempted by the other tradition to such an extent that we have made it our own, and yet, we do not leave our own tradition. It is in such a challenging and creative tension where we find real *koinonia,* and the common good becomes a common concern.

One of the failures of the current ecumenical situation is the temptation for particular denominations to act in a unilateral way on issues of immense gravity that affect the whole church, either by claiming to be prophetic or by claiming a new revelation with respect to the truth. Such actions are not ecumenical. They are the result of selfish individualism, a spirit of independence, an unwillingness to exercise self-control, and a complete disregard of the wisdom of the rest of the church. Ecumenism is not about individualism. It is not about making a name or being prophetic. It is about respecting one another. It is about bringing clarity to difficult subjects between traditions that see things from differing perspectives. It is about healing past rifts or schisms. It is about building a future together. As a result, good ecumenists know their strengths, but they do not bask in them. They know their weaknesses and are not shamed by them. They know how to use both effectively and allow them to be supplemented by the strengths of others.

2. The Study of Church and Ecumenical History. It is no accident that ecumenism is most frequently linked to church history. It has been roughly two thousand years since the church came into existence. Its earliest manifestation was Jewish, but after the Jerusalem Council of Acts 15, it quickly spread among Gentiles. Even in Scripture, Gentile culture was not homogeneous. It was Greek and Roman. As the church spread, so did the number of cultures with which the church came into contact, and with its growing diversity the question of how to maintain its unity grew in importance.

The apostolic fathers urged various congregations that were full of hardheaded individuals to submit to the leadership of their bishops *for the sake of unity.*[42] Irenaeus, the foremost Christian apologist of his day encouraged submission to the bishops even as he developed the outlines of *regulae fidei* to help maintain unity in an expanding church.[43] Tertullian viewed the episcopacy as a sign of the church's unity.[44] Cyprian, who confronted schismatics and met the problems posed by those who had lapsed, argued that those who broke with the bishop were not part of the church. Fellowship with the bishop was critical to any understanding of the church's unity![45] The Council of Nicaea in 325, with the subsequent support of the Cappadocian Fathers, ultimately led to the development of the Nicene-Constantinopolitan Creed, once again in the interest of Christian unity.[46]

Today the church can be found in literally thousands of cultural contexts, each with a unique history colored by the Divine leading and human responses that have played a part in the history of the church. As a result, the church stands today as a magnificent jewel, fractured into many pieces by factors such as language, culture, politics, and personal ambition. These pieces have little or no understanding of the whole and often express little or no desire to be reunited.

The church historian Henry Chadwick once said, "Nothing is sadder than someone who has lost his memory, and the church which has lost its memory is in the same state of senility."[47] The history of the church and the mutual understanding of its divisions are critically important to the ecumenical task. Yet one of the current ecumenical weaknesses is the temptation for all denominations to be paralyzed by the divisions and arguments of the past. This should come as no surprise; it is part of the human condition. Some denominations are open to rereading the past, working toward the healing of their historical memories or perspectives in new ways with their ecumenical partners; others are unable to do so because they are unwilling to acknowledge any fault from the past or any possible error in their historical memory or perspective. They refuse to change. History, however, can be used in a way that opens up the future rather than hold the church captive to the past, and Pentecostals should be able to lead the way in this regard precisely because they often hold history at arm's length.

While questions of unity have been with the church from the beginning and there were foretastes of the concern for unity as early as the eighteenth century, it was not until the beginning of the twentieth century that the subject of ecumenism received such widespread discussion and support. The 1910 Edinburgh Missionary Conference gave significant impetus to the subject. The ecumenical patriarch also gave it impetus when in his 1920 encyclical he called for greater efforts on the unity question. The most significant events of the twentieth century, though, were the founding of the WCC in 1948 and, a decade later, Pope John XXIII's call for the Second Vatican Council.

An effective ecumenical methodology for Pentecostals requires not only some knowledge of this history but also some knowledge of its ecumenical vocabulary. What is the difference between a *convergence* document like *Baptism, Eucharist, and Ministry* (BEM), as opposed to an agreement such as the *Joint Declaration on Justification by Faith* that was signed by representatives of the Lutheran World Federation and the Roman Catholic Church? What is the difference between "Tradition" and "tradition"? What is a bilateral dialogue over against a multilateral dialogue, and how effective are they? What is meant by the term *reception,* and how important is it?[48] Is there a hierarchy of truths?[49] What is meant by "canonical territory"? What is the basic content of such documents as *Lumen gentium, Unitatis Redintegratio,* and *Nostrae Aetate,* the Toronto Statement, the Lund Principle, the Lima Liturgy, the Apostolic Faith Study, the Leuenberg Agreement, the Porvoo Common Statement, *Ut Unum Sint, Dominus Iesus,* or *The Nature and Mission of the Church?* These are all shorthand for some of the significant steps taken along the ecumenical path over the past seventy years.

It is essential that one know both the contributions and the limitations that each of these items brings to the question of Christian unity in order to be an informed and effective ecumenist. By reading about the leading ecumenists, sur-veying the critical events, and studying the more important ecumenical docu-ments, it is possible for the Pentecostal ecumenist to appreciate how the work has proceeded to date, what the most fruitful streams of exploration have been, where the most difficult battles have been fought, where the most intractable problems lay, and where the best direction for the sake of unity might next unfold.

3. Knowledge of the Pentecostal Tradition. An effective methodology demands a well-developed knowledge of one's own denomination, how it came into being, what its worldview encompasses, and how it has changed over time. But good ecumenists must go beyond their specific denomination or group of congrega-tions. They must recognize and acknowledge the topography of the larger Pente-costal tradition, including its strengths and its weaknesses, its wisdom and its shortcomings in all their diversity.

The Pentecostal tradition is neither stagnant nor homogeneous. It does not consist of a single denomination (even a dominant one) or a single family (e.g., Holiness, Finished Work, Oneness). *It is a movement that is in motion.* Thus it is vital that Pentecostal ecumenists understand its rich and varied quality and its global character. New developments continue to appear around the world, colored by particular histories and specific cultural realities. The reality of global migra-tion, for instance, is changing the face of Pentecostalism in many parts of the world.[50] It is important for Pentecostal ecumenists to be conversant with all these changes, and it may be useful to speak of Pentecostalisms, in the plural.

Differences in baptismal practice are common. Seating arrangements in the gathered community vary, with mixed seating in some countries and separation according to gender in others. The role of women differs, with some denomina-tions granting equal rights to women in all things, others placing limits on their ministerial credentials, and still others requiring that they be silent and keep their heads covered. Who may participate in the Lord's Supper also differs, often reflect-ing the practice of the majority religious tradition (Orthodox, Catholic, etc.) in the cultural context. Who is allowed to preach, or teach, the length and style of sermons, and how many sermons are delivered in a particular service varies from place to place. Differences over the number of gifts (charisms) of the Spirit that are accepted, whether all charisms have been "restored" and are to be accepted today (e.g., apostleship), how these gifts are defined, and who is expected or allowed to manifest them and under what circumstances elicit a plethora of responses. Even the question of what if any evidence is necessary to determine whether a person has been baptized in the Holy Spirit is debated within Pente-costal circles. It is critical, therefore, that Pentecostal ecumenists be aware of such differences and be able to explain them.

An effective ecumenical methodology requires that those engaged in ecumeni-cal dialogue undergo some minimal training in the field in order to be effective.

This does not necessitate a complete course of study. I have found it useful to assign a reading list to team members and to bring the Pentecostal team together one full day before a specific dialogue. By doing this, team members can get acquainted, pray together, talk about what they have learned, agree on a common language or a common approach regarding how to address the subject on the table, and bring to the surface any differences that might prove substantive in the midst of discussion. An effective methodology requires that the team have some sense of where it is going before it begins discussions and both recognizes and appreciates whatever differences of opinion there are. Nothing is more difficult to manage than a surprise that one person unleashes on his or her own team. It can scuttle days of work.

4. Honesty of Presentations. I am convinced that a good ecumenical methodology for Pentecostals requires complete honesty. This is much more difficult than it initially appears. In all ecumenical gatherings three temptations quickly surface. First, there is the temptation to idealize one's own tradition. This fact needs to be noted when it is done, and the distance between the ideal and the real needs to be described. Second, there is the temptation to share only what is good about one's own tradition and compare it with what is less good in the other tradition. Falling to either of these temptations is the same as bearing false witness. Third, there is the temptation, sometimes brought on by denominational pressure, to smooth out one's own tradition so that it looks exactly like the ecumenist who makes the presentation or the group exerting the pressure. Those who submit to such pressures jeopardize the integrity of the dialogue results. It is a foundation built on sand.

In 1988 Jerry Sandidge and I were asked to present a paper on the subject of baptism and baptismal practice within the Pentecostal tradition at the International Roman Catholic–Pentecostal Dialogue.[51] I had included a survey of Pentecostal baptismal practices from around the world. What I found was that some Pentecostal denominations practice infant baptism, whereas the majority of them offer believers baptism. Some baptize by means of pouring or sprinkling; the majority immerse. Some immerse three times; the majority immerse only once. Some invoke only the name of Jesus Christ; the majority of Pentecostals use the Trinitarian formula.

Since the majority of denominational leaders who were on the Pentecostal team at that time practiced believers baptism by single immersion using the Trinitarian formula, they were upset with me for naming this diversity. They accused me of not showing a unified front. They told me that I had let them down. At least four of them told me that I was unfit to hold Pentecostal credentials and that if I were part of their denomination, they would have me defrocked. But my understanding was that if we were to be true to the belief and practice of the Pentecostal tradition rather than to one or another denomination, and if we were to be honest with our dialogue partner, who would inevitably run into these Pentecostals who differed from our "norm," it was critical for us to be honest. The forthrightness of our paper led to a breakthrough that week. When the Catholics applauded us for giving them a realistic view of the diversity that is a genuine part of the Pentecostal movement, those who had earlier criticized me changed their minds.

A good Pentecostal ecumenist speaks from the heart of his or her tradition with love and respect but also with honesty. To speak of Pentecostals as though they were all the same or as though they were perfect is to be dishonest. For the ecumenical task to succeed, ecumenists must acknowledge and address their genuine differences. In the fifth round of dialogue with the Catholic Church, their acknowledgment of the pastoral problems that accompany their practice of infant baptism and the improvements that came with their use of the Rite of Christian Initiation for Adults had an equally disarming effect that led to a deeper level of trust, even though it did not change Catholic practice.

5. Development of Communication Skills. Many though not all differences that separate churches today come down to the issue of communication. In any good ecumenical methodology, we communicate so that we may be understood. That, too, may sound easy, but it is not. For one thing, the church is a global reality. As a result, ecumenists soon find that they are up against language problems. It is impossible to find one language that is universally known and understood with the same level of nuance that a native speaker of that language typically possesses. This disadvantages some people. Even if it were possible to settle this issue, we are quickly confronted by the fact that because of our different histories and cultures we often use the same words to describe different realities. It is vital that anyone entering into ecumenical dialogue understand this fact. Terms like *conversion, member, proselytism, evangelization,* and *unity,* to name but a few, are often given very different meanings by different denominations. Thus an effective ecumenical methodology requires awareness of these differences in every ecumenical encounter. The key to effective ecumenism is to listen, listen, and listen some more, teasing out the nuances of meaning that come from different contexts. Only when these differences are understood can they become effective tools that contribute to greater unity.

A considerable amount of ecumenical work is also accomplished through writing. Drafting and redrafting documents that will survive the limited span of a typical dialogue and make a contribution to a broader audience often requires hundreds of hours. Because so much work toward unity is done through theological discussions, ecumenists often employ a shorthand theological vocabulary that only they will ultimately understand. Ecumenical vocabularies can be effective communication tools between specialists. But if the intention of ecumenism is to affect the church at the grassroots level, to communicate clearly and articulately where the problems lie or where the agreements rest, then a good ecumenical methodology requires talented wordsmiths, who communicate just as clearly with ordinary readers.

I remember well the argument that took place in the International Roman Catholic–Pentecostal Dialogue on the verb *persuade* and the adjective *persuasive.* I wanted to say that Pentecostals often engage in "persuasive preaching," by which I meant, their task in preaching was an apologetic task intended to bring people to a point of decision, just like we find in Acts.[52] One of our Catholic counterparts was equally adamant that the word could not, and therefore would not, be used. His reading of the word was that in all cases in which persuasion was involved, undue pressure that amounted to "proselytism" was being applied, something that both of us wanted to condemn. We fought over this word for an entire day— looking at possible alternatives, what words would be used to translate the idea, how it might be understood in this or that language, and what would be gained and what lost if we left it out—before we finally resolved the issue. All words hold some level of importance in any ecumenical document, and their meanings must be made clear and find some kind of agreement.

An effective ecumenical methodology for Pentecostals requires drafters to employ terms that are simple enough to communicate what is intended but specialized enough to carry the freight of what needs to be communicated. This takes training and skill. Effective ecumenical drafting may require input from laypeople for simplicity of language, from pastors for anecdotes that help make a point, from scholars to explain or nuance concepts, and from denominational leaders to point out political realities. In the end, for an ecumenical document to be effective, all parties must see their concerns faithfully represented in language that they understand. If this is not done, the work will not be received.

It is important to find people who can articulate positions clearly; however, it is equally important that all drafters recognize the service that they bring to the ecumenical task. When they speak or write, good drafters cannot afford to be afraid to be everything when it is absolutely necessary. The debate over the words *persuade* and *persuasive* was an important one to have, even if it took a full day. But in the end, all ecumenical documents are group projects. All members of the group must have a sense of ownership of what is written. Thus those who serve as primary drafters must be willing to become nothing. While it may be their words and their thoughts that find ultimate articulation in the document, in the end, the document is the product of the dialogue in which all have participated and not the work of a single individual.

6. Broadening the Base of Participants. Ecumenism is not intended to be the work of a single person or a small handful of specialists. It belongs to the whole church. For the church to be "catholic," the whole church must be present at the local level. As a result, it is important not to think about either a personal or a denominational legacy but about how to expand the pool of those who are able to make an effective contribution to the unity of the church. This means that every Pentecostal ecumenist needs also to become an ecumenical mentor. This mentoring process can take place at the level of denominational leadership, within the Pentecostal scholarly community, in the local congregation, within the family, or in one-on-one conversation with others. It is important that seasoned ecumenists identify and empower younger people and that Christian leaders become effective ecumenists so that the work toward visible Christian unity continues when they retire or move on.

Like any good mentoring, ecumenical mentoring takes time and patience. One does not have to be old to provide good mentoring. Ecumenical mentoring requires an investment of energy that challenges others to grow. I learned much from watching David and Justus du Plessis work, though they were more than two decades my senior. But I have also learned a great deal from peers such as Jerry Sandidge (Assemblies of God) and Cheryl Bridges Johns (Church of God). Sometimes my ecumenical learning came from my students, for example, Edmund Rybarczyk and David Cole. And in my case, it has not always been Pentecostal mentors who have taught me the most. I learned much from Donald W. Dayton, a Wesleyan theologian and fellow ecumenist; Jeffrey Gros, F.S.C., a Catholic lay brother and former director of Faith and Order in the National Council of Churches of the United States; Fr. Kilian McDonnell, O.S.B., longtime co-chair of the International Roman Catholic–Pentecostal Dialogue; Mary Tanner (Anglican), who entrusted me with a very difficult task at the Fifth World Conference on Faith and Order; and Hubert van Beek (Reformed), a lay staff person responsible for church and ecumenical relations within the WCC; and a host of other colleagues.

Part of broadening the pool of effective Pentecostal ecumenists will involve investing in Pentecostal partners who recognize and reflect the global reality of the Pentecostal movement. Most studies of the movement make it clear that Pentecostalism is composed of far more women than men, yet it is largely the men who lead the movement in the offices they hold, the pulpits they fill, the classrooms they occupy, and the dialogues in which they participate. And though sociologists paint a compelling picture showing that the majority of the movement is in the developing nations of the "Global South," global leadership is still dominated by white males from Europe and North America. There are many reasons for this imbalance—theological, sociological, financial, and cultural, to name but a few. But it should be acknowledged that lack of trust, the preservation of power, and the bigotry of prejudice continue to play a role. Consequently, it is important that those who convene dialogue teams take great care to balance them with those from the margins of the movement as well as from the center, and when those voices are not able to be present, by those who will represent their concerns with integrity.

7. Evaluation of Each Ecumenical Encounter. Ecumenism is expensive. Most denominations cover the expenses of their representatives, but because of their fears and suspicions of the ecumenical movement, most Pentecostal denominations do not. There are exceptions, but often those Pentecostals who have been actively involved in ecumenical discussions have had to raise their own funds or pay their own expenses. Thus an effective ecumenical methodology for Pentecostals must ask the effectiveness question. It is a matter of stewardship.

As we work for greater Christian unity, both short- and long-term goals are legitimate. It is important at the end of each encounter to ask how well these goals are being met. To what extent have the discussions that have been held and the actions that have been taken contributed to or furthered the unity of the church? To what extent have these discussions and actions contributed to the pentecostal movement's participation in God's plan for his church? If there is a sense of accomplishment, then it may be worth continuing the discussion. If there is no discernible progress, it *may* be necessary to look elsewhere for a more effective place to invest your time, energy, and finances.

Clearly, the unity of the church is not something that can or should be measured solely by how much money we spend, or how much time and effort we give, but it can be an important measure. It should also be acknowledged that if reconciliation and unity are on the heart of God, as Pentecostals frequently profess, then ecumenism should find a place in their denominational agendas. So far it has found very little space on these agendas. The reasons for this failure are varied. Factors such as ignorance, fear, misunderstanding, and potential power shifts are every bit as important to consider as are history, sociology, culture, or theology.

Part of an effective ecumenical methodology, then, must include the development of an ecumenical strategy that makes sense of the words and actions that are intended to aid in the rediscovery of the other, the articulation of a common vision of unity, and the coordination of the work to participate with God in making that vision a reality. An effective ecumenical methodology must evaluate the various visions of unity that are in play. It must also involve a variety of people who will lead leaders to a greater understanding of what is at stake, who will educate educators to train their students to become pastors that are ecumenically open, who will minister to ministers who show their flocks that they are part of something much larger than the local congregation and that by being ecumenically open they express their catholicity. This will require that Pentecostals think more seriously about the nature of their current ecclesiological forms, which are currently highly individualistic.

At the moment, there are thousands of independent Pentecostal congregations and many independent Pentecostal ministries. Many of them view the local congregation as constituting "the Church." They see no need to cooperate with others, nor do they desire any input from outside their own circle, a position condemned by the apostle Paul in 1 Corinthians 12:14–27. The question that needs to be asked of all such Pentecostal groups is whether they really are able to be "catholic." How far are they willing to go in order to be "catholicized"; that is, how willing are they to think beyond the boundaries of their individual, local congregations and be willing to be part of an ecclesiology that is truly global? Unity is only possible when catholicity is also a part of the discussion.

8. Exploration of New Possibilities. When the modern ecumenical movement came into being, it was something new. At no time previously had anyone succeeded in getting so many ecumenical partners to the table. It was a major advance over the status quo. Similarly, when the Catholic Church decided to become a participant in the ecumenical movement, few had expected it to do so, and fewer still expected that its role would be so positive. But these new things brought about unprecedented partnerships between denominations around the world. Times have changed, however, and many historic denominations, especially Protestant ones, seem to be pulling back from their earlier ecumenical commitments. The ecumenical movement has harvested much fruit, but it may be that the current configurations, the current institutions, and the current methodologies have given all the help that they are capable of giving. As a result, there has been considerable talk about an ecumenical malaise for several years.[53]

A healthy ecumenical methodology that is fully informed by Pentecostalism should work against this malaise. It should keep the future open. While Pentecostalism necessarily looks back to that first Christian Pentecost (Acts 2), it has always looked toward the future. This ability is fully in keeping with Joel's prophecy concerning the dreams of the old and the visions of the young (Joel 2:28; Acts 2:17). Any effective ecumenical methodology worthy of the name "Pentecostal," therefore, will be one that thinks seriously about how to participate with God in crafting the future of the church. To think in lesser terms is to squander the Pentecostal vocation.

Konrad Raiser, former general secretary of the WCC, observed in the mid-1990s that the ecumenical movement needed to broaden the table of participants if it was going to live up to its calling.[54] It was clear that the Catholic Church was not going to join the WCC, even if it was a full member of the Commission on Faith and Order and the Joint Working Group. It was equally clear that the majority of Pentecostal denominations would never join the WCC. As a result, Raiser convened a consultation in 1998 that opened new possibilities.

The question that needed to be asked was whether there were other ways of engaging a broader representation in a shared ecumenical vision. That discussion ultimately gave birth to the Global Christian Forum. This forum is another new idea, a new way of doing things. It is not intended to replace or to detract from the work of any other existing ecumenical organization. Its intention is to broaden the discussion by bringing participants to the ecumenical table that normally would not be found there. It provides a safe ecumenical environment free from the commitments that have been made without full participation of the whole church, including Pentecostals.[55]

In keeping with this "dream," participants decided that it was necessary to develop a new ecumenical methodology, one that was heavily informed by Pentecostalism with input from the global South. First, instead of inviting only seasoned ecumenists from historic denominations to the table, Pentecostal and evangelical leaders were invited in sufficient numbers to empower them with a critical mass. Second, instead of using traditional ecclesial or academic titles, which lend themselves to power plays and political posturing, participants were requested to use first names, thereby aiding all participants to view one another as peers. Third, instead of beginning with major theological papers (the traditional methodology used by professional ecumenists), participants were asked to share a personal testimony on one of two subjects: how they came to faith or how they discerned their call to ministry. These changes empowered the ecumenical novices who participated while at the same time destabilizing professional ecumenists because it was a new methodology with which they were unfamiliar. What resulted was a broader, more equitable table as well as a new sense of speaking and listening that may in the end prove more fruitful than earlier methodologies.

CONCLUSION

It is time for Pentecostals to take their rightful place at the table of the church. In order for them to do so successfully, they will need to change the ways they have traditionally viewed other Christians. Such a change calls for humility and openness before the Holy Spirit. To aid in this regard, Pentecostals who desire to serve the church through an ecumenical vocation need to adopt a methodology that takes seriously the efforts that have been made by others to bring about greater unity and yet reflects the Pentecostal promise to dream the impossible dream: One Church of Jesus Christ, visibly united in such a way that its call for reconciliation to God and neighbor through Jesus Christ no longer falls upon deaf ears.

NOTES

1. In *Ut Unum Sint,* 79, John Paul II enumerated the following issues: (1) Scripture and Tradition, (2) the Eucharist, (3) Ordination, (4) the Magisterium, and (5) Mary. Others could be added.

2. Michael Kinnamon, *Truth and Community* (Grand Rapids: Eerdmans, 1988), 1–18.

3. H. A. Gross, "Whither Are We Bound, Brethren?" *Herald of Faith* 9:6 (June 1944): 2, 20–22; Joseph Mattson Boze, "Too Big to Bag: A Vigorous Attack on the Assemblies of God?" *Herald of Faith* 10:6 (June 1945): 20–32; Lewi Pethrus, "No Pentecostal World Organization," *Herald of Faith* 12:7 (July 1947): 7; Joseph Mattson, "Shall Pentecostal Bodies Consolidate?" *Herald of Faith* 13:10 (October 1948): 7.

4. The WEF (now Alliance), in which a range of Pentecostal denominations hold membership, provided an alternative between "theological liberalism" and "unreformed Catholicism." Its Web site is www.worldevangelicalalliance.com. See W. Harold Fuller, *People of the Mandate* (Grand Rapids: Baker, 1996).

5. Most Pentecostal groups contend that conversion and baptism in the Holy Spirit provide access to the power of the Risen Christ and may be more effective as a means of determining readiness for ministry than is any particular level of degree completion. The Assemblies of God has institutionalized this commitment. See Bylaws, art. VII, sec. 2, par. h, *Minutes of the 52nd Session of the General Council of the Assemblies of God Convened at Indianapolis, Indiana, August 8–11, 2007* (Springfield: OGS, 2007), 111.

6. In 2000, among senior pastors, 12 percent had no education beyond high school and 4.3 percent claimed no ministerial training. While 30.6 percent claimed some training in a college or technical school, 27.4 percent had taken a certificate or correspondence courses; and 55.6 percent had attended a Bible college, with 41.3 percent completing a degree. While 12.4 percent held a master's degree, only 9.9 percent held a seminary degree (often in counseling), and 2.8 percent held an advanced degree in ministry. "Fact* Survey Results: A 2000 Survey of Assemblies of God Churches" (Springfield: OGS, 2000), 9.

7. *Confessing the One Faith,* F&O Paper 153 (Geneva: WCC Publications, 1991), 139 pp.

8. See, e.g., John R. Mott, "New Forces Released by Cooperation," in *The Foreign Missions Convention at Washington 1925,* ed. Fennell P. Turner and Frank Knight Sanders (New York: Revell, 1925), 209–22; and J. W. Welch, "The Present Great World Crisis," *Pentecostal Evangel* 590 (28 March 1925): 2–3, 8–9.

9. See Cecil M. Robeck Jr., "The Assemblies of God and Ecumenical Cooperation: 1920–1965," in *Pentecostalism in Contexts,* ed. Wonsuk Ma and Robert Menzies (Sheffield: SAP, 1997), 132–48.

10. Francesco Toppi, *E Mi Sarete Testimoni* (Rome: ADI-Media, 1999), 61–67; Giovanni Traettino, "The Fascist Regime and the Pentecostal Church," (Mattersey Hall: SPS-EPCRA, 1995), 26 pp.; Giorgio Rochat, *Regime fascista e. chiese evangeliche* (Torino: Claudiana, 1990), 113–26. The Assemblies of God made repeated resolutions in the *Minutes of the General Council of the Assemblies of God Convened at Springfield, Missouri, September 13–18 1945* (Springfield: OGS, 1945), 39.

11. In 1957 the Assemblies of God passed a resolution on the persecution of Protestants in Colombia. *Minutes of the Twenty-seventh General Council of the Assemblies of God Convened at Cleveland, Ohio, August 28–September 3, 1957* (Springfield: OGS, 1957), 52.

12. "Building the Church in Bulgaria," *Mountain Movers* 35:9 (September 1993): 5.

13. Francesco Toppi, *E mi sarete testimoni,* 200–205. They belong neither to L'Alleanza Evangelical Italiana nor La Federazione della Chiesa Pentecostali.

14. Robeck, "Assemblies of God and Ecumenical Cooperation," 123–24; R. T. McGlasson to David T. Scott, 3 May 1961. When David Yonggi Cho sought to bring the Yoido Full Gospel Church into the KNCC, he faced stiff opposition from the Assemblies of God in the United States.

15. From 1965 to 2005 the Assemblies of God included a statement on the ecumenical movement under the title "Doctrines and Practices Disapproved." See Bylaws, art. IX.B, sec. 11, "The Ecumenical Movement," *Minutes of the 50th Session of the General Council of the Assemblies of God Convened in Washington, D.C., July 31–August 3, 2003* (Springfield: OGS, 2003), 131–32. For the current statement, see Bylaws, art. IX.B, sec. 11, "Interdenominational or Ecumenical Relationships," in *Minutes of he 51ˢᵗ Session of the General Council of the Assemblies of God Convened in Denver, Colorado, August 2–5, 2005* (Springfield: OGS, 2003), 125–26.

16. Among them are Iglesia Pentecostal de Chile, the Misión Iglesia Pentecostal, the Iglesia de Misiones Pentecostales Libres de Chile, the Asociación "Iglesia de Dios" and the Iglesia Cristiana Bíblica from Argentina, and the Missão Evangélica de Angola.

17. G. W. H. Lampe, ed., *A Patristic Greek Lexicon* (Oxford: Clarendon Press, 1961), 944.

18. Dieter T. Hessel and Rosemary Radford Ruether, *Christianity and Ecology* (Cambridge, MA: Harvard University Center for the Study of World Religions, 2000); Calvin B. DeWitt, ed., *The Just Stewardship of Land and Creation* (Grand Rapids: REC, 1996).

19. *Gaudium et Spes,* 1.

20. See Michael Kinnamon and Brian E. Cope, eds., *The Ecumenical Movement* (Geneva: WCC Publications, 1997), 211–324.

21. Kinnamon and Cope, *The Ecumenical Movement,* 393–422; Edward Idris Cassidy, *Ecumenism and Interreligious Dialogue* (New York: Paulist, 2005).

22. Kinnamon and Cope, *The Ecumenical Movement,* 79–210.

23. Marlin van Elderen, *Introducing the World Council of Churches* (Geneva: WCC Publications, 1990), 4.

24. Ray H. Hughes, "Pentecost and Ecumenism," *Church of God Evangel* 56:45 (1967): 12–13, 15; Thomas F. Zimmerman, "The Holy Spirit: Unifying the Church," *Church of God Evangel* 57:35 (1967): 12–14, 17; Opal L. Reddin, "Church Unity," *Enrichment* 1:2 (spring 1996): 68; Francesco Toppi, *E mi sarete testimoni,* 199.

25. For an interesting perspective, see Margaret O'Gara, *The Ecumenical Gift Exchange* (Collegeville: Michael Glazier, 1998).

26. I have drawn these models from *Called to Be One* (London: CTE Publications, 1996), 47–49.

27. For a summary of the debate, see W. H. T. Gairdner, *"Edinburgh 1910"* (Edinburgh: Oliphant Anderson and Ferrier, 1910), 178–214.

28. So, *Baptism, Eucharist, and Ministry,* F&O Paper 111 (Geneva: WCC Publications, 1982).

29. Nicholas Lossky, Jose Miguez Bonino, John Pobee, and Tom Stransky, eds., *Dictionary of the Ecumenical Movement* (Geneva: WCC Publications, 2002).

30. Huibert van Beek, ed., *A Handbook of Churches and Councils* (Geneva: WCC, 2006).

31. Ruth Rouse and Stephen Charles Neill, *A History of the Ecumenical Movement, 1517–1948,* vol. 1, 3rd ed. (Geneva: WCC, n.d.); Harold E. Fey, ed., *The Ecumenical Advance,* vol. 2, 2nd ed. (Geneva: WCC, n.d.); John Briggs, Mercy Amba Oduyoye, Georges Tsetses, Routh Rouse, and Harold Edward Fey, eds., *A History of the Ecumenical Movement, 1968–2000,* vol. 3 (Geneva: WCC, 2000).

32. Günther Gassmann, ed., *Documentary History of Faith and Order, 1963–1993* F&O Paper 159 (Geneva: WCC Publications, 1993).

33. Austin Flannery, ed., *Vatican Council II* (Northport: Costello, 1996).

34. William G. Rusch and Jeffrey Gros, eds., *Deepening Communion* (Washington, DC: U.S. Catholic Conference, 1998); Jeffrey Gros, Harding Meyer, and William G. Rusch, eds., *Growth in Agreement II* (Geneva: WCC Publications, 2000); Jeffrey Gros, Lorelei F. Fuchs, and Thomas Best, eds., *Growth in Agreement III* (Geneva: WCC Publications, 2007).

35. Generale Synode der Nederlandse Hervormde Kerk, *De Kerk en de Pinkstergroepen* (The Hague: Boekencentrum, 1960); Broederschap van Pinkstergemeenten, *De Pinkstergemeente en de Kerk* (Rotterdam: Volle Evangelie Lectuur, 1962); Generale Synode van de Gereformeerde Kerken, *Het Werk van de Heilige Geest in de Gemeente* (Kampen: J. H. Kok, 1968).

36. "The Official Discussions between the Evangelical Lutheran Church of Finland and the Pentecostal Movement of Finland 1987–1989," in *Dialogues with the Evangelical Free Church of Finland and the Finnish Pentecostal Movement,* Documents of the Evangelical Lutheran Church of Finland 2 (Helsinki: Church Council for Foreign Affairs, Ecclesiastical Board, 1990), 33–56; Risto A. Ahonen, "Appraisal of the Discussions between the Evangelical Lutheran Church of Finland and the Pentecostal Movement of Finland," in *Dialogues,* 57–63; also published in Finnish as *Päätösasiakirja* (Vantaa: RV-Kirjat, 1989).

37. Arnold Bittlinger, *Papst und Pfingstler* (Frankfurt: Peter Lang, 1978); Veli-Matti Kärkkäinen, *Spiritus ubi vult spirat* (Helsinki: Luther-Agricola-Society, 1998); Veli-Matti Kärkkäinen, *Ad ultimum terrae* (Frankfurt: Peter Lang, 1999); Paul D. Lee, *Pneumatological Ecclesiology in the Roman Catholic-Pentecostal Dialogue* (Rome: Pontifica Studiorum Universitas A.S. Thoma Ag. in Urbe, 1994); Jerry L. Sandidge, *Roman Catholic/Pentecostal Dialogue (1977–1982)* (Frankfurt: Peter Lang, 1987).

38. See "Word and Spirit, Church and World," *Pneuma* 23:1 (spring 2001): 9–43; and *AJPS* 4:1 (2001): 41–72; "Word and Spirit, Church and World," *Reformed World* 50:3 (September 2000): 28–156; and "'Word and Spirit, Church and World," *CPCR* 8 (September 2000). See www.pctii.org/cyberj/index.html; www.warc.ch/dt/erl1/20.htm. Related articles include Frank Macchia, "Spirit, Word, and Kingdom: Theological Reflections on the Reformed/Pentecostal Dialogue," *Ecumenical Trends* (March 2001): 1–8; Gesine Von Kloeden, "Geistes Gegenwart: Endrücke von der 4. Konsultation zwischen dem Reformierten Weltbund und den Pfingstkirchen," *Reformierte Kirchen Zeitung* (15 July 1999): 269–71; Gesine Von Kloeden, "Pfingstlerisch und reformiert: Eine Standortbestimmung," in *Pfingstkirchen und Ökumene In Bewegung*, ed. Christoph Dahling-Sander, Kai M. Fundschmidt, and Vera Mielke, special issue of *Beiheft zur Ökumenischen Rundschau*, no. 71 (Frankfurt am Main: Otto-Lembeck Verlag, 2001), 82–99.

39. For the report of JCG: www.oikoumene.org/en/resources/documents/assembly/porto-alegre-2006/3-preparatory-and-background-documents/joint-consultative-group-wcc-pentecostals-jcgp-2000–2005.html.

40. Ken Appold, "Institute Begins Lutheran-Pentecostal Study Group," *Building Bridges* 6 (summer 2005): 2–3; Ken Appold, "Second Lutheran-Pentecostal Conversation Held at Strasbourg Institute," *Building Bridges* 7 (winter 2005): 4.

41. Richard Howell, ed., *Global Christian Forum* (New Delhi: Evangelical Fellowship of India, 2007).

42. Clement, *Epistle to the Corinthians* 12, 37–38; Ignatius, *To the Ephesians* 3–6; *Magnesians* 6–7; *Philadelphians* 2:7; *Smyrnaeans* 8–9.

43. Irenaeus, *Against Heresies* I.10.1–2; III.3.2–3; IV.33.8.

44. Tertullian, *Prescription against Heretics* 20.30; 32:1–2.

45. Cyprian, *Letter* 66 (68).5.1; 8.3.

46. Anthony Meredith, *The Cappadocians* (Crestwood: St. Validimir's Seminary Press, 1995).

47. Douglas Martin, "Henry Chadwick, Scholar of Early Christianity, Dies at 87," *New York Times*, 22 June 2008), 28.

48. William G. Rusch, *Ecumenical Reception* (Grand Rapids: Eerdmans, 2007).

49. Cf. *The Notion of "Hierarchy of Truths,"* F&O Paper 150 (Geneva: WCC Publications, 1990), 16–24; also David Argue, "Truth 101," *Pentecostal Evangel* 4229 (28 May 1995): 14–15.

50. J. Kwabena Asamoah-Gyadu, "An African Pentecostal Mission in Eastern Europe," *Pneuma* 27:2 (fall 2005): 297–321; Paul Brodwin, "Pentecostalism in Translation," *American Ethnologist* 30:1 (2003): 85–101; Edward Opoku-Dapaah, "Ghanaian Sects in the United States of America and Their Adherents within the Framework of Migration Challenges since the 1970s," *African and Asian Studies* 5:2 (2006): 231–53; Anne Parsons, "The Pentecostal Immigrants," *JSSR* 4 (1965): 183–98; André Droogers, Cornelis van der Laan, and Wout van Laar, eds., *Fruitful in This Land* (Zoetermeer: Boekencentrum, 2006); Michael Bergunder and Jög Haustein, eds., *Migration und Identität* (Frankfurt: Otto Lembeck, 2006); Mark Hutchinson, *Pellegrini* (Sydney: Australasian Pentecostal Studies, 1999); Daniel Ramierez, "Borderland Praxis: The Immigrant Experience in Latino Pentecostal Churches," *Journal of the American Academy of Religion* 67:3 (1999): 573–96; Claudia Währisch-Oblau, *The Missionary Self-Perception of Pentecostal/Charismatic Church Leaders from the Global South* (Leiden: Brill, 2009); Michael Wilkinson, *The Spirit Said Go* (New York: Peter Lang, 2006).

51. For an edited version, see Cecil M. Robeck Jr. and Jerry L. Sandidge, "The Ecclesiology of *Koinonia* and Baptism: A Pentecostal Perspective," *JES* 27:3 (1990): 504–34.

52. Acts 2:14–39; 3:13–26; 4:10–12; 5:30–32; 10:36–43; 13:17–41. See C. H. Dodd, *The Apostolic Preaching and Its Developments* (New York: Harper & Row, 1964), 7–35.

53. Konrad Raiser, *Ecumenism in Transition* (Geneva: WCC Publications, 1991), 1–30; Mark Heim, "Montreal to Compostela: Pilgrimage in Ecumenical Winter," *Christian Century* 109:11 (April 1992): 333–35; Kathleen Hurty, "Local Invitation Stimulates National Ecumenical Consultation," *Corletter* 7:2 (April 1992): 1.

54. Mark Heim, "The Next Ecumenical Movement," *Christian Century* 113:24 (14–21 August 1996): 780–78; Konrad Raiser, *To Be the Church* (Geneva: WCC Publications, 1997), 101.

55. See www.globalchristianforum.org.

CONTRIBUTORS

ALLAN ANDERSON is Professor of Global Pentecostal Studies at the University of Birmingham.

MICHAEL BERGUNDER is Professor of History of Religions and Mission Studies at the University of Heidelberg.

ELIZABETH BRUSCO is Professor in the Department of Anthropology at Pacific Lutheran University in Tacoma, Washington.

MARK J. CARTLEDGE is Senior Lecturer in Pentecostal and Charismatic Studies at the University of Birmingham.

ANDRÉ DROOGERS is Professor Emeritus of Cultural Anthropology in the Department of Social and Cultural Anthropology, Vrije Universiteit Amsterdam.

HENRI GOOREN is Assistant Professor of Anthropology in the Department of Sociology and Anthropology at Oakland University in Rochester, Michigan.

ODILO W. HUBER is Researcher at the University of Fribourg, Switzerland.

STEFAN HUBER is Adjunct Professor at the Center for Religious Studies (CERES), University of Bochum, Germany.

STEPHEN HUNT is Reader in the Sociology of Religion based at the University of the West of England, Bristol.

VELI-MATTI KÄRKKÄINEN is Professor of Systematic Theology at Fuller Theological Seminary, Pasadena, California, and Docent of Ecumenics at the University of Helsinki.

CORNELIS VAN DER LAAN is Professor of Pentecostal Studies in the Faculty of Theology at Vrije Universiteit Amsterdam and Lecturer at Azusa Theological Seminary.

BIRGIT MEYER is Professor of Cultural Anthropology in the Department of Social and Cultural Anthropology at Vrije Universiteit Amsterdam.

TONY RICHIE is Adjunct and Guest Lecturer at the Pentecostal Theological Seminary and Lee University in Cleveland, Tennessee.

JOEL ROBBINS is Professor and Chair of the Department of Anthropology at the University of California, San Diego.

CECIL M. ROBECK JR. is Professor of Church History and Ecumenics and Director of the David du Plessis Center for Christian Spirituality at Fuller Theological Seminary in Pasadena, California.

AMOS YONG is J. Rodman Williams Professor of Theology and Director of the Ph.D. Program in Renewal Studies at Regent University School of Divinity in Virginia Beach, Virginia.

TEXT
10/12.5 Minion Pro

DISPLAY
Minion Pro

COMPOSITOR
Toppan Best-set Premedia Limited

INDEXER
Kevin Millham

"An important read." —*Journal of the American Academy of Religion*

Global Pentecostalism
The New Face of Christian Social Engagement
DONALD E. MILLER and TETSUNAO YAMAMORI

"Miller and Yamamori are explorers bringing word to the First World of a large Third World religious development that, until now, has barely broken the surface of our awareness."—**Jack Miles, Pulitzer Prize winner for** *God: A Biography*

Includes a DVD featuring footage of Pentecostal religious worship, testimony, and social activism, and interviews with Pentecostal pastors and leaders from around the world.

978-0-520-25194-6 paper   www.ucpress.edu

Milton Keynes UK
Ingram Content Group UK Ltd.
UKHW040140141024
449609UK00005B/139